Explaining Irish Democracy

Explaining Irish Democracy

Bill Kissane

University College Dublin Press
Preas Choláiste Ollscoile
Bhaile Átha Cliath

First published 2002
by University College Dublin Press
Newman House
86 St Stephen's Green
Dublin 2
Ireland

www.ucdpress.ie

ISBN 1 900621 69 X (hardcover)
1 900621 70 3 (paperback)

Cataloguing in Publication data available
from the British Library

Typeset in Ireland in Adobe Garamond and Trade Gothic
by Elaine Shiels, Bantry, Co. Cork
Text design by Lyn Davies
Index by Helen Litton
Printed on acid-free paper in Ireland by ColourBooks Ltd.

To my mother and father

Contents

List of tables

Acknowledgements

This book originated in a PhD thesis completed in the Department of Government at the LSE. I was lucky to have in Professor Brendan O'Leary an exemplary scholar, supervisor and friend, someone whose faith in the project never wavered. I am also grateful to the Scholarship Office of the LSE for the award of a postgraduate scholarship between 1992 and 1994, and to CIMO of the Finnish Department of Education for providing me with a grant which enabled me to spend a year in Helsinki in 1996–97. In Finland, Risto Alapuro, Eino Lyytinen, and Elina Haavio-Manila were unfailingly hospitable and I can only regret the comparatively short space in this book devoted to Finnish–Irish comparisons. I also acknowledge a grant provided by STICERD at the LSE, which enabled me to travel to Dublin to research the development of Irish civil society in 2001. Thanks are also due to the staffs of the National Archives, UCD Archives, the National Library, and Trinity College Library, in Dublin, as well as to the staffs of the British Library's newspaper library at Colindale, and of the British Library of Political and Economic Science. I would like to thank the editors of *Civil Wars*, *Democratization*, and *Irish Political Studies* for allowing me to reproduce longer versions of earlier articles in chapters six, eight, and nine respectively, and Blackwater Press for permission to use the quotation from P. Hannan and J. Gallagher (eds), *Taking the Long View: 70 Years of Fianna Fáil* at the beginning of Chapter Eight.

The thesis was examined in 1998 by Professors Eunan O'Halpin and Fred Halliday who both made useful suggestions for improvement. The manuscript has also been read for UCD Press by Professors Alan Bairner and Tom Garvin, and I'm grateful for their comments. I also thank Barbara Mennell at UCD Press for her hard work, efficiency, and high professional standards. Over the years I have been fortunate to know a number of people whose support and friendship made life as a young academic less fraught with difficulty: Stefan Hanvey, Brídeen Kiernan, Anne Kissane, Niall Kissane, Karen Lopez, Michael Middeke, Eoin Moore, Joan O'Mahony, and Nick Sitter, all of whom helped in various ways. Beyond that I would also like to thank many friends and colleagues who have made the LSE a congenial place for postgraduate research: they include Katharine Adeney, Sumantra Bose, Alan Burke, Thomas Crothers, Rosie Gosling, Jim Hughes, Scott Kelly,

Dominic Lieven, Chun Lin, John Madeley, Peter Mair, Paul Mitchell, Terry Mulhall, Tom Nossiter, Brendan O'Duffy, Mads Qvortrup, and Erik Ringmar. The responsibility for what follows is of course mine alone. Finally, I have to thank my parents for their unstinting support throughout these years. Without them this book could not have been completed. It is dedicated to them.

BILL KISSANE
London School of Economics and Political Science
November 2001

Abbreviations

ASR	*American Sociological Review*
CP	*Comparative Politics*
D/T	Department of An Taoiseach
D/J	Department of Justice
D/E	Dáil Éireann files
ESR	*Economic and Social Review*
EJPS	*European Journal of Political Research*
GAA	Gaelic Athletic Association
FJ	*Freeman's Journal*
IHS	*Irish Historical Studies*
IRA	Irish Republican Army
IRB	Irish Republican Brotherhood
IPS	*Irish Political Studies*
JCH	*Journal of Contemporary History*
JIH	*Journal of Interdisciplinary History*
NA	National Archives
NL	National Library
PSQ	*Political Science Quarterly*
PR	Proportional Representation
RDS	Royal Dublin Society
STV	Single Transferable Vote
TD	Teachta Dála
UCD	University College Dublin
UCDA	University College Dublin Archive Department

Chapter 1

Introduction

When, in January 1922, the Sinn Féin party split in two over the terms of the Anglo-Irish Treaty, Winston Churchill hastened to denounce its leadership as 'Irish terrorists', men who were 'naturally drawn to imitate Trotsky and Lenin'.[1] In his view the Irish were 'members of a race who have a genius for conspiracy rather than government'.[2] The claims of Irish nationalists to Home Rule had long been countered with the assertion that the Irish were entitled to, but incapable of, self-government. Lord Salisbury had put it this way in 1886:

> The confidence you repose in people will depend something upon the habits they have acquired. Well, the habits the Irish have acquired are very bad. They have become habituated to the use of knives and slugs which is wholly inconsistent with the placing of unlimited confidence in them.[3]

The apparent extremism of Irish politics under the Union also convinced many in Ireland itself that an independent state would not be stable. These included previously ardent nationalists who withdrew their support for Home Rule during the Land War of 1879. As the historian William Lecky wrote, 'the last few years have quite cured me of the notion that either property or liberty could be safely entrusted to an Irish popular chamber . . . I do not believe in democratic Home Rule . . . and Home Rule which is not democratic would never be tolerated'.[4] Unionist opposition to Home Rule had been predicated on the idea that Home Rule would be 'Rome Rule', and during the Treaty negotiations of 1921 it was further argued that the Irish could not be trusted to behave decently towards their Protestant minority.[5]

The early disintegration of the new state into civil war in June 1922 convinced many of the accuracy of these predictions. On the eve of the conflict, Kevin O'Higgins, a senior member of the Provisional Government, described the outlook for the new state 'as unquestionably very grave'. The internal morale and the international reputation of the country were 'at a very low ebb indeed'. Economically things were 'heading straight for ruin'. The situation in the north-east, established as a separate area of administration under the terms of the Government of Ireland Act of 1920, was 'drifting from bad to worse'. Murders and burnings were following each other with 'dreary monotony', and refugees were fleeing the country altogether, or pouring across the Irish border into counties already 'menaced with famine'.[6] The number of casualties of sectarian violence, most of them Roman Catholic, may have exceeded five hundred in the first two years of Northern Ireland's existence, and the possibility existed that the Free State would intervene.[7] However, on 3 February 1922, the northern premier, James Craig, warned that 'if any attempt were made by the people in the south to take away large proportions of the six counties, there would be no other result than a renewal of Civil War'.[8]

Apart from the possibility of a clash between northern unionists and southern nationalists over the question of partition, O' Higgins saw three other possibilities for the new state. The first consisted of a full-scale civil war within the area of the Free State itself. For O'Higgins such a war would come about as a result of the determination of a republican section of the Sinn Féin movement, which had orchestrated the movement towards independence since 1916, to oppose the new Provisional Government set up in conformity with the Treaty. The second possibility was that of social revolution. Organised labour had followed the reformist path up to the Great War, but since then the radical potential of the Irish workers' movement had become more pronounced. On 25 May 1922, the Provisional Government raised the spectre of waging civil war against 'bolshevism sheltering under the name of republicanism'.[9] A third possibility consisted of reoccupation by the British. This would be effected by force, but if disordered conditions continued it could be accompanied with a moral mandate such as the British never before possessed with regard to Ireland.[10] Irish independence would vanish before it ever became a living reality.

The Irish state was founded then in conditions that made the consolidation of a democratic political system apparently unlikely. The initial move to independence had led to the declaration of a Republic in 1919. The following year, the British government legislated for the existence of two separate parliaments, north and south, both clearly subordinate to the crown. While northern unionists accepted that the northern body met their demand that they not be governed by Dublin, for nationalists partition was unacceptable and the powers vested in the southern parliament were too limited. The following year, negotiations led to the signing of the Anglo-Irish Treaty on 6 December 1921, which created a 26-county dominion of the British Empire in Ireland. While this compromise just about received majority support in the Irish parliament, Dáil Éireann, it was not acceptable to many of those who had sworn allegiance to a 32-county Republic between 1919 and 1921. Before the June 1922 election, Eamon de Valera, the anti-Treatyite political leader, provided a classic summary of the republican position:

> Republicans maintain that the proposed 'Treaty', which involved the abandonment of the Republic and the acceptance of the British Crown and the British Empire, should not be put to the people whilst England's threat of war prevents the free

will of the people from being truly expressed. They maintain further, that there are rights which a minority may justly uphold, even by arms, against a majority, and that such a right is that of defending and preserving for themselves and for all those who come after them, the precious heritage of belonging to a nation that can never be said to have voluntarily surrendered its territory or its independence.[11]

Despite majorities in favour of pro-Treaty candidates in the June 1922 election, and again in August 1923, throughout the 1920s republicans would still maintain that 80 per cent of the people were really in favour of breaking every connection with Britain, and would signify that preference when circumstances changed.[12] Such elitist attitudes to democracy were widespread among radical nationalists and they were not devoid of logic.[13]

As elsewhere the extent to which a state which was considered insufficiently 'national' was able to contain the forces of 'unsatisfied nationalism' within democratic politics would determine the degree of political stability achieved by the new state. Two variables affected this process. One was the ability of the regime-founding coalition to surmount the initial challenges to the authority of the state within a democratic framework. Another was the extent to which the disloyal opposition became committed to the defence of existing institutions. Rather surprisingly, in view of the dire predictions of O'Higgins, the Free State was to score rather well on both counts. Full-scale civil war followed in 1922–23, but a victory for the Provisional Government seemed a certainty by September 1922. Perhaps as many as two thousand people died during the war, but this pales in comparison with the 25,000 people that lost their lives as a result of the Finnish civil war of 1917–18. Armed resistance to the Free State subsided late in April 1923, and the bulk of the republicans confined themselves to peaceful opposition afterwards. In the shape of the Fianna Fáil party they entered the lower house of the Irish parliament, Dáil Éireann, in 1927, and formed a government from 1932 onwards. The fact that the changeover took place only ten years after the civil war, and was accompanied by no retribution, was a sign of the political maturity of the new state.[14] By 1938 most of the controversial issues stemming from the Treaty had been resolved, and the state entered the coming world crisis with an impressive degree of political unity. The long period of political instability dating from before the First World War was then over.

Eighty years later the consolidation of a democratic system is remembered as the chief accomplishment of the Irish state since independence:

The institutions of the state were soon established, an uncorrupt public administration and judicial system was in place, and within four years a public appointments system based on merit had been extended from the Civil Service to local government. Moreover, an unarmed police force had established its moral authority; and by the end of the decade tight discipline had been secured within the ranks of a greatly reduced Army. This ensured a smooth handover of power to those defeated nine years earlier; the great bulk of whom within three years of the end of the Civil War had taken their seats in the Dáil as the principal opposition party . . . Within ten years of the foundation of the state a second government, composed of men who had been defeated in the Civil War, was demonstrating similar commitment and skill in securing, through the introduction of a new Constitution, the domestic legitimation of the State in the eyes of the one third of the population who had initially been alienated by the manner in which it had been brought into being.[15]

On the other hand critics have been less than complimentary about the Free State's political culture. Fred Halliday compares the Irish state to 'the smaller, less belligerent, European states of the right', such as Spain and Portugal. While he concedes that the Irish 'allowed political pluralism and a measure of constitutional liberty from independence in 1922', in other respects the political culture was authoritarian:

particularly under the Fianna Fáil government of the 1930s and 1940s, it was engaged in a mild version of semi-peripheral escape: ideological repression through censorship and clerical control of education, economic delinking through import substitution and trade controls, all of this topped off with nationalist cant about Hibernian exceptionalism, in the economy and in the eyes of God.[16]

Arguably, however, the Free State did satisfy the four main criteria of democratic politics.[17] Firstly, elections were decisive in determining who would govern, despite the fact that pressures to ignore this procedure, particularly in 1922 and 1923, were great. Secondly, after 1923 the opposition was allowed to organise freely and compete on equal terms with the government, although the loyalty of the anti-Treaty republicans to the Free State was clearly in doubt. Thirdly, a defeated government stood down in 1932, even though members of the outgoing government had viewed the changeover with trepidation. Shortly before the election, Patrick Hogan, the Minister for Agriculture, told voters in Galway that, 'if we are beaten in this election, we will accept the decision of the majority of the people. The Army and the Garda will go over to the new Government and the Military Tribunal, if it is there to function.'[18] An effort to organise a preventive coup d'état from within the ranks of the Free State army came to nothing, and was opposed by William Cosgrave, President of the Executive Council.[19] Lastly, after 1922, the ultimate authority of Dáil Éireann was never in doubt. This was demonstrated emphatically in 1924, when an abortive 'army mutiny' was accompanied by the resignation of the Minister of Defence and several commanding officers.[20]

In contrast in Finland, a useful control case for the Irish experience, the army and the civil guards – the civil war winners – remained beyond civilian control and were able to influence government policy until 1931, when the Lapua crisis enabled the President to assert the authority of the government.[21]

The conception of democracy used in this study is an empirical not a normative one. It refers to the efficacy of institutions that allow voters' preferences to be translated into public policy rather than to the effects of those policies themselves. Dahl defined such a 'polyarchy' as:

> a system of political control in which . . . as a consequence of the set of institutions mentioned earlier, the highest officials in the government of the state face the prospect of their own displacement by means of popular elections, and hence tend to have strong incentives to modify their conduct in such a way as to win elections in political competition, with other candidates, parties, and groups.[22]

The basic institutions of 'polyarchy' – inclusive elections, a competitive party system, and a wide range of civil liberties – have all existed in independent Ireland since 1923, despite the state's continued reliance on emergency powers to deal with subversives. Between 1922 and 1939 there were eight general elections and the STV system made them relatively competitive. If we accept the percentage of votes won by parties other than the largest one in each election as a basic indicator of competitiveness, the Irish decennial figures were in line with those of other European democracies at the time. Among European democracies the mean figure for political competitiveness in the 1920s was 62.6 per cent, while for non-democracies the figure was 32.0 per cent. The Irish figure for the 1920s was 61.2 per cent. In the 1930s the European democratic mean for competitiveness was 62.5 per cent while the undemocratic mean was 19.6 per cent. The Irish figure of 53.0 per cent is still much closer to that for the democratic sample.[23] Political pluralism rested on a much surer foundation in inter-war Ireland than people have usually assumed. Indeed of all the 'successor' states that were created in the wake of the First World War, the Irish Free State was the only one that remained fully democratic. Czechoslovakia would have been an exception, but it collapsed under German pressure in 1939. Finland was a partial exception too, but its large communist party was banned for most of the inter-war period. It was only during the Second World War that the communists were allowed back into the system. The rest of the successor states all became authoritarian between the wars. Table 1.1 shows the fortunes of democratic government in that era. With the exception of the Irish case, none of the full democracies was a successor state. Iceland was still under Danish sovereignty, while Norwegian autonomy dated back to the beginning of the nineteenth century. In contrast Czechoslovakia and Finland, which are both classified as 'unstable democracies',

Table 1.1 **Democracy in Europe in 1938**

Full democracies	Male democracies	Unstable democracies	Failed democracies
1. Denmark	1. Belgium	1. Bulgaria	1. Italy
2. Iceland	2. France	2. Czechoslovakia	2. Poland
3. Éire	3. Switzerland	3. Finland	3. Lithuania
4. Luxembourg			4. Yugoslavia
5. Netherlands			5. Germany
6. Norway			6. Portugal
7. Sweden			7. Estonia
8. United Kingdom			8. Greece
			9. Austria
			10. Spain
			11. Latvia
			12. Romania

Source: adapted from Dahl, *Democracy and its Critics* (1989), table 17.1, p. 239.

were successor states, as were most of the states where democratic government collapsed in the inter-war era. There was a clear relationship between the newness of the state and democratic breakdown.

As the only 'successor state' to have remained continuously democratic since independence, the Irish case should stand as a useful test case for theories of democratic survival and breakdown in the inter-war period. Curiously, however, it usually does not feature at all in comparative analyses of the fate of democracy in the period, and is generally ignored in the wider area of empirical democratic theory.[24] Rarely have explicit comparisons of the Irish case with other European states at the time been made, and only twice have attempts been made to explain the Irish case in terms of comparative democratic theory.[25] Why is this so? Firstly, it has been argued that the Irish experience was atypical of the European experience, and that meaningful parallels can be made only with the developing nations in the Third World.[26] As Ireland is the only European country that is a former colony of Great Britain, comparisons with the colonial world are more suitable. This involves the additional assumption that Irish society, not simply Irish political structures and habits, was also post-colonial.[27] Secondly, we have the anglo-centric view that the Free State remained democratic because of its proximity to Great Britain. This view ignores the fact that British influence did little to shore up democratic practice in the part of Ireland that remained part of the UK, as well as underestimating the difficulties British policy created for democratic state-building in independent Ireland.[28] Thirdly, while Irish social science has absorbed many Anglo-American intellectual influences, it has only recently begun to look at the development of the Irish state in a European context.[29] Irish insularity has been the fundamental precondition of comparative neglect.

What is missing from the literature is a full discussion of the explanatory power of comparative theories of the genesis and consolidation of democracy for the Irish case. The chapters which follow attempt to correct that failing by selecting a number of the most influential perspectives on democratisation and testing their explanatory power against the Irish evidence. Ever since Hermens's diatribe against the effects of PR in the inter-war period most mainstream theories of democratic stability have addressed the issue of why the era proved to be so disastrous for democratic government.[30] However, the explanatory power of such theories, when tested against a wide number of cases, has proven to be of limited scope.[31] This does not necessarily imply that their explanatory power for individual cases can be dismissed from the start. What follows can be considered a test of how well existing theories of democratisation and democratic consolidation can explain the Irish experience between the wars.

In general, two main approaches to democratic transitions exist in the comparative politics literature: the functionalist and the voluntarist. The former sees stable democracy as the outcome of long-term processes of socio-economic development, while the latter emphasises the importance of elite choices in the transition process. From the first perspective, Irish democracy can be seen as something that emerged quite spontaneously out of the socio-economic changes that transformed Irish society in the decades between the Famine and the First World War. From the second perspective, Irish democracy was 'born' under traumatic circumstances between 1918 and 1923, and elite commitment was crucial in bringing it about.[32] What is offered here is an integrated analysis, which argues that functionalist theories tell us a lot about the process of democratisation, while voluntarist theories explain much about the process of democratic consolidation.[33] The Irish case provides a particularly dramatic illustration of this truism since the relationship between democracy and socio-economic development after independence was clearly weaker than at practically any time since the mid-nineteenth century. Ultimately, functionalist and voluntarist perspectives should not be seen as mutually exclusive. If democracy cannot survive without the requisite commitment on the part of the political elite, there is no reason why it should emerge in the first place if the traditional social structure remains unchanged.

Broadly speaking, the chapters that follow can be evenly divided into two types: those that emphasise structural preconditions for democracy, and those that highlight the importance of elite variables. After reviewing the existing literature in Chapter Two, Chapter Three tests the conventional argument that economic development and democracy were positively related by comparing Irish rates of economic development with those of the democratic and

of the undemocratic European countries. Chapter Four discusses Barrington
Moore's thesis that democracy can only emerge when the traditional structure
of agrarian class relations has been radically overturned, by looking at the
impact of land reform on Irish political development.[34] Chapter Five traces
the development of a civil society in Ireland between 1800 and 1921 and assesses
the extent to which it was democratically organised. Chapter Six assesses the
now fashionable claim that elite decision making is the crucial variable in the
consolidation of any democratic system by looking at the efforts made to
prevent the outbreak of civil war in the first half of 1922. Chapter Seven
discusses the view, found in Prager and Garvin, that the civil war expressed
the clash of two poles of Irish political culture, one a pre-modern communitarian one, the other a modern liberal-democratic one.[35] Chapter Eight
analyses the strategies elites can employ to reshape chronically unstable
political systems and focuses on de Valera's reform of the Free State after the
civil war. Hermens's thesis that the sources of democratic survival and breakdown were to be found in the institutional structures of the inter-war states is
discussed in Chapter Nine.[36] My conclusions are presented in the final chapter.

The sources used reflect the eclectic choice of theories discussed in this
book. The first chapter is based mostly on secondary material. Chapters Three
and Four rely mostly on statistical evidence of the social structure of the Irish
state as well as secondary historical sources. Some is taken from comparative
volumes of historical statistics, and some from official statistical collections
such as Irish census data. The subsequent chapters rely more on conventional
historical sources and contemporary publications. There is no claim here to
be unearthing masses of fresh primary material, or to be providing a new
narrative of Irish political development. Throughout the book, primary
sources are used not to chronicle or illuminate the unfolding of events but to
illustrate and clarify theoretical arguments. As a result, the book's arrangement
follows the logic of comparative enquiry rather than of narrative: it assumes
that democratisation in Ireland reflects general laws of social development
rather than local and specifically Irish circumstances, and its focus is on the
circumstances in which Irish politics developed rather than on the personalities
of the day. In short, the book is a work of comparative political science, not a
study in the development of Irish political consciousness.

Chapter 2

Democratic theory and the Irish Free State

'We have had to contend not merely with the absence of a State sense amongst large sections of the people, but with positive propaganda of a more insidious character against the members of the Government'

William Cosgrave, 1931

In the 1930s a spate of books on the crisis of European democracy appeared in the English-speaking world. Most of them ignored the Irish Free State entirely while those that mentioned it did so in a cursory fashion.[1] Since the Irish state was not challenged by a strong communist or fascist movement in the period, perhaps it was concluded that the Free State was ideologically 'immune' to the sorts of pressures that led to democratic breakdown on the continent. As a later account put it, the experience of British rule, the underdeveloped nature of the society, and the fact of geographical isolation, all meant that the Irish state 'never experienced a genuine crisis of its political system' between the wars.[2] Such an 'immunisation theory' has been applied in various ways to cases as different as inter-war Finland, France, and Ireland, and could probably be applied to most of the surviving democracies between the wars. Taken to extremes it implies that democracy survived the inter-war period only in those states that did not experience a genuine crisis. This rules out the possibility that some states overcame periods of crisis and emerged with greatly strengthened democratic institutions as a result. This was certainly the case in the Free State, which went through recognisable periods of crisis between the wars, but by the late 1930s the long era of political instability dating back to the Home Rule crisis had definitely reached an end. Indeed, as I show below, the Irish Free State was far more vulnerable to the general crisis of European democracy than the immunisation theory suggests. The issue of why it remained democratic, and the answers given to that question by Irish specialists, have therefore a significance far beyond Ireland.

2.1 Ireland and the inter-war crisis

The collapse of Empires in the wake of the First World War gave rise to violent conflicts throughout the area of the former Hapsburg and Romanov Empires. The problems of the new Irish state were bound up with the wider crisis of the inter-war era. Foremost among these was the intensification of national feeling brought about by the First World War and the Versailles settlement. That settlement was to establish an international order based on the principle of self-determination. This concept had played a central part in Sinn Féin's campaign for recognition of a 32-county Republic between 1919 and 1921.[3] The 1918 election, the first election to be held under conditions of near universal adult suffrage, had resulted in a landslide victory for Sinn Féin and for their Republican programme. There were, however, two problems with their demand. First, before 1916 the traditional nationalist claim had been for Home Rule only. The new mandate for a Republic was produced by exceptional and short-lived circumstances. Chief among these was that the British 'first past the post' electoral system had seriously exaggerated the size of Sinn Féin's mandate by allowing it to obliterate practically all other parties.[4] A second problem with the Sinn Féin demand was that the First World War also radicalised opposition to independence on the part of Ireland's large minority of Unionists, who constituted a majority in the north-east of the country. As a result, the British government introduced partition in 1920 as a 'provisional' solution to the conflict between two national loyalties in Ireland.

Neither 'the Partition Act' of 1920 nor the Treaty which followed was satisfactory to radical nationalist opinion. Republicans continually referred to the 1918 election as the founding election of a putative 32-county Republic. Disputes over the peace treaties were common throughout the inter-war era. Most of the successor states were 'nationalising states', which were 'conceived by their dominant elites as nation-states, as the states of and for particular nations, yet as incomplete or unrealised nation-states, as insufficiently national'.[5] The achievement of foreign policy objectives, the revision of demeaning peace treaties, the enlargement of state boundaries to include lost irredenta, or the possession of overseas colonies, were all part of this compensatory complex which proved fatal to democratic government in many of the new states. The signing of the Treaty in December 1921, which established an Irish Free State with jurisdiction over 26 counties of Ireland, but gave Northern Ireland the right to 'opt out' from this state, did little to assuage southern nationalist grievance at partition. A Boundary Commission in 1925 failed to redraw the boundary line to the satisfaction of nationalists, and this issue, alongside that of the Treaty, remained controversial right down to the eve of the next war. Over time, the Treaty came to be gradually revised, but not without causing a major conflict in Anglo-Irish relations between 1932 and 1935.

The First World War had been accompanied by widespread social and psychological changes. The war had a radicalising effect 'on an important stratum of largely middle class, nationalist soldiers or young men who after November 1918 resented their missed chances of heroism'.[6] The problems posed by demobilisation and peacetime re-employment were especially pronounced. In Ireland, apart from the Great War itself, the 1916 Rising, the War of Independence, and the subsequent civil war, all added to the militarisation of political life and to a sense that 'the experience of fighting' was 'central and inspirational' to political life. By the spring of 1922 peacetime conditions had produced an IRA that was 'in danger of becoming popular', as 'trucileers' or 'sunshine soldiers', young volunteers who had played no part in the War of Independence, flocked to its ranks.[7] One correspondent described the circumstances, which led to the IRA challenge in 1922:

> To understand how they came into being one must look back to the years from 1914 onwards. During the European war emigration was stopped and thousands of farmers' and labourers' sons who used to go to Australia, America, New Zealand, had perforce to remain in Ireland. There was no land for them and little work. Further, Ireland did not suffer in men or material in the European war in proportion to other countries. The Conscription Act was, rightly or wrongly, not applied here. And when the Armistice came there were at least thirty thousand youths between the ages of sixteen and twenty-two, who for four years had read of war, talked of war, seen war on the pictures, played at war as volunteers, but have never smelt real war or seen its horrors. They were, thanks to the repeal of the Arms Act, almost all armed. They had little education and as I have pointed out previously, owing to the method of Government in Ireland, could have no sense whatever of civic responsibility. Into this soil, ripe for the sowing, fell the seeds of the Republican doctrine preached from 1916 onwards.[8]

The civil war also saw the creation of an Irish national army, which was over thirty thousand strong by November 1922.[9] It contained within it a small and pivotal group, which continued to see the role of the army as an instrument for the realisation of nationalist objectives. As elsewhere in Europe, how the civilian authorities handled such a *Frontsoldat* mentality within and without the state would be crucial to the course of Irish political development.[10]

Political controversy would also be intensified by the delay of the economic recovery of Europe, a recovery shattered by the experience of economic depression in the late 1920s. In Ireland the civil war placed the Free State under severe fiscal stress from the beginning and in today's terms took several billion pounds out of the economy.[11] The war was followed by years of stagnation during which thousands of republicans were forced to emigrate. Then in the late 1920s the Irish experience of the world depression was comparatively severe: in February 1932 a government minister, Patrick McGilligan, told voters in Newcastle West that people might have to die through starvation.[12] The effects of the depression were greatly exacerbated by the closing off of traditional emigration routes in the early 1930s, and then by the Fianna Fáil government's willingness to wage a tariff war with the UK after 1932. This policy placed sectors of the agricultural population in great difficulties, which helps to explain why sections of the farming community were willing to give their support to a radical right-wing movement, the Blueshirts, in the 1930s.[13]

Another threat to the political stability of the new states was posed by their political structures. Before 1918 only a handful of European states were in any meaningful sense democratic, and the post-war settlement encouraged a boom in constitutional experimentation. This was marked by an enthusiasm for radical and French models of democracy which then failed to provide political stability afterwards. As a result they were gradually replaced by less democratic institutions, but this process was a controversial one in many cases, such as in the Baltic states, leading to authoritarian forms of government. In Ireland, having adopted some radically new institutions between 1919 and 1922 – including an elected judiciary, provisions for direct democracy on fundamental matters, and an experimental constitution – the Irish political elite gradually came to discard its experimental institutions in favour of more traditional British ones. While these reforms fulfilled the important function of bringing constitutional law into line with political practice, they also gave rise to a centralisation of power which led to further polarisation between the two main political parties. In June 1928, de Valera complained that the policy of the pro-Treaty government was to concentrate power as far as possible in themselves, but in power after 1932 his party was accused of doing exactly the same.[14] Irish party competition up to 1937 took place in an increasingly authoritarian institutional framework, a context that often led to the emergence of undemocratic systems of government elsewhere.[15]

The Irish state was certainly not immune to the general crisis that affected Europe in the inter-war years. The main source of instability was a basic lack of consensus among the political elite regarding the legitimacy of the new state. A 32-county Republic had been declared in 1919 and most of the revolutionary movement had sworn allegiance to it. Now they were being asked to swear allegiance to the Free State constitution and fidelity to the British crown as head of a 26-county Irish dominion. Such 'conflicts of principle' were widespread throughout the successor states of the time, but in Ireland a republican form of government had been for many the guiding ideal since the establishment of the Irish Republican Brotherhood in 1858.[16] In 1921 acceptance of the Treaty was justified on pragmatic grounds, but the type of Irish republicanism that had emerged after the Easter Rising of 1916 was not known for its capacity for compromise. In December 1922 a republican newsletter asked:

> What is the argument for the Treaty? Is it not materialism, root and branch? Was it not openly said that we are getting the practical things, the essentials of freedom, the resources of the country, the power over education, industry, police, judiciary? And what are we asked to give in exchange? Nothing, a shadow, an oath of allegiance. 'All these will I give thee if falling down thou shalt adore me'. Do you think that a state rooted in materialism can evolve anything but a bitter materialism?[17]

To differing degrees all the successor states suffered from 'regime-crises' which existed where elites were either semi-loyal or disloyal to a new state that did not fulfil all of their expectations. In these states the extent to which the new states fulfilled the expectations of the traditional political elites was an important factor in explaining their political fortunes. Regime crises of this type arose in states that had lost out in the reorganisation of the European system after the First World War. Such was the case in Germany, Italy, Hungary, and Austria. In Austria, the rump state of the Hapsburg Empire, there was little consensus on the desirability of an independent Austrian state at the outset, rather than unification with Weimar Germany. In comparison with imperial Vienna the new Republic was a provincial affair and but for external pressure the name of the new state would have been 'German Austria' rather than the Austrian Republic. The *Grossdeutsch* idea appealed to both left and right at different times but became highly divisive after Hitler's coming to power.[18] After a brief civil war in 1934 an authoritarian system emerged and it was not surprising that many Austrians welcomed the Anschluss with Germany in 1938.

Even in some of the longer-established European states there was no elite consensus on the nature of the regime. Spain, for example, had never had a stable liberal regime in the nineteenth century and in 1931 became a Republic without any convinced republicans. The largest socialist party, the PSOE, had supported the dictatorship of Primo de Rivero in the 1920s and saw the concept of a democratic Republic in instrumental and highly conditional terms.[19] Even after the establishment of the Second Republic in 1931 the left's attitude to the regime was a half-hearted one. For the right on the other hand, the conception of a Republic was just part of that wider mix of modern ideologies which was considered *Anti España*, antithetical to the traditional order. The Spanish Republic's inability to gain and maintain the loyalty of its political elites in the 1930s was a chief source of political instability.

Elsewhere, the formation of new states after the First World War led to a variety of constitutional crises which resulted in civil wars being fought between rival contenders for governmental authority in the new states. According to

Coakley, the transition to independence in Finland, Czechoslovakia and the Baltic states took place in confused conditions, allowing a situation of 'multiple sovereignty' to emerge. The succession process was 'typically contested', with different claimants arising with regard to the exercise of governmental authority.[20] This meant that different institutions emerged to provide rival foci for national sentiment: left wing and republican elements favouring more radical institutions and right wing and conservatives favouring more limited and traditional models of independence. Even where the lines of division in these conflicts were clearly social, as in Finland, the confusion involved in the transition to independence had allowed these conflicts break out in the first place.[21]

As in the other successor states then, the Irish state had been established under conditions that made its future success unlikely. The early experience of civil war made the initial divisions over the Treaty all the more acute and the legality of the process of regime change was 'sufficiently ambiguous' for the losers in the civil wars to claim a moral victory and to continue to deny the legitimacy of the new regime.[22] Republicans pointed out that pro- and anti-Treaty candidates had stood on the same platforms in the June 1922 election, and that the Provisional Government had gone back on its promise to establish a coalition government after the election. Then, without convening the new parliament, the Provisional Government, at Britain's bidding, attacked the anti-Treaty forces. On 4 July 1922 de Valera complained that:

> Dáil Éireann has not been allowed to meet, and the Provisional Government, relying on English powers, has unconstitutionally assumed a military dictatorship, and with English big guns, English armoured cars, English ammunition, and English methods of press censorship and false propaganda, has made war on the voluntary soldiers of the Republic who are simply keeping their oath to the Republic and preventing the sovereign independence of the country from being surrendered.[23]

On the other hand the Free State represents a case, such as that of Finland, in which a defeated opposition was gradually reintegrated into the political system. Despite its civil war past, Finland was in many respects a typical Nordic democracy by 1937. In that year the Social Democrats formed a coalition with one of their opponents in the civil war, the Agrarian Union. Likewise in Ireland, the losing side in the civil war regrouped and embraced democratic rules of political competition as a means of revising the Treaty settlement. Their entry into the Dáil in the summer of 1927, their formation of a minority Fianna Fáil government in 1932, and their attainment of an overall parliamentary majority in 1933, were all-important steps in their integration into the structures of the new state. By 1938 those features of the 1921 Treaty that had been objected to by republicans, the oath to the British crown, the place of the crown in the 1922 constitution, and British possession of Irish ports, no longer existed.

In summary, if the Irish political system had been founded under conditions that made the consolidation of a democratic system unlikely, it is difficult to sustain the argument that the Irish state was 'immunised' against the wider crisis of democracy in the inter-war era. Arguably the Free State remained democratic, not because it did not experience a genuine crisis of the democratic order, but because it overcame one by democratic means. If this was so, then two questions arise: firstly, why were Irish political elites so committed to the defence of democratic institutions between the wars, and secondly, why did this defence succeed? To answer these questions we have first to turn to the literature provided by Irish specialists

2.2   Irish democratic theory

Four distinct interpretations as to why the Free State remained democratic can be found within Irish political science literature. Two argue that Irish democracy survived because of the development of a strong democratic culture under the Union, while another two emphasise the importance of the civil war and its aftermath. The first, 'the British tutelary theory', stresses the importance of the British legacy. The Free State had a majoritarian political system rooted in English common law. Under the terms of the 1921 Treaty all previously existing legal decisions were declared still valid. The bulk of the state's civil servants had joined the service before independence and the standards and procedures of Whitehall were put in place. After 1922 the British nature of Irish political practice, in terms of constitutional conventions, decision making and party competition, became more pronounced. Irish MPs had been attending the Westminster parliament since 1801 and elections had been popular events in Irish life since the 1820s. Democratisation was gradual, and since it coincided with the replacement of Irish with English as the language of the masses, the British system became 'internalised':

> As is the case of the white communities of the British Commonwealth, many of the currently held political traditions and values were inculcated and absorbed during a most critical and formative period: the period of the advent of mass democracy . . . Extensions of the franchise in Britain were followed by extensions, with modifications, in Ireland; and Irish people acquired democratic habits and values. Political ideas were almost wholly expressed in British categories, for, from O'Connell to Parnell and beyond, the political experience of most Irish leaders was gained in British political life, and they practised the parliamentary ways of Westminster.[24]

A second, constitutional nationalist, interpretation stresses that the progress of Irish nationalism towards self-government was inherently democratic. Home Rule meant a sovereign parliament based in Dublin, such as had existed in the past. Farrell argues that 'it was through parliament and largely within parliament that Ireland grew to both nationhood and full independence'.[25] The Irish state no longer endorses the romantic view of revolutionary struggle, and is now embarrassed by ceremonies such as the commemoration of the 1916 Rising which suggest that the revolutionary Fenian tradition was the central one in Irish political life. Farrell argues that if this had been the case the outcome would have been different: 'that work could scarcely have been accomplished if the central Irish political tradition had been so robustly rebellious, so chronically violent and so demanding of change as has been usually suggested'.[26] This view is essentially the one adopted by the state itself. A government sponsored report on the constitution in 1967 declared:

> the republican status of the State, national sovereignty, the supremacy of the people, universal franchise, fundamental rights such as freedom of speech, association, and religion, the rule of law and equality before the law, were all part and parcel of this nation's struggle for independence and it is not surprising, perhaps, that, in the minds of the people, they are now to be regarded as virtually unalterable.[27]

For Farrell the Irish state's achievement of political stability after 1922 'was primarily part of Ireland's British inheritance from the nineteenth century', but a parliamentary tradition 'which Irish leaders and parties in parliament had done much to shape'.[28] His argument focuses on the importance of a sovereign parliament, Dáil Éireann, during the nationalist struggle from 1919 to 1921. It represented more than a *de jure* claim to statehood since in some respects it exercised a *de facto* authority over areas of Irish life such as local government and justice. It was 'a Westminster import' rather than a revolutionary parliament: in it 'a consistent effort was made to maintain Westminster standards' and procedures; the Speaker's rulings were accepted by the members; priority was given to parliamentary questions, and above all, the authority of the Dáil over the military campaign was continuously stressed during the War of Independence. The creation of the Dáil courts also showed 'a concern to preserve as far as possible the existing and accepted system'.[29] Both the survival of the Cosgrave government during the civil war and Fianna Fáil's decision to enter the parliament in 1927 were evidence of the non-ideological, gradualist nature of Irish political culture: according to Farrell, 'the willingness to accept what cannot be changed, the commitment to empirical solutions is paramount'.[30] This was dramatically revealed by the general acceptance of the Treaty's terms in 1922 and of the ruling of the Boundary Commission in 1925.

Arguably, both these interpretations underestimate the problems faced by the Free State. Kevin O Higgins described the Provisional Government which took over from the British as:

> simply eight young men in the City Hall [the adjoining Dublin Castle's centuries-old association with British oppression made it unsuitable as a seat of government for Irish ministers] standing amidst the ruins of one administration, with the foundations of another not yet laid, and with wild men screaming through the keyhole. No police force was functioning through the country, no system of justice was operating, the wheels of administration hung idle, battered out of recognition by rival jurisdictions.[31]

The achievements of the pro-Treaty governments between 1922 and 1932 have been widely praised by historians.[32] Britain had left the Free State with a lot of problems: partition, a discredited parliamentary tradition, and a monarchical constitution repugnant to its sense of nationality. The Anglo-Irish Treaty of 1921 had solved the Irish question by stabilising 'Ireland', but temporarily destabilising the two states. After 1916 'the wild men' had seized the initiative and now turned their guns on the pro-Treatyites. More generally, in those areas where an experience of good government would be most obvious – respect for the law, faith in the political process, and an acceptance of the ultimate writ of the state – the inheritance was an ambiguous one. A key feature of the British tutelary model was the creation of bureaucratic structures that 'stressed the legitimate role of state authority in the preservation of order in societies that left to themselves, would have descended into anarchic violence'.[33] However, the pro-Treaty elite believed that British rule left behind an ambivalent attitude to central authority, an attitude described by a *Round Table* correspondent in 1923 who asked of the Irishman:

> How could he have civic responsibility? A Chief Secretary appointed by England today imprisoned him for doing what a previous Chief Secretary had praised him for. He was taught that the only way to gain anything was by the back door, by wire-pulling. The Irishman was not taught the theory of the state, the necessity for government. The policeman at the street corner was not his policeman, he was the policeman appointed and paid by the Castle, which in turn was controlled by whatever party was in power at Whitehall. The barrister who prosecuted in a criminal case was not a public prosecutor, appearing for the people to see that right was done. He was looked on, and not without cause, as a prosecutor appearing for some mysterious entity known as 'the Crown' determined to convict by whatever means possible, and the juries thought it was their duty to save the prisoner from his clutches. No one thought of the Government as our Government. It was always the English Government. [34]

The apparent existence of this syndrome forced the Free State elites into a tutelary attitude themselves. They were concerned with order, legality, and the irresponsible and irrational nature of Irish political traditions. Indeed for many Free State politicians, the civil war was not about anything as such, but the product of fantasy and lawlessness. O'Higgins commented that 'leavened in with some small amount of idealism and fanaticism', there was 'a good deal of greed, envy, and lust, and drunkenness and irresponsibility'.[35] In December 1922 he summarised the Provisional Government's interpretation of the civil war:

> The actual position is that a body of people in this country, though numerically insignificant, refuse to accept the majority will as the deciding factor in our political affairs, and declare that there is to be no peace on the basis of a Treaty signed by five Plenipotentiaries, endorsed by the Dáil, and accepted by the people.[36]

For O'Higgins, Irish democracy had to be taught: 'the problem is psychological rather than physical, we have to vindicate the idea of law and order to government, as against anarchy', he declared.[37] According to Garvin the Republican tradition opposed by O'Higgins had more in common with the secret society mentality of Southern Europe. Fenianism, the IRB, and the IRA were part of a 'public band' tradition which saw society as a 'moral community' and republicans as guardians of that community's highest values and aspirations. The nature of their commitment was expressed by the role of the secret oath: they were answerable only to themselves. As de Valera put it, 'the majority had no right to do wrong'. The Treaty split can be seen then as a conflict between 'the public band' tradition personified by the anti-Treatyite IRA, and the world of 'civil society' – the church, the business community, the ex-Unionists and the electorate, who supported the Treaty in 1922. For Garvin the survival of Irish democracy was not inevitable but a product of the defeat of one way of thinking by the other in 1923. After this the 'unenthusiastic democrats' of the Fianna Fáil party rejoined civil society in 1927.[38]

A fourth interpretation, that of Fianna Fáil, sees the progress towards the Republic as the main theme of the inter-war era. It was later said that the 'primary misfortune' of the new Irish state 'was that from the very beginning its existence constituted a violation of the principles of its founders'.[39] It is common to see signs of a healthy civic spirit in public participation in state holidays, which celebrate independence days and re-enact foundation myths in the US vein. There is no such thing in independent Ireland. For decades the commemoration of the 1916 Rising was the only such ritual. On the walls of Irish primary schools are hung copies of the 1916 Proclamation of the Irish Republic, not the constitutions of 1922 or 1937. There are also photos of the martyred heroes of 1916, but not of the real founding fathers of the Irish state,

Cosgrave, Mulcahy, Collins, and O'Higgins. The terms 'the Free State' or 'Free Stater' were used by some either to denigrate the state's status or to question someone's nationalist credentials.

For some in 1922, de Valera had unleashed a 'wild and destructive hurricane . . . from a thin insubstantial vapour',[40] yet for republicans the degree of British power implicit in the Treaty was substantial. The shelling of the Four Courts at the beginning of the civil war, Britain's dictatorial amending of the 1922 constitution, and the Boundary Commission fiasco, were all signs of Ireland's continued subordination to Britain. When de Valera tried to challenge the oath to the British crown in 1928 by using the constitutional right to initiate a referendum on it, the relevant article was removed from the constitution by Cosgrave. The Fianna Fáil view argues that the Free State government was strong, although not legitimate. How did it became so, and how in turn did Irish republicanism, at least in the South, become a purely constitutional form of politics?

The constitutional republican view credits the Fianna Fáil party with this achievement. Along with the Blueshirts, between 1932 and 1936 Fianna Fáil was under threat from the IRA, which had over 30,000 members in 1933.[41] Faced with opposition from both the left and the right, it was necessary to put the state on a more legitimate footing. Repression, which had been the policy of Cumann na nGaedheal in the 1920s, was not enough. Positive constitutional measures undermining the Treaty settlement of 1921, especially the removal of the oath and the introduction of a new constitution, would have the effect of marginalising republican opposition to the Free State. This view suggests that the bulk of the population, including those who initially saw the Treaty as a stepping-stone towards greater freedom, were in favour of undoing the Treaty. The leadership provided by de Valera was the *sine qua non* of this process:

> Indeed, if we take together de Valera's move away from 1916 militarism to the constitutionalism of elections in 1916 and 1918, his break with abstentionist and extra-parliamentary Sinn Féin in 1926 and the stern, if professedly anguished, steps against the IRA in the 1940s, we can say that not only did he epitomise at the outset of his career the ambivalence of constitutionalist and violent traditions of Irish nationalism but that he also bridged and transcended them, and finally and firmly asserted the supremacy of the civil over the military tradition, the constitutionalist principle, over that of physical force, and majority rule over the people have no right to do wrong assertion.[42]

In summary, four distinct perspectives exist within Irish democratic theory as to the sources of democratic stability in the Free State. The first two argue that the survival of Irish democracy was due to the development of a strong democratic political culture under the Union: from this perspective the consolidation of democracy after 1921 was no surprise. The latter perspectives emphasise the touch and go nature of the outcome and concentrate more on how the political elite overcame the crisis of the civil war and its aftermath. Which emphasis is correct? Should stable democracy be seen as a culmination of political developments under the Union, or was the outcome of the civil war more relevant to the politics of the new state? To answer this question we have to turn again to comparative perspectives on the pattern of democratisation in inter-war Europe.

2.3   Comparative analysis

European democracies went through three stages in their development up to the Second World War. The first began in the mid-nineteenth century and ended around 1920, a period which seemed to presage the universal triumph of the democratic ideal; by 1914 even the three imperial polities of Russia, Turkey and Iran had formally adopted parliamentary models of government. This sense of democratic optimism was added to by the adoption of highly democratic constitutions in Eastern Europe after the war, the introduction of proportional systems of election throughout the west, and by the formation of social democratic governments in many countries after 1918. By 1920 most of the area west of the Soviet Union was under democratic rule.

However, the following decade was largely a period of political retrenchment, a process accelerated by the recession of the late 1920s and early 1930s.[43] In the Catholic countries of Austria, Portugal, and Spain, a reversion to the clerical authoritarianism of the nineteenth century took place in the 1920s. In Spain it resulted in the dictatorship of Primo de Rivera, in Portugal Salazar established an authoritarian Catholic state in 1929, while Austria did not become formally an authoritarian state until 1934. Elsewhere, political systems, democratic or authoritarian, were consolidated on a nationalist and conservative basis. From the mid- to late 1920s conservative governments emerged in the UK, France, Germany and Hungary. Authoritarian coups took place in Poland and Lithuania in 1926, and in Yugoslavia in 1928. By the late twenties the democratic model of government was under serious assault.

If, in the 1920s, 'security was apparently wrested from profound disorder and turbulence', the third phase, the period between 1930 and 1938, proved to be one of ideological polarisation.[44] The early experiment with mass democracy turned out to be a prelude to dictatorship in countries such as Spain and Germany. Then, in response, democracy, often containing a strong social democratic element, especially in the Nordic and Benelux countries, was consolidated in north-western Europe. European states became more clearly divided into democratic and authoritarian categories but the long-term direction of change was certainly authoritarian. Overall, 'in 1918–20 legislative assemblies were dissolved or became ineffective in two European states, in the 1920s in six, in the 1930s in nine, while German occupation destroyed constitutional power in another five during the Second World War'.[45]

The place of Ireland within this pattern is clear. Between 1918 and 1921 its political life was democratised and radicalised. The first Dáil was elected by universal suffrage, it adopted a 'Democratic Programme' which seemed to place limitations on the right to private property, and in 1919 it enacted a short constitution for the whole island based on the principle of popular sovereignty. Between 1919 and 1921 directly elected republican courts were established, local government was reformed, and a proportional electoral system was introduced for local and national elections. However, the period between 1922 and 1932 proved to be one of retrenchment.[46] The republican courts were abolished, local government was emasculated, and the 1922 constitution dropped the radicalism of the Democratic Programme. Ideologically Cumann na nGaedheal governments advocated a mixture of tough law and order policies and economic liberalism, although they did not share the radical nationalism of the European right. As elsewhere, 'reaction against the subversion of the old social order in 1917–1920', was at the root of this regime, as it was of the Stormont system in Northern Ireland. [47]

In the depressed socio-economic conditions of the late twenties the competition between the civil war parties reflected a clear right-left divide, William Cosgrave, President of the Executive Council, alleging in September 1927 that the Fianna Fáil party had in mind 'the establishment of socialism in this country'.[48] In 1931 the government introduced a new Public Safety Bill aimed at subversive organisations. Cosgrave stated that he and his colleagues believed:

> that the future of the country is linked up with the traditions and teachings of the Christian religion which have governed the minds of its people for fifteen hundred years. We believe that the new patriotism based on Muscovite leanings with a sugar coating of Irish extremism is completely alien to Irish tradition. The right to private property is a fundamental of Christian civilisation and so long as the government remains in power it will maintain that sacred right for its people.[49]

The rising Fianna Fáil party was able to take advantage of the economic distress in the country as well as the unpopularity of the government's coercive measures. Its period in office between 1932 and 1938 saw the consolidation of Irish democracy, as well as the introduction of measures designed to counteract the depression. A radical right-wing movement, the Blueshirts, temporarily linked to the Fine Gael party, emerged, but proved unsuccessful, as elsewhere in democratic Europe of the time.

In short the Irish went through the general sequence of aspiration, retrenchment and polarisation that was experienced by European democracies in the inter-war period. As elsewhere, the First World War had a fundamental effect on the prospects for political stability in Ireland, and 'bourgeois defence' quickly became central to the politics of the new state.[50] However, it was only in those societies where liberal parties had been historically dominant before the First World War, such as in America, Britain or France, that liberal solutions to the problem of mass democracy were institutionalised in the inter-war era. Elsewhere, the First World War had a radicalising effect on political opinion, particularly on the left, and 'corporatist' institutions which took either social democratic or fascist forms, had to be established in the 1930s.[51] In Ireland there had been both radical and liberal elements in the nationalist movements of the nineteenth century, but between 1881 and the First World War, liberal assumptions, reflected in the electoral monopoly of the Home Rule Party, were in the ascendant. The Home Rule crisis of 1911 and then the First World War greatly radicalised political life, which undermined the hegemony of Ireland's rather conservative parliamentary elites.

If, as Farrell suggests, the Sinn Féin elite between 1919 and 1921 were bent on institutionalising a democratic political order based on the Westminster system, by 1922 the control of that elite over the nationalist movement had weakened considerably. What followed in the summer of 1922 was precisely the reassertion of liberal hegemony and an attempt to reimpose a purely liberal solution to the problems of the new state afterwards. Yet liberalism Cumann na nGaedheal style failed. The one factor that could sustain a liberal polity, middle-class unity, was absent. Significant sections of the middle or lower middle class refused to give their allegiance to the Free State. Irish democracy could only be stabilised if an alternative coalition of interests could construct an illiberal alternative. In 1927, it appeared that this might take the form of a rainbow coalition of socialist, nationalist and liberal elements. Later it appeared that an alliance of Labour and Fianna Fáil would govern, but ultimately an alternative emerged only under the Fianna Fáil governments of the 1930s.

Irish developments between the wars owed their dynamics, as they did elsewhere, to the impact of the First World War and the promise of radical change it brought about. According to Maier:

> That long and gruelling combat imposed parallel social and political strains upon the states of Europe, and for years after dictated a common rhythm of radicalism and reaction. All Western nations experienced new restiveness on the left after the Russian Revolutions of 1917 and continuing radical turmoil from the 1918 Armistice through the spring of 1919. The 'forces of order' had to make their peace either with political overturn, as in Germany, or, at the least, new attacks on

capitalism. Yet, by 1920–1921, they had recovered the upper hand and pushed the 'forces of movement' onto the defensive. By 1922–1923 a new wave of nationalist, sometimes authoritarian, remedies replaced the earlier surge of leftist efforts. Right-wing schemes, however, could not durably settle the economic and social dislocations the war had left. By the mid-1920s each country had to find a new and precarious equilibrium, based less on the revival of traditional ideological pre-scriptions than upon new interest-group compromises or new forms of coercion.[52]

As in other countries where the First World War undermined the tradi-tional liberal route to stable democracy, Irish democracy was consolidated 'in the midst of economic and political crises', which emerged in the late twenties and early thirties.[53] However, the new equilibrium in Ireland appeared in the form of protectionist policies after 1932 rather than in corporatism per se. Indeed what Maier calls 'bureaucratically sponsored interest group mediation' was never institutionalised in the Free State.[54] Fianna Fáil's economic policies were sufficiently different from Cumann na nGaedheal's to lead to intense domestic opposition in the mid-1930s, but they signalled more a reconstruction of Irish society according to bourgeois criteria rather than a social transfor-mation. In those countries where politics had been radicalised by the Great War, stability could be achieved in one of two ways: by repressing change entirely, or by disarming the left-wing challenge with reformist initiatives.[55] The Irish experience was a classic example of the latter.

Although this perspective points to the importance of analysing Irish developments right into the 1930s, the question of why the Irish response to the usual problems of the period remained a democratic one still remains unanswered. As Maier points out, in most European countries 'the strains left in the wake of the First World War were almost insuperable', and democracy could not be maintained, regardless of changes in economic policy.[56] Perhaps the answer lies in the possibility that the impact of the First World War on Ireland was less profound than elsewhere, and that less obvious tendencies towards stabilisation were at work below the surface between 1914 and 1921. Mair argues that the ease with which the Free State established its authority after 1921 can be related to the fact that in the two areas where the Irish public was most likely to come into contact with the state – legal arbitration and local government – the Sinn Féin movement had succeeded in effectively replacing the British state apparatus with one of its own by 1921. According to Mair there was an 'inevitable link' between the means used to repudiate the authority of the crown between 1918 and 1921 and the ability of the successor state to sustain its own authority.[57]

If the ability of the Free State to have its authority accepted after independence was dependent both on its practical effectiveness between 1918 and 1921, and on the normative framework which legitimised such activity (as

Mair suggests), then it also follows that in 1922 the Free State's de facto authority was fundamentally undermined by its loss of the legitimising symbols which had sustained 'the separatist Republic' during the War of Independence. Indeed in the two areas where Sinn Féin had succeeded in effectively replacing the British administration with its own by 1921 – local government and the administration of justice – the Cosgrave governments were quickly forced into rearguard action. The republican courts were abolished in 1922, and local government was totally emasculated in the years after the civil war. In other words, the legacy of the 'revolutionary' era was more complicated than Mair's thesis allows for, and this was compounded by the fact that in Ireland 'there was no tradition of political control of armed nationalism; nor had there been any experience of effective centralised control over armed movements' before 1921.[58]

Two factors then – a disjuncture between the de facto and the de jure basis of the new state's authority, and the Sinn Féin leadership's lack of real authority over the IRA – were the key ingredients of that potent mix of circumstances which led to civil war. A firm institutional basis for democratic government still had to be constructed in 1922. 'A key group of almost forgotten but brilliant people, principal among them William Cosgrave, Hugh Kennedy, Kevin O'Higgins, and Kevin O'Shiel', are credited by Garvin with this achievement.[59] During the civil war they were forced to defend, in quite a Hobbesian way, the prerogatives of the state against internal disorder, and, in their minds, against possible outside attack. This, they argued, was what prompted their initiation of the civil war on June 28, Richard Mulcahy claiming in the Dáil in September that the attack on the Four Courts on 28 June was motivated by the fear that the actions of the anti-Treatyites would eventually bring the British back into the country.[60] The institutions subsequently created by the pro-Treatyites were all conceived as institutions belonging to the state not to a political party. Commenting on de Valera's peace proposals at the end of the civil war O'Higgins told Cosgrave to inform de Valera that the army was not 'the army of a party, but the army of the people and that it will be the instrument of the will of any government returned with a democratic mandate'.[61]

Clearly the Free State government did succeed in establishing, in a basic sense, a viable state in southern Ireland. Since a democracy can only exist in the context of such a state, Garvin's emphasis on the achievement of the pro-Treaty elite is self-evidently justified.[62] It is a telling fact that when Cosgrave outlined the conditions under which he would be willing to support a Fianna Fáil administration in 1927, that four of his five conditions – a balanced budget, a single army, an independent judiciary, and an impartial administration of the law – had to do with the autonomy and authority of the state.[63] Indeed the de Valera governments built on these achievements, and it is difficult to believe that the changeover in 1932 could have gone so smoothly had they not been accomplished. The introduction during the civil war of an unarmed police force, in a society which had had a paramilitary police force under the Union, was the most dramatic of these achievements, but the creation of a meritocratic and apolitical civil service, along with the establishment of a small and purely professional army, were also important events in the development of the Irish state.[64]

According to Garvin, 'the character of elite political culture is central to any estimate of the prospects of democracy in any nascent polity, quite apart from economic conditions or even traditions of civic strife'.[65] However, another view of pro-Treatyite elite culture was put forward by Gavan Duffy, a Treaty signatory who resigned from the Provisional Government in the summer of 1922. He believed that the 'bellicose republicans' were to blame for the start of the civil war, but personal enmities that infected several of the leaders on both sides were 'of more lasting effect'. After the death of Collins, the leaders of the Free State were not 'qualified by education and training to take part in constitutional controversies'. They were 'utterly perplexed by the problems of statecraft'.[66] After Collins's death, they abandoned all thought of reconciliation between the wings of Sinn Féin, and stuck to a policy of criminalising their opponents, which only intensified opposition to the Free State. At the end of the war, their refusal to remove the oath of allegiance from the constitution in return for IRA decommissioning meant that the civil war did not end in a negotiated peace.[67]

The tension between authoritarian and democratic impulses within the pro-Treaty elite was a strong one. De Valera later characterised their initiation of the civil war as 'an executive coup d'état', and if the pro-Treatyites were 'constitutionalists', it was constitutionalism with a sting in the tail.[68] Reneging on an explicit agreement to form a coalition government with the anti-Treatyites after the June 1922 election, refusing to summon the third Dáil in the summer of 1922 until the decisive battles in the south-west had been won, and preventing a referendum on the oath of allegiance in 1928, were hardly a great vindication of pro-Treatyite political culture. While the Provisional Government justified the assertion of centralised authority in June 1922 in the name of 'the people's rights', the reality of their position between June and September was revealed by Eoin MacNeill's remark that 'the people' didn't want an immediate meeting of the Dáil.[69] According to Garvin himself, what emerged after the civil war was a political system 'rather authoritarian and secretive in its political style, and sceptical of the public-spiritedness of the population to which it owed its right to rule'.[70]

If the pro-Treaty elite tended to respond to crisis situations in an authoritarian manner, and if this was true of the political elite as a whole, the question of why democratic impulses ultimately proved stronger than authoritarian ones remains unanswered. Ultimately Garvin's explanation is ambiguous. On the one hand he suggests that the Irish public was 'ready' for democracy in 1921 and that the assumptions which legitimised electoral democracy were widely shared in pre-independence Ireland.[71] On the other hand, he relies on the concept of elite political culture to explain why Irish democracy survived the civil war crisis.[72] Can one really hold both arguments at the same time: that democratic institutions had widespread legitimacy in Irish society before 1921, and that the reason they survived the civil war was due to the nature of elite political culture? Arguably the pro-Treaty elite did succeed in installing democratic institutions under difficult circumstances in 1922–23, but they did so in an environment that was generally supportive of democratic institutions. Crucially, the sub-elites in Irish society – the civil servants, the professions, and the clergy – remained committed to democracy after the civil war, whereas in a case like that of the Weimar Republic, they were hostile to democracy from the beginning, and abandoned it when it entered a period of crisis in the late 1920s. If this is the case then we have to question the very concept of 'elite political culture' in Ireland, since during the civil war the Provisional Government were clearly dependent on the moral support of the Church, the financial support of the banks, and the ideological support of the national newspapers.

On closer inspection it is clear that Garvin's conception of democracy is not an elitist one at all, but one that is premised on the idea of the sovereignty of the electorate and with that on the strength of civil society. It is true that the pro-Treaty elite took many decisions that were crucial to the long-term evolution of the system, but in so doing they did not override the preferences of any major social institution, and explicitly defended the civil war as a defence of 'the people's rights'. In a democratic system elites are constrained by the preferences of the electorate, as well as by those of the most powerful social institutions. Those preferences can only be articulated if a democratic infrastructure is already in place. In early 1922, the vast majority of local government bodies, most of the senior clergy, and almost all the national and provincial newspapers, came out in favour of accepting the Treaty, thus providing the Provisional Government with a high degree of moral authority from the start.[73] Arguably, the Provisional Government's subsequent ability to mobilise popular support behind the defence of the economic status quo and of established institutions during the 1922 and 1923 elections, also presupposes a well-developed civil society. If this is so, why emphasise the importance of elite political culture, since the strength of civil society was decisive?

The fact that Irish elites got it right in the end should not lead people to assume that elite political culture, with its 'legitimist claims, abandoned oaths, and rival authorities', was the key factor in explaining the successful outcome.[74] Elites operate in a given social context and in Ireland this context was a relatively advanced one. Much of the literature on the Irish case suggests that

Irish democracy emerged out of an essentially unmodern society.[75] Carty, for example, sees Ireland as an exception to the rule that democracy blossoms only in modern developed societies.[76] Schmitt argues that Ireland displayed many of the features of post-Second World War developing nations.[77] Prager also puts Ireland firmly within a Third World perspective.[78] Independent Ireland is regarded by these authors as the India of western Europe. Garvin's judgement is more ambiguous, although he argues that 'the social reality of Ireland in the 1920s was that it was slowly emerging from serfdom and pre-literate culture and could only be built up slowly by the gradual and long-term efforts of large numbers of people'.[79] In contrast I argue that Irish democracy emerged out of a society that was relatively modernised by 1921, with high levels of education and urbanisation. Moreover, it emerged after a half-century of land reform had thoroughly reformed the Irish agrarian class structure, and by independence had a democratic civil society that reached into practically every area of Irish public life. The relative modernity of the Irish state is precisely what distinguishes the Irish case from the less fortunate states in Eastern Europe, a point emphasised by Lee.[80]

This does not imply, however, that stable democracy was the inevitable outcome of long-term processes of socio-economic development. Such social factors can only provide favourable conditions for consolidation. What is offered here is an integrated analysis that combines an analysis of structural variables with an appreciation that voluntarist factors can also have explanatory power. One voluntarist perspective that can be applied with modification to the Irish case was developed by Rustow. He argued that the factors which bring a system into being are very different from the factors which keep it in place.[81] In the Irish case, sociological theories can tell us a great deal about the genesis of democracy in the decades before independence, but they tell us little about the process of democratic consolidation afterwards. In particular Rustow emphasised how important the experience of a phase of 'severe and deeply entrenched conflict' was to the life of a democracy. That experience can be positive if it is followed by the 'conscious adoption of democratic rules' by partisan elites. In this respect de Valera's formulation of a 'constitutional republican' alternative to the Free State after the civil war was a decisive aspect of the consolidation of Irish democracy.

Rustow also stipulated, however, that 'national unity' was a precondition for stable democracy and it is hard to believe that the civil war helped create a sense of national unity. By October 1922 the Provisional Government had abandoned Collins's interpretation of the Treaty as a stepping-stone towards greater freedom, while in the same month the IRA leadership rejected de Valera's Document No. 2 which proposed a Republic associated with the Empire.[82] The problem with applying Rustow's model to the Irish case lies in the fact that the Irish conflict was not just 'a hot family feud' such as that between the

Social Democrats and conservatives in Sweden, but a violent civil war where the basic authority of the state was at stake. In Rustow's model 'national unity' means that the state must not suffer from contested boundaries and that the citizenry should have no doubts as to the political community to which they belong.[83] However, 'stateness' should refer to much more than the issue of borders, since other aspects of the 'stateness' variable can also be divisive. In the Irish context, partition was just one aspect, since acceptance of the Treaty also meant inclusion in the British Empire, a limited British military evacuation, a potential external veto on domestic legislation, and the requirement that Irish elected representatives take an oath to the British crown.[84] What Rustow's model seems to exclude is the possibility that national unity can be the outcome rather than the cause of consolidation. In the Free State 'national unity', broadly understood, came about only when the Treaty had been significantly revised. A basic consensus on foreign policy was then manifest between 1939 and 1945 when the state pursued a policy of neutrality in the war. De Valera's creation of a 'constitutional republican' alternative to the Free State provided a necessary source of re-legitimation and one that was ultimately successful.

In summary, the Irish state went through a three-phase experience in the inter-war period: the genesis of a democratic system between 1918 and 1921 was followed by civil war in 1922, which was then followed by the 're-equilibration' of the democratic system between 1932 and 1938. Democratisation in Ireland can be likened to the progress of a train that, travelling over an ostensibly straight line after 1918, finds itself derailed in 1922 as the train turns sharply to the right, but finds itself back on the track as the train completes a full semi-circle and then its progress straightens out in the 1930s. I have borrowed the term 're-equilibration' from Juan Linz to describe this process.[85] The Irish political elite proved unable to prevent their particular train going off the tracks in 1922, but were able to find their way back again. Fundamental changes in British policy towards Ireland were an important reason why the 're-equilibration' of Irish democracy proved successful in the 1930s, just as British policy was a major factor in the origins of the civil war.

In saying that the sequence was one of genesis, followed by civil war and then 're-equilibration', I am setting myself at odds with two lines of inter-pretation in Irish political science. The first argues that the Sinn Féin elite achieved a significant degree of democratic institutionalisation between 1919 and 1921.[86] The second represents the civil war as a conflict 'between majority right and divine right' and credits the pro-Treatyites with the consolidation of Irish democracy.[87] While it is indisputable that the Cosgrave governments created a strong institutional basis for Free State democracy in the early 1920s, how plausible is the argument that Irish democracy was consolidated in 1924, only a year after the end of the civil war? Neither the failed attempts of the revolutionary Dáil government to establish a democratic government after 1919, nor the more successful efforts of the Cumann na nGaedheal elite to create a strong institutional base for Free State democracy, can be considered 'consolidations' of a democratic system. Both consolidation and legitimacy came only in the 1930s and were largely the work of de Valera.

To conclude, the Irish went through the general sequence of aspiration, retrenchment and polarisation that was experienced by European democracies between the wars. Historical analysis has tended to concentrate on the first phase of this sequence, but this emphasis underplays the challenge posed by the civil war to democratic stability in Ireland. From the pro-Treaty point of view, only resolute action in defence of majority rule saved Irish democracy from collapse in 1922. From the losers' perspective, it was primarily de Valera's legitimising strategy that stabilised the situation in the 1930s. Either way the key variable is how the elite responded to the crisis of the civil war and its aftermath. What is indisputable is that Irish democracy was consolidated at exactly the same time as democracy was secured on the continent. If this is so, one has to be wary of explanations that suggest a specifically Irish route to democracy or that rely on explanatory factors which were absent in the wider democratic sample. Democratisation, then as now, was not a local process, and its causes can only really be understood with reference to forces at work in the wider world. As a result, any explanation of why the Free State remained democratic should begin first with comparative theories on democratisation and democratic consolidation. It is to such theories that our attention must now turn.

Chapter 3

Economic development and democracy in Ireland

'Ireland belonged to a group of countries which until the Second World War had been largely unaffected by the main currents of industrial growth in the past century.   **United Nations Report, 1961**

Writing in 1971 Robert Dahl reflected that 'it is widely assumed that a high level of socio-economic development not only favours the transformation of a hegemonic regime into a polyarchy but also helps to maintain – may even be necessary to maintain a polyarchy'.[1] The relationship between economic development and democracy has taken three divergent patterns. First, economic development can lead to the permanent transition from an undemocratic to a stable democratic system. Second, where significant economic development does not take place, an undemocratic regime persists. Third, if the economic conditions are only 'mixed or temporarily favourable' then three more possibilities exist: (*a*) democracy would break down and be replaced by an undemocratic system; (*b*) the same process occurs, but in this case the undemocratic regime also breaks down and is then replaced by a democratic system; (*c*) the second process continues without any type of system lasting long.[2]

Which pattern does Ireland fit into? While Lee argues that between 1848 and 1918 'southern Ireland modernised probably as quickly as any other western European society',[3] other writers argue that independent Ireland is relevant to democratic theory precisely because it is an exception to the rule that democracy blossoms only in modern developed societies.[4] Irish democracy can be seen either as the normal outcome of processes of modernisation which transformed Irish society in the latter half of the nineteenth century, or as a modern polity which emerged out of an essentially backward society. In the latter case 'unique historical events', rather than socio-economic processes, 'may account for either the persistence or failure of democracy'.[5]

This chapter tests which of these possibilities is true, by comparing Irish rates of economic development with those of the democratic and those of the undemocratic European countries in the twentieth century. The first section tests the relationship between democratisation and economic development in

Ireland, while the second examines the relationship between economic development and the consolidation of Irish democracy. The third section provides a critique of the use of quantitative indicators in comparative politics. The emphasis throughout is on clarifying the comparative position of the Irish state with respect to the levels of development existing in the democratic and the undemocratic world.

3.1 Economic development and democratisation ·

The most influential developmental theory of democracy was published by Lipset in 1959. He asked why democracies are in general much wealthier, more urbanised, more educated, and more industrialised than non-democracies. His answer was that the 'economic development complex', consisting of industrialisation, increased wealth, urbanisation, and education, provides a crucial support for democratic politics by creating a larger middle class:

> Increased wealth . . . also affects the political role of the middle class through changing the shape of the stratification structure so that it shifts from an elongated pyramid, with a large lower class base, to a diamond with a growing middle class. A large middle class plays a mitigating role in moderating conflict since it is able to reward moderate and democratic parties and penalise extremist groups.[6]

Lipset speaks of 'social requisites' rather than necessary conditions, but it is clear he believes that both the emergence of a democratic system and its maintenance are closely related to this 'economic development complex', whose components are so highly correlated with each other 'as to form one common factor'. For example, he argues that although individual characteristics, such as a high level of education, may not be sufficient conditions for democracy, 'the available evidence does suggest that it comes close to being a necessary condition in the modern world'.[7]

Lipset hypothesised that 'the more well-to-do a nation, the greater the chances that it will sustain democracy'.[8] In his view the diffusion of wealth is what makes democratic compromise possible since it leads to a more open class system, educational opportunities for more people, and more economic security for the working class:

> From Aristotle down to the present, men have argued that only in a wealthy society in which a relatively few citizens lived in real poverty could a situation exist in which the mass of the population could intelligently participate in politics and could develop the self-restraint necessary to avoid succumbing to the appeals of irresponsible demagogues. A society divided between a large impoverished mass

and a small favoured elite would result either in oligarchy (dictatorial rule of the small upper stratum) or in tyranny (popularly based dictatorship).[9]

Lipset defined democracy procedurally as 'a political system which supplies regular constitutional opportunities for changing the governing officials', and substantively as 'a social mechanism for the resolution of the problem of societal decision-making among conflicting interest groups which permits the largest possible part of the population to influence these decisions through their ability to choose among alternative contenders for political office'.[10] Since Lipset took durability to be one indicator of stability, he took his data from sources for the late 1950s. These data were used to answer the very different questions of why some states became democratic while others did not, and why some democracies remained democratic while others did not. In contrast the data I use to analyse the relationship the emergence of democracy and economic development is taken from the beginning of the inter-war period, whereas I use Lipset's own data to explore whether the survival of democracy in some states had anything to do with their subsequent economic performance. Throughout, I follow Lipset's method of testing his basic hypothesis: the higher the level of development the greater the chances for democratic politics, by comparing mean scores for his indices of development for samples of 'more democratic' and 'less democratic countries'. 'More democratic' includes states considered democratic and stable by Lipset in 1959 while 'less democratic' includes states classified by Lipset as unstable democracies and dictatorships.

This first section tests whether there was also a close connection between the initial process of democratisation and industrialisation. Lipset's data showed that the level of industrialisation was much higher for democracies than for non-democracies in 1959. Lipset's indices for industrialisation were the percentage of males employed in agriculture, and per capita energy consumed. It is impossible to find historical data for the latter, so I will concentrate only on the first, albeit for the whole of the workforce rather than only for males. Table 3.1 shows the mean percentage of the workforce employed in agriculture for a sample of European democracies and non-democracies around 1920, as well as figures for the Free State in 1926, and Ireland as a whole, in the last census year before partition, 1911. Clearly in 1920 the democracies were much more industrialised than the non-democracies. The figure for Ireland as a whole is exactly the same as that for Sweden in 1920, but none of the other democratic states included in the sample – Belgium, Denmark, the Netherlands, Norway, Switzerland, Sweden, or the UK – had as high a proportion of its workforce in agriculture as the Free State, which has a figure midway between the democratic and the undemocratic mean. Ireland as a whole was quite industrialised, but the independent state was significantly less industrialised than other democracies at the time.

Table 3.1 **Percentage of the economically active population employed in agriculture around 1920**

	Mean Percentage	Range
More democratic mean	27.5	7–44
Less democratic mean	71.2	57–82
Irish Free State[1]	52	
Ireland[2]	44	

1 Figures are for 1926, and include those employed in forestry and fisheries.
2 Figures are for 1911, and include those employed in forestry and fisheries.

More democratic sample: Denmark, Norway, Sweden, Belgium, The Netherlands, Switzerland and Britain.
Less democratic sample: Bulgaria, Hungary, Poland, Yugoslavia and Austria.

Sources: M. Alestalo, *Structural Change, Classes and the State: Finland in an Historical and Comparative Perspective* (1986), table 2, p. 26. For Ireland, Mitchell, *International Historical Statistics: Europe 1750–1933* (1998), table B1, p.152.

Most of the industries that had existed in the early nineteenth century, such as cotton, wool, silk, tanneries, and coach making, had gone into long-term decline after 1801.[11] The decline in industrial employment was particularly striking in Connacht where in 1881 only 15.2 per cent of the labour force were employed in industry compared to 42.9 per cent in 1821. These western areas were 'those most reliant upon foreign markets to absorb their surplus labour [and] were least successful in developing alternative sources of employment at home'.[12] Only in the province of Ulster was there a similarly dramatic decline in the percentage of the labour force employed in industry, from 55.3 per cent to 37.1 per cent, yet that decline was only in the border counties of Cavan, Derry, Donegal, Fermanagh, Monaghan and Tyrone (three of which would be included in the Free State).[13] The closer one got to Belfast, the only example of large-scale industrialisation in Irish history, the more decline gave way to growth.

Partition, which removed the north-east from the territory of the new state in 1920, left the Free State without a highly industrialised region. The census figures on the occupation of males in the future area of the Free State, published in 1926, showed a stagnant situation. In 1881 approximately 59 per cent of males worked in agriculture. By 1901 the percentage had increased to 60 per cent. In 1911, the last census year before independence, as many as 56.4 per cent of males still worked in agriculture.[14] In short, if Ireland did industrialise, the process was limited to certain areas, especially in the north-east. Areas of the Free State were probably industrialised by European standards; others were certainly less industrialised than the norm in Western Europe. As a result, outside the future area of Northern Ireland industrialisation could only have had a marginal impact on democratisation.

Max Weber argued that the modern concept of citizenship was closely related to the emergence of cities. Similarly Lipset maintained that occupational groups such as farmers are more receptive to extremist ideologies and less tolerant of differences since they, 'like workers in isolated industries, tend to have a more homogenous political environment than those employed in most urban occupations'.[15] The more cosmopolitan social groups are exposed to a variety of influences and are therefore less likely to accept all or nothing views. As a result the more urban a society the less likely it is to be exposed to fundamental conflicts. Table 3.2 shows the levels of urbanisation of eighteen states around 1920, ranked according to the size of the total population living in urban settlements of ten thousand or above. Figures are given for the percentage of the population living in areas of less than ten thousand inhabitants, ten thousand to a hundred thousand inhabitants, in areas of a hundred thousand to a million inhabitants, and in areas with over a million inhabitants.

Table 3.2 **Distribution of total population by size of locality as a percentage of total population in European states around 1920, ranked according to size of total population in urban centres of 10,000 or above**

Country	Less than 10,000	10,000– 100,000	100,000– 1,000,000	More than 1,000,000
England & Wales			39.1	13.5
Netherlands	41.3	34.5	24.2	
N. Ireland	56.6	10.3	33.0	
Italy	54.4	32.3	13.3	
Belgium	57.9	30.2	11.9	
Germany			18.6	08.2
Austria	58.7	08.3	02.6	30.4
Denmark	64.6	14.0	21.4	
France	65.4	19.2	08.0	07.5
Irish Free State	68.2	08.9	22.9	
Switzerland	72.4	16.1	11.5	
Norway	75.3	14.9	09.8	
Sweden	76.5	11.0	12.5	
Hungary	69.3	16.3	14.4	
Finland	87.5	06.8	05.9	
Czechoslovakia	81.1	10.7	08.2	
USSR	85.6	07.9	06.5	
Yugoslavia	92.7	05.3	02.0	

Sources: for Western Europe, P. Flora et al., *State, Economy and Society in Western Europe* (1987), pp. 251–80; for Eastern Europe and the USSR, Schoup, *The East European and Soviet Data Handbook* (1981), table H, pp. 397–407.

Rather surprisingly, Northern Ireland had one of the most urbanised populations in Europe, which was more typical of Great Britain than of Ireland as a whole. Moreover, the Free State was more urbanised than Sweden and Norway, and was not, contrary to popular belief, an exceptionally rural democracy. A relatively large proportion of the Free State's population, fifteen per cent, lived in cities of a hundred thousand inhabitants or more. This is above average for our sample of states and higher than that of Italy, Switzerland, and Denmark. There might therefore have been some connection between urbanisation and democratisation in Ireland. Lee estimates that the overall proportion of the Irish population living in towns increased from 15 per cent in 1841 to 35 per cent in 1914.[16] Dublin, with a population of 300,000 in 1914, and Belfast, which saw its population grow from 100,000 to 400,000 between 1850 and 1914, were the largest population centres. Their growth was exceptional compared to the rest of the country.

Indeed the geographical pattern of urbanisation reveals a similar pattern to that of industrialisation. Royle estimates that the mean rate of urbanisation for an Irish town between 1841 and 1911 was only 0.47 per cent per annum. In other words a town would grow to 133 per cent of its 1841 size by 1911. Yet most Irish towns failed to grow at all in this period and most were smaller in 1911 than in 1841. Only twelve out of 32 counties had any town with a growth rate above the mean. Moreover, all the five counties with a positive general rate of urbanisation were in the east of the country. Those towns that grew at a rate higher than the national mean clustered around commercial centres such as Dublin, Limerick, Cork, Galway or Belfast.[17] This suggests again that while the Irish figures do not disprove the general thesis that urbanisation and democratisation are positively related, internal variation in the rate of urbanisation suggests that this relationship was stronger in some areas than in others.

According to Lipset, increased wealth also has positive effects on a society since it moderates the political outlook of the working class. He argues that 'a belief in secular reformist gradualism can only be the ideology of a relatively well-to-do lower class', and the presence of a well-to-do working class also affects the upper classes' attitude towards democratisation:

> The poorer the country, and the lower the absolute standard of the lower classes, the greater the pressure on the upper strata to treat the lower classes as beyond the pale of human society, as vulgar, as innately inferior, as a lower caste. The sharp difference in the style of living between those at the top and those at the bottom makes this psychologically necessary.[18]

Only rough international comparisons are possible with respect to wealth. Here I rely on the figures for national income calculated by a group of Irish economic historians.[19] Two estimates of GNP are provided in table 3.3. The first set in column A relates to GNP per capita valued at US prices. The second set, in column B, is based on different sources, and relates to GDP per capita. Kennedy et al. showed that the two measurements led to different results. The first set of figures, A, suggests that Irish GNP per capita in 1913 was only slightly below the European average, and sixty per cent higher than the level of Eastern Europe as a whole. Ireland comes tenth out of 23 European countries and its per capita GNP was about 15 per cent higher than the European mean level. It is only slightly behind that of France, Austria, and Sweden. However, the second set of figures, B, leaves Ireland in twelfth position. Its product per capita is marginally below the mean level.

Table 3.3 **Average real product per capita in states classified by Lipset as more democratic and less democratic, and Southern Ireland relative to the UK in 1913**

	A	Range	B	Range
More democratic mean	83.5	57–126	81.6	52–122
Less democratic mean	44.7	23–72	47.3	26–67
Ireland	61		55	

More democratic sample: United Kingdom, Switzerland, Denmark, Belgium, The Netherlands, Sweden, Southern Ireland, Norway, United States, Canada, Australia, New Zealand.

Less democratic sample: Austria, West Germany, France, Finland, Czechoslovakia, Italy, Spain, Poland, Hungary, Romania, Greece, Portugal, Yugoslavia, Bulgaria.

Source: K. A. Kennedy et al., *The Economic Development of Ireland in the Twentieth Century* (1988), table 1.1, p. 14.

The authors conclude that:

> both sets of figures are consistent with the broad conclusion that average income per capita in Ireland was not widely different from the European average in 1913. Thus, while it would be going too far to imply, as Lee does, that Ireland in 1913 was in the first division among European countries in terms of per capita income, nevertheless its relative standing was surprisingly high for a country commonly thought of as a very poor and undeveloped country.[20]

Nevertheless, after including the non-European democracies, the United States, New Zealand, Canada, and Australia, the figures show that Ireland is really in an intermediary position between the democratic and the undemocratic groups. Next to Norway it has the lowest score for per capita GNP on both measurements, while its position vis à vis the mean scores is midway between the democratic and the undemocratic countries on the first measurement, and clearly closer to the undemocratic mean on the second. In short, as a European democracy the Irish state was not poor, but as a member of a larger world of democracies, it was quite a poor relation.

Table 3.4 **Educational enrolment levels around 1920, ranked according to per capita number of enrolled students (.0001) in each educational sector**

Primary enrolment per capita (.0001)		Secondary enrolment per capita (.0001)		University enrolment per capita (.0001)	
USA	1974	USA	247	USA	65
New Zealand	1877	Switzerland	198	New Zealand	32
Netherlands	1629	Greece	167	Austria	23
Ireland	1608	Czechoslovakia	166	Switzerland	18
Germany	1572	New Zealand	128	Germany	15
Belgium	1502	Germany	117	Hungary	12
Norway	1449	Italy	108	Italy	11
Switzerland	1388	Finland	102	Belgium	11
Austria	1381	Bulgaria	101	UK	11
Bulgaria	1347	UK	83	France	11
UK	1279	Norway	83	Poland	11
Sweden	1211	Poland	75	Sweden	10
Hungary	1211	Hungary	70	Czechoslovakia	10
Italy	1113	Ireland	69	Finland	9
France	1025	Austria	65	Ireland	9
Czechoslovakia	1017	Sweden	61	USSR	8
Poland	899	Romania	60	Netherlands	8
Greece	888	Yugoslavia	56	Romania	7
Finland	708	Belgium	52	Denmark	6
Yugoslavia	674	USSR	51	Portugal	3
Romania	642	Netherlands	43	Greece	1
USSR	417	France	38	Bulgaria	0
Portugal	313	Portugal	18	Norway	0

Source: A. S. Banks, *Cross Polity Time-Series Data* (1971), Section 6, pp. 208–36.

The widely held view that the better educated a society, the better the chances for democracy, is shared by Lipset. Today democratic countries are almost entirely literate and have consistently higher rates of enrolment at all educational levels than non-democracies. Education is usually regarded as an indispensable requirement of citizenship.[21] Political literacy, reading newspapers, registering to vote, and voting itself all require basic functional literacy. Education also broadens outlooks, makes people see others' points of view, and enables them to appreciate the need for tolerance in a political system. Perhaps the most important educational qualification for democracy is the possession of literacy. The inter-war data suggest that near-universal literacy is the norm for democratic countries. Diverse countries, such as Australia, Czechoslovakia, the Irish Free State and the United States, all had literacy rates well over 90 per cent around 1920. In contrast, those Eastern European countries that were undemocratic show a consistently lower level of literacy. In 1928 the USSR and Portugal had more illiterates than literates, Yugoslavia had almost as many illiterates as literates, while Romania's literacy rate was only just above 50 per cent. Greece's level of basic literacy at this time was only 56.1 per cent. Poland and Italy, which had both reverted to authoritarian rule by 1928, score highest among non-democracies, with 71.7 per cent and 75.7 per cent respectively. Remarkably, the individual figures for democracies do not vary much, and are in almost all cases close to 95 per cent of the population.[22]

Lipset also uses three other indicators to measure the level of education in a country – primary enrolment, secondary enrolment, and higher education enrolment. Table 3.4 gives figures for enrolment levels in these sectors per ten thousand persons. The figures suggest a strong relationship between the level of basic education and democratisation, but also suggest that while basic educational development is a necessary condition of democracy, increases in the level of secondary and university education will not necessarily increase the prospects for democracy unless this first hurdle is passed. With regard to primary enrolment, Ireland came fourth out of twenty-three states in this table. A system of primary education was established in 1831, and in the 1890s eight years of schooling was made compulsory. Where there had been 4,500 schools and 500,000 pupils in 1848, by 1914 this had doubled to around 9,000 schools and 1,000,000 pupils. However, poor attendance rates were common. The majority of children before 1918 received only four to five years' schooling, the absolute minimum necessary to cross the threshold of literacy. The average school attendance under the age of fourteen in 1921 was only 15 per cent.[23] After independence the 1927 School Attendance Act tried to enforce attendance on children. Poor attendance aside, the figures suggest that the Free State had achieved a comparatively high level of basic educational development by 1931, and that the vast majority of the population were at least functionally literate.

Having reviewed the Free State's position on the four elements of Lipset's 'economic development complex', what conclusions can be drawn from these figures? Firstly, there is little statistical backing for the argument that:

> as a twentieth century nation faced with the problems of decolonisation, it is more comparable in character and conviction, in many respects, to the new nations of the Third World than to Denmark, Switzerland, or other small Western demo-cracies to which it is more frequently compared. Its economy and social structure

bear the strong imprint of its colonially dependent status. It still remains a largely rural, agriculturally orientated nation, unlike most of its Western counterparts.[24]

In 1921 the Irish Free State was a more developed entity than the successor states in Eastern Europe, never mind the post-colonial states in Asia and Africa. In comparison to the other 'small Western democracies' the Free State was also a highly educated and urbanised society, although the figures for industrialisation suggest that it was in an intermediary position between the western and eastern European countries. All in all the figures suggest that those European countries that were undemocratic were less developed than the Free State, while those that were more developed were democratic. An analysis of another set of quantitative indicators of the social structure of the Free State in the 1920s would arrive at exactly the same conclusion.[25]

On the other hand, comparative historical statistics do not support Lee's argument that southern Ireland modernised at a comparable rate to other Western societies between the Famine and independence.[26] Central to the concept of development is the idea of growth. Most European countries saw their populations grow by an average of one per cent per annum in the nineteenth century. In contrast, the Irish population decreased on average by one per cent per annum, and between 1849 and 1911 the population almost halved in size. This decline affected the pattern of economic development. Although Ireland's GNP levels were close to the European average in 1913, the annual growth rate of total product in the century before was only estimated to have been 0.7 per cent, which was the lowest among European countries. With Spain, Ireland was the only country to stay behind the one per cent rate. If the per capita growth rate was one of the highest in Europe for the same period this was largely due to population decline:

> Given the wide disparities in income levels in 1841, and the fact that the bulk of the population decline was concentrated in the poorer half of the population, a significant increase in overall average income per capita would emerge even if the better half of the population had experienced no improvement in income per capita.[27]

Although Ireland may have been as wealthy as Norway in 1921 and was certainly wealthier than Finland in 1918, this was not a product of greater development. Rather, the vicissitudes of persistent underdevelopment were mitigated by large-scale emigration from the areas worst affected. The picture that emerges from the historical statistics of Irish development is not one of overall growth, but one where

> a declining rural economy associated with the loss of population at and after the Famine, contrasted with extensive urbanisation based around the commerce of Dublin, and more particularly, the industrialisation of Belfast and eastern Ulster.[28]

What developed then were not so much two economies – a commercially viable one in the East, and a subsistence economy in the West – but a continuum in which economic backwardness became more pronounced the further one moved westward. National statistics do not reflect this complex pattern. Some areas of the future state may have been developed by West European standards while others may have resembled Eastern Europe more.

3.2   Economic performance and the consolidation of democracy

It is frequently argued that continued economic growth is a necessary precondition of political stability in democratic states. Lipset analysed democratic persistence and breakdown in terms of two concepts, legitimacy and effectiveness. The first, legitimacy, 'involves the capacity of a political system to engender and maintain the belief that existing political institutions are the most appropriate or proper ones for the society'. The second, effectiveness, was defined by Lipset as 'the extent to which it satisfies the basic functions of government as defined by the expectations of most members of the society'.[29] The question Lipset then asks is 'how the degree of legitimacy of a democratic system may affect its capacity to survive the crisis of effectiveness, such as depressions or lost wars'. [30] Lipset uses a four-fold table to analyse the fortunes of countries during the depression of the thirties. The four possible combinations of his variables are represented graphically in figure 3.5 by positions A, B, C, and D. In A he places states such as the United Kingdom and the USA, possessing both legitimacy and effectiveness. In C he places states such as Austria and Germany, which were low in legitimacy but which remained 'reasonably effective'. In D Lipset would place ineffective and illegitimate regimes which needed to maintain themselves by force, as with the Stalinist regimes of Eastern Europe. No mention is made of regimes in B, which were low in effectiveness and high in legitimacy during the 1930s.

Table 3.5 **The relationship between different degrees of effectiveness and legitimacy in different political systems**

		Effectiveness	
		+	−
	+	A	B
Legitimacy			
	−	C	D

Source: S. M. Lipset, 'Some social requisites of democracy: economic development and political legitimacy', *APSR 53* (1959), p. 90.

Lipset summarised the inter-war experience as follows:

> When the effectiveness of the governments of the various countries broke down
> in the 1930s, those countries which were high on the scale of legitimacy remained
> democratic, while countries which were low such as Germany, Austria, and Spain,
> lost their freedom, and France narrowly escaped a similar fate. Or to put the
> changes in terms of location in the four-fold table, countries which shifted from
> A to B remained democratic, while the political systems which shifted from C to
> D broke down.[31]

The Weimar Republic failed to survive the crisis of effectiveness during the
Great Depression even though its economy did not suffer to the extent of
those of the USA or The Netherlands which 'entered the depression high in
legitimacy and their regimes consequently endured intact'.[32] So at first Lipset
suggests that a high degree of legitimacy can compensate for short-run deficiencies in effectiveness. Later he reverses the argument by hypothesising that:

> Prolonged effectiveness which lasts over a number of generations may give
> legitimacy to a political system; in the modern world, such effectiveness mainly
> means constant economic development. Thus those nations which adapted most
> successfully to the requirements of an industrial system had the fewest internal
> political strains, and either preserved their traditional legitimacy, the monarchy,
> or developed new strong symbols of legitimacy.[33]

This suggests that the legitimacy of traditional institutions is due to successful
modernisation, and that effectiveness is really a side effect of economic
growth. Lipset later explains the redemocratisation of Western Europe and
Japan after 1945 in these terms. Post-war Germany, Italy, and Japan, 'clearly
had no legitimacy at birth. But they have had the advantage of the post-war
economic miracles, which produced jobs and a steadily rising standard of
living. They have been economically effective for over four decades'.[34] So
regimes which lack traditional legitimacy must be effective if they are to
be stable.

What is noticeably absent from Lipset's analysis is a consideration of
states such as the Irish Free State that did not begin the inter-war period with
a high degree of legitimacy, and were therefore in either position C or D to
begin with, yet did not break down during 'the crisis of effectiveness'. In
contrast the Free State became more stable as the 1930s went on. This leaves
two possibilities. It could have moved from C or D to A or to B. If the former
happened, its achievement of legitimacy could be explained by an increase in
effectiveness, or if it moved to B it became more legitimate without an
improved economic performance. In this section I test which of these

possibilities was true by comparing the Irish state's comparative position on the main developmental indicators around 1959 with its position around 1920.

Table 3.6 shows the figures for industrialisation for 1956, which also include figures for per capita energy consumption, measured in terms of tons of coal per person per annum. These figures show that the position of the Irish state had changed dramatically since 1920. On both measures its position is typical of non-democratic states, whereas the 1920 figures had suggested it was in an intermediary position between the two samples. Clearly there was little significant industrialisation between 1920 and 1956. This rules out the possibility that the survival of Irish democracy after 1921 could be explained by the state's economic growth.

Table 3.6 **Irish level of industrialisation compared with European states classified by Lipset as 'more' or 'less' democratic, 1956–59**

	% males in agriculture	*Per capita energy consumed*
More democratic mean,	21	3.6
Less democratic mean	41	1.4
Republic of Ireland	46	1.4
Ranges		
More democratic	6–46	1.4–7.8
Less democratic	16–60	.27–3.2

More democratic sample: Belgium, Canada, Denmark, Ireland, Luxembourg, The Netherlands, Norway, Sweden, Switzerland, United States

Less democratic sample: Austria, Bulgaria, Czechoslovakia, Finland, France, West Germany, Greece, Hungary, Romania, Spain, Yugoslavia

Sources: Lipset, 'Some social requisites of democracy: economic development and political legitimacy', *APSR 53* (1959), table 11, p. 76; UN *Demographic Yearbook* (1956), table 12, pp. 350–70; UN *Statistical Yearbook* (1956), table 127, pp. 308–10.

Although the Irish educational data in table 3.7 show moderate increases in all respects on the 1920 data, the basic pattern shown by the 1920 data continued. The Irish Republic had a very high level of basic educational development in the late 1950s, but this had not been translated into growth in other sectors since independence. The second generation in independent Ireland were probably not better educated than the first. Although the level of secondary education was probably not low by democratic standards, university education seems severely restricted by European standards, democratic or undemocratic. The Irish experience between 1921 and 1959 then was more one of educational frustration than educational development.

Table 3.7 **Irish levels of education in 1959 compared with those of states classified by Lipset as 'more' and 'less' democratic countries**

Means	% Literate in 1959	Primary enrolment per capita (.0001)	Secondary enrolment per capita (.0001)	University enrolment per capita (.0001)
More democratic mean	98.5	1347	367.9	49.7
Less democratic mean[1]	90.1	1240	181.3	45.2
Republic of Ireland	98.8	1767	256	35
Ranges				
More democratic	97.6–98.8	925–1839	123–677	0–177
Less democratic	61.3–98.8	916–1603	60–446	22–108

1 Less democratic literacy mean excludes Hungary

More democratic sample: Australia, Belgium, Canada, Denmark, Luxembourg, The Netherlands, New Zealand, Norway, Sweden, Switzerland, United Kingdom, Republic of Ireland, United States

Less democratic sample: Austria, Hungary, Bulgaria, Czechoslovakia, Finland, France, West Germany, Greece, Italy, Poland, Portugal, Romania, Spain, USSR, Yugoslavia

Sources: A Banks, *Cross Polity Time Series Data* (1971), Section 6, pp. 206–36.

Table 3.8 **Irish levels of urbanisation compared with 'more' and 'less' democratic European states around 1960**

Country	–10,000	10,000–100,000	100,000+
More democratic mean	54.3	24.4	21.2
Less democratic mean	63.7	18.9	17.4
Republic of Ireland	64.3	10.3	25
Ranges			
More democratic	24.7–72.3	10.3–42.6	9.3–32.7
Less democratic	40–77.4	10.7–35.3	8.4–32

More democratic sample: Belgium (1961), Denmark (1960), Republic of Ireland (1961), The Netherlands (1960), Norway (1960), Sweden (1960), Switzerland (1961).

Less democratic sample: Austria (1961), Albania (1960), Bulgaria (1956), Czechoslovakia (1961), Finland (1960), France (1962), Hungary (1960), Italy (1961), Poland (1960), Romania (1960), Yugoslavia (1961).

Sources: For Western Europe, P. Flora et al., *State, Economy and Society in Western Europe 1815–1975* (1987) vol. II, pp. 251–80; for Eastern Europe and the USSR, P. Schoup, *The Eastern European and Soviet Data Handbook* (1981), table H, pp. 397–407.

Lipset does not specify a date for the figures for urbanisation but the year 1959 is assumed to be a good guide. The Irish figures are for 1961. Again the figures in table 3.8 show a changed situation. Whereas in 1920 the state was a relatively urbanised society, more so than Sweden for instance, by 1959 the number of people living in areas of ten thousand or less had declined by only four per cent. Over the same period the Swedish figure for people living in areas of ten thousand or less dropped from over three quarters of the population to less than half. In 1920 almost a third of the Irish state's population lived in urban areas of 10,000 or more; by 1959 the figure was still only 35.7 per cent. This figure is much closer to the non-democratic mean. The percentage of the Irish state's population living in urban areas between 10,000 and 100,000 inhabitants increased only slightly in this period, and in 1961 it was below the mean figure for the undemocratic sample. Moreover, the percentage of the Irish state's population living in large cities of 100,000 or more also increased only slightly. This figure is still clearly closer to the democratic mean, but does not negate the overall impression of a society that failed to urbanise at a rate comparable to other Western democracies. In 1920 the Irish Free State was an urbanised society by European standards. By 1959 the Irish Republic was an exceptionally rural democracy.

Table 3.9 **Irish levels of wealth compared with 'more' and 'less' democratic countries, 1957–64**

	Per capita income in $	Thousands of persons per doctor	Telephones per thousand persons	Radios per thousand persons	Newspaper copies per thousand persons
More democratic mean	695	.86	205	350	341
Less democratic mean	308	1.4	58	160	167
Republic of Ireland	550	1	71.8	176	225

More democratic sample: Australia, Belgium, Canada, Denmark, Ireland, Luxembourg, The Netherlands, New Zealand, Norway, Sweden, Switzerland, United Kingdom, United States.

Less democratic sample: Austria, Bulgaria, Czechoslovakia, Finland, France, West Germany, Greece, Hungary, Iceland, Italy, Poland, Portugal, Romania, Spain, Yugoslavia.

Sources: While all the mean figures are taken from Lipset, 'Some social requisites of democracy', *APSR 53* (1959), the following figures for the Irish Republic are taken from different sources. GNP per capita for the year 1957, thousands of persons per doctor for the year 1959, radios per thousand persons and newspaper circulation per thousand for the year 1960, are from B. Russett et al., *World Handbook of Political and Social Indicators* (1964), tables 44, 59, 35 and 31. The national figures for telephones per thousand are from C. L. Taylor and M. C. Hudson, *World Handbook of Political and Social Indicators* (1972), table 4.7, and are for the year 1965.

It is easier to obtain figures for Lipset's numerous indicators of wealth for the post-war period than it was for 1920. Some of these indicators are more appropriately considered measures of social mobilisation, such as newspaper copies per thousand persons. Nevertheless, social mobilisation can still be considered a dimension of economic development, and is relevant to the maintenance of a political system that requires at least periodic mass participation. Table 3.9 shows that around 1960 the Irish Republic was not poor by European standards: most of the figures place the Irish state in an intermediary category between democracies and non-democracies in terms of wealth. However, some decline is apparent regarding GNP per capita. In 1913 it was placed about tenth out of 23 European countries in terms of GNP per capita. From these figures it had dropped to seventeenth out of 27 countries, but its figure was still higher than those of most Eastern European countries, with the exceptions of East Germany and Czechoslovakia. What is noticeable is that the Irish state's system of communications, measured by the number of radios, telephones and newspapers per thousand people, was relatively undeveloped.

Taken together, do these figures support Lipset's hypothesis that improved effectiveness gave legitimacy to the system? Clearly this is disproved by the Irish figures which show a decline since 1920 on practically all aspects of development. Rather than moving from C to A on Lipset's scheme – from being a state with a high degree of effectiveness and a low degree of legitimacy, to being a state with a high degree of both effectiveness and legitimacy – the figures suggest that the Irish case moved from C to B. It went from being a state with a low degree of legitimacy and a high degree of effectiveness, to being a state with a high degree of legitimacy and a low degree of effectiveness. This suggests that the achievement of legitimacy had next to nothing to do with economic performance. Coakley also tested the hypotheses that the collapse of European democracies was related to the severity of the inter-war economic crisis, by comparing the economic fortunes of three democracies that survived the depression (Czechoslovakia, Finland and Ireland), with those of three that collapsed (Estonia, Latvia and Lithuania). He noted that the survivors' external trade experienced a slump of the same degree as that of the Baltic Republics.[35] His examination of the cost of living index for the latter group also suggests that the material conditions of people in the Baltic Republics may actually have been improving when the Estonian and Latvian coups took place. Furthermore, data on unemployment levels show that unemployment increased at a dramatically higher rate in Ireland and Czechoslovakia, 'where, ironically, the authoritarian threat was weakest – to a point enormously above the Baltic and Finnish levels'.[36]

From Coakley's analysis there seems to be no relationship between the two variables Lipset uses to explain the fate of democracy during the depression.

Indeed the economic crisis caused by the depression in Ireland was deeper than that in Finland, but it was in Finland that the emergence of a small right-wing party, the Lapuas, proved 'almost fatal to parliamentary government' in 1930.[37] In contrast, the emergence of the Blueshirts did not present as serious a challenge to democratic government in Ireland. The general consensus is that the Finns did not suffer heavily from the depression and that this was an important source of stability.[38] Between 1922 and 1928 their economy recovered from the wartime crisis and its export goods found new markets in Western Europe to replace the Russian ones.[39] The inter-war period actually ended well for the Finnish economy.[40] The immediate reason for the greater severity of the depression in Ireland was the state's dependence on agricultural exports, which took up about 86 per cent of total exports and made up over a third of national income in 1929. Agricultural income declined by 12.8 per cent between 1929 and 1931 and its fall accelerated after that.[41] The situation was compounded by the fact that traditional routes of emigration dried up in the early 1930s, leaving the state with more and more unemployment. Whereas in 1929 over twenty thousand people emigrated, by 1932 this figure had dropped to less than one thousand per annum.[42]

In other words, Irish democracy was consolidated during a time of economic hardship and high unemployment. In contrast, economic trends before and immediately after the emergence of the Lapua movement in Finland were more favourable than in Ireland, but it was in Finland that the right-wing challenge was strongest. It is difficult then to explain the more severe nature of the political crisis in Finland in economic terms. Linz also suggests that there was no simple relationship between economic performance and democratic stability:

> The world depression that presumably destroyed democracy in Weimar and Austria created more unemployment in Norway and in the Netherlands and in fact consolidated the Norwegian democracy. The Dutch government was one of the most long-lasting after the depression. The degree of institutional legitimacy was more decisive than the economic crisis.[43]

Barry reflects that regimes that were low in efficiency and high in legitimacy in the 1930s may have been the rule rather than the exception in the democratic world, since in the 1930s all the 'stable democracies' had serious unemployment problems.[44] The United States is the only case Lipset acknowledges, but all three Scandinavian countries can be considered states that were low in effectiveness but high in legitimacy. This suggests that for most of the inter-war democracies what was important was that these systems had consolidated themselves prior to the depression, that the sole source of stability was simply the legitimacy of the existing arrangements, or as Coakley puts it, 'the extent to which it [i.e. the population] had had the opportunity of absorbing liberal democratic norms', and not a combination of legitimacy and effectiveness at all.[45] If a state's effectiveness is bound to vary, as it did in most states in the 1930s, then any stable state 'must be legitimate though it may or may not be effective'.[46] What explains long-term stability in democratic countries is therefore legitimacy on its own.

In summary, the consolidation of Irish democracy cannot be explained by the economic performance of the Irish state after 1921. MacDonagh argues that between 1921 and 1959 independent Ireland's economy grew by only one per cent.[47] In 1961, just two years after the publication of Lipset's article, the UN's annual *Survey of the World Economic Situation* published a report on the development problems of Europe. It grouped Ireland with the peripheral countries of Turkey, Greece, Yugoslavia, Spain, and Portugal:

> Per capita income in Ireland is roughly twice as high as in the countries of southern Europe, but still only one-half of that of the industrial countries of western Europe. Though climatically Ireland resembles more the countries of north-western Europe, it is closer to those of southern Europe in economic structure and its lack of economic development. In particular, as in those countries, agriculture predominates in employment, output and exports, and under-employment and unemployment are only partly offset by emigration.[48]

Despite the structural similarities, none of these southern European countries was democratic whereas the Irish Republic certainly was. Peillon came to the paradoxical conclusion that 'Ireland displays major institutional features which are closely associated with advanced societies, although it cannot be defined as an advanced capitalist economy'. He pointed to a 'striking disjuncture' between the processes of capitalist development and institutional development, a disjuncture which is even more pronounced for the post-independence period than it was for before 1921.[49]

3.3   Minima and maxima of democratic development

For most of the last three decades the Irish case has been considered an exception to the rule that democracy blossoms only in modern industrial conditions. As 'a poor new nation' it serves as a useful test case for theories of democratic breakdown in the Third World.[50] Such a view suggests that there is no relationship between the processes of capitalist development and institutional development in Ireland. Although it is true that the consolidation of Irish democracy had next to nothing to do with economic growth, conventionally understood, Irish society was still a relatively developed entity in 1921. Why then has the state so often been considered, like India, an exceptional case for democratic theory? Part of the reason for this belief lies in the country's self-perception as a post-colonial state. Part also lies in the fact that the comparisons normally made between Ireland and the democratic world are with the very developed world of Anglo-American democracy, and not with the smaller European democracies where levels of economic development before 1921 were comparable to Ireland's. A third reason lies in the nature of comparative indicators which exaggerate the discrepancies between the Irish case and the developed world. The manner in which this statistical fiction is maintained forms the subject of this section.

Lipset was trying to measure the shift from predominantly agrarian societies to industrialised societies. The key indicator of this is the size of the labour force employed in agriculture. This is a misleading indicator of industrialisation. For example in 1920 Finland's agricultural labour force was enormous by any standards, yet this should not be taken as an indication of retarded industrialisation because large parts of Finnish agriculture were in fact industrialised. This fundamentally important aspect of Finnish industrialisation is missed out on by Lipset's indicator which, à la Marx, lumps the world's agrarian populations into a sack of potatoes. The poor and rural image of Ireland is also reinforced by the use of GNP per capita as a measure of wealth. GNP per capita measures only the commercial value of goods and services produced. As the proportion of goods that are commercialised increases with the level of industrialisation this leads to the undervaluing of agricultural production.[51] Farming families' consumption of their own produce, family members' work on the family farm, and goods and service that are exchanged informally, are not included. Agricultural countries appear poorer than they are.

Lipset's work has been criticised on other grounds, the most important of which is that his mean scores uphold a general relationship between development and democracy, which individual figures prove is not a necessary one. It has been pointed out that while the means of the two groups may differ:

> the spread in the values on almost every indicator is so extreme that it appears that it would be very difficult to place a single nation in either the democratic or non-democratic category knowing, for example, only its score on the number of telephones. In the European and English-speaking table democracies a nation may have from 43 to as many as 190 per 1,000. One wonders about the stable European democracies that have only 43, 60, 0, 130, 150 or even 195 telephones. How do they manage while dictatorial European nations can at the same time have as many as 196 per 1,000.[52]

The mean difference suggests a correlation between the variables, but it could be demonstrated that this is not a necessary one for practically all of Lipset's indicators. If, for example, independent Ireland's communications system was undeveloped in 1959, this is not such a problem, since the sheer variance in the values for each indicator suggests that democracies can have undeveloped communications systems and semi-developed communications systems, as well as developed communications systems. So Lipset's own figures do not support the argument that a high level of any of the four variables is a necessary condition for democracy.

The quantitative theorist who wants to clarify necessary levels of development must try to specify the levels of each variable at which the emergence of a democratic system becomes inevitable. Unfortunately, attempts to do this lead to mixed results. In a review of the explanatory power of Lipset's theories for the inter-war period, Berg-Schlosser and de Meur suggested the following threshold level for one indicator of each of Lipset's variables for the year 1930:

per capita GNP must be $200 or above.
fifty per cent or more of the population must be resident in towns with a population of 20,000 or above.
seventy-five per cent of the population must be literates.
the industrial labour force must be 30 per cent of the active population or more.[53]

Six countries (Belgium, the Netherlands, Britain, France, Czechoslovakia and Germany) had reached these levels by 1930. All of them had become democratic, even if Germany would not remain so. The negative cases which did not pass any of the levels (Greece, Portugal, Romania, Spain and Italy) failed to become democratic, which would also confirm Lipset's theory. However, there are many cases which reach the levels on some indicators but not on others. Hungary, Poland, and Finland passed only the literacy threshold. Austria was not industrialised enough. Sweden, Denmark, Norway and Ireland were cases with high levels of wealth and education but low levels of industrialisation and urbanisation. The only clear positive result from this test is that states must have three quarters of their population literate if they are to become democratic. The authors conclude that:

> On the whole these socio-economic indicators seem to have a rather limited explanatory power. They discriminate relatively little between the actual instances of democratic breakdown and survival in the universe of cases analysed. The industrialisation variable, for example, adds very little over and above the differentiations already provided by the other three indicators.[54]

If all the aspects of the economic development model which Lipset identifies as necessary conditions for democracy are relevant to democratisation, then we have as many anomalous cases within the democratic sample as we have explained cases. If Sweden, Norway, Ireland and Denmark are unexplained then the theory is simply wrong. Rather, the results suggest that a high level of two of Lipset's indicators and a moderate score on the other two may be sufficiently high to sustain a democracy. At the very least the evidence suggests that the relationship between a high level of development and democracy is not a necessary one.

If it is true that the more the relationship is tested in terms of individual states the weaker the thesis, then the more it is tested in terms of a large universe of cases, the stronger the thesis. After all, Lipset pushes the burden of proof onto the fact that 'in each case, the average wealth, degree of industrialisation and urbanisation, and level of education is much higher for the more democratic countries', not on the possibility that in each democratic state the levels for each of his variables are higher than the levels in this or that 'less democratic state', which would be a more stringent test. He is also reassured by the fact that had he combined Latin America and Europe in one table, the differences between the democracies and the non-democracies may have been greater.[55] So the sampling affects the outcome. The relationship between democracy and development in Europe, the English-speaking world, and Latin America combined, is therefore stronger than the relationship between democracy and development only in Europe and the English-speaking world.

For Ireland the consequences of the sampling are clear. Irish GNP per capita was about average by European standards in 1913, but in terms of the universal democratic world it was low. There is no reason why the fact that Irish levels of development were less than those of the more advanced countries should be held to be more significant than the fact that their levels were considerably higher than those of the European non-democratic countries. In fact the inclusion of the English-speaking democracies, that would have passed the thresholds chosen by Berg-Schlosser and de Meur on all variables by 1930, heightens the discrepancy between the democratic world and countries like Ireland. The case of university education brings this out quite well. In comparison with both the more democratic and the less democratic sample, the Irish level of secondary and third-level education was low in 1956. The mean figure for higher education per thousand was about one and a half times higher than the Irish figure. This would lead one to believe that the state failed to provide adequate higher educational opportunities for its citizens. However, if we change the more democratic sample by including only the European stable democracies we find that the Free State's level of higher education turns out to be above the European democratic average.[56] In general the contrast between the Irish state and the European democratic sample was one of small rather than large differences.

Lipset's argument was that a high level of development would produce a strong middle class, a reduction in material inequalities, more fluid class-boundaries, and political moderation on behalf of the working-class leadership. This liberal model of development assumes that increases in the overall wealth of a society would necessarily result in greater distribution of wealth within that society. GNP per capita, for example, does not measure the distribution of wealth as opposed to its national level. Lipset is making an assumption that is crucial for his theory. Without greater diffusion of wealth political moderation is unlikely. Consider the case of education. In contrast to the literacy figures, the data on educational enrolment rates in table 3.4. do not unequivocally support the theory that the higher the level of education, the better the chances for a democratic regime. Rather, the data show that a high level of basic education may be a necessary, if not sufficient, prerequisite of democracy since, as with the literacy figures, there seems to be a clear difference between democracies and non-democracies in respect of primary education. All democracies had high levels of primary education. Most of the democracies in 1920 are in the top half of table 3.4 and the four countries with the lowest level of primary education were undemocratic. Although those countries that had a high level of enrolment at all educational levels had become democratic by 1920, they also had high literacy and primary enrolment rates. There is no example of a democratic country with a high ranking in secondary and university education and a lower ranking in primary education. Conversely, all those countries that have a relatively high ranking for secondary or university education and a relatively lower ranking for primary education, such as Greece, Italy, Poland or Hungary, were either authoritarian or short-lived democracies.

On the other hand, extensive primary education cannot be a sufficient condition for democracy, since countries such as Bulgaria, Hungary and Italy had relatively widespread primary education in the 1920s, but were not democratic. In the sections on secondary and university education, the ranking of the countries does not give us a clear picture of the relationship between democracy and educational development, since the democracies do not cluster at one end and the non-democracies do not cluster at the other. In short there is a random distribution of states in these tables. Non-democracies like Greece had high rates of secondary education, while France, Belgium, and The Netherlands are ranked near the bottom. The third column is less random, but the ranking of Denmark, Norway, Ireland, Finland, and The Netherlands in the bottom half of the table suggests that extensive university education is not a necessary condition of democratic politics, while the high position of Hungary and Italy suggests it is not a sufficient condition either for democracy.

So the pattern of educational development is a better guide to the political outcome than the overall levels. Why should that be? Consider the data on university education that Lipset himself uses in 1959. Table 3.10 shows the paradoxical result that in the Europe of 1959 the higher the rate of third-level

Table 3.10 **Mean figures for higher education per thousand for European states classified as 'more democratic' and 'less democratic' by Lipset, 1949–52**

More democratic mean	2.9
Less democratic mean	3.5
Republic of Ireland	2.6

More democratic sample: Belgium, Denmark, Iceland, The Netherlands, Norway, Sweden. Switzerland, England & Wales.

Less democratic sample: Austria, Bulgaria, Czechoslovakia, Finland, France, West Germany, Greece, Hungary, Italy, Poland, Portugal, Romania, Spain, Yugoslavia.

Source: UNESCO, *World Survey of Education*, vol. 1 (1955), table M, pp. 24–5.

education the greater the chances for an undemocratic regime. What happens if advanced educational opportunities are extended to a minority before basic education is extended to everybody? Writers on inter-war Eastern Europe have pointed out the dangers of a large underemployed educated class in societies where basic education was not widespread. This class was prone to political extremism and political debate was confined to this circle.[57] What seems to matter is the educational distance between elites and masses which in turn leads to an ideological gulf between town and country. So economic development will only reduce the inequalities between elite and mass if it is accompanied by a greater distribution of the benefits of wealth. Redistribution is as important as development. It may be that in societies such as Britain and the United States, increases in wealth did reduce inequalities because the societies were so affluent, but this can hardly be the case for poorer countries where an egalitarian pattern of development may make up for deficiencies in the overall level.

On the whole the wide divergences between the Irish state and the universal democratic means for socio-economic development should not lead one to see it as a completely anomalous case for developmental theory. Lipset's method exaggerates both the necessary levels of development and the extent to which the Irish state fails to meet these levels. Attempts at specifying minimum levels have led only to doubt not so much about whether there are such levels, but about the relevance of some of the variables themselves. There is no proof that any of these variables apart from universal literacy are necessary requisites for democracy. A combination of a high level of two variables with a low level of the others may be sufficient in itself. This suggests that the specific combination of developmental processes found in Ireland in 1920 – high levels of basic education and urbanisation alongside moderately high levels of wealth and industrialisation – might have been sufficient in itself. In other democratic states, particularly in the Nordic region, the specific combination could have been different, but the overall level of development was no higher. The evidence suggests that these patterns are not uniform for all successful cases.

3.4   Conclusion

We can arrive at three conclusions about the relationship between economic development and democracy in independent Ireland. Firstly, we could argue that Irish democracy was the unsurprising outcome of processes of modernisation that transformed Irish society in the decades between the Famine and independence. If so the Irish case was a normal case for developmental theory. Secondly, we could argue that since independent Ireland remained a largely agrarian society until the 1960s, it was in fact an anomalous case, which can only be explained by some extraordinary factor not present in other under-developed states. Democracy may have developed because of 'a syndrome of fairly unique historical factors, even though major social characteristics may favour another form'.[58] Thirdly, we could argue that whereas there may be some relationship between the genesis of a democracy and economic development, there is no determinative relationship between the two. Independent Ireland fits into a third pattern with only 'mixed or temporarily favourable conditions' for stable democracy. In short, Ireland could be an impressive case, or if Irish democracy survived merely because the favourable conditions for authoritarian rule – a powerful military, a severe depression or an irredentist cause – were not present, it could be considered a lucky case.

Independent Ireland was not a normal case for developmental theory because, while its institutional development followed that of the advanced capitalist countries after 1900, its economic development was characterised by a very late shift from agraria to industria. On the other hand, it was not an anomalous case either, since independent Ireland possessed a relatively high degree of socio-economic development at the outset. The fact that Ireland experienced a severe depression in the inter-war period rules out the possibility that Ireland was simply lucky. Independent Ireland was in fact an impressive case. Economic conditions in 1922 were 'mixed or temporarily favourable' but did not guarantee the survival of a democratic system. The genesis of Irish democracy could have been predicted by Lipset's theory, but not necessarily its survival.

Clearly, the relationship between democracy and development is not a unilinear one. An increase in a state's overall level of development does not make a state more democratic. Some writers prefer to advance a threshold thesis which accepts that certain minimum levels of socio-economic develop-ment are necessary conditions for democratisation but that the subsequent performance of a democracy is unrelated to further increases in those levels.[59] Exploring the relationship between development and social equality, Jackman writes that:

> while the initial stages of economic development may lead to a more equitable distribution of material rewards, a threshold is reached at moderate levels beyond which continued economic expansion and growth do not produce a corresponding reduction in material inequality.[60]

The same may apply to the relationship between democracy and development. The early stages of social development may lead to a democratic break-through, but it does not follow that all further industrialisation will be as strongly supportive of democratic institutions, as the experience of highly developed states such as the Weimar Republic would suggest.[61] Conversely, a state like Ireland may have reached the necessary level of development by the time it became democratic, but its failure to keep up with the rate of change after that may not have mattered since in those stages the relationship between the two is much weaker. The factors which bring a system into being are not the same as those that keep it in place.

There is no evidence in any case that quantitative theory can succeed in its attempts to specify conditions which are sufficient to bring about a democratic system or conditions without which democracy is impossible.[62] No economic model can satisfactorily explain why the fortunes of democracy varied so much in such broadly comparable inter-war states as Czechoslovakia, Ireland, Finland and Hungary. Of these the most developed and prosperous state was Czechoslovakia but:

> In all, the Czech experience suggests that even with patterns of development close to those of the West, especially industrialisation and the existence of a native entrepreneurial class, these do not in themselves guarantee the evolution of a Western-style political system.[63]

The record suggests that the experience of democratic breakdown in the inter-war period as a whole is not explained by economic variables. Institutional structures, constitutional choices, and political strategies must have had some bearing on the outcome.[64] These variables cannot be reduced to economic factors.

Finally, Lipset hypothesised that in some cases democracy may survive because of 'a unique historical syndrome'. However, in the Irish case a crucial factor of this type is obscured by his theory. About a third of the population emigrated between 1922 and 1960. Precisely because the average Irish person lived in an international as well as domestic labour market, social mobility was possible without growth at home. Polarised class conflict could never happen if the Irish working class was content to improve its position in other countries. Because of emigration Irish democracy was perfectly compatible with constant underdevelopment. This aspect of the Irish experience is probably unique: in the words of one economist, 'there is simply no similar demographic experience anywhere in the world, so far'.[65]

Chapter 4

The Barrington Moore thesis
and Irish political development

*'It is better to destroy serfdom from above, than to wait until that time when
it begins to destroy itself from below.'*   **Alexander II 1861**

Since its publication in 1966 Barrington Moore's *Social Origins of Dictatorship
and Democracy* has been regarded as a classic of modern social science.[1]
Moore's emphasis on the importance of changes in the character of agrarian
class relations for democratisation has been shared by his detractors as well as
by his admirers.[2] Indeed it is debatable whether later refinements of his thesis
have ever departed from his fundamental contention that the nature of the
relationship between lord and peasant had a crucial bearing on the development
of democracy in the western world.[3] On the other hand, Moore's neglect of
smaller countries was considered a fundamental flaw in his account of democratic development in the Western world.[4] Accordingly, in recent years his
theory has been used to explain the democratisation process in several small
European cases, hitherto ignored, where the nature of landlord–peasant relations
also had a fundamental impact on their political development.[5] What follows
is an attempt to extend that process one step further, by analysing how
Moore's arguments can be applied to one more European case, that of Ireland.

4.1 The Barrington Moore thesis

Although primarily the work of a historical sociologist, Moore's book was also
a contribution to modernisation theory. Rejecting prevalent assumptions
which suggested that all societies would experience essentially the same
process of modernisation, Moore described different 'routes' to the modern
world. The social costs and achievements of these routes were explicable by the
pattern of social class development experienced by each society. Moore took
social classes as the basic units of analysis, which involved two assumptions.
The first was that particular classes favour those political systems which enhance
their economic interests. The second was that the switch from subsistence to

commercial agriculture was the key event which shaped the subsequent development of class relations within societies. The manner in which this change affected prevalent class relations determines later political outcomes.

In particular Moore set out to

> explain the varied political roles played by the landed upper class and the peasantry in the transformation from agrarian societies . . . to modern industrial ones. Somewhat more specifically, it is an attempt to discover the range of historical conditions under which either of these rural groups have become important forces behind the emergence of Western parliamentary versions of democracy, and dictatorships of the right or the left, that is, fascist or communist regimes.[6]

Moore saw three possible routes to the modern world: 'the bourgeois revolution', 'revolution from above', and 'peasant revolution'. The first, the 'bourgeois democratic route', took place in Great Britain, France and the USA. In these countries violent social upheavals resulted in the destruction of the traditional landed elite. Democracy and industrialism emerged after a revolution in which the bourgeoisie, or a bourgeois-led coalition, was the leading element. The second route, followed by Germany and Japan, saw industrialism achieved without revolution, through a fascist dictatorship of landlords and industrialists. The traditional landed elite retains its political and economic power and thwarts popular revolution. Instead it forms a modernising alliance with the industrial class. The third route, followed by Russia and China, proceeds first through a peasant revolution which destroys landlord domination, and then through a communist revolution which undermines peasant proprietorship as well, ending up with an industrialised but not a democratic system.

Moore identified three separate sets of preconditions leading to the emergence of democratic, communist, or fascist systems. The difference between them rests on the strength of the respective social classes and their relationship with the state apparatus. The conditions leading to a peasant revolution identified by Moore were: the existence of a weak bourgeoisie; a powerful agrarian elite; and a highly centralised state, combined with high peasant revolutionary potential. In contrast the critical precondition for the emergence of a fascist dictatorship is the development of an alliance between large landowners, the crown (or the state apparatus), and a politically depen-dent bourgeoisie. The most important feature of the authoritarian route is that landlords must remain a politically powerful group into the modern era. Their dependence on 'labour repressive' means of exploiting the peasantry makes them seek an alliance with the state in order to maintain the peasants in a politically subordinate position. The bourgeoisie also become dependent on the state for different reasons. In countries like Germany and Japan where the process of industrialisation begins late, the state plays a heavy role in encouraging industrial enterprises and the bourgeoisie therefore loses its incentive to mobilise against the state.

When a society has undergone an initial stage of industrialisation and avoids peasant revolution, it will develop in a democratic direction if it lacks the preconditions leading to authoritarianism. Moore outlined five preconditions for the democratic route: (1) the development of a balance to avoid too strong a crown or too independent a landed aristocracy; (2) a turn towards an appropriate form of commercial agriculture either on the part of the landed aristocracy or the peasantry; (3) the weakening of the landed aristocracy; (4) the prevention of an aristocratic–bourgeois coalition against the peasants and workers; (5) a revolutionary break with the past. Moore recognises that the course of democratisation has consisted of quite different causal elements in the various countries analysed, and attempts to identify 'only the background conditions against which a variety of different configuration of forces have generated similarly different outcomes'.[7] Nevertheless, some basic causal hypothesis can be gleaned from Moore's statement, 'no bourgeoisie no democracy'. When applied to Ireland, Moore's analysis suggests that the two classes most hostile to the survival of bourgeois democracy, landlords and landless peasants, had been eliminated as serious political forces from the scene by independence.

4.2 Lord and peasant under the union

The political problems of nineteenth-century Ireland had their origins in the Cromwellian and Williamite land settlements of the seventeenth century. In the 1640s Cromwell had proposed 'an almost universal transfer of land held by Catholics to Protestants'.[8] His ambition was to reduce the dominance of the native population, deprive it of leadership, and establish a 'decisively large Protestant majority on the island'.[9] The land settlement which followed transferred 'nearly all landed wealth from Catholics to Protestants' and created a new Protestant Ascendancy which ruled over the majority native and Old English Catholic population'.[10] Within the following decade the Protestant share of Irish land doubled from forty to eighty per cent. Furthermore, from the 1690s to the 1720s a succession of 'penal laws' succeeded in further reducing the area of Catholic ownership to five per cent.

In Europe as a whole the seventeenth century had seen an intense struggle between the centralising forces of royal absolutism and the landed aristocracy. In general 'neither throne nor nobility triumphed' but 'an uneasy compromise between *étatisme* and administrative centralisation on the one hand, and seigneurial privilege and private proprietary rule on the other, worked itself out'.[11] In Britain, however, the century witnessed two successful revolutions against crown authority, one asserting the rights of a gentry-dominated parliament, the other establishing the Protestant succession. Although the legislative power of the eighteenth-century Irish House of Commons was limited, Ireland remained a separate kingdom controlled by a landed aristocracy. The penal laws were approved 'under pressure from the protestant gentry who formed the majority of the Irish House of Commons and whose relish for anti-popery legislation had its grounds in a desire to avenge past humiliations as well as to prevent future threats to their economic and social ascendancy'.[12] The Irish House was overwhelmingly composed of the Anglo-Irish gentry or those aspiring to enter that class. Catholics were debarred from its ranks by oaths of allegiance and supremacy. Local government, the administration of justice, and the means of defence – British militias based in Ireland – were also under gentry control. The bulk of the population was excluded from 'the nation' and from participation in its political life on specifically politico-religious grounds. As in eastern Europe, the assertion of crown authority in the seventeenth century undermined the traditional communal freedoms of the poor, and concentrated seigniorial power over the peasantry to a degree unknown in the West.[13]

Throughout the colonial world challenges to the power of the imperial metropolis emerged in the late eighteenth century. The Anglo-Irish aristocracy was not alone in being dissatisfied with the economic and legislative relationships which existed between Britain and Ireland. It drew back from revolt, however, because 'the only security by which they hold their property, the only security they have for the present constitution in Church and State, is the connection of the Irish Crown with, and its dependence on the Crown of England'.[14] This suited the British too, who were alarmed as much by the tendency of the independent parliament to go its own way, as by the threat posed to her western coast by French revolutionaries. A proposed Act of Union between the two kingdoms would also appeal to middle-class Catholics who hoped for emancipation from disabling laws which the Ascendancy had denied them, as well as the Catholic hierarchy who were promised state support for their clergy. After the 1798 Rising, which was inspired by the French revolution, it was decided that a union of the two kingdoms under the same parliament would be the best way to strengthen the link between the two islands and consolidate the power of the British Empire. The island would continue to be governed indirectly through the Lord Lieutenant at Dublin Castle, but the Irish parliament was abolished.

The Act of Union was emblematic of a change in the conception of Empire which would occur in the nineteenth century. After the American and French Revolutions, which promoted the principles of liberty and equality, 'imperialists needed to justify their seizure of land and mastery of areas which were inhabited with large number of *indigenes*. Old ideas of limited liability fell away as imperial power 'took responsibility for the colonial societies they now held in trust, as well as for the extension of the full benefits of citizenship to all, regardless of race'.[15] The hopes vested in the Act of Union by Catholics were initially disappointed. For example, Catholics were not emancipated until 1829 and when emancipation came the Catholic Association, which can be credited with this achievement, was forced to disband. Nevertheless, the attempted integration of Ireland into the United Kingdom had profound consequences for the development of agrarian class relations within the island. Indeed it resulted precisely in the creation of a set of conditions which Moore held was most likely to favour democratic development.

The first of these was the creation of *a balance to avoid too strong a crown or too independent a landed aristocracy.* The Act of Union placed the whole of Ireland under the authority of the Westminster parliament and in the course of the next century or so the British state, responding to popular demands and to international pressure, took the institutions of government out of the hands of the Anglo-Irish aristocracy. The militias, whose activities were previously co-ordinated by the county gentry, were disbanded. In their place a centralised constabulary service under the control of the Lord Lieutenant was introduced in 1836. It was renamed the Royal Irish Constabulary in 1867. The British government also slowly introduced a separation of church and state, and after 1829 Catholics were entitled to hold all offices except those of regent, chancellor, and lord lieutenant, although strict controls on the behaviour of Catholics who held public office were retained.[16] In 1869 the Protestant Church of Ireland was disestablished, and over the following decades, religious tithes (taxes paid by Catholics to that Church) were eased out. As Catholic education developed and meritocratic reforms were introduced, more and more Catholics were recruited into the civil service itself. This happened slowly but was an unmistakable trend in the last decades before independence.[17]

Moore's argument was that a balance of power must emerge between the crown and the landed aristocracy. The British aristocracy, which had close links with the Anglo-Irish landed elite, retained its power throughout the century, and in Northern Ireland landed elites remained important well into the next century. The House of Lords succeeded in blocking three Home Rule Bills for Ireland, in 1886, 1893, and 1912, and as late as 1874, out of six occupational categories, large landowners with over 1,000 acres were the second largest group in the parliamentary Home Rule Party. Until the introduction of secret voting in 1872 landlords possessed a high level of influence over parliamentary elections; they could use their prestige to promote favoured candidates, they could provide such candidates with financial assistance, and they could instruct their better-off tenants how to vote.[18] Dramatic change came about only in 1880 when the proportion of MPs from the middle and lower-middle classes dramatically increased.[19] Before 1898 the main governing body at county level was the 'grand juries' whose chief role was to finance and supervise public works. As these bodies were composed almost entirely of landowners, the landed class had the deciding say in the choice of public works to be carried out, and in the distribution of local patronage.[20] Anglo-Irish institutions, such as Trinity College, the Bank of Ireland and the Church of Ireland, also retained their importance in Irish life, and at the end of the century senior positions in the Irish civil service and the professions were still disproportionally staffed by Protestants.[21] In 1907 the Catholic Defence Society claimed that, in the Irish legal profession, out of 22 County Court Judges there were only seven Catholics, out of 44 Benches of the Kings Inns there were only nine Catholics, and out of 66 Resident Magistrates there were only 19 Catholics.[22] It was only in the last two decades before independence that the demise of the Ascendancy was rapid. For the rest of the century a balance between the crown and the landed elite existed.

The second precondition discussed by Moore was *a turn towards an appropriate form of commercial agriculture.* By commercial agriculture Moore meant the production of agricultural produce for the market rather than for family consumption. Commercialised agriculture allows for capital accumulation to take place and stimulates further industrial growth. Indeed Moore's analysis of the English case led him to conclude that 'getting rid of agriculture as a major source of social activity is one pre-requisite for successful democracy'.[23] However, Moore also suggested that if the peasant is turned into a farmer producing for the market rather than for his own consumption or that of his landlord, small-scale proprietorship need not be incompatible with capitalist development. If the opportunities for market production, as well as the existence of market towns, appropriate financial institutions, and an adequate transport system, are present, then peasants can become part of the democratic capitalist system. Moore accepts that this is what happened in Scandinavia and Switzerland where the peasantry 'have become part of the democratic system by taking up fairly specialised forms of commercial farming, mainly dairy products, for the town markets'.[24] Arguably it also happened in Ireland where a large market for the export of Irish livestock had developed in Britain by the late nineteenth century, alongside an internal network of market towns for the consumption of all forms of agricultural produce. Hoppen notes that banks greatly increased their activities in this period, the number of branches rising from 179 in 1859 to 404 in 1879.[25]

Moreover, the Famine ushered in a rapid reduction in the size of those lower agricultural classes who survived mainly through subsistence farming. Table 4.1. shows lower agricultural classes by acres between 1845 and 1910. What is most noticeable is that over the 55 years after the famine it was the poorer agricultural peasants that declined in numbers, whereas the medium-sized farmers holding more than 15 acres tended to become more numerous. In addition, whereas the largest occupational class in 1845 were the agricultural labourers, by 1910 farmers with over 15 acres had become the largest farming group. The class which experienced the most dramatic fall in their numbers were the 'cottier' class of farmers with less than five acres. Moreover, in the period between 1841 and 1911, while the number of farmers declined by just over a quarter, the number of farm workers or agricultural labourers fell by nearly two thirds.[26]

Table 4.1 **Lower agricultural classes by acres, 1845–1910**

	Labourers	Cottiers (–5 acres)	Farmers (5–15 acres)	Farmers (15+ acres)
1845	700,000	300,000	310,000	277,000
1851	500,000	88,000	192,000	290,000
1910	300,000	62,000	154,000	304,000
change	–400,000	–238,000	–156,000	+27,000

Source: adapted from Lee, *The Modernisation of Irish Society* (1973), p. 2.

The statistics point to a steady consolidation of larger agricultural units, but this process was not exponential, since very large farms remained the exception rather than the norm. A report on the state of agriculture in the Free State in 1932 concluded:

> Farms of between fifteen and 100 acres, of which there are 194,200 in the Irish Free State comprising about 7,000,000 statute acres, constitute the agricultural mainstay of the country. They are mostly economic, and many of them are well worked on a mixed system of farming. As a class they constitute more, in ratio, to the stable upkeep of the country than either smaller farms or those that are larger in extent.[27]

In short the turn towards an appropriate form of commercial agriculture after the Famine led to the emergence of the medium-sized family farm as the basic unit of production. Large-scale *latifundia* estates became unsustainable, while farms of less than 15 acres were also decreasing in number. There is no doubt also that this process was aided by the massive emigration of the poorer rural classes in the decades after the Famine. Fitzpatrick suggests that two and a half million people left the country between 1846 and 1855, and another four million would leave between 1855 and the First World War.[28] Most of these emigrants were young unmarried adults who were listed as labourers and servants and their departure between 1846 and 1854 helped the reorganisation of estates, the consolidation of farms, and the shift in agriculture away from subsistence farming.[29] While the resulting depopulation of the countryside did nothing to further the industrialisation of the larger part of Ireland, the political consequence of emigration was that it provided a safety valve, draining the country of the young and those with no stake in its economy. [30] Three groups of people in particular could avail themselves of this safety valve: the cottiers who after the Famine could no longer survive on the fruits of a tiny potato garden; farm workers who were denied work by landlords and commercial farmers more interested in using their land for pasturage; and those pauperised by the course of industrialisation in the north of Ireland.[31] There is no doubt that the effect of emigration was to reduce the size of the rural proletariat in Ireland, an outcome that might be compared with the more modest Swedish case, where between 1860 and 1910 more than 750,000 rural Swedes (or about one in five) emigrated to the United States, 'thus greatly alleviating the problem of rural poverty and removing the basis for a peasant revolution'.[32]

The weakening of the landed aristocracy was the third precondition for democratisation identified by Moore. Over a period of seventy odd years, fifteen million out of a total of nineteen million square acres were transferred from landlord to peasant by the British state.[33] The scale of these changes is indicated in table 4.2, which shows the shift in agricultural proprietorship between 1870 and 1929. Whereas in 1870 only three per cent of Irish farmers owned their land, by 1929 this had increased to 97.4 per cent. These changes in land ownership reflected political developments. The electoral franchise was extended in 1850, 1868, 1884, and 1918, and these reforms, combined with the introduction of secret ballots and the abolition of rotten boroughs, meant that the Ascendancy lost the ability to control voters. Whereas in 1868 69.5 per cent of Irish MPs at Westminster came from the landed classes by 1885 this figure had been reduced to 15.5 per cent.[34] Moreover, the Local Government Act of 1898 'transferred local administration from the grand juries, landed oligarchies, to elected country, urban and rural councils'.[35] By 1911, out of a total of 707 elected local councillors in the future area of the Free State, only fifteen were Unionists which meant that they would have only a limited influence on local government appointments.[36]

The fourth precondition for democratisation discussed by Moore was *the prevention of an aristocratic–bourgeois coalition against the peasants and workers.* Once land reform was introduced the Irish landed elite no longer required the state to repress a large agrarian labour force. In any case an authoritarian alliance of the bourgeoisie and the landed elite in Ireland would have been unlikely. From the beginning of the century Catholic politicians had suc-cessfully mobilised and united the Catholic peasants and the inchoate middle

Table 4.2 **Percentage of Irish farmers as owner-occupiers, 1870–1929**

Year	% Owner-occupiers	% Other
1870	3	97
1906	29.2	70.8
1911	63.9	36.1
1929	97.4	2.6

Source: Hooker, cited in Rumpf and Hepburn, *Nationalism and Socialism in Twentieth-Century Ireland* (1977), p. 227

class against the Protestant Ascendancy and the British state. On the basis of pre-existing religious, ethnic and class-based grievances, Catholic nationalist politicians were able to maintain the support of the Catholic masses to their political goals. Even where a common material interest might have brought Protestants into this alliance, as with the Tenant League of the 1850s, Catholic politicians were unable to recruit long-term Protestant support. Why did the Catholic middle class consistently turn to broader social classes for support in their campaigns for social and political equality? Basically, the small Catholic middle class, which consisted of a tiny number of shopkeepers, usurers and merchants, and a much larger number of lawyers, doctors and journalists, was far too weak to challenge the social and political ascendancy of the landowners on its own.[37] Strauss has provided a insightful portrait of the attitudes of the Catholic middle class to political mobilisation:

> In normal times it was content to play second fiddle to the landlords and to gather the crumbs which fell down from their still very well-spread table. But the Anglo-Irish gentry was so strongly imbued with the arrogance of the ruling nation and its native imitators that it refused to fulfil the modest ambitions of the Catholic middle class, and times were as a rule far from normal. In periods of crisis the poorer and more enterprising elements of the middle class could not resist the temptation of mobilising the forces of rebellious discontent, which were always at work among the peasantry, in support of middle class claims. The Irish middle class was, therefore, torn between servility towards the landlords and their English backers, because it wanted to share in the exploitation of the peasants, and agitation amongst the peasants in order to blackmail the landlords and the English Government, whom it could not bend to its will by its own strength.[38]

In Moore's account, for a democracy to emerge 'the monopoly of power of a small group of arbitrary rulers must be broken'.[39] In the early stages the aristocracy and the bourgeoisie must ally to prevent the growth of royal absolutism, but the bonds between these classes must not be so secure as to prevent the formation of a common front against the popular classes, since in the later stages the bourgeoisie must be able to turn to broader social classes for support in its struggle for an extension of democratic rights. The Irish case represents a colonial variation on this theme. The arbitrary power of the Protestant Ascendancy was broken by a periodic alliance between the forces of Catholic nationalism and a reformist British state. Since the British state did not sponsor industrialisation, no sizeable Catholic bourgeoisie developed which could have allied itself with the landed elite. A decade after independence a constitutional lawyer reflected that, 'the more wealthy classes had tended to oppose national aspirations, and the movement had, therefore, been in essence one in which the mass of the people was arrayed against a small but powerful aristocracy'.[40]

The main reason why the emergent Catholic elite opposed the status quo in Ireland was that the British state in nineteenth-century Ireland was only relatively autonomous from the Protestant interest. Catholic emancipation came a quarter of a century after the Union, and religious equality was not attained until the disestablishment of the Church of Ireland in 1869. The Catholic Association, the first mass organisation to represent Catholic interests, had emerged half a century before any significant suffrage extension or land reform had taken place, and almost a century before they had been completed. The Catholic masses were mobilised into political movements well before mass enfranchisement, a fact which structured the pattern of political mobilisation for the next century.[41] From the outset, then, both Catholic elites and Catholic masses faced a type of double domination, whereby the subordination of Ireland within the UK at the macro-level was reproduced at the micro-level by the subordination of one religion to another, of the peasantry to their landlords, and with respect to finance, status, and opportunities, of the Catholic elite to the Protestant elite.

On the other hand it was equally important that the British state was relatively autonomous from the Protestant interest in Ireland and was therefore responsive, at times, to Irish public opinion. Indeed, although many of the reforms were made in response to popular pressure, the British state played a role in pioneering social reform within Ireland. This fact is particularly relevant to Moore's conception of the state's role in 'late industrialisers'. In the cases he discusses, state intervention in the economy resulted in modernisation 'from above' because the state gets drawn into imperialist expansionism and arms production as a result of its involvement in promoting economic growth. In Ireland the British state, while ostensibly concerned with maintaining its sovereignty, was not involved in industrialisation efforts but merely in social reform. For example in 1831 a central Board of Works was set up and given funds to make loans to grand juries or to private individuals for public works. In time the Board began to take on many of the functions hitherto performed by the grand juries and became an important element in the whole Irish economy.[42]

It has been suggested that a factor necessarily present in any authoritarian coalition was the state's capacity to repress popular protest, but this was not totally absent in nineteenth-century Ireland, particularly after 'the Kilmainham Treaties' of 1881, when the scale of popular unrest greatly decreased.[43] What was more important was that the state was relatively autonomous from the landed elite and had an autonomous conception of its role. No reactionary alliance between the state, the bourgeoisie and the landed elite could have emerged in Ireland. Only in Ulster did an alliance against Catholic peasants and workers develop between the Protestant bourgeoisie and the landed elites. Again the confessional divide in Irish society determined that the Protestant working class would support this alliance in the form of Ulster Unionism.[44] In the rest of Ireland the Anglo-Irish elite proved unable to resist the trend towards Catholic democracy. After 1885 Unionist electoral majorities in the future area of the Free State emerged only in urban constituencies.[45] Their decline on the land, however, was tempered by their dominance of the professions. According to the 1911 census, almost half the lawyers, over a third of doctors, and over two thirds of bankers in Ireland were Protestants.[46] This situation continued after independence when in 1926 the Protestant minority of just over eight per cent accounted for 18 per cent of the entire professional class in the Free State.[47]

The final precondition for democratisation discussed by Moore was a *revolutionary break with the past*. If the term 'revolutionary' implies violent social change rather than peaceful reform, this factor was absent in the Irish case. Indeed if a transformation of the social structure is an essential ingredient of a social revolution, 'the Irish revolution' between 1916 and 1923 was not a revolution at all.[48] The fall of 'landlordism' came about through legal reform not revolution, and the war of independence did not significantly alter the Irish social structure. The high tide of agrarian disorder had occurred between 1879 and 1882; after that it subsided. According to Rumpf and Hepburn, 'with the widespread establishment of peasant proprietorship the social base of the forces calling for change had narrowed down to landless men and small uneconomic smallholders'.[49] The socialist republican interpretation of the civil war had been that the wider conflict with Britain was inextricably bound up with the existence of rural class conflicts within Irish society.[50] From this perspective the civil war had 'revolutionary potential' and a victory for the anti-Treatyites might well have resulted in far-reaching social change. Garvin also argues that 'there was a marked agrarian radicalism hiding behind the anti-Treaty cause' in 1922–23, on the basis that the anti-Treaty Sinn Féin vote in 1923 correlated heavily with areas where agrarian outrages were perpetrated during the Land War of 1879–1882.[51] In 1967, Richard Mulcahy, Chief of Staff of the Irish Army during the civil war, also argued that though social differences were not openly expressed during the conflict, class variables went some way towards explaining the ferocity in which the war was fought, particularly in the west. According to Mulcahy, the anti-Treatyites were supported by the urban intellectuals, urban revolutionaries, and the small tenant farmers in the west of Ireland. The pro-Treatyites on the other hand were supported by the urban middle class, state functionaries, landowners, and the Irish 'Kulaks', the upper layer of small farmers.[52]

It is not clear, however, how this interpretation can explain key features of the conflict. For example those areas where agrarian disorder existed during the war and those where militant opposition to the Free State was strongest did not coincide. Army reports reported serious agrarian trouble in Cavan, Leitrim, Monaghan, and Roscommon, for example, but electoral support for the republicans was weak in all these counties in 1922, and military resistance to the Free State thereafter was also weak.[53] Military opposition was confined mainly to the west and south-west, more specifically to counties Cork, Kerry, Limerick and Tipperary in the south-west, and Galway, Mayo and Sligo in the west. Wexford was the one Leinster county where fighting continued to the end. Like Munster it cannot be considered an area of great agrarian disorder.

Table 4.3 **Number of persons engaged on farms in each province in 1926 and their proportionate distribution on certain sizes of farms**

	Number	1–15	15–30	30–50	50–100	100+
Leinster	155,442	14.4	17.5	18.0	22.1	25.5
Munster	207,365	10.7	16.8	21.7	28.4	20.6
Connacht	187,384	34.9	35.6	17.1	7.5	4.1
Ulster	96,104	34.7	29.9	17.3	10.6	5.7
Saorstát Éireann	646,295	22.2	24.4	18.8	18.1	14.8

Source: Census of Population: vol. 10, *General Report* (Dublin, 1926), p. 28.

Table 4.3 shows the distribution of various sizes of farms by province in the Irish Free State. It suggests that there were two areas of relative agrarian poverty in the Free State (Connacht and the Border Counties), and two areas of relative agrarian prosperity (Leinster and Munster). In both Leinster and Munster just under fifty per cent of those engaged in agriculture were employed on farms of between fifty and one hundred acres. In contrast, well under twenty per cent of those employed in agriculture were employed on farms of this size in Connacht and the border counties. Rather, over two thirds of all farmers were employed on farms between one and thirty acres in both areas. The relevant figure for Leinster and Munster is 32 per cent and 37 per cent respectively. Significantly these sharp differences are not reflected by positions on the Treaty. In Connacht and much of Munster (Kerry, Clare, Tipperary and Cork) support for anti-Treaty candidates was strong in 1922 and 1923. Not all of this area can be considered poor. Moreover, the border counties did not show strong support for republican candidates in 1922 or 1923 and were quiet during the fighting.

A close analysis of the statistics does not then support the thesis that opposition to the Free State was strongest where smallholders were more preponderant. Rather, it suggests that military opposition to the Free State was strongest in the counties of the south-west where medium-sized farms of 50–100 acres were more numerous, while in the Border counties and Donegal, where small farms of 1–30 acres were most common, military opposition to the Free State was weak. Farm workers were plentiful in both areas but more so in the second group of counties.[54] The south-west had been the area where nationalist violence was at its height between 1918 and 1921, and Munster was the province where the Sinn Féin organisation was most extensive. The decision of Liam Lynch, Chief of Staff of the IRA in July 1922, to maintain a defensive line running from Waterford to Tipperary, behind which 'the Munster Republic' could exist, reflected this geographical reality. The profile of republican resistance to the Free State in 1922 was as much southerly as westerly, the area in the south-west proving to be the stronghold of the anti-Treatyites, as it was to remain over the next year. Connacht was also affected by much fighting, particularly in Galway, Mayo, and Sligo, but never displaced counties such as Cork, Kerry, and Tipperary as the heartland of IRA resistance.

Table 4.4 **Average number of prisoners per county in military custody, November 1923**

Area	County Average	Range
Connacht	224	55–395
Leinster	168	20–896
Munster	385	197–821
Ulster	29	8–127
Ireland	178	8–896

Source: List showing number of prisoners from each county at present detained in military custody 28 Nov. 1923 (NA, D/T, S 3435).

This argument is supported by an analysis of the geographical backgrounds of the 5,699 IRA men still detained in military custody in November 1923. As table 4.4 shows, the average number of prisoners per county in Munster was clearly higher than in the other provinces, and the figures for each Munster county were uniformly high, with 821 coming from Cork, 498 from Tipperary, 496 from Kerry, 198 from Limerick, and 197 of the prisoners coming from Clare. Connacht comes second with 395 prisoners coming from Mayo, 303 from Galway, 301 from Sligo, 65 from Leitrim, and 55 from

Roscommon. With the exception of the 896 prisoners coming from Dublin and the 200 from Wexford, the figures for Leinster are very low. There were few prisoners from Ulster. Although further analysis would be required before coming to a definitive conclusion, the figures suggest that outside Dublin the anti-Treaty IRA was strongest in Cork, Kerry and Tipperary, and this fact cannot be attributed to agrarian poverty.

There is thus little empirical support for the view that the Irish civil war was a veiled class war. In 1926 Kevin O'Higgins reflected that anti-Treaty opposition in 1922–23 had consisted of three elements: republican fundamentalists, document number twoites, and socialist republicans.[55] The latter were only a minority element, whose aspirations were not shared by the majority of anti-Treatyites. None of the peace terms proposed by members of the IRA during the civil war made any mention of socio-economic issues, and the IRA leadership failed to develop a coherent programme for capitalising on the economic distress that undoubtedly existed in the country in 1922–23.[56] Over the previous half century, a combination of land reform and emigration had dramatically reduced the size of the one constituency that could have enabled a social revolution to take place – the landless peasantry. As for the rest

> the discontent of the small farmer population, particularly in the west, would give rise to some localised and sporadic 'anti rancher' manifestations, but it had neither the social depth nor geographical reach to turn the countryside upside down. The small farmer and landless labourer were still mesmerised by visions of piecemeal land acquisition which were easily assimilable by anti-rancher rhetoric that had been the stock-in-trade of Irish nationalism since the days of the Land League.[57]

To return to Moore's thesis, the elimination of landlord and peasant from the Irish countryside meant that there was no revolutionary break with the past between 1918 and 1921. The Treaty split might have created the conditions in which a revolutionary challenge would emerge, but the leadership of both sides remained committed to the existing social order. On 9 June 1922 Michael Collins denounced Soviet-style direct action on the part of workers, recommending instead co-operative schemes.[58] On the anti-Treaty side, in April 1923 an IRA officer from Cork actually proposed that the IRA intensify its campaign by directing it against Labour. Liam Lynch opposed the plan, citing the possible reactions of public opinion.[59] If the prerogative of the Provisional Government during the civil war was to assert the authority of the new state, the main aim of the anti-Treaty IRA was to subvert that authority, but Labour was not persuaded to take part in their campaign. Considering the polarising effects of such a challenge from the left in inter-war Austria, Finland, and Germany, this can only be considered a benign development.

4.3   The Irish 'route' in comparative perspective

Moore had asked, 'what are the pre-requisites for entry into the modern, industrialised, urban world; what changes needed to be effected in the countryside to make such revolution possible, and what is the necessary social cost of such a process?'.[60] His conclusion was that getting rid of agriculture as a major social activity is an essential prerequisite of successful democracy. Either the landed elite or the independent peasantry adopts commercial methods of agricultural production or they are violently removed from the scene. However, Moore's emphasis on the overriding need for the independent peasantry to adopt commercial methods of agriculture or be eliminated from the countryside can be questioned, since in Ireland there seemed to be no connection between the process of land reform and industrialisation. As late as 1946 out of 1,298,367 employed persons in independent Ireland, 593,653 were still employed in agriculture.[61]

In Europe as a whole,

> there are three different patterns in the development of the structure of the agrarian population: (1) the Western European development, which means that industry could absorb the workforce which was released from farming. The modernization of farming gave an impetus to industrialization and facilitated its development. (2) The east European development meant that only farming was developed. At the same time, it became heavily dependent on demand in western Europe. (3) The development in Finland, which represented an intermediate form and meant originally that the modernization of farming and industrialization took place almost simultaneously. The development of agriculture gave no significant impetus to industrialization, which was slower than in western Europe in general. The solution to the problem of the landless population was sought in turning the landless, a whole class in the society, into independent farmers.[62]

The Irish 'route' was clearly more like that of Finland where in 1940 almost two thirds of the economically active population were still employed in agriculture.[63] In both countries land reform was a politically expedient solution to the agrarian issue but in neither case did it give much impetus to industrialisation. While in Finland it was part of a programme of 'national reconciliation' backed by the Agrarian Union and the National Progressives after the civil war, in Ireland land reform had been part of a long-running policy of 'killing Home Rule by kindness'.[64] In 1918 the Finnish *Eduskunta* passed a Crofters Act which enabled tenant farmers to buy their own land. Four years later, a second act, the *Lex Kallio*, led to the creation of new smallholdings for the landless population. As a result of both acts, about 100,000 new farms were created. 'There is no doubt that the reforms had significant political consequences. The population which had previously formed the agrarian proletariat in rural areas began to accept the existing system in the society as legitimate, and worth defending.'[65] Much the same is true for Ireland. In 1923 the government passed a Land Act that created up to 100,000 new holdings and reportedly transferred 3,000,000 acres from landlord to peasant.[66] This policy was continued on a smaller scale by Fianna Fáil after 1932. By 1938 the political scientist, James Hogan, who had been greatly alarmed at the influence of communism in Ireland only a few years earlier, could reflect that 'if it be true that the small business, with a peasant proprietorship, is the necessary backbone of a free country, the best training ground for character and the best safeguard of the variety of life, we in Ireland have reason to be grateful.[67]

The crucial difference between the two cases, however, was that in Ireland land reform had advanced very far by 1921, whereas in Finland agrarian problems were allowed to mount up in the decades before independence. As a result, the Finnish civil war of 1917–18 had a strong social dimension that was lacking in the Irish case. From the 1870s on Finland's economic development was based on a thriving export trade, especially in timber. The forests from which this timber was extracted were owned by the farmers and peasants.[68] The sawmill industry led to the creation of a rural capitalist class among median-sized farmers who in turn invested their profits into the local banking, educational, and co-operative movements. As the distinction between these independent farmers and the traditional manorial farmers becoming clouded owing to the increased wealth from timber, the gap between those that had land and those that did not became more acute. This gap increased because of a number of factors, foremost among them being the decreasing death rate which created rural overpopulation. As the numbers of the rural population began to grow, the practice of sub-division was not sufficient to generate employment for all. As a result the landless population began to increase.

Table 4.5 **Agrarian households in Finland by class, 1815–1901**

Class	1815	1870	1901[2]	Increase / decrease
Landowners	57%	39%	35%	−22%
Crofters[1]	28%	32%	17%	−11%
Agricultural workers	15%	29%	48%	+33%

1   Includes other 'tenant farmers' too.
2   In 1901 scrapholders, previously classified as crofters are now classified as labourers, thereby exaggerating the relative decline of the former and the relative increase of the latter.

Source: adapted from R. Alapuro, *State and Revolution in Finland* (1988), table 4, p. 40.

Indeed the Finnish rural class structure became increasingly stratified towards the end of the century. Alapuro has provided a breakdown of the figures for changes in the sizes of agrarian social classes in the nineteenth century, part of which I have reproduced in table 4.5. Between 1815 and 1901 the proportion of Finnish landowners among the agrarian population decreased from well over half to just over a third of the total number of households, while the proportion of crofters also declined. Agricultural labourers, who comprised only 15 per cent of agrarian households in 1815, made up almost half of agrarian households by 1901. By the turn of the century half of the rural population were landless. Alapuro has described the consequences of this overpopulation:

> As the landless population expanded without being effectively absorbed into industry, it remained in the countryside, producing a large number of agricultural workers. In 1910 there were 2.3 agricultural workers and 0.5 crofters and other tenant farmers for every landowner, and in the southwest the proportion was much higher, with 4.6 agricultural workers to every landowner.[69]

Table 4.6 **Persons engaged in agriculture and agricultural labourers in the future area of the Free State, 1881–1911**

	1881	1891	1901	1911
Total	684,206	643,196	606,612	554,059
Agricultural	160,757	116,239	106,069	99,848
Labourers	(23.4%)	(18%)	(17.4%)	(18%)

Source: Irish Free State Census 1926.

The Irish situation was very different. Table 4.6 shows the total number of persons employed in agriculture and the number of agricultural workers in the future area of the Free State between 1881 and 1911. In this period the number of agricultural labourers fell from a total of 160,757 in 1881 to 99,848 in 1911. Whereas in 1881 their proportion of the total agricultural labour force was 23.4 per cent, by 1911 this had fallen to 18 per cent. This means there was less than one agricultural labourer for every five farmers in 1911, whereas in Finland there were more than five for each one. Before the Great Famine there had been at least two male farm workers for every farmer in Ireland: by 1911 that was true of only four counties. Moreover farm workers, who were often 'labour occupiers' in reality, had as a class become far less distinct from the farming class after the Famine.[70]

In 1906, however, only about a quarter of Irish farmers owned their own farms.[71] This figure compares poorly with the Finnish figure in 1900 where 'there were two comparable strata of peasant farmers in Finland – over

100,000 independent landowners and about the same number of tenant farmers'.[72] However, due to land reform, by 1911 the proportion of Irish owner-occupiers increased to almost two thirds of the total number of farmers. In contrast, a number of ill-conceived reforms of tenancy arrangements aggravated the tenant–landlord relationship in Finland, without increasing the number of independent farmers. According to an official enquiry around 14,000 tenant evictions took place between 1909 and 1915.[73] The Finnish parliament intended to pass a Land Reform Bill improving tenancy conditions in the months before the civil war, but this proved impossible in the uncertain conditions of the time. During the civil war of 1918 both industrial workers and agricultural labourers were on the Red side, with the independent peasantry and the upper classes in general supporting the Whites. Tenant farmers were found on both sides.[74] The Irish civil war lacked this clear social basis. Perhaps if the proportion of farm workers had not shrunk from over half the occupied male workers in 1841 to less than a third in 1911, the situation might have been comparable. According to Fitzpatrick, 'the survival of the class of rural labourers might well have engendered a social revolution still more far-reaching than that which resulted from its collapse'.[75]

Moore had suggested that the commercialisation of agriculture was necessary in order to further industrialisation, but the Finnish–Irish comparison suggests that it was more important that the independent peasantry found its political identity before the industrial working class was mobilised. Where this did not happen, as in Finland where the Social Democratic Party gained the support of both urban and rural workers between 1906 and 1917, violent class conflict between socialists and the rural middle classes ensued. In inter-war Europe, where Social Democratic parties became involved in rural class conflicts, the independent farmers typically opposed both democracy and socialism. Social democratic regimes could only be consolidated if they had the support of the independent farmers. This was forthcoming only where socialist parties stayed out of rural class conflict.[76] In the three Scandinavian cases strong peasant movements had emerged before the development of socialist parties and the agrarian parties that followed remained committed to democracy. The violent outcome in Finland was due to a combination of domestic and international factors. The country's political development was retarded by its dependence on Tsarist Russia, while the 1917 revolution intensified opposition to socialism among the bourgeois parties.

In the Irish context agrarian politics had been dominated by nationalist parties long before the Labour Party had a chance to organise in rural areas. This may explain why there was no significant agrarian opposition to democratisation in 1918, and why the larger farmers supported the move to independence between 1919 and 1921. Indeed the Sinn Féin party and the IRA opposed the claims of 'landgrabbers' during the War of Independence, and once the Free

State had been established, the pro-Treaty IRA were quick to suppress land agitation and 'cattle driving'. For example, in May 1922 the pro-Treaty IRA in Clare issued a proclamation threatening 'drastic action' against cattle drivers should their activity continue.[77] The attitude of the anti-Treaty IRA was not that different. In January 1922, with the support of their Chief of Staff, they proclaimed a state of martial law in Kilmallock as a means of dealing with a labour dispute.[78] Labour opposed these actions, but in the June 1922 election, the first general election contested by the party, Labour failed to contest seats in the west of Ireland and the Border counties where agrarian distress was most prevalent. After its disappointing performance in the August 1923 election, the party had to remind itself that if it wished to form a 'Workers' Republic' it had to appeal to the rural poor in the west.[79] With the anti-Treaty Sinn Féin party already strong in the poorer and peripheral areas of rural Ireland, there was little possibility that Labour would displace them after 1923. The failure of Labour to mobilise the rural poor was one reason for the weakness of the left in independent Ireland, but it may also have defused a potential source of conflict within the new polity. As the 'Blueshirt' episode of the 1930s showed, sections of rural society in Ireland could be mobilised by authoritarian elites, but with Labour a marginal player in rural class conflict, there was little likelihood that agrarian class conflict would destabilise the system.

The dominance of bourgeois values in the Irish countryside was also clearly evident from the ideology of national integration that came to be espoused after the civil war. This ideology was essentially similar to that propagated by the bourgeois parties in Finland where, despite acute class divisions, a relatively united nationalist culture had developed by the early years of the twentieth century, and was solidified by a common fear of Soviet Russia after 1917.[80] Finnish and Irish nationalist ideologues had long romanticised the nature of rural life and celebrated the free-farming peasant as the model citizen, assuming in both countries that each nation's most authentic traditions were rooted in the rural way of life. In Finland, the agrarian ideology of the inter-war years derived from the *Fennoman* movement of the nineteenth century its idealisation of the Finnish peasant, its stress on the need for moral regeneration in society, and the need to protect the national culture from external sources of contamination.[81] In Ireland a stress on the virtues of the family farm, a belief in the need to preserve rural life in the face of modernisation, and a celebration of spiritual values over material ones, were all part and parcel of a world view that had its origins in the Gaelic Revival of the 1890s.[82]

In both Finland and Ireland, then, after the civil wars nationalist ideologues propagated a view of their societies as 'interclass communities' and this image was made plausible by the relatively egalitarian pattern of land distribution in both countries.[83] The promotion of the national culture was a token of the bourgeois elite's determination to counter what they regarded as the pernicious influence of class distinctions.[84] In 1933 de Valera announced that:

> The Communist policy is directly opposed to ours. Our policy is to plant as many families as possible on the soil, to give them food, and to respect private property and to interfere only in the way the State has a right to interfere – for the general good of the community. As a matter of fact, our policy is the alternative to Communism, and those who support our policy are doing the best thing to save this country from any advance of Communism.[85]

Consciously or not, this affirmation of rural values was an Irish restatement of a familiar theme in modern European political propaganda where arguments advanced for land reform often tended to stress a social ideal as much as the practicalities of land provision. For example, the leading ideologue of the Finnish Agrarian Union, Santeri Alkio, also committed himself to the search for a 'third way' between capitalism and socialism: 'a vision of society that would guarantee the protection of private property, but at the same time promote inter-class harmony through general social reform'.[86] As early as 1930 an outside observer could remark that Finland had already achieved a considerable degree of national consolidation:

> Finland is basically governed by the peasants for the peasants, and the fact that Finns are essentially a highly educated peasant nation seems to have prevented any class distinctions in the ordinary sense of the word. This, combined with the fact that there is no great wealth and comparatively no poverty, has greatly contributed to that quality of solidarity to which I have already referred.[87]

Moore himself acknowledged that 'democracy and an independent peasantry have not been incompatible bedfellows in France; rather it is modernisation and peasantry which seem to be necessarily incompatible'.[88] Indeed the possibility that democracy could flourish in rural conditions has been long considered by political theorists. Aristotle, for example, maintained that 'there is no difficulty in constructing a democracy where the bulk of the people live by arable and pastoral farming'.[89] Travelling through America in the nineteenth century, de Tocqueville reflected that 'among the novel objects that attracted my attention during my stay in the United States, nothing struck me more forcibly than the general equality of condition among the people'.[90] Before him Rousseau specified what he thought were the most ideal social conditions for a democratic system: 'a very small state, in which the people may be readily assembled, and in which every citizen can easily know the rest; secondly great simplicity of manners, which prevents a multiplicity of affairs and thorny discussions; next, considerable equality of rank and fortune, without which equality in rights and authority could not long subsist'.[91] Why should democracy flourish in such agrarian societies? Dahl has identified two features that may sustain a democratic system:

> As Tocqueville observed (among many others), the agrarian society of the United States possessed the two crucial features that make an MDP society favourable to polyarchy. It produced a wide dispersion of power and it strongly fostered democratic beliefs. In fact, ideologues of agrarian republicanism like Thomas Jefferson and John Taylor were so firmly convinced that an agrarian society of independent farmers was absolutely essential to the existence of a democratic republic that they were unable to foresee the possibility that a republic might continue to exist in the United States even after farmers became a miniscule minority.[92]

Widespread dispersal of property ownership and strong beliefs in equality are thus the two main ingredients of the agrarian model of democracy. Arguably both existed in inter-war Ireland and formed the basis for a stable but rural political system until the 1960s.

In summary, the Irish case does not support Moore's argument that getting rid of agriculture as a major social activity is an essential prerequisite of democratisation. Democratic values have thrived in free farming communities of widely different cultural backgrounds, including the world's earliest modern democracies – France, Iceland, Norway, the United States, and Switzerland. Indeed, without the possibility of an alignment with a politically committed agrarian middle class, urban liberals or urban socialists in the Third World are unlikely to be able to stabilise a democratic regime on their own.[93] Moreover, there is little evidence to justify the view that the costs involved in the transition to democratic capitalism must be borne by the peasantry as a whole. In Ireland they were borne by the poorer agricultural classes only. The Irish also benefited from the early timing of land reform and the strong nationalist consensus that had developed in the late nineteenth century survived the civil war. In contrast the Finns had greater difficulty integrating the defeated side into the system, since the Finnish workers retained separate social clubs, sports organisations, and financial institutions after 1918.[94]

4.4   Conclusion

The basic contention of this chapter has been that the creation of a large class of independent farmers was a basic precondition for the emergence of a stable democratic system in Ireland. British reformism succeeded in eliminating the two social classes, the landed aristocracy and the landless peasantry, who would have had least stake in a democratic system. The story of Ireland under the Union is one of Catholic advance at the expense of a dominant minority and to nationalists this appeared synonymous with the progress of democracy itself. Writing in 1906 Tom Kettle reflected that

> If we now turn to Irish history it is easy to see that it is a passage from feudalism to democracy. Thus, when Mr. Michael Davitt came to write the story of the Land War, he inevitably called it, 'The Fall of Feudalism in Ireland'. Under the same title you might gather every stream of agitation, every Act that could be in any sense called beneficial from the Abolition of Tithes and Catholic Emancipation to the Local Government Act. They are all parts of a process which is shifting the centre of power from privileged arbitrary classes to responsible, representative classes.[95]

Whether Moore would have considered the Irish 'revolution' a modernising revolution is more open to debate. It seems just as likely that he would have compared it to the Indian case: democratic but unmodern. However, in so far as fundamental changes in agrarian class relations are concerned, the Irish experience was probably more like the Nordic cases, where the individualisation of agriculture was a basic starting point for democratic political development.[96] In these countries, although historical and topographical factors were also important, the modernisation of agriculture was also carried out by the crown, often in alliance with the nobility. In the Irish case the state was a major actor too, but Moore's theory, which limits itself to the analysis of class relations, actually tells us little about why the state should act in this way.[97] As a recent theory has put it, 'the transplantation of state structures' was a crucial aspect of democratisation in the colonial world, and the same was true for Ireland.[98]

Arguably the choice in independent Ireland was not between fascism, democracy and communism at all, but between democracy and social democracy. The agrarian class system did not fully determine which of these regimes emerged after independence, since two other factors – a deeply divided middle class and a politically weak working class – added further elements to the equation. The former, a divided middle class, prevented a purely liberal regime being stabilised after independence and would have allowed for the emergence of a social democratic regime had there been a more radical urban socialist party to fight for it. There wasn't and rural assumptions about political life continued to dominate political debate thereafter. The new state has been described as 'a periphery-dominated centre', but all the Nordic democracies were based on an alliance between town and country, more specifically of Social Democratic and Agrarian parties.[99] As in Ireland these regimes incorporated this positive evaluation of the role of the small farmer into their self-image.

On the other hand the extent to which rural society dominated political life in independent Ireland was probably unequalled among European democracies. Even in inter-war Finland, a much more rural society, the Social Democrats, the Swedish People's Party, and the liberal National Progressives, were important sources of ideological variety. In independent Ireland in contrast there were few strong ideological rivals to the former Sinn Féin elite. However, it is also true that no agrarian parties flourished either. The two largest parties have always been composed of rural and urban interests. Moreover, political representatives have tended to come from the ranks of the professions and politics as a profession has traditionally been dominated by the middle class. The characteristically Irish pattern of political representation, with a middle-class 'national' political elite representing rural constituencies, developed in the nineteenth century and continues today. In a rustic way it does little to disprove Moore's dictum 'No bourgeoisie no democracy'.

Chapter 5

Civil society and democratic practice under the union

'The civic sense, the community conscience is feeble in Ireland.'

Kevin O'Higgins, 1925

One of the stock-in-trade reflections of the founding fathers of the Irish Free State was that civic culture in Ireland was notoriously weak. Kevin O'Higgins described the social convictions behind Irish democracy as 'an unquestionable mixture of feudalism and brigandage in one quarter, and a deplorable amount of grabber and gombeen morality generally'.[1] Naturally, our evaluation of the performance of Irish governments after 1921 will depend to a large extent on our estimation of the political aptitudes of the public and, if O'Higgins was right, Irish democracy was an amazing achievement. The problem is that political cultures are notoriously difficult to reconstruct, and the only way we have of doing so is by recourse to civil society. Emerging in the 'long nineteenth century' between 1800 and 1921, Irish civil society, that set of social and political institutions lying between the individual and the state, has never been systematically studied, and what follows is necessarily an incomplete analysis.[2] The issue of whether Catholics and Protestants shared a common civil society, the extent to which gender and class inequalities underpinned the growth of Irish associational life, and the support of the Catholic Church for this civil society, cannot be fully explored here. Nevertheless, some crucial questions – whether a genuinely civil society developed before 1921, the extent to which it was democratically organised, and how it related to the general progress of democratisation – can be resolved. Given that the United Kingdom was a parliamentary rather than a democratic state before 1918, and since nationalist Ireland lacked any form of self-rule before 1898, it was only through civil society that a democratic political culture could have emerged. If O'Higgins was right, Irish civil society was unequal to this task and the result was a state built on very shaky foundations. If O'Higgins was wrong, the survival of Irish democracy after 1921 was no surprise.

5.1 Democracy and civil society

The concept of civil society is a protean one, put to many uses. Keane describes it as an 'ideal-typical' concept employed to mean different things in different contexts. For some, civil society is primarily an analytical concept that is used to analyse and interpret 'the empirical contours of past, present, or emergent relationships between social and political forces and institutions'. For others civil society is a pragmatic term, to be used 'as a guide in formulating a social and political strategy or action programme'. For others yet again, civil society is a normative term, one that is used to highlight 'the ethical superiority of a politically guaranteed civil society compared with other types of regime'.[3] It is primarily in the first sense of the term that civil society is used here, as a concept that describes a legally protected but spontaneously generated set of social and political institutions that are separate from the state. In pre-independence Ireland such institutions ranged from organisations such as the Christian Brothers Past Pupil Union, to bodies with a more serious purpose, such as the 'Pioneer' temperance movement, to organisations that were directly engaged with the state, such as the United Irish League. However, although civil society is always conceived of as a realm of collective action separate from the state, it is not synonymous with 'society' as a whole. Civil society is concerned with public rather than private ends and the emphasis here is on public organisations which contributed in some way to the shaping of the wider political culture of Irish society.[4]

There is no doubt that by 1921 Ireland had developed a civil society that touched on practically every area of Irish public life. Indeed it is impossible to write the political history of the country under the Union without discussing the role of mass movements, such as the Catholic Association, the Land League, and the National League, to name just a few. Other less political organisations, based mainly in Dublin, also provided the 'intellect' of an improving society at a time of general social distress, such as Primate Marsh's Public Library (1707), the Royal Dublin Society (1742), and the Royal Irish Academy (1786). By the middle of the nineteenth century these organisations were joined by a plethora of other organisations, such as the Geological Society of Dublin, the Royal Irish Art Union, the Dublin Statistical Society, and the Royal Horticultural Society of Ireland.[5] In the second half of the nineteenth century Irish professional life became regulated by a number of organisations, some recently formed, some long-standing, such as the Architectural Association of Ireland, the Incorporated Law Society, the Institute of Bankers, the Institute of Civil Engineers, the Institute of Journalists, the Insurance Institute of Ireland, the Irish Medical Association, and the Society of Incorporated Accountants in Ireland. Then the period between the late 1880s and independence saw the emergence of a number of nationalist organisations, such as the Gaelic Athletic Association (1884), the Gaelic League (1892), the Feis Ceoil (1897), and the National Literary Society of Ireland (1892). A number of women's organisations emerged in this period too, such as the Irish Central Bureau for the Employment of Women, the Irish Women's Suffrage and Local Government Association, and the Women's National Health Association. A remarkable aspect of this period was also the strong growth of the trade union movement, with over seventy unions being formed or registered with the Registrar of Friendly Societies between 1890 and 1921.[6]

A number of observations can be made about these developments. Firstly, none of the mass organisations so prominent in the nineteenth century, from O'Connell's Catholic Association, to the Land League and the National League, survived for long. Most lasted less than ten years, and it was the nominally 'apolitical' organisations that were formed in the closing decades of British rule, such as the Gaelic League, that provide the essential continuity between the pre- and post-independence periods. Indeed the tradition established by O'Connell, of building parliamentary movements on the edifice of mass civil organisations, died out before 1921, since all subsequent Irish parties were independent of civil society organisations. Secondly, although the ideological temper of the Free State clearly reflected the mood of the 1890–1914 period, with its themes of cultural revivalism, economic protectionism and temperance, there is also continuity between the movements that promoted those values and earlier organisations. This was most obviously the case with regard to the 'pioneer' temperance movement founded at the turn of the century, but organisations such as the Royal Agricultural Improvement Society founded in 1841, which had around 110 subsidiary local farming societies by 1848, were not that different in spirit from Horace Plunkett's Irish Agricultural Organisation founded in 1894.[7] Thirdly, many of these earlier organisations emerged under the tutelage of the British state, either through being incorporated by Royal Charter, through being registered with the Registrar of Friendly Societies, or simply in response to government policy. Since the United Kingdom as a whole was to develop a civil society in the nineteenth century, we have to assess how the norms and structures of its 'subscriber democracy' influenced Irish organisations.[8] Lastly, although this sketch has largely omitted the myriad religious organisations that emerged, some analysis of the contribution of organised religion to Irish civil society is essential, since in Europe as a whole the contribution of religion was a key variable affecting the prospects of a democratic civil society developing.[9] By the middle of the nineteenth century, organisations such as the Association for Discountenancing Vice and Promoting the Knowledge and Practice of the Christian religion (1792), the Vincent de Paul (1833), and the Irish Temperance Union (1839) were playing an important role in Irish public life, and their role was complemented by a host of charitable or religious societies, too numerous to mention.[10]

Inevitably the question will arise as to how democratic this civil society was. The earliest extant rulebook in the Registry of Friendly Societies is that of the Ancient Moira Society established in 1804. Its 1812 rulebook provided for a government of a President and two stewards 'who shall act with strict justice and impartiality to the society in general according to these rules'. Members who felt mistreated by any of the officers of the society had a right of appeal to 'a superior council' of 12 members and all members were expected to serve a term in office. The membership was limited to 100 and no person could be admitted to membership but by the votes of a majority of the members.[11] We see here, in embryonic form, the basic tenets of constitutionalism: that rules are binding on all members regardless of rank, that executives are accountable for their behaviour, and that decisions should be decided by majority rule. It is interesting to look forward to the 1833 rule book and observe a number of further rules: that the secretary be chosen annually by majority vote, that there be no objection to any prospective member on the basis of his trade or religion, and that there be no change allowed to the fundamental principles of the rules.[12] Clearly a number of further ideas that are fundamental to a democratic constitution – that executives be elected by majority vote, that societies should not discriminate against prospective members on the basis of religion, and that rules be changed only by extra-ordinary procedures – are foreshadowed in self-governing bodies of this kind. The 1873 rule book then specified the conditions under which members could be expelled (ultimately by ballot), the number of 'general meetings' each year, and the size of the majority needed to change the rules (two thirds of members), all of which appear in more elaborate form in the constitutions of later organisations.[13] The Ancient Moira Society was a benefit society not a political organisation, but its constitutional history, taken with the records of similar organisations, proves that the basic tenets of constitutionalism were valued at a very early stage in Irish life.

Of course any analysis of Irish civil society must also focus on organisations that were public in the sense that they used public funds and performed functions later taken over by the state. Here the norm was also for executives to be chosen by ballot among the members who paid voluntary subscriptions, but there was a wide range of practices when it came to admission of members. Primate Marsh's Public Library admitted readers gratuitously and without religious distinction, the only requisite being a reference authenticated by a parochial clergyman. The Dublin Mechanics Institute, founded in 1837, also admitted members gratuitously but required a subscription of ten shillings per annum. The Chemico-Agricultural Society of Ulster offered membership to landed proprietors at an annual subscription of £1 per annum and to tenant farmers at a subscription of not less than five shillings annually. In contrast, the Archaeological Society founded in 1840 required a subscription of £1 per annum, an entrance fee of £3 on election, and membership was limited to 500 in 1848 ('Noblemen and gentlemen' who wished to become members could forward their names to a Dr Todd at Trinity College, Dublin). The practices of electing new members by ballot and of requiring an annual subscription of at least £1 from members were common to most learned Dublin societies in the middle of the nineteenth century. The Royal Zoological Society of Ireland, for example, required members to pay £1 on admission alongside an annual subscription of £1 or a life subscription of £10.[14] Clearly, although such societies were funded by public subscriptions, and although membership implied a commitment to the ends of the organisations and a willingness to obey their rules, they could also be regarded as closed shops and this point will be elaborated upon later.

The democratisation of Irish civil society proceeded more rapidly in societies that were both public and 'populist'. The Gaelic League is a classic example of an organisation that was committed to public ends and achieved a mass membership of over 100,000 by independence. Its 1899 constitution provided for a regular representative structure with an executive committee (Coiste Gnótha) elected annually by a delegate conference (Ard Fheis). The delegates to this Ard Fheis were elected by the branches (craobhacha) in proportion to the certified membership of the branches.[15] In 1900 the consti-tution was revised but the basic structure remained the same. The representative congress remained the supreme governing body; it would meet at least once a year, and at its annual meeting it would elect an executive committee charged with the daily running of the organisation. The members of this committee would not be entitled to vote for the election of executive officers at the succeeding annual meeting. Membership of a branch would not be made conditional upon membership of any other body, but would be open to persons of every class or creed.[16] In 1921 the constitution was again revised, this time allowing members of the Coiste Gnótha to vote in the election of succeeding executives. Two new representative tiers (coiste ceanntiar and coiste duitche) were also formed, which would supervise the work of the branches. A special meeting of the Ard Fheis would be convened at any time at the request of one third of the members of the Ard Fheis or by resolution of the Coiste Gnotha. Special representation in the election of the Coiste Gnotha was given to the four provinces of Ireland, and to Dublin, Great Britain, and the United States. The new rules reaffirmed that the League (Conradh na Gaedhilge) would be strictly 'non-political and non-sectarian'.[17] Despite the corralling of the organisation by the Irish Republican Brotherhood in 1915, the basic structure of the organisation proved remarkably durable and formed a blueprint for later political parties.

While there is no doubt that there was a democratic civil society in nationalist Ireland by 1921, the question remains as to why it should have developed at all. Putnam traces the civic culture of Northern Italy to a centuries-old tradition of municipal self-government, but Irish Catholics had no such tradition and Garvin argues that civic tradition in Ireland was uniquely weak in western Europe.[18] Where then did civil society come from? The romantic view of civil society, which sees voluntary groups emerging from below out of the decisions of citizens who spontaneously decide to join associations and get things done outside the sphere of government and politics, is criticised by Skocpol. She relates the development of American civil society to the activities of the state: the beginning of competitive national and local elections, the openness of the Congress to petition drives, and the spread of public schooling.[19] In other words, civic traditions are not independent variables which explain the growth of civil society, but are offshoots of wider processes and structures. In the Irish context, with no native tradition of local government, with no memories of statehood to draw on, and with a retarded process of economic development until the 1870s, the emergence of civil society is all the more remarkable. Part of the explanation obviously lies in the diffusion of British constitutional values to Ireland, part may derive from the commitments of elite sections of Irish society themselves, but the main explanatory variable must be the nature of the British state itself.

5.2   Roots of constitutionalism

The rulebooks contained in the Registry of Friendly Societies are probably the best guide we have to the emergence of a constitutionalist culture in Ireland under the Union. At least 486 such 'friendly' societies were registered with the authorities in 1844 and perhaps as many as twice that number were in existence.[20] A number of factors explain their emergence: religious revivalism spread ideas of personal initiative and moral obligations to the community among both Catholics and Protestants; the growth in artisan activity made it imperative for members of trades to pool their resources together and regulate their businesses; and the encouragement of the British state itself, which passed legislation aimed at them in 1793, 1819, 1829, 1834, 1846, 1850 and 1855, and which offered tax breaks in return for registration, made the formation of such societies more attractive. Behind all this was a process of cultural diffusion, since the 1820s and 1830s saw the emergence of a strong associational culture in Britain. Irish developments were probably a decade or two behind, but the main elements of Britain's associational culture were clearly present in Ireland too. British associations, like their Irish counterparts, were open to those who supported their aims, followed their rules, and paid subscriptions.

Accountability was a key issue, expressed by the election of officials and the publication of annual reports and accounts. Decisions were reached by debate, and the emphasis was on debating issues on which there could be consensus.[21] Much the same was true of Ireland. The first rulebook of the Moira Society read:

> Whereas it hath been a standing Maxim that no Government can well support itself without love and unity among several Members, so likewise the same Maxim must certainly stand good in relation to all Civil societies in general. It having been found by many examples that Mankind Uniting themselves into Civil Societies has been of great advantage to them in their several private Capacities.[22]

Friendly societies were typically self-governing societies of males, which raised funds to help members in distressed circumstances and often provided funeral expenses for deceased members and their wives. The funds were raised by periodic subscriptions by the members and were entrusted to a democratically elected treasurer. All executive positions were occupied only temporarily and members who refused to serve on management committees were often fined. Regular meetings, visits to sick members and attendance at funerals encouraged the kind of face-to-face interaction among the members that underpins a sense of solidarity. The character of new members was vetted before their admission was put to a ballot, and all new members were expected to possess a copy of the societies' rulebooks and to abide by them. These rules typically emphasised the importance of tolerance, respect and decorum in social relations. Drunkenness, violence, swearing and gambling were typically met with fines. In particular, disrespect towards the office of President was punished. The 1844 rulebook of the Emerald Society read:

> Any member not standing up while addressing the Chairman and who shall interrupt a brother whilst addressing the chairman or who shall wear his hat while the chair is occupied or who offers to lay wages in the Society soon shall for each of these several offences be fined sixpence.[23]

The workings of the friendly societies seem to epitomise many of the values commonly associated with 'social capital' – solidarity, egalitarianism, and trust.[24] What underpinned their rule-based culture was a sense of the importance of reciprocity and consent in social relations. By avoiding permanent hierarchies within organisations, by making officers accountable to members, and by making membership conditional only on testimonies of good character, these societies were all subscribing to an egalitarian and harmonious view of social relationships. The 1848 rulebook of the Protestant Pembroke Society of Tradesmen began:

And as concord and unanimity form the basis whereon the tranquillity and happiness of the society depend – we therefore the members of this society, in order to obtain those desirable ends, agree to be governed and regulated by the following rules.[25]

It is significant that the British practice of 'no religion and no politics' at meetings was adopted and is present in the constitution of nearly all Irish societies registered up to 1921. Likewise, the acceptance of legal norms, through the practice of expelling felons, was a characteristic feature too: the 1850 rules of the Friendly Brothers of Saint Jerome society specifically prevented members of secret societies from becoming members.[26] A clear sense of reciprocity with the state also obtained, these societies usually submitting changes in their rules, the names and occupations of their officers, and their annual accounts, to the Registrar for inspection. The 1843 rule book of the Caledonian Benevolent Society specifically stated that the majority of the members could change the rules provided there was nothing therein contrary to the most recent Act of Parliament relative to friendly societies.[27] In other societies the rulebooks stipulated that disputes between members could be referred to justices of the peace or the petty magistrates.

In design the friendly societies tried to avoid many of the worst features of 'politics': conflict over issues that could not generate consent, unaccountable executives, and factionalism. The rulebook of the Protestant Pembroke Society of Tradesmen established in 1848 read:

That if any member, publicly or privately strives in any way to promote the dissolution of this society or introduces any improper conversation likely to promote division, and disturb the peace and Brotherly love that exists in this society, or in any way endeavour to separate them from each other, he or she shall be excluded or fined.[28]

All of them avoided the permanent division of the societies into ex-officio and ordinary members. The Friendly Brothers of the Society of Saint Michan after 1859, for example, elected their government by taking four members in alphabetical order and whoever received a majority of the votes would be elected President, others becoming stewards. These would remain in office for only four weeks. However, not every office, particularly that of secretary, could be subject to re-election at such short intervals, but in all cases there was a clear ethos of accountability with respect to officials. The Treasurer of the Dean's Grange Society in 1861 was elected for life by a majority of the members at the first general meeting of the society after the rulers were certified, but could still be removed by a majority of the members at a meeting convened for that purpose.[29] Similar rules existed for practically every other friendly society whose records have survived and in some instances there were extraordinary procedures for holding officials to account. After 1848, in the Protestant Pembroke Society of Tradesmen, if the President should neglect any part of his duties, causing a meeting to be disturbed, a member who complained and whose complaint was seconded could get the meeting to discuss the issue in the absence of the President with 'the Father' taking the chair. If the President were found at fault he would be fined and removed from his post.[30]

In short, the rudiments of democratic practice – that executives be elected, that they be held accountable for their actions through clear procedures, and that only members deciding by majority vote had a right to alter constitutions – are all present in the constitutions of the friendly societies that have survived to this day. Moreover, these practices are present, in more elaborate form, in practically all the organisations that were registered later in the nineteenth century. In the Caledonian Benevolent Society the basic features of the rules adopted in 1843 survived into the twentieth century. These 1843 rules provided for the appointment every quarter of a President and two stewards from nine members taken from the membership list who would each serve for one month in rotation as they appeared on the list.[31] The 1860 rules provided for the selection of seven members from the membership list in rotation to serve as stewards and the President. The President would be chosen by a majority of the members from among the seven. The remaining six would take turns (two by two) as stewards for one month while the president would serve for three months.[32] The 1888 rules provided for the election of a President from three names taken alphabetically from the membership roll who would serve for three months unless removed by a majority at a meeting convened for that purpose. A secretary, treasurer, and assistant treasurer would also be chosen by ballot, but would remain in office unless removed by a two-thirds majority at a meeting convened for that purpose.[33] The 1906 rules made no fundamental changes to the governing structure save for the introduction of an 'annual meeting' which by then had become the norm in similar societies.[34]

Of course it could be objected that such societies were unrepresentative and that the larger nationalist organisations that emerged later on were different in ethos. However, the records of organisations such as the Irish National Foresters Benefit Society, established in 1878, show a similar if more recognisably modern ethos. Its 1878 rules allowed for a committee of management, consisting of ten persons, to be elected every year by an annual general meeting. Its officers would be elected at half-yearly intervals, but the treasurer, trustees, and secretary would remain in office during the pleasure of the society unless removed by a majority of the members at a specially convened meeting. No political or sectarian debates would be allowed and rules could be changed only by a majority at a meeting specially convened for that purpose.[35] Then the 1898 rules also provided for an 'annual convention' consisting of delegates from branches throughout the country which had the right to send at least two delegates to the convention. As with most large organisations of that era, the convention had the power to appoint officers (now called the Executive Council), administer the funds, and alter the rules of the society. Canvassing for the appointment to executive positions was not allowed and the rule forbidding 'political' or 'sectarian' debates was retained.[36] The case of the Foresters is a good example of how the ethos of the smaller societies was transposed onto a much larger body, and there are other cases. The constitution of Horace Plunkett's Irish Agricultural Organisation Society, founded in 1894, also bears testimony to their influence. Some aspects of its 1912 constitution – the role of the annual general meeting in deciding policy, the branch structure with delegate representation, and the provisions for provincial representation on the management committee – were new and to be expected in an organisation that would have almost 300 branches by 1921.[37] However, the basic legacy of the friendly societies was still there; membership was dependent on subscription (£1 shares), executives were replaced and elected annually, and religious and political motions could not be introduced at meetings of the society.[38]

The values promoted by the friendly societies, such as thrift, self-reliance, reciprocity, self-government and civility, could also be wedded to the more general objective of integrating the working classes into capitalist society.[39] The friendly societies mostly regarded overcoming class divisions as a precondition for the development of harmonious social relationships and the evidence suggests that many subscribed to a basically reciprocal view of employer–employee relations. For example the 1863 rules of the Dublin Grocers' Assistants' friendly association stated:

> It is an acknowledged fact that the position occupied by the Grocers' Assistants is, from the peculiar nature of the trade, one of considerable trust and serious responsibility, and that every employer must necessarily place implicit confidence in their integrity. It is evidently, therefore, a matter of the first importance to every grocer to procure the services of respectable young men, properly trained, and of unimpeachable character.[40]

Between 1820 and 1850 Dublin artisans as a whole hoped for a society in which their labour would be protected, in which worker–employer relations would be based on mutual agreement, and in which disputes would be settled by arbitration; this ethos seems to have lasted.[41] The rule book of the Metropolitan House Painters Trade Union, established in 1893, for example, stated that if it be necessary to seek any increase in wages, reasonable notice 'should be given to employers and should they resist every effort should be made to avert a strike or lock out, by arbitration or otherwise'.[42] The 1905 rules of the Irish Drapers Assistants Benefit and Protective Association, which claimed over 4,000 members and had branches in nearly all the principal cities and towns in Ireland, stated that 'our idea is not to work in a spirit of aggression to our employers'.[43] The 1907 constitution of the United Corporation Workmen of Dublin Trade Union committed itself 'to raise the social status of its members' and expressly forbade members from engaging in strike action without the permission of its committee and general body.[44]

Since many Irish trade unions were initially formed as sections of their British counterparts, it is not a surprise to find that many shared the same ethos of constitutionalism. For example the Dublin, Wicklow and Wexford Railway Friendly Society, established in 1863, was open to railway employees under 45 whose wages did not exceed sixty shillings per week, but any members convicted of a felony had to quit and disputes between members were to be referred to justices of the peace.[45] In terms of governance a similar ethos prevailed. The 1888 rule book of the Ancient Guild of Incorporated Brick and Stonelayers Trade Union provided for the election at the first annual general meeting of a committee of management consisting of a Master, a Book Steward, a second Steward, Secretary, Treasurer, two trustees, and six council members. In line with the practice of rotating officers, the Master would hold office for only three months after which his place would be taken by the book steward, whose place would then be taken by the second steward and so on. All officers were removable by a majority of votes at a meeting specially convened for that purpose.[46] The 1903 rules of the Dublin Operative Poulterers' Trade Union stipulated that the officers of the society would be elected annually at a general meeting, but would be removable by a majority of the members at a meeting specially convened for that purpose.[47] The 1902 rules of the Operative Stonecutters of Ireland Trade Union vested supreme decision-making power in its 'annual congress' consisting of delegates from its Provincial Councils or County Associations.[48] It is a short journey from these rules to the 1912 constitution of the Irish Transport and General Workers Union, which would have 100,000 members by 1921.[49] The General Executive would be annually elected by the branches of the four provinces, it would have the power to interpret the rules (but its decisions could be challenged by a referendum), and all decisions made by a National Convention of delegates would be binding.[50]

All this considered, it is not surprising then to find that organised labour came to have a very constructive attitude towards the state and a positive attitude towards democratisation in general. On 1 March 1899 a meeting of the Dublin Trades Council, established in 1885 (renamed the Dublin United Trades Council and Labour League in 1989) and which represented around 16,000 workers, passed a resolution demanding that the existing municipal franchise qualifications in Ireland be abolished and replaced by the existing parliamentary qualifications. At its first meeting on 31 May 1886 only 25 trades had been represented, but by 1914 over seventy labour organisations were affiliated with this 'parliament of labour'.[51] It subscribed to the view that trade unions were not only the best friends of the workman, but 'the best agency for the employer and the public'.[52] The cause of suffrage reform was also adopted by the Irish Trade Union Congress, which from its inception in 1894 represented over 60 unions. It consisted of delegates from these unions who each year elected a standing committee of five. It also formed a parliamentary committee of seven to try to give practical effect to the resolutions of the Congress, to scrutinise legislation affecting Irish labour, and to initiate legislation. At the end of the year this committee (increased to nine in 1899) would present a committee report to be debated by the congress. The 1894 congress declared itself in favour of manhood suffrage, the assimilation of parliamentary and municipal franchises, labour representation in parliament and on local boards, and the payment of members of parliament by the state.[53] At its 1897 congress 'this annual parliament of labour', now claiming to represent around 50,000 workers, adopted the motto 'defence not defiance'.[54] So closely interwoven were the interests of the Congress with the general progress of parliamentary reform that it subsequently adopted the practices of interviewing candidates for public positions, and issuing circulars to prospective MPs asking them for support for legislative reform relating to fair wages, housing, protectionism and pensions.[55]

The reformist nature of the trade union movement may be evidence of the long-term assimilation of British constitutional norms by the Irish public, but it is important not to exaggerate the role of the friendly societies. Their concerns were mostly private rather than public, and although they undoubtedly affected members' conceptions of the wider polity, they did not encourage the kind of debate that might have stimulated a fully fledged civic consciousness among the members. As in Britain, their social philosophy was an ethical rather than a political one, 'concerned with gaining and sustaining a stable and ethical relationship between the individual and a coherent and orderly wider society'.[56] This outlook did not require that relations between government and governed should be democratic, but merely that the two commit themselves to common ends. Moreover, since the rules forbidding religious debates seem to indicate a pessimism regarding the wider prospects for consensus in society, we have to be careful not to attribute too much influence to them in terms of their ability to reshape the wider political culture. Civil society is a sphere where values such as tolerance, moderation, and a willingness to compromise can develop, but not all societies furthered such values.[57] In 1907, for example, a critic alleged that the large Ancient Order of Hibernians, formally registered as a charitable society with a democratic constitution, actually operated like a secret cabal within the Home Rule movement, had secret initiation ceremonies, and was open only to Irish Catholics.[58] In other words, however great the constitutional legacy, other issues – the nature of nationalist civil society, the development of a recognisable public sphere, and the influence of both on the process of democratisation – can only be understood with reference to societies that were arguably less 'fraternal' but more political.

5.3 Towards a public sphere?

If the early nineteenth century saw the progressive influence of British constitutional ideas on Irish political development, that process would still not have amounted to an Irish civil society, were it not for the emergence of another set of societies, also based on public subscriptions, which seemed to herald the arrival of an Irish 'public sphere'. By public sphere we mean, first and foremost, a sphere of social interaction and communication in which something like public opinion can be formed.[59] Public opinion of course can only emerge when the means of communication – learned societies, periodicals, newspapers – already exist, and by the middle of the nineteenth century such an infrastructure was already in place in Ireland. However, public opinion can only imply a political public sphere when it deals with areas connected to the activities of the state, and in this sense the process does not reach fruition until the next century. Moreover, the idea of a public sphere as something that provides a counterweight to the state is rather an anomaly in nineteenth-century Ireland, since many of the subscriber organisations were eventually incorporated by royal charter. Indeed, the related idea that this public sphere is inevitably democratic is questionable, since not only were the mass of the public through lack of resources unable to join these societies, but the principle of general accessibility, while present in some bodies, was lacking in others. Indeed it was the British state itself which was the best guarantor of accessibility, but in a highly stratified society the extent to which this was realised before 1900 is a moot point.

According to Morris, by 1810 one form of association, the 'subscriber democracy' of the urban middle classes, had begun to dominate British public life. These bodies were 'public' in the sense that they were open to all who paid a cash subscription, published annual reports, and met in public spaces with motions debated in a formal manner.[60] While the early appearance of the Royal Dublin Society (1742) and the Royal Irish Academy (1786) suggests that Irish developments kept apace with British ones, in truth Ireland was a decade or two behind. The 1830s and the 1840s saw a dramatic increase in the number of such organisations, with the Royal Zoological Society of Ireland (1831), the Dublin Natural History Society (1838), the Dublin Mechanics Institute (1837), the Irish Archaeological Society (1840), the Dublin Scientific

Association (1841), the Royal Society for the Promotion and Improvement of the Growth of Flax in Ireland (1841), the Royal Agricultural Improvement Society (1841), the Society of Irish Artists and Royal Irish Institutions (1842), the Dublin Oratorical and Literary Institute (1844), and the Celtic Society (1845), all being formed in those decades. Like their British counterparts, these bodies depended on voluntary subscriptions, elected their officers by ballot annually, and publicised their activities. Religious and charitable organisations also mushroomed in the first half of the century, with the Hibernian Bible Society (1806), the Charitable Association (1806), the Sunday School Society for Ireland (1809), the Society for Promoting the Education of the Poor in Ireland (1811), the Association for the Relief of Distressed Protestants (1836), Irish Trinitarian Bible Society (1837), the Additional Curates Fund Society (1839), the Protestant Total Abstinence Society (1839), and the Protestant Registration Office (1844), all being formed in this period.[61] A remarkable development was the number of societies formed to encourage the study of Irish art and literature, with the Irish Archaeological and Celtic Society (1854), the Irish Institution (1853), the Ossianic Society (1853), and the Irish Antiquarian and Historical Society (1879) all being formed for this purpose.

The key contribution of such societies was to provide the intellect of an improving society at a time of widespread poverty. In the all-important area of agriculture a number of associations emerged that encouraged the diffusion of advanced methods of agricultural production. The Royal Agricultural Improvement Society of Ireland, founded in 1841, was committed to the formation of local farming societies, the opening of an Agricultural Museum and Library in Dublin, and the establishment of an agricultural college. It held prizes whereby premiums would be given to innovative farmers and these prizes were limited to those who held not more than 20 acres. The Royal Society for the Promotion and Improvement of the Growth of Flax in Ireland, established in 1841, hired a group of Belgian agriculturalists to give instructions to farming societies and landed proprietors in the best method of handling flax. The Chemico-Agricultural Society of Ulster tried to apply the theory of chemistry to the practice of agriculture and offered tenant farmers membership at a reduced rate.[62] The Royal Dublin society was primarily concerned to 'educate those concerned in the first principles of successful farming'.[63] In 1800 a Farming Society was formed under its patronage which was committed to improving cattle breeding and sent itinerant instructions out into the countryside. Between 1801 and 1832 the society also gave money premiums to farmers successful in competitions, it held lecture series on practical topics, and it established a public veterinary school as well as a school for agriculture and chemistry. Such associations were arguably forerunners of later organisations devoted to improving the lot of the farming population, such as the Irish Agricultural Organisation Society, the United Irishwomen and the Irish Farmers Union.

On the surface these associations must also have contributed to the spread of a democratic culture in Ireland. Morris explains their emergence in Britain as part of a strategic plan for the urban middle classes to consolidate their power and incorporate the working classes.[64] Certainly, the role of some Irish organisations seems similar. Formed in 1837, the Dublin Mechanics Institute promoted the 'scientific and literary improvement of the operative classes' and sought to attract members with tickets to public baths, gymnasiums and Portobello Gardens at reduced prices. The ethos of improving the ethical level of the population was also clearly shared by the religious organisations too, not all of which were exclusively denominational. In 1848 the Church Education Society for Ireland stated that it had 1,899 affiliated schools with 100,755 children on the rolls, of whom 12,691 were dissenting Protestants and 30,057 Roman Catholics.[65] However, the very large number of organisations that were specific to one religion suggests that Ireland's 'subscribing democracy', such as it was, did not transcend the religious divide. For example, the Protestant Registration Office, founded in 1844, was established to find employment for Protestants only, and similar organisations would appear later on the Catholic side, such as the Catholic Association (1902), and the Catholic Defence Society (1905). Moreover, it is debatable to what extent subscriber associations really signalled a switch, as in Britain, from closed to more open forms of association. The record of the Dublin Chamber of Commerce, founded in 1783, suggest that such bodies were less enthusiastically democratic than one would expect. Initially formed with a subscription fee of one guinea, open to any trader in Dublin, and committed to electing a ruling council, the practice of non-elections soon prevailed, and in 1805 it was decided that 16 of the 21 members of this council would be elected by the council itself and only five by the general assembly.[66] After some reforms in 1820 there were no real contests between 1826 and 1855 and between the 1850s and the 1870s the Chamber was associated with 'a very narrow world of old established business and wealth'.[67] Even after a change of the rules in 1878, regular elections, which took place at times in the 1880s, were not common in the 1890s. Indeed it was not until after 1910 that elections were contested each year.

The history of the Royal Dublin Society suggests that there was no neat equation between public subscription and accessibility either. Since 1731 its rules had allowed for members to pay an annual subscription, for membership to be decided by ballot, and for executive officers to be elected. The society was incorporated by Royal Charter in 1750 and received parliamentary grants from 1761 onwards. The list of its 267 members in 1773 was a veritable 'who's who' of the Irish establishment, with Anglican clergymen, peers, senior judges and other prominent professionals prominent.[68] However, a major dispute between the government and the society arose when the Catholic Archbishop of Dublin, Dr Murray, was rejected for membership in 1836. A Select Committee of the House of Commons subsequently required of the society that 'no individual be excluded, notwithstanding one-third of the members present may have voted for his rejection unless at least forty members shall have voted against his admission'.[69] The society was forced to accept this decision, but another controversy erupted in 1861 over the question of opening the society's Botanical Gardens on Sundays. A petition for reform had been signed by all the police magistrates of Dublin, by 43 out of the 60 municipal representatives, and by 22,000 citizens.[70] Robert Peel was reported to have said that the RDS was not suitable for 'the grand design of erecting temples of science, literature, and art in Ireland, perfectly free and open to all-comers, whatever their creed, their class or their party'.[71] The government informed the society that the grant of £6,000 for that year was conditional upon changes being made and again the society acquiesced. However, the society retained the reputation for being an exclusive body, 'a body which has several ornamental Catholics on its Council but no Catholics at all on its official staff' according to one critic in 1902.[72] Its decision to expel Count Plunkett, who was associated with the 1916 Rising, in January 1917, led the Markets Committee of Dublin Corporation not to allow members of the society's Committee of Agriculture to make use of their markets. Peace was only established when the society made election by ballot unnecessary unless objection to a candidate was expressed in writing by six members. Since then no ballots on membership have taken place.[73]

In short, the extent to which such organisations contributed to the emergence of a genuinely public sphere before 1921 can be debated, since the public they represented was, socially, a rigorously demarcated one. Indeed the ideal of a public sphere in which citizens rationally debate the fortunes of their society, irrespective of their particular religious, gender, or class background, finds its nemesis in nineteenth-century Ireland, where social exclusiveness was a reflex of polite civil society.[74] Indeed some were convinced that an inclusive civil society would only come about, not spontaneously, but through the agencies of the state in alliance with wider public opinion. The organisers of the 1861 petition stated:

> More than thirty years ago the grants for national education were taken from the management of a private society; and although we have had thirty years of preaching and praying, of platform and newspapers denunciation, the State holds the ground it then gained; and year after year draws round her an increasing mass of independent public opinion, on behalf of the great principle that no private society whatever its pretensions, should be entrusted with duties which belong alone to the Executive, responsible to the elected representatives of the people for such acts.[75]

In nineteenth-century Ireland, the wider political background, a restrictive franchise favouring Protestants, Anglican Ascendancy, and an iniquitous land settlement, formed the backdrop against which any political principle, including accessibility, had to be judged, and it is not surprising to find that a donation of £10 from Dr Murray to Daniel O'Connell may have been a reason for the rejection of his membership in 1836.[76] Until the formation of the Catholic Commercial Club in 1881 most Dublin clubs were regarded by Catholics as hostile to their national aspirations and religious feelings, but by this time other movements had already articulated the demands of this more restive and inclusive public.[77] Not surprisingly, these movements bypassed the various bodies discussed in this section and vested their hopes for reform directly in the state. Subscriber organisations such as the learned Dublin societies may have contributed to the intellect of Irish society at a time of social stasis, but when it came to voicing its aspirations, the country threw up organisations with few parallels in British experience.

5.4 The mobilisation of public opinion

If the liberal idea of the public sphere ran aground in the highly stratified society of nineteenth-century Ireland, it could be said that it also acquired a deeper democratic resonance in other sectors for exactly the same reason. With the assistance of an educated and centralised clergy, Catholic politicians from the 1820s on were able to construct political movements that were expansive rather than restrictive in their attitude towards membership, geared towards politicising the people rather than excluding them, and seeing mass participation as the most effective proof that they represented public opinion. It was clearly understood by them that the only real weapon they had against the British state was public opinion, and the Catholic Church was the organisational substratum upon which that public opinion would be roused. It seemed in the 1820s, the 1880s, and the 1890s, as if the public was suddenly organising itself as the bearer of public opinion, but political leadership, organisational factors, and ideological resources were key variables. Movements that promised immediate benefits only to the educated strata of Catholics, such as that of Catholic emancipation, struck a popular cord among a peasantry long attuned to dreams of deliverance from Protestant dominance.[78] Organisations such as the Land League could overcome the deep-rooted class divisions of Irish rural society, because peasant proprietorship could be represented as the restoration of an ancient right rather than the integration of some tenants into the alien world of commercial agriculture.[79] And the United Irish League could represent a Home Rule parliament as 'national self-government', not only something that existed in the past, but a state of affairs that would, along with land reform and a new local government franchise, be the surest catalyst for the transfer of power from the Protestant minority to the Catholic majority in Ireland. It would be too strong to argue that such movements consolidated civil society among Irish Catholics, since all proved short lived, but if the main Irish political tradition is that of 'mobilising everybody in the community for political action', these movements undoubtedly made a vital contribution.[80]

Founded in 1823, Daniel O'Connell's Catholic Association was a classic case of a middle-class subscriber democracy which transcended the limits of that genre. Financed by subscriptions of one guinea a year, it initially had the appearance of a middle-class club with familiar rules and modest aims. The association was open to Protestants and Catholics alike, newspapers were invited to its meetings, and the books of the association were always open to inspection.[81] Its aim was 'to adopt all such legal and constitutional measures as may be useful to obtain Catholic emancipation' but this association, never intended to be a community of equals, was later converted into 'a complicated mechanism designed to transform the elemental power of mass discontent into political pressure on the British government in the interests of the Irish middle class'.[82] This transformation was largely due to the support of the Catholic clergy which enabled O'Connell to convince his associates of the wisdom of popularising the association.[83] Since priests were admitted as members without payment of a subscription such clerical support was not surprising. Yet there were two other reasons why the transformation was possible. First was a change in the finances of the organisation in February 1824, to include members who were encouraged to join at the cost of a penny a month. This 'Catholic rent' would then be forwarded to the central body from every parish by a committee headed by a parish priest, who would also post the names of the subscribers in or near as possible to the Catholic chapel. This rent was then used to forward petitions to the government, to pay a parliamentary agent in London, and to secure legal representation for Catholics injured by Orange violence.[84] Secondly, O'Connell made use of the votes of the 'forty-shilling freeholders' who were less than ten per cent of all landowners to mobilise Catholics at election times. Forty-shilling freeholders included not only owner-occupiers, but also leaseholders who had leases for life and were willing to swear that their farms were worth at least forty shillings more than the rent reserved in their lease.[85] It was customary for local priests to canvass these voters, and in the run-up to voting day a team of speakers, lay and clerical, visited the chapels, and addressed the congregation after Mass.[86] Then, with the assistance of the local clergy, who often accompanied voters to the poll, these freeholders could be persuaded to vote against their landlords and Catholic candidates (who were not entitled to take their seats) would be returned. Very quickly, since voting was open and since factions would gather to support the various candidates, elections became popular events.[87]

The Catholic Association began the tradition, which would last into the next century, of involving the clergy in politics. They provided essential organisational and leadership skills in the localities 'and in return exercised considerable influence over the choice of candidates and the character of the programme and tactics'.[88] Moreover, at a time of great regional diversity, the Catholic clergy could build on the organisational frameworks provided by local groups, while at the same time transcending these boundaries and uniting people from different parts of the country.[89] Secondly, through the association, a large section of the population, much wider than those entitled to vote, gained a broad education in methods of political organisation and propaganda, since below the central committees and parish clergy many were involved as wardens, marshals, collectors, readers, and 'constables'.[90] O'Connell's movement pioneered the widespread use of political meetings, at parish, county, provincial and national level, and in many areas liberal clubs formed after 1826 survived into the 1840s and beyond.[91] Moreover, the involvement of the public in elections and the practice of pressurising candidates to declare their position on general issues signified a switch towards the concept of general elections 'as confrontation between national parties on national issues rather than that of a series of local contests'.[92] This should inevitably have entailed a diminution in other forms of protest, but the scale of such a switch should not be exaggerated.[93] What O'Connell did achieve, however, was the establishment of a link, however conditional, between Irish public opinion and parliament. This was a vital precondition for the development of a civil society in Ireland, since in Europe as a whole the establishment of 'an internalised link between the citizenry and the formal arenas of representation, was decisive in determining whether groups would be supportive of democracy or not'.[94]

However precocious in comparative terms was O'Connell's achievement, the obstacles in the way of any sustained mobilisation remained formidable. Firstly, when emancipation came in 1829 it was accompanied by a change in the electoral law, undercutting the position of the forty-shilling freeholders by raising the county property qualification to ten pounds. The ability of any popular movement to affect electoral outcomes afterwards was accordingly greatly reduced and uncontested elections remained the norm for some time. Hoppen notes that between 1852 and 1868 only 38.5 per cent of all elections were contested, compared to a figure of 69.9 per cent for the more politicised period between 1869 and 1885.[95] It was really the 1872 Ballot Act, which allowed tenants the freedom of conscience provided by the polling booth, that revitalised elections.[95] Secondly, the trick of combining spontaneous local agitation with strong central co-ordination, the hallmark of every successful movement under the Union, was difficult to repeat. The anti-tithe movement of the 1830s, for example, never succeeded in establishing the kind of commanding national headquarters of O'Connell's Association, while the Home Rule League of the 1870s failed to develop a grass-roots organisation. Thirdly, the Catholic Association and the Repeal movement were strongest in areas such as Leinster and east Munster, where communications were developed and large farmers numerous, but both failed to mobilise the rural poor in the west.[97] Indeed the peasantry as a whole was unmoved by the Catholic Association and it was only with the appearance of the Amnesty Association, in response to the failed 1867 rising, that a truly nationwide movement emerged.[98] In 1870, its President, Isaac Butt, could claim that between 1 August and 31 October 1870 alone, his association held as many as 40 meetings at which over a million people attended.[99] Lastly, the resolve of the British state itself should not be underestimated. In 1843 alone O'Connell's Repeal movement organised 32 meetings with attendance estimated at over 100,000 persons, but the movement failed in its objective.[100] A popular cause was not sufficient to build a durable organisation, and if O'Connell had established a link between the Irish public and Westminster, the reverse process, that of parliament becoming responsive to Irish public opinion, was very much in the balance.

Arguably it was the alliance between the Land League and the Home Rule Party during the Land War of 1879–82 that recovered the earlier momentum of the Catholic Association.[101] The Irish National Land League was formed in Dublin on 21 October 1879 with the aim of uniting the various local groups that were staging land demonstrations and in 1880 alone hundreds of branches were formed.[102] The movement sought to disrupt the land system by assaulting landowners and their agents, persuading tenants to withhold their normal rents, and by organising them to resist evictions. Its overall aim was 'to facilitate the ownership of the soil by the occupier' and the concession of a Land Act in 1881 which conceded the three Fs – fair rent, fixity of tenure, and freedom of sale – went some way towards satisfying grievances. The League had formed an alliance with the Home Rule Party and in the general election of 1880 helped its leadership by issuing a manifesto urging its supporters to vote against landlord candidates, by secret financial subvention, and in places by the electoral support of its local branches.[103] At its core, the league consisted of seven executive members and 54 committee members based in Dublin. Meetings of the League were public in the sense that the press could attend, anyone who paid a subscription of £1 could be elected to membership, and the League publicly declared itself a non-sectarian body.[104] However, a characteristic feature of the League was the dominance of its executive. The League had no written constitution, the original committee of 54 never again met, and the executive had no stated responsibility to the committee or to the one thousand or so local branches. The seven executive members were appointed from a prepared list at the inaugural meeting and retained control of the organisation until its suppression in 1881.

According to Lee, 'the land agitation achieved the largest active mass participation of any movement in Irish history, mobilising sectors of the population and areas of the country just beginning to be politicised'.[105] Newspaper sales rocketed in the period, a Ladies' Land League was formed, and the League consciously incorporated labouring interests by renaming itself the Land League and Labourers and Industrial Movement in 1880. Its founder, Michael Davitt, saw American influence in all of this:

> The Irish in the United States were steadily climbing upward socially and politically. They were being inoculated with practical ideas and schooled in democratic thought and action. American party organisations were training them for an active participation in public life, and in proportion as they lifted themselves up from the status of mere labourers to that of business pursuits and of professional callings did they find the opportunities and means of taking an active part in the government of cities and States. These experiences and advantages reacted upon public opinion in Ireland, through the increasing number of visitors, letters, and newspapers crossing the Atlantic, and in this manner cultivated the growth of more political thought and purpose in our political movements at home.[106]

Lee also notes that during the Land War the priests lost their traditional role in arbitrating land disputes as the League set up its own land courts.[107] Indeed, just as agrarian secret societies had disappeared from the countryside by the 1870s, the clergy were now playing less of a role and in their place the formidable 'shopkeeper-publican-politician' trio was coming into its own.[108] Moreover, the branch structure of the League represented the further encroachment of democratic practices into rural Ireland. The central executive stipulated that each branch was to have an executive committee composed of a president, vice-president, treasurer, and secretary, plus at least seven other members. This committee was supposed to be elected annually by all members who had paid their subscriptions.[109] The evidence suggests that the branches took these central regulations seriously.[110] Finally, if the essence of the League's success was that of subsuming local grievances within a nationwide campaign, the flip side of this was a conception of politics fundamentally engaged with the state. Apart from the obvious demand to resolve agrarian issues through legislation, the League took as its remit the scrutiny of the British state in all it workings. The original league, founded in Mayo in August 1879, had as one of its aims:

> To act as a vigilance committee in Mayo, noting the conduct of the grand jury, poor-law guardians, town commissioners, and members of Parliament, and pronouncing on the manner in which their respective duties are performed,

whenever the interests, social or political, of the people represented by this club render it expedient to do so.[111]

While the modernisation of Irish political consciousness may be regarded as the greatest achievement of the Land League, another consequence was that it gave a fillip to Parnell's Home Rule Party and that party, supported by its ancillary organisations – the National League and the United Irish League – was to dominate Irish political life until 1918. The original Home Rule League of the 1870s was controlled by an elected governing council of 50 (who could then co-opt another 50), was open to everyone who paid a subscription of £1 annually, and special procedures existed for holding officers to account.[112] It failed, however, to develop a grass-roots organisation and was replaced by the Irish National League in October 1882. The National League was a sophisticated mass organisation which 'combined the appearance of local spontaneity with the reality of centralised control'.[113] Each branch had its own officers, its roll of members with membership cards, and regular meetings that were recorded in the minutes.[114] Yet with the parliamentary party having the nomination of 16 members out of its council of 45, it never found it difficult to control the League. On the other hand, an innovative aspect of the new League was the role it now gave delegates of branches in the selection of electoral candidates at county conventions. The number of such branches increased from 818 in 1885 to a massive 1285 in July 1886 and the League enabled the parliamentary elite to convert what was 'a loose conglomeration of independent and sometimes discrepant elements into a well-knit political party of a modern type'.[115] What was equally important, however, was the wide range of demands besides Home Rule that the party now made of the British state. Not only were the provisions of the Land Acts to be extended to more sections of the farming population, but the process of democratisation was to be extended so that the grand juries would be replaced by elected county boards, nomination to civil service positions would be in the hands of these bodies not the government, and the Irish parliamentary and municipal franchises would also be assimilated to those of Britain.[116] Much of this simply meant that the Irish would be governed by 'British' standards, but it also heralded the transfer of power from a hitherto dominant minority to politicians that were more broadly representative, a process that would culminate in the reform of local government in 1898.

Nevertheless, the Irish National League found itself in ruins soon after the local government reform. With the disintegration of the parliamentary party into three factions with the Parnell split of 1890, a new body, the United Irish League, was formed in 1898 to restore the cohesion of the nationalist movement. As well as reuniting the parliamentary party, the objectives of the League were to decide which candidates stood for parliament, to determine the strategy of the overall movement, and to enforce discipline on MPs.[117] The 1900 constitution of the League explicitly stated that its central executive would have no power to make suggestions as to parliamentary candidates, a power vested in provincial directorates composed of delegates of its various branches, alongside members of the clergy and MPs.[118] After the 1900 election the League lost its control of the parliamentary party and power returned to the politicians of the early 1890s.[119] As with its predecessor, the League provided a vital service to the parliamentary party by mobilising voters at election time, but hopes that either League, through their democratic structures, would shift power away from the parliamentary caucus proved unfounded.

Yet to arrive at a negative conclusion about the role of civil society before 1900 would be to underestimate what had been achieved. Organisations such as the National League clearly provided a model for the development of later movements, such as the GAA, which was founded in 1884. Like the League, the GAA combined strong central co-ordination with a considerable amount of local democracy. Only one GAA club was allowed in each parish, the central committee fixed the subscription fees (and took 20 per cent of them), and monthly reports from the branches had to be submitted to the central committee. On the other hand, the hundreds of clubs also possessed their own elected committee of management consisting of a president, vice-president, treasurer, secretary, and six other members.[120] Not only did the Leagues provide a blueprint for later bodies, they also strengthened elements in Irish political culture set in train by O'Connell. A tradition of involving everyone in the community in politics, a habit of seeing electoral contests in terms of issues as much as personalities, and an ability to link local grievances with nationwide campaigns, were all a product of this emergent civil society and proof that, politically at least, Ireland was fast becoming a modern society. Common to all the movements discussed in this section was also the assumption that effective political action in a parliamentary system revolved around mobilising public opinion in the broadest possible sense. The 1900 constitution of the United Irish League remarked on the

> universally acknowledged fact that no Irish Parliamentary Party can be maintained in an effective condition, or can command the respect of English Ministers, without the support of a people strongly organised and prepared with every legitimate weapon of public opinion to give unceasing battle to the enemies of our National rights and obligations.[121]

This was evidence that the impetus created by O'Connell had been consolidated by 1900 and no less significant was the nature of the demands being made by its architects. The League's most immediate goal in 1900 was to secure the election of nationalists to the recently created county councils, and then to bring these councils together once a year on a national council to agitate for: (*a*) popular control of the police (*b*) the transfer of spending power from government departments to the county councils and (*c*) the upgrading of the county councils so that they have the same status and powers as their counterparts in Britain.[122] To Ireland's 'national rights and obligations' were added the demand for further democratisation and, given the still restricted nature of the parliamentary suffrage in the UK, this stance was all the more remarkable.

Moreover, in terms of governance, the League's constitution, with its extensive branch structure, its elaborate directory system, and the centrality of its nomination conventions, bore testimony to how far the populist impulse of O'Connell was now becoming converted into schemes of political organisation of a genuinely accountable and representative nature. Decades later, Eoin MacNeill, a leading light in the Gaelic League, argued that his organisation should take lessons from the United Irish League:

> It seems to me that the League could do worse than take a leaf out of the book of the Irish Parliamentary Party and the United Irish League. The directory of that body is constantly engaged in arranging with local supporters for the holding of public meetings and appoints reliable speakers to address them. For the most part, these speakers seem not to be rich men and I assume that their experts are paid in connexion with the meetings. We have hardly any Gaelic League speakers who can afford to go to meetings in distant places at their own cost. We should therefore provide a fund for such expenses, but where the local supporters can afford it, they should be asked to assist.[123]

So even if the League had failed in its efforts to subject the parliamentary elite to democratic control, its aspirations should be seen part of a wider process of political maturation. The process had begun in the 1820s with the practice of mobilising public opinion in the broadest sense against the state. It found its most dramatic expression with the widespread agitation of the Land War and, with the Home Rule movement, it clearly became interwoven with the general struggle for democratisation. The preconditions for all of this were a parliament sometimes responsive to public opinion, a political system sufficiently liberal to allow that opinion to be organised, and a franchise broad enough to make popular participation in elections meaningful. As a result, the custom of popular participation in elections, the habit of seeking election pledges from candidates, and the general desire to hold parliamentary elites accountable to genuinely democratic organisations, all became part and parcel of Irish politics by 1900. This did not mean that Irish democracy was a foregone conclusion, but in so far as democracy is a political system in which the public, through elections, periodically involves itself in the selection of governing elites, the tradition established by O'Connell of involving as many people as possible in that process was obviously crucial.

5.5 The final phase

The last stage of the process, from the 1880s on, involved the final democratisation of Irish civil society, the increasing specialisation of its various parts, and the crystallisation of a sophisticated and constructive attitude towards the state. While the associations and leagues of the nineteenth century had essentially been props for parliamentary elites, and saw their role as conduits for the communication of public opinion in the broadest sense, the most important movements of the last phase, while no less concerned with the business of legislation, acted independently of the parliamentary party, were functionally specialised, and stood for social values not reducible to 'mere politics'. Between 1884 and 1921 the various strands of Irish nationalism came together to give rise to a civil society whose foundations were more durable, whose workings were internally more democratic, and whose aspirations were more practical. No doubt much of this was due to the 'modernisation' of Irish society after the Famine, but the final phase should not be seen in isolation.[124] The friendly societies of the nineteenth century had provided much of the values of such a civil society, and if societies such as the Royal Dublin Society had also contributed to its intellect, this last phase saw the fusing of these two qualities with the broader public aspirations embodied by people such as O'Connell, Davitt, and Parnell. The result was a genuinely democratic civil society that in many ways is still with us today.

While the era between the fall of Parnell in 1891 and the passing of the Third Home Rule Bill in 1912 has often been regarded as a fallow one in political terms, tranquillity on the surface concealed a dynamic with portentous consequences for the new state. Not only were all the main organisations committed to the revival of traditional Irish culture formed before 1921, but their size also rapidly increased in this period. Between 1900 and 1901 alone, the number of clubs affiliated with the United Irish League increased from 892 to 1150, the number of GAA clubs rose from 311 to 411, and the number of Gaelic League clubs rose from 99 to a massive 258.[125] As it turned out, well over a third of the elected members of the political elite in independent Ireland were members of the GAA or the Gaelic League in their youth, and since great political changes are usually preceded by fundamental changes in civil society, such a statistic is not a surprise.[126] Ever since the formation of the Catholic Commercial Club in 1881 Catholics had been making inroads into the commercial and professional life of the country, and in the short period between 1899 and 1905 three bodies fundamentally concerned with the temporal interests of Catholics – the Catholic Association, the (Board of Erin) Ancient Order of Hibernians (unbanned in 1904), and the Catholic Defence Society (with the more spiritual Catholic Truth Society) – emerged. Other organisations, more economic in nature, also had a marked impact on the nature of Irish rural life. Horace Plunkett founded the co-operative movement in 1894, and by 1923 there were 222 creameries and stores, 340 agricultural supply societies, and 72 farming societies registered with the Free State authorities.[127] Trade union activity also became steadily stronger after the foundation of the Irish Trade Union Congress in 1894, and by 1923 there were 46 registered trade unions, a number that would rise in the 1920s. This figure, combined with a total of 471 friendly societies and 831 industrial and provident societies in 1923, suggests that a vast and complex structure of associational life emerged in the last decades of British rule.[128]

The reasons behind these developments are often reduced to the presence of a new spirit of 'individualism, initiative and self-reliance' in Irish society.[129] That spirit must in turn be related to the growth in the numbers of educated Catholics in the country and their determination to revive a land often felt to be culturally stagnating in the wake of the development of commercial agriculture.[130] For example, the founders of the Cork Industrial Development Association stated in 1903 that their worst enemy was 'the awful apathy of the general public' and this lament was frequently made by contemporaries.[131] The apparently moribund nature of parliamentary politics after the Parnell split may also have convinced people that effective political action could best be accomplished outside the parliamentary arena, and the introduction of a democratic local government franchise in 1898 definitely gave many the confidence that their objectives could now more easily be achieved. A background factor too was the growing involvement of the British state itself in Irish life from the 1880s onwards, through land reform, through the creation of the congested districts board and the department of agriculture, and through the improvement of rural housing by the various labourers' acts.[132] In such a context mobilisation for practical policy objectives became more realistic, and arguably a clear sense of reciprocity with the state obtained until the First World War. Remarkably, Horace Plunkett, the founder of the co-op movement, was made first secretary of the first Irish Department of Agriculture and Technical Instruction in 1899.

The close interaction between the democratisation of the state and this emergent civil society can best be seen by looking at the activities of the Gaelic League. Founded with the aim of reviving the Irish language and literature, the practical measures it supported were the teaching of Irish in schools, the introduction of Irish as a matriculation subject in the national university, and the support of the language in areas where it was still spoken. The first public act of the League was its protest in October 1893 against the fining of a

Corkman for having his name in Irish on his cart. In 1900 the League intervened in the municipal elections in Dublin by publicising the names of candidates who had pledged support for the language. This was how Dublin acquired bilingual street names.[133] In 1905 candidates in the local government elections were specifically asked whether, if elected, they would support the making of Irish a criterion for appointments in the board's gift.[134] Eventually Irish was made compulsory for posts in Dublin Corporation and some other local bodies introduced similar rules. By 1900 the League was also putting pressure on all parts of the education system to introduce Irish into schools. It supported a change in the composition of the National Education Board, which it felt was unsympathetic to its cause, and in 1905 its Ard Fheis called for its replacement with 'a board in the election of which the people of Ireland would have a voice'.[135] As a result of the League's activities, the number of children being taught Irish in primary schools rose from 1,825 in 1899 to 180,000 in 1911, the National Board sanctioned a bilingual programme in the Gaeltacht, and schools managers began to put pressure on teachers to use the language.[136] In pursuing its goals the League had always cultivated the support of mainstream nationalist politicians in the hope that when Home Rule was granted, it would help to turn the League's programme into national policy.[137] The support of local government bodies then proved crucial when the League called for Irish to be introduced as a matriculation subject in the National University. Hundreds of local bodies passed resolutions in support and the Senate decided in its favour in June 1910 after nine county councils awarded 138 scholarships on the condition that they would not be paid unless Irish was obligatory in the university.[138]

The tactics of the League, and the crucial connection between the structure of the state and the realisation of its goals, are evidence yet again of how closely interwoven were the process of democratisation and the growth of Irish civil society. On the other hand the League found it increasingly difficult to defend its 'non-sectarian' and 'non-political' character.[139] A police report from August 1902 remarked that while the League was 'harmless' in country areas, in the cities and the towns it was under the control of men 'whose constant endeavour is to inculcate extreme hatred of England and everything British'.[140] Defending the League, its President, Douglas Hyde, argued in 1914 that the majority of the members were moderates 'whose ideas on political matters are much the same as those of their own County Councils'.[141] However, the League was effectively taken over by the Irish Republican Brotherhood at the July 1915 Ard Fheis, and the following year six of the seven signatories to the Proclamation of the Republic in Easter 1916 had been members of the League, and four had been members of its Coiste Gnotha.[142] Arguably, though, it was only the circumstances of the war that allowed the IRB to gain the upper hand, and even after July 1915, the majority of the members still tried to make the executive more accountable by devolving power to the county committees.[143] The League was much more than a front for extreme nationalism. According to Murray,

> The number of such movements – including those promoting agricultural co-operation and industrial revival, as well as the Gaelic League – that adopted, and adhered to, a non-political and non-sectarian constitutional stance suggests that contemporaries perceived political realities differently. Emerging during the 20 years separating the second from the Third Home Rule Bill such movements adopted an approach which was simultaneously broad and narrow. It was broad in so far as they sought to be national rather than nationalist or unionist, defining their identities outside the control of the stalemated party political monoliths of the religion-bounded ethnic polarisation to which these parties gave expression. But in another way the new movements were narrower than the older parties. While the latter were primarily concerned to defend or oppose the way in which the state was constituted, the former were oriented towards the operation of the state within particular, delimited policy fields.[144]

Indeed such movements were also continuing the impetus towards demo-cratisation we have already observed in the home rule and trade union movements. The clearest example of this is the cause of women's suffrage. A Dublin Women's Suffrage Association had been formed in 1876 which initiated the strategy of petitioning parliament whenever a women's suffrage measure was under consideration.[145] In 1896 a Women's Poor Law Guardian Bill was passed, in 1898 the new local government franchise included women, and, in the spring of 1899, 85 women were elected as Poor Law Guardians.[146] The organisation became more expansive when it became the Irish Women's Suffrage and Local Government Association in 1901 and over the next decade another set of bodies was formed, such as the Irish branch of the Conservative and Unionist Suffrage Association, the Irish Women's Suffrage Association, and the Irish Women's Reform League.[147] In line with the existing practice of trade unions, the latter initiated a committee to monitor legislation affecting women, and a courts committee to observe cases involving injustice to women and girls was also formed. The key issue for women proved to be their exclusion from the parliamentary suffrage under the third Home Rule Bill. A mass meeting of Irish women was held in Dublin in June 1912 to demand their inclusion and unanimously passed a resolution calling on the Government to amend the Home Rule Bill by adopting the local government register as the basis for the new parliament.[148] The resolution failed and John Redmond, leader of the Home Rule Party, turned his back on the suffrage movement, a sign once again of how out of touch the party was with advanced Irish opinion.

The politicisation of Irish women was also carried forward by organisations such as the Women's National Health Association, the United Irishwomen, and Cumann na mBan, which also saw preparing women for participation in Irish public life as a key part of its activities.[149] By 1914 the methods used by these organisations had become the stock-in-trade of Irish civil society. In 1912 Hanna Sheehy-Skeffington remarked that the Irish Women's Franchise League had since 1908 'run the gamut' of constitutionalism: 'meetings, petitions, country campaigns, deputations, open-air demonstrations, processions, resolutions from public bodies, heckling of Cabinet Ministers sojourning in Ireland, election propaganda'.[150] The extent to which these tactics were being employed in the general struggle for democratisation is also apparent from the history of the Irish Women Workers' Union, founded in 1911 and which claimed 5,300 members by 1918. In 1894 a major state investigation into the conditions of women's work had been carried out, and the union became affiliated with the Dublin Trades Council and the Irish Trade Union Congress. It was led by prominent feminists and was as committed to getting the parliamentary vote for women as it was to labour issues. After the establishment of new machinery to regulate wages under the Trade Boards Act of 1918, it joined with the Labour Party and the Trade Union Congress in its campaign for a representative Irish Industrial Board.[151] On St Brigid's day in 1920 a convention of delegates from its various branches held 'a parliament of working women in Ireland' and its 1921 constitution retained its highly democratic representative structure, with a central executive committee being elected by an annual convention of delegates from the various branches in proportion to their size. Only women workers, not honorary members, were allowed a controlling vote in the union's affairs.[152]

By 1921 such a representative structure was typical of most civil society organisations in nationalist Ireland, which were now clearly influenced by American modes. Table 5.1 shows the constitutional structure of the most important of these organisations. Almost all gave the deciding say in making policy to a delegate congress of some kind, most had a mass base in branches or affiliated societies, and special procedures were typically retained for changing constitutions. The Irish National Teachers Organisation was unusual in that it allowed all members a postal vote in the annual election of its officials, a reform instigated in 1899 in response to excessive canvassing and corruption. Over the next hundred years such an election would take place every year, the only exception being 1915. The majority of these organisations also adhered to some version of the 'no religion no politics' code, and there is no discernible difference in constitutional structure between organisations that were cultural, religious or economic in nature. Even organisations such as the Catholic Defence Society, which submitted its constitution before ratification to the standing committee of the Bishops in 1905, subscribed to a basically democratic ethos.[153] What is also apparent is the fact that nationalist organisations which were clearly under the control of the IRB, such as the GAA, operated much in the same way as apolitical bodies like Horace Plunkett's.[154]

Table 5.1 **The constitutional structure of nationalist organisations, 1868–1921**

Organisation	Date of formation	Supreme decision-making body	Election of executive	Repre-sentative structure	Rule changes	No politics/ religion rule?
Gaelic Athletic Association	1884	General Committee	By votes of delegates from clubs	Central Executive, county committees	Required vote of three quarters of members of General Committee	No politics
Gaelic League	1892	Repre-sentative Congress	By votes of delegates and by co-option	Branches and Executive Committee. (regional tiers later added)	Information not available	'Strictly non-political and non-sectarian'
Irish National Teachers Organisation	1868	Annual Congress	By postal vote of members	Central Executive Committee, county associations, local associations	Information not available	Present
Irish Agriculture Organisation Society	1894	Annual General Meeting	By votes of delegates and by co-option	Central Committee and affiliated societies	Changed by majority vote at AGM	Present
United Irishwomen	1910	Ordinary General Meetings	By votes of delegates	Governing Committee, branches, special members	Require two-thirds majority at special general meeting	Present

Table 5.1 **(cont.)**

Organisation	Date of formation	Supreme decision-making body	Election of executive	Representative structure	Rule changes	No politics/ religion rule?
Irish Farmers Union	1920	Annual Congress	By votes of delegates, by votes of county associations, and by co-option	National Executive, provincial councils, county farmers associations, and branches	Changed by majority vote at Congress	Absent
Irish Industrial Development Organisation	1903 (renamed 1906)	Annual General Meeting	By vote of members at AGM	Ruling Council and affiliated societies	By special resolution of association	Present
Catholic Association	1902	Annual Convention	By vote of delegates at Convention	National Council, affiliated societies and branches	Requires support of two thirds of delegates	No politics
Catholic Defence Society	1905	Annual Convention	By vote of delegates at Convention	Branches, Central Branch and Council	Decided by Convention	Absent
(Board of Erin) Ancient Order of Hibernians	1904	National Convention	By vote of delegates at Convention	Divisions, funeral districts, county boards, national board	Requires two-thirds majority at Convention	Absent

Sources: T. J. O'Connell, *History of the Irish National Teachers Organisation 1868–1968* (1970); Rev. Monsignor Hallinan, *The Catholic Defence Society* (1907); Catholic Association, 1902; *General Rules of the Ancient Order of Hibernians (Board of Erin) Friendly Society* (1908, Belfast); Ancient Order of Hibernians 1908–19, Registry of Friendly Societies; Gaelic League (see notes 14 and 15, p. 241); *Rules of the Irish Agriculture Organisation Society, Limited* (1912) (NA, Registry of Friendly Societies, RF8 R88); *Irish Farmers Union Rules* (Dublin, 1920) (NA, Registry of Friendly Societies, 346TA); *The United Irishwomen: Rules* (Dublin, n.d.) (NA, Registry of Friendly Societies, F 1230).

Indeed the constitution drafted by Maurice Davin for the GAA in 1888, has served the organisation, with modifications in 1895 and 1903, very well. All this is evidence that a relatively homogeneous political culture, of Anglo-American provenance, had matured, and also that the promise shown by the Home Rule Leagues in combining central co-ordination with local democracy had finally borne fruit. The most controversial body was the Ancient Order of Hibernians, whose Catholic, nationalist and right-wing ethos attracted many working-class men throughout the island. Garvin sees it as a significant link 'between the new nationalist organisations and the century old tradition of popular militant societies' but its formal structure was recognisably modern.[155]

The extent to which advanced democratic ideas influenced civil society in this final phase becomes even clearer from an analysis of organisations founded for a purely commercial purpose, where issues of accountability are absolutely crucial. For example, the rules of the Irish Agricultural Wholesale Society Limited, founded to further the aims of the co-operative movement, gave ordinary shareholders the power to elect six of the ten directors, gave them a veto on resolutions at annual general meetings, and vested the power to change the rules in the AGM as a whole by a two-thirds majority.[156] In the same vein, the rules of the National Land Bank, founded in 1919 to assist societies or individuals purchasing land, allowed ordinary members to acquire a £1 share in the bank, vested the right to annually elect five of the nine directors of the bank in them, and effectively gave them a veto power over decisions made at special general meetings, by allowing for their votes to be counted separately from corporate members, and if a two-thirds majority of them favoured a decision, such a vote would be binding on the meeting.[157] Finally, the rules of the Irish Farmer Limited, founded to assist farmers and the co-operative movement generally, limited the number of shares individual members could have to fifty preference shares, gave each society total freedom to choose its representative at general meetings, and gave all members one vote irrespective of the number of shares possessed by the society. The committee of management was elected annually at general meetings from ordinary members who held at least five preference shares.[158] Such organisations may not have survived the passing of the economically buoyant mood of the 1914–21 period, but their rules are evidence yet again of the strong commitment to democratic values in rural Ireland.

Arguably, membership of such societies gave people a practical experience of democracy hitherto possible only in the friendly societies. The mass organisations of the nineteenth century had similar ambitions, but their connection with parliamentary politics inevitably meant that popular input was limited. Nor, with its restricted suffrage and typically uncontested elections, did parliamentary life give a programme of political action for the ordinary individual. In contrast, organisations such as the Gaelic League involved their members in constant propaganda campaigns and were not unlike modern political parties in their workings: its 1921 constitution exhorted members to form alliances with local bodies, to encourage, by house to house canvass, the habitual speaking of Irish, and to organise an annual collection of funds.[159] Eoin MacNeill, elected president of the League in 1916, remarked that 'as a people we have got into the habit of thinking that laws, regulations, constitutions, boards, councils, governments, elections, majorities, resolutions, and all such formally instituted things are the deciding factors in a nation's life'.[160] It is impossible to know to what extent these bodies actually conformed to their rules, but when the constitution of the GAA was clearly flouted by the IRB in 1887, strong opposition soon emerged and the Executive was forced to accept a new set of rules the following year.[161] Moreover, involvement in organisations that were committed to specific policy objectives gave people a new ability to depersonalise political questions. According to Horace Plunkett:

> Until the past few years, for example, it was our habit – one which immensely weakened the influence of Ireland in the Imperial Parliament – to form extravagant estimates of men, exalting and abusing them with irrational caprice, not according to their qualities so much as by their attitude towards the passions of the hour . . . Even now public opinion is too prone to attach excessive values to projects of vague and visionary development, and to underrate the importance of serious thought and quiet work, which can be the only solid foundation of our national progress. In these new associations – humble indeed in their origin, but determined to play a large part in the peoples lives – projects professing to be fraught with economic benefit, have to be judged by the cruel precision of audited balance sheets, and the worth of men is measured by the solid contribution they have made to the welfare of the community.[162]

On the other hand, the rapid growth of so many organisations may not have been compatible with political stability were it not for the extraordinary degree of reciprocity between them. Douglas Hyde, the founder of the Gaelic League, maintained that the values associated with language revival, such as initiative, self-reliance, and self-respect, were also those promoted by the causes of temperance and Irish manufacture.[163] Revealingly, it was from the head office of the Gaelic League that in 1903 invitations were sent out to Dublin's businessmen and industrialists to attend the first meeting of the Irish Industrial Development Association.[164] The Gaelic League in its turn was supported by a variety of organisations such as the Ancient Order of Hibernians, Cumann na mBann and the Catholic Association. In 1902, of the 53 societies registered with the League in Dublin, the Purveyors' Assistants Association, the Grocers' Assistants, the Antiquarian Cyclist Society of Ireland, the

Leinster Choral Union, and the Commercial Club were all on the list.[165] Even the general secretary of the Irish Women's Workers Union, 'Cumann ban-oibre Éireann', called for the revival of the language and the national dress.[166] The cohesion of such a civil society was also due to the support of the Catholic Church which shared its basic commitment to revitalising the countryside. The Church did not unconditionally lend its support to new organisations – it was initially lukewarm about the co-op movement – but its view of society as a harmonious whole of interlocking parts, in which class conflict would be submerged, fitted nicely with the kind of civil society that was developing.[167]

Not only was the cohesive nature of nationalist civil society in this last phase conducive to stability, but it also provided the intellect of the state that would emerge in 1921. In March 1893 the Gaelic League had publicly thanked all those shopkeepers, traders and business people, who had helped make St Patrick's day that year a national holiday by closing their shops, and evidence that such concerted action presaged a genuinely national civil society was provided by the line-up, thirteen years later, for the 1906 St Patrick's Day Parade, which consisted of the League, the GAA, educational bodies with a nationalist bent, temperance bodies, industrial societies, friendly societies, representative bodies and political parties.[168] This was the raw material on which the independent state would be built and as early as 1907 a commentator pointed out that Sinn Féin was the only party to express the qualities of individualism, initiative, and self-reliance embodied by movements like the Gaelic League and the co-op movement.[169] Since the nation states between the wars were usually regarded by their political elites as instruments for the creation of a moral community among their citizens, the Irish state was, to a large degree, constituted by the kind of civil society that emerged after 1884. That civil society was highly democratic, functionally specialised, and free of the ideological polarisation that led to instability in other Catholic countries. The Free State would largely share these features.

5.5   Conclusion

With its localist horizons, extensive brokerage practices, and supposedly irrational party system, it is often tempting to arrive at the conclusion that in Irish politics the nineteenth century persisted into the twentieth, modernity was subverted by tradition, and a basically cyclical pattern of political development reasserted itself after 1921.[170] Nothing in this chapter justifies such a perspective. There was a clear connection between the values of the early friendly societies and the more elaborate structures of the late nineteenth century. The organisational structures of bodies such as the Irish National League provided blueprints for later movements, and the movements that emerged after 1884 mostly proved, for one reason or another, remarkably durable. Clark argues that there was a fundamental transformation from collective action based on small communal groups to action based on broadly based interest groups, organised associationally, and the analysis here supports his hypothesis.[171] The key evidence that political modernisation was uneven is provided by the fact that movements like the National League proved so short lived, but in the demise of such bodies one can also discern positive developments: the increasing autonomy of parties from ancillary bodies, the functional specialisation of civil society, and an increasing pluralism in nationalist politics, all of which are features of the last phase. Moreover, the link between the process of democratisation and the emergence of this civil society was clear from the word go, and climaxed in the activities of the Home Rule, women's suffrage, and trade union movements in the last decades of British rule.

If civil society is a sphere in which democratic practices can develop, in which an autonomous public opinion can be formed, and in which people acquire the skills that make them effective citizens in the modern polity, then the development of Irish civil society should be regarded as a precondition for the emergence of Irish democracy between 1918 and 1922. Irish civil society, with its egalitarian values, its populist impulse and national conventions, provides the clearest answer we have to the general question of why a population totally outside the provinces of law and politics in the eighteenth century should become pioneers of free elections, modern political parties and democratic politics in the subsequent two centuries.[172] Much of this was due to the absorption of British and American values in the nineteenth century, much due to the support of the Catholic Church, but the main explanatory variable was the nature of the British state itself. Regular local and national elections, administrative structures increasingly subject to popular control, and a parliament at times responsive to Irish public opinion, were all crucial incentives for the politicisation of Irish society, and the connection between this process and the general progress towards democratisation was plain to see. Democratising states makes for democratic civil societies and by 1914 the basic tenets of constitutionalism, civil rights, and parliamentarism were taken for granted in Irish society.

From this perspective Lieven argues that 'the wars of 1919–23 were an aberration, the return to constitutional politics a reassertion of the Irish norm'.[173] Indeed it is impossible to understand stances taken during the civil war, such as O'Higgins's declaration in September 1922 that the Treaty would stand 'until publicly repudiated by the majority will of the nation', without reference to the deep vein of democratic practice in Ireland.[174] Political elites, even at times of national crises, do not invent rules of the game from scratch, but make choices 'in the context of traditions and institutions that shape their preferences', and it is hardly credible that Irish elites after 1921 were uninfluenced by the political culture that had developed over the previous one hundred and twenty years.[175] The fact that the workings of this civil society had long been regulated by constitutions with the rights of members clearly stated in the rules must have contributed to a political culture which conceived of democracy as 'lucid constitutions' and 'rights and duties set down clearly on paper', an attitude which influenced both the 1922 and 1937 constitutions.[176] Not only did the triumph of constitutionalism after 1923 fulfil a potential long present in Irish civil society, but the turbulent events from 1916 onwards left the basic contours of Irish civil society unchanged. When the Free State government initiated its reform of Dublin Corporation in 1923, for example, it routinely consulted ten separate civic organisations as well as fifteen local government bodies.[177] Crucially, the civil war split did not divide Irish civil society into two and this sturdy set of institutions arguably provided a basis for the healing of wounds later on.[178] The GAA, for example, was never at the forefront of radical nationalism between 1916 and 1921; it tried to remain neutral during the civil war, and in the 1920s and 1930s, Gaelic football teams representing a bitterly divided county like Kerry were typically composed of men who had been enemies during the civil war.[179] Civil society had provided the cultural platform on which the new state was built and its importance after 1921 should not be underestimated.

Chapter 6

Voluntarist democratic theory and the origins of the civil war

'Coalition Government is probably the most suitable method of carrying over the period of stress.' **Michael Collins, 1922**

Democratic theory has undergone a paradigm shift in recent decades. Eschewing attempts to find structural preconditions for the consolidation of democratic regimes, it concentrates on elite behaviour and elite strategies as the crucial variables in explaining the fate of regimes. The structural characteristics of societies 'constitute a series of opportunities and constraints for the social and political actors, both men and institutions, that lead to one or another outcome'. Within those constraints, elites have a number of choices that 'increase or decrease the probability of the persistence and stability of a democratic regime'.[1] With this voluntarist perspective has come a new optimism with regard to the ability of elites to consolidate democratic regimes in areas traditionally considered inhospitable to democracy. In *To Craft Democracies* di Palma suggests that a democracy need not enjoy from birth 'rare conditions of legitimacy' nor need such legitimacy be the product of 'hard fought consolidation'. Instead, he stresses the rewards that the open political game of democratic politics can bring to those who play it. The appropriate 'crafting' of the rules of the game can bring reluctant players into the political game and establish a democratic consensus from the outset. This consensus is sufficient reason for a stable democratic system to be institutionalised.[2]

This chapter applies di Palma's perspective to the events leading to the outbreak of the Irish civil war. In that period the Collins–de Valera electoral pact represented an attempt to stabilise a new polity by elite pact and prevent the outbreak of civil war. The pact failed but there has been no systematic attempt to unravel the reasons why. Some have suggested that the pact was merely an expedient which enabled an election to take place, while others suggest that it represented a genuine attempt to avert civil war, one scuppered by British intervention.[3] Similarly, some maintain that civil war was a virtual certainty from the time the IRA refused to give their allegiance to the new Provisional Government, while others argue that civil war came about only because of the collapse of the pact.[4] Which perspective is true? Could civil war have been averted by Irish elites or was it the inevitable consequence of the Treaty split? What part did elite error play in creating the circumstances which led to the Irish civil war? What does the Irish case tell us about di Palma's argument that a capable elite can quickly stabilise a new democracy regardless of the conditions into which it is born?

6.1 The making and unmaking of the Collins–de Valera pact

The Anglo-Irish Treaty signed on 6 December 1921 made the 26 counties of Ireland a British Dominion. Its constitutional status within the Empire was to be analogous to that of Canada. The decision to sign the Treaty resulted in an immediate division within the Irish cabinet. Three members opposed, while four supported the Treaty. Eamon de Valera, the President, was in a minority. The Cabinet nevertheless agreed to recommend the Treaty to the Dáil. Debate on the Treaty continued as the Dáil went into recess from 22 December to 3 January. An open split in the Sinn Féin parliamentary party was feared. A meeting between four pro-and four anti-Treaty deputies was held on 4 January in order to find a basis for party unity. It was suggested that the services of de Valera should be retained as President of the Dáil. A majority vote on the Treaty would be avoided and the President would suggest abstention from the vote on the basis that the new Provisional Government be permitted to function by the Dáil. Only members of the Provisional Government need sign acceptance of the Treaty.[5] The proposals were agreed to by Arthur Griffith and Michael Collins, who had signed the Treaty, but de Valera insisted that an alternative document be accepted instead. The peace conference failed.

In the Dáil debate on the Treaty on 7 January, 64 members supported the Treaty while 57 members rejected it. The Treaty was accepted by the Dáil. As a result de Valera immediately resigned as President, and failing to secure re-election, led his side in a walkout from the Dáil. His place was taken by Griffith. A Dáil cabinet composed entirely of pro-Treaty members was elected. The anti-Treatyites would continue to attend the Dáil until June. De Valera later remarked that this was evidence 'that we accepted the principle of majority rule, and the right of the people to decide finally on the question at issue'.[6] The truth, however, was more complex. Under the terms of the Treaty a Provisional Government could only be elected by 'the parliament for Southern Ireland', a body which had been created by the Government of Ireland Act of 1920. The parliament had been boycotted by the Sinn Féin members, but now the pro-Treaty deputies, together with four unionists, attended in order to elect a Provisional Government. Collins became

Chairman of this Provisional Government. The authority of his Government was not derived from the Dáil, but from the Treaty. The anti-Treatyites refused to accept that the Provisional Government was the legitimate government of the country, or that the Dáil had the power to disestablish the Republic, which could only be done by the votes of the people.

On 22 February a general convention of Sinn Féin agreed to delay the election for three months, so that when the vote on the Treaty came, the public would have the new constitution before it. Collins hoped to produce a constitution acceptable to republicans. He was encouraged to do so by de Valera who stated that if Collins was to persuade the anti-Treatyites that the King was not part of the Irish constitution, then the best way to do so was 'to frame a constitution in which he will not be there, and then it may not be too difficult for us to agree with this afterwards'.[7] Since late January a non-party constitutional committee chaired by Collins had been drafting a new constitution. It was hoped it would be available by the end of April, so that 'people will be free to examine it in its entirety', and 'neither Mr de Valera nor anybody else will be able to complain that the issues are being concealed from the country'.[8]

At this stage, as the British withdrew from the country, the attitude of the IRA to the Provisional Government became crucial. Army barracks were immediately occupied by local brigades, regardless of attitudes towards the Treaty. The Provisional Government, unsure of its military strength, allowed this to happen, leaving a country divided between armed camps, with most areas under the control of anti-Treaty commanders.[9] In late February leaders of the IRA demanded that Richard Mulcahy, Minister for Defence, hold an army convention with a view to establishing a new army council. They hoped the convention would show the Provisional Government that the majority of the IRA were against the Treaty. Mulcahy eventually agreed, fearing that not to do so would threaten the position of the Free State. On 15 March, however, this decision was reversed by the cabinet, Griffith's objection being that the purpose of the convention was to remove the army from the control of the elected government. The banned convention met on 26 March anyway with over two thirds of IRA brigades represented. It unanimously agreed that the army 'shall be maintained under an Executive appointed by the convention'.[10] The IRA was no longer under the authority of the Ministry of Defence and on 13 April the Executive occupied a number of buildings in Dublin, including the Four Courts. Asked whether this occupation constituted a *coup d'état,* Rory O'Connor, their leader, equivocated.

Differences over the election reached a head in late April when a conference was held at Dublin's Mansion House. The Provisional Government proposed that in keeping with the February agreement, 'a plebiscite on the issue of acceptance or rejection of the Treaty shall be taken within a month and a full opportunity be afforded to every adult to vote'. The plebiscite would be held on a Sunday, and all persons over 21 would be entitled to vote. Voters would have to walk through gates to register their preferences. The Labour Party, the Catholic Church, and local authorities would be entrusted with supervising voting. The anti-Treatyite delegates rejected the idea 'both in principle and in detail', ridiculing the scheme as a 'stone age plebiscite'. In response the Provisional Government refused to continue with the conference. They issued a statement stating that the Provisional Government 'has now cast upon it the duty of seeing that the people of Ireland who are and must be the sovereign authority shall be free to vote their approval or disapproval of the Treaty'.[11]

At this time, however, the idea of an 'agreed election' began to take hold. Late in March Harry Boland, an anti-Treatyite, had met with Mulcahy and suggested that the two Dáil sides should avoid further party meetings and co-operate on one platform on the basis of a proactive Ulster policy. An agreed constitution would be produced by the Dáil. As an afterthought Boland proposed that the anti-Treatyites be guaranteed around 20 per cent of seats in the new Dáil.[12] On 12 April it was then suggested to Collins that all members be returned unopposed. They would be free to attend the Free State parliament but the Dáil would also continue to exist, having control of the IRA and 'all matters dealing with English relations'. Collins replied that he was 'interested' in the scheme and would, with qualifications, do his best to secure it. Significantly he didn't oppose the idea of an agreed election.[13]

On 1 May a document was drawn up by officers of the Irish Republican Brotherhood. It proposed:

(1) Acceptance of the fact – admitted by all sides – that the majority of the people of Ireland are willing to accept the Treaty.
(2) An agreed election with a view to –
(3) Forming a government which will have the confidence of the whole country.
(4) Army unification on the above basis.

On 3 May these officers were permitted to address the Dáil. A motion proposing that the Dáil approve their statement led to immediate division over the first clause. However, the Dáil approved of their efforts and subsequently appointed a committee, five from each Treaty side, to explore the possibilities of agreement. After eleven sessions the peace committee reported to the Dáil on 10 May having failed to agree a basis for peace. The previous day talks had broken down over the pro-Treaty delegates' insistence that the preamble to the agreement state that the majority of the country accepted the Treaty. The IRB officers had been asked to mediate and Sean McKeon proposed the following compromise preamble:

accepting the fact that Dáil Éireann has by a majority approved of the Treaty which is the vehicle of these advantages, and accepting also the position created in the country by this approval, we are of opinion that a contested election now would be attended by civil strife which would result in a dissipation of these advantages and a worsening of our National position.[14]

This was still rejected by the anti-Treatyites. Harry Boland, the most prominent of the anti-Treaty delegates, insisted that the 'it be accepted and understood that no issue is being determined by the election'. Moreover, he resuscitated Labour's proposal at the Mansion House conference that the Provisional Government be replaced by a Council of State with the Minster of Defence elected by the delegates entitled to attend the banned IRA convention of 26 March. Neither proposal was agreed to by the pro-Treaty delegates. The two sides could only agree that all legislative power was derived from the people of Ireland and that Dáil Eireann was the supreme governing authority in Ireland.[15] In the end both sides prepared separate reports which were presented to the Dáil on 17 May. A long debate followed. There was no consensus on the necessity of an election.

At the same time, however, a secret meeting was taking place in the Oak Room of the Mansion House. Representing the Provisional Government were Arthur Griffith, Michael Collins, Richard Mulcahy, and Eoin O'Duffy. Eamon de Valera, Liam Lynch, Cathal Brugha, and Rory O'Connor represented the anti-Treatyites. Five men from the North also attended the meeting, and stressed the importance to the others of maintaining unity in view of the situation developing in the six counties. As a result of their plea, discussion between the two Treaty sides focused on the conditions under which an agreed election could be held. Progress was initially stalled on Collins's insistence that he retain a working majority in the new Dáil. On 17 May Collins finally agreed that both the Treaty sides could be represented on the joint panel for the new Dáil in the same proportion as they were represented in the existing Dáil. This concession on Collins's part, which gave the anti-Treatyites the share of representation they had demanded on the Dáil peace committee, broke the impasse.[16]

The next day de Valera and Collins formally agreed at University College Dublin to put forward a united slate of candidates at the election and to form a coalition government afterwards. On 19 May the Dáil met to consider their agreement. Despite some vitriolic speeches, Boland stated that the coalition was still possible if Collins's constitution showed that 'the independence of the country can be gained by parliamentary methods'.[17] The following day the Dáil approved the agreement. The agreement was signed on 20 May and contained seven clauses:

We are agreed :

(1) That a National Coalition Panel for this Third Dáil, representing both parties in the Dáil and in the Sinn Féin Organisation be sent forward, on the ground that the national position requires the entrusting of the Government of the country into the joint hands of those who have been the strength of the national position during the last few years, without prejudice to their present respective position.

(2) That this Coalition panel be sent forward as from the Sinn Féin organisation, the number of each party being their present strength in the Dáil.

(3) That the candidates be nominated through each of their existing party Executives.

(4) That every and any interest is free to go up and contest the election equally with the National–Sinn Féin panel.

(5) That constituencies where an election is not held shall continue to be represented by their present Deputies.

(6) That after the election the Executive shall consist of the President, elected as formerly; the Minister for Defence, representing the army; and nine other Ministers – five from the majority party and four from the minority, each party to choose its own nominees. The allocation will be in the hands of the President.

(7) That in the event of the Coalition Government finding it necessary to dissolve, a general election will be held as soon as possible on adult suffrage.

The agreement represented a clear victory for the anti-Treaty side since it contained in essence 'the terms already proposed by the republican section of the peace committee and rejected by the pro-Treaty section'.[18] The preamble had been dropped and the pro-Treaty Sinn Féin TDs were not guaranteed a majority in the third Dáil. Moreover, the anti-Treatyites also believed that the Treaty would not be an issue in the election so the vote could not disestablish the Republic. For the pro-Treatyites the pact was a means by which an election could be held. In certain areas electoral registers which had been raided were returned after the pact, with the result that an election could be held in those districts.[19] The pact was also a means by which responsible figures on the republican side could co-operate with the Provisional Government in bringing ordered conditions back to the country. It was in that spirit that de Valera publicly endorsed it on 10 June, as a means of restoring power to a central authority and of bringing the two sides together on the basis of a law and order policy.[20] The pact was also approved by a general convention of Sinn Féin held on 23 May.

It soon became clear that the British Government was not happy with the pact. The Provisional Government were soon to meet their British counterparts and their policy was to stress the fact that the pact had been agreed 'to enable the Provisional Government to carry out the terms of the Treaty and to restore order'.[21] The two sides met in Downing Street on 27 May. Churchill pointed out that article seventeen of the Treaty obliged all members of the Provisional Government to sign a declaration of adherence to the Treaty. There was no requirement in the pact that the four republican ministers would sign the Treaty. Churchill stated that if clause seventeen did not apply 'the process of transfer of function does not go forward anymore'. On the other hand, the British did not want to be seen to be interfering in the internal affairs of a dominion. Their acceptance of the pact was subject to one fundamental condition: the conference agreed that acceptance of the pact did not prejudice the British Government's right 'to raise any question of non-conformity between the constitution and the Treaty'.[22]

Collins came under a different pressure when he returned to Dublin. Although pro-Treaty Sinn Féin would not hold a majority of seats in the new Dáil, at the UCD meeting de Valera had assured him that the third parties could be called upon to support his government if the pact failed. Collins was not convinced.[23] As soon as campaigning began, these third parties became subject to a range of intimidatory tactics. Collins warned his legal adviser, Kevin O'Shiel, that 'clause four must be absolutely adhered to. I cannot agree to any appeal, joint or otherwise, that is not seen by me and that does not fairly protect the principle contained in clause four'.[24] Despite this, on the eve of the nominations for the election, he approved a draft of a joint statement which was given to the press on 9 June. It was also signed by de Valera and stated that 'in view of the fact that one of the most obvious aims of the agreement was the avoidance of electoral contests which could not fail to engender bitterness and promote discord and turmoil, the signatories had hoped that the spirit of the pact would have ensured that such contests would be reduced to a minimum'.[25] Collins had again given ground to the republican side and had gained the assent of his government colleagues to this appeal. In a speech at the Mansion House on 9 June he told his audience that 'practically there is only one party' and advised them to vote for the candidates put forward by that party.[26]

Collins soon had reason to revise his position. An advertisement issued by the anti-Treaty party Cumann na Poblachta appeared in the Dublin papers on 12 June asking voters whether they would play 'the enemy's game' and destroy the pact by voting for a Dáil of 'warring sections and interests'.[27] The next day Collins denounced the advert as 'not in keeping with the spirit of the pact and to suggest that non-panel candidates by contesting the election branded themselves a national enemy was obviously contrary to the agreement'.[28] Then on 14 June, two days before the election, Collins renounced the pact in Cork, stressing that 'the country must have the representatives it wants'.[29]

Garvin argues that this statement represented the explosion of Collins's 'essentially democratic instincts' against the elitism of the IRA.[30] However, there were other relevant factors. On the election day Collins's new constitution was published. Collins's original draft had contained no references to the Treaty, no mention of the oath to the British crown, and the office of Governor General was omitted. However, the British had severely amended it, and the final draft contained a clause stipulating that if in any respect the constitution conflicted with the Treaty, it would be 'void and inoperative'. Republican objections to this new draft 'were mainly grounded in the fact that the King is to be part of the Parliament, that he is to have a veto on legislation and that executive authority is to be vested in him'. Rory O'Connor declared that 'its only merit was that it gave a holiday every four years'.[31] A key part of Collins's strategy, that of producing a constitution acceptable to republicans, had already failed before he renounced the pact.

Moreover, behind the scenes negotiations had been going on between the Ministry of Defence and the Four Courts Executive. On 14 April the army council of the IRA had informed the Provisional Government of the terms under which they were prepared to discuss the unification of the pro and anti-Treaty IRA. These included demands that the existing Republic be upheld, that the IRA be under the control of an elected independent executive, and that no election on the Treaty be held while Britain's threat of war existed.[32] These terms were initially ignored by the Provisional Government.[33] Following the Dáil's decision of the previous day to establish a peace committee, negotiations began on 4 May when both sides agreed to suspend all operations except training. Harry Boland argued that if the political issue could be solved by the Dáil committee 'the question of army unification will present no insuperable difficulties to the soldiers'.[34] After the pact was signed, an army council was set up to consist of Richard Mulcahy, Gearoid O'Sullivan, and Eoin O'Duffy on the pro-Treaty side, and Liam Lynch, Liam Mellowes, Rory O'Connor, and Sean Moylan on the anti-Treaty side. Initially, the army council unanimously agreed to accept de Valera as the Minister of Defence but this was rejected by the Provisional Government.[35] As a basis of unity a GHQ staff memo proposed that a unified Army Council would be periodically elected by an IRA convention. Eight members were proposed by Mulcahy, four from each Treaty side. The overall scheme of army organisation was agreed to by the Four Courts Executive on 9 June, but they demanded that the Chief of Staff would be chosen by them.[36] The demand was accompanied two days later by a warning that negotiations could not be prolonged after 12 June.[37] The IRA Executive would hold another convention on 18 June.

Mulcahy believed that the anti-Treatyites wanted Rory O'Connor as Chief of Staff. At the end of May O'Connor had stated publicly that the truce was only 'an interlude before the final coup for the Republic', and Mulcahy suggested Eoin O'Duffy as an alternative.[38] On 12 June Mulcahy replied to the IRA Executive that the original list of members was only a probable one, subject to overall agreement. As early as 5 June the cabinet was concerned at the 'excessive representation' given to the IRA Executive on the proposed Army Council.[39] Now Mulcahy informed the IRA Executive that his side had 'gone in this matter as far as it is possible for us to go'.[40] Mulcahy believed that five members of the proposed Army Council were prepared to agree to his proposals, and two of those from the IRA Executive were prepared to recommend to the IRA convention on 18 June that unification be proceeded with on the proposed basis. On 14 June, however, the IRA Executive rejected the proposals by 14 votes to 5 and informed the Ministry of Defence that not only were negotiations to cease, but the IRA Executive had resolved to take 'whatever action may be necessary to maintain the Republic against British aggression'.[41] On 17 June it was then indicated that because of objections on the part of Sean Moylan and Liam Lynch to portions of the draft constitution, the proposals would not be recommended to the IRA convention.[42] In short, negotiations on army unification had also broken down before Collins's renunciation of the pact, and irretrievably so before the election results became known.

The election on 16 June returned pro-Treaty Sinn Féin as the largest party with 58 seats out of 128, while the anti-Treatyites got 36, a loss of 22 seats. The Provisional Government interpreted the results as giving them a clear mandate to implement the Treaty. Republicans interpreted the result as a mandate for a coalition government. The Treaty, they maintained, had not been an issue in the election. Panel candidates had been returned in a majority of 73 per cent, and the 17 Labour candidates had also pledged to support the pact. Republicans have since maintained that republican voters gave their support to pro-Treaty candidates as a means of supporting the panel. In practically all constituencies pro- and anti-Treaty Sinn Féin candidates had stood on joint platforms and there was a high degree of transfers between coalition candidates.[43]

On 18 June a motion was put to the IRA army convention that unless Britain withdrew from the island within seventy hours, resumption of war should occur. This proposal originated with Tom Barry who was afraid that Liam Lynch would put the Beggars Bush proposals to the convention.[44] Liam Lynch, Sean Moylan, and Liam Deasy opposed the motion, while Barry, Rory O'Connor and Liam Mellowes argued in its favour.[45] The convention was divided between those who felt that further negotiations on army unity were futile and that peace moves only gave their opponents a chance to prepare for war, and the delegates of the IRA's 1st southern division, who followed their Chief of Staff, Liam Lynch, in his belief that negotiations should continue. Lynch had been one of those who had been willing to recommend the Ministry of Defence proposals to the convention. In general the Four Courts men preferred to force national unity by renewing the conflict with Britain, while the 1st southern men felt that unity could be based on the coalition government to be established on 1 July. The majority of the Executive and a slim majority of the delegates seemed to back war, but on a second ballot the motion was narrowly defeated. It was opposed by the majority of the delegates of the 1st southern division. After that the defeated minority walked out and returned to the Four Courts.[46]

The Provisional Government's decision to attack the Four Courts on 28 June was prompted by the assassination of Field Marshal Wilson on 22 June and Lloyd George's subsequent demand that the sham government in the Four Courts no longer be tolerated. Two days later the election results were published. On 26 June Lloyd George warned that further tolerance would mean the Treaty would be 'formally violated' and the British government would resume 'liberty of action'. Following the kidnapping of their assistant Chief of Staff, the Provisional Government attacked on 28 June. The attack was not simply the result of British pressure, but was also the culmination of months of failed efforts at mediating between opposing sections of the IRA and Sinn Féin . The external factor, in the shape of Britain's veto on Collins's constitution, was one reason why these proposals failed. It was not, however, the only one. The IRA had rejected Mulcahy's proposals for army unity and had not kept to the terms of the truce of 4 May. Nevertheless the anti-Treatyites were still divided on whether they wanted a showdown. According to Sean MacBride, there was a fundamental policy difference among the IRA Executive at this stage, with those close to Lynch ultimately willing to accept the Beggars Bush proposals, and Tom Barry and his allies hoping to renew the conflict with Britain rather than let this happen.[47] Unfortunately, this split may have been one reason why the Provisional Government attacked on 28 June and in so doing precipitated civil war.

6.2   Elite tactics and the failure of the pact

Civil war having begun, to what extent was its outbreak an inevitability, or to what extent was it the product or elite error, elite misdeed, or elite short-sightedness? This brings us to the question of elite tactics. Di Palma's *To Craft Democracies* is an influential approach to the politics of democratic transition. In his view the task of democrats in transitional situations is that of transferring loyalties to the new democratic regime. This task requires an understanding of democracy's strength as a system of 'co-existence in diversity'. If, during a transitional situation, 'the first object is not or does not soon become co-existence, it is axiomatic that the democratic experiment will be short-lived'.[48] Concentrating on co-existence means finding rules of the game that promise to preserve it. The more concerned those who craft the transition are with guaranteeing representation, the more attractive the rules will be to a variety of players. Di Palma argues that 'the essence of the democratic method is to regulate and institutionalise uncertainty of outcome'.[49]

Avoiding a situation that keeps winners always winners, and losers always losers, is the chief merit of a competitive political system. It is also the prospective *sine qua non* of any successful transition. 'By choosing the democratic method, political actors are also choosing a degree of calculated uncertainty'.[50] Democracy has two features which allow this uncertainty to prevail:

> Institutional dispersion and the removal of politico-institutional monopolies curb institutional sources of uncertainty. At the same time by legalising equal access to institutional positions and by deploying them to countervail socio-economic positions, democracy also corrects the unequal effects of social and economic privilege.[51]

The rules of the game that are chosen must accentuate these two features of a democratic system. Ideally such rules should be able to balance two contradictory pressures – the desire of the majority to govern, and the desire of a minority to get rules that curb majority rights. In the latter case the task of democrats is to find rules that gain the consent of small parties to lose as a condition for winning later.

> It stands to reason that reluctant players will be more attracted to the democratic game if the representation of their interests in a democratic form is a paramount concern. It stands to reason that if some players worry that their interests will be disregarded or minoritarian, all players, whatever their investment in democracy, may be better served by rules that embrace fair and equal representation.[52]

The rules that satisfy these requirements are called *garantista* rules – rules which stress the competitiveness of the political market. Institutional *garantismo* aims 'to avoid prejudging or loading the future wins or losses of anyone who abides by the market's intentionally easy rules for admission'.[53] This can be done in two ways. One way is to choose representative institutions such as proportional representation, a multi-party system, a strong parliament, and a weak executive combined with a policy role for the opposition. Another way is to introduce checks and balances within the system, or countervailing powers such as an active constitutional court and a strong role for regional assemblies.

Di Palma also welcomes transitional pacts in conflict-ridden situations as means by which parties can give a sign of a mutual commitment to democracy. In his view 'decisions can be embodied in pacts that will signal a firmer and clearer collective commitment'.[54] At its simplest, pacts are chosen 'to provide some orderly exit from divisive times'.[55] They may be merely transitional coalition arrangements which enable a fledging democracy to achieve a measure of civil order before the development of an openly competitive political system. Pacts are also a means by which 'breakdown games' are avoided if recalcitrants are included in a transitional government. In such a way, political behaviour that is openly hostile to democracy, or merely fearful of lopsided outcomes, can be constrained. In this sense the more extensive and durable the pact the better.

Di Palma assumes that successful elite agreement on the rules of the game is a sufficient source of democratic stability. If there is a precondition for a transition to democracy, it is that rules must be designed to achieve a wide and fair representation of interests. Without an attractive set of rules, reluctant actors will not be brought within the democratic game. Logically, the failure of a transition must be due to one of two factors: either elites have not concentrated on devising appropriate rules for the political game, or elites have erred in choosing the rules. The failure of the transition must be due to one or other of these factors: this amounts to a negative version of his minimalist hypothesis. How true was this of the Irish case? The situation that faced the Provisional Government was not altogether different from that discussed by di Palma. Under the terms of the Treaty, the Irish Free State would come into being no later than 18 December of the following year. In the transition, the government of southern Ireland would be gradually encharged to a Provisional Government. It became agreed between the British and Irish representatives that an election should take place in that period, although no fixed date was established. The task of the Provisional Government became that of gaining the assent of their republican opponents to the election. A government guaranteed majority support faced a recalcitrant minority that would agree to an election only if it were guaranteed a share of representation proportionate to its existing position in the Dáil, and if it were guaranteed future participation in a coalition government.

By conceding the ground to the republicans on both counts, Collins created his own *garantista* solution to the problem posed by republican opposition to an election. He also constructed a transitional pact which would secure the co-operation of republicans in the management of the transition after June. This was understood on both sides to mean that anti-Treatyites would co-operate in the maintenance of ordered conditions in the country. It was in that sense that de Valera welcomed the pact. Collins for his part indicated that he thought coalition government 'probably the most suitable method of carrying over the period of stress'.[56] From di Palma's perspective then the Irish political elite employed the correct tactics, chose the right options, and found the right rules of the game to enable a transition to take place. Attention had been focused on securing precisely the kind of co-existence in diversity that di Palma believes is important. No party dissented from the consensus on the desirability of these rules. Labour also pledged its allegiance to the pact. This was a reward for Collins's insistence that 'there be no inherent thought or wish to interfere with the free choice of the electorate'.[57] For the time being both Treaty sides had suspended their search for majoritarian solutions to the Treaty question. The pro-Treaty side had sacrificed an absolute parliamentary majority in return for republican co-operation in the pact. The anti-Treatyites had suspended what was in effect a campaign to curb majority rights, once convinced that the Treaty would not be an issue in the election. Their delegates' report on the peace committee stated that:

> There is a real necessity, also, to meet that body of opinion in the country, which considers that the present Dáil is not, in any sense of the word, sufficiently representative and to show them that, taking cognisance of the national position, we have interfered with the electorate's full right only to the most limited possible extent.[58]

The failure of a transition then could be due to one of two factors: either elites had not concentrated on finding the right rules of the game, or they had erred in choosing those rules. At first glance, neither was true of the Irish case. The problem lay rather in the institutional basis of the pact. As already noted, the agreement followed almost two weeks of failed efforts at mediation by a peace committee which could not provide a united report. When the committee reports were presented to the Dáil they gave rise to bitter debates about the necessity for an election. On two occasions, 17 and 19 May, it seemed that the Dáil would abandon its efforts for peace. It is significant that Griffith's motion approving the electoral pact on Saturday 20 May did not follow a lengthy Dáil debate that day. Far from renewing the authority of the Dáil, the signing of the pact reflected the reality that only a backroom agreement between elites could avert civil war.

For some pro-Treatyites a straight contest was preferable to the endless negotiation that preceded the pact. For Kevin O'Higgins the Treaty conferred 'very great benefits, very great advantages, and very great opportunities on the Irish people and I would not declare off-hand that it was not worth civil war'.[59] For some republicans a renewal of the struggle with the British was preferable to the loss of national honour involved in accepting the Treaty. Some of these had a relatively exalted view of politics, denouncing each other for 'haggling' for extra seats on the peace committee. One anti-Treatyite, Cathal Brugha, declared that he was 'absolutely sick of politics' on 17 May, and favoured a return to war.[60] Another, Liam Mellowes, denounced the IRB peace scheme as a way of turning the country again 'into the mire of rotten politics'.[61] The spokesman for the IRB delegation referred to 'an atmosphere of absolute hostility' combined with 'a sense of utter irresponsibility' existing in the Dáil.[62]

How faithfully then did de Valera and Collins reflect the views of their supporters? Opposition within Collins's cabinet was a known fact. Griffith was reportedly 'appalled' by the pact when he read it.[63] Cosgrave had protested that 'no party in the Dáil ever has the power of the authority to get members returned unopposed'.[64] The day before the pact was signed, O'Higgins told the Dáil that they had come close to 'trifling with a thing that cannot be outraged without serious reactions, trifling with the absolute right of the people to choose their own representatives and their policy in any given circumstances'.[65] The anti-Treatyites were basically undemocratic: 'We were threatened with terrible and immediate civil war if we did not ram certain gentlemen down the necks of their reluctant constituents'.[66] On the other side, Cathal Brugha used the phrase 'when we take the field again', in the Dáil debate on 19 May, suggesting that peace with the British was only temporary. Another republican delegate stated that civil war was 'a certainty' if an election takes place. De Valera, as is known, had not been consulted when the Four Courts Executive was set up, and had not persuaded the hardliners to accept his 'Document No 2'.[67] By late June most of these republicans regarded the pact as 'a dead letter'. The hardline republican attitude to peace talks was later captured in a recollection of Ernie O'Malley's: 'whatever alliance could have been made with Collins, civil or military, some section of the country would possibly have fought, and I knew that I would have joined them'.[68]

According to di Palma, the legitimacy of the rules of the game is extraneous to any consideration of substantive ends. In his view 'legitimation must come from shared institutional guarantees for competitiveness before coming from anything else'.[69] Such legitimation is threatened by those who see democracy as 'a tool of social upheaval' or as 'a majoritarian lever of wilful social progress'.[70] In particular, the radical view that legitimation can only come with the achievement of certain policy ends, is likely to be counterproductive. The problem in Ireland was that both sides were unable to consider the rules of the game separately from a consideration of policy ends. There was deep divergence of opinion with regard to the purpose of an election. Churchill saw it as a means by which the Provisional Government would mobilise national support in defending its 'just and lawful position'.[71] The Provisional Government saw it as a means of giving the public a chance to give or withhold their assent to the Treaty. Collins believed that they had a right to know if the people would give them a mandate for the course they were taking.[72] The anti-Treatyites feared that an election in the 26 counties would signify the disestablishment of the Republic. An election would be a misrepresentation of the free choice of the Irish people and would give the British an opportunity of claiming that the Irish had freely chosen to remain within the

British Empire. If the people were free to choose, they claimed they would 'get for the independence of Ireland and a continuation of the Republic as overwhelming a vote as you got in 1918'.[73]

Both sides expressed very majoritarian attitudes to the electoral process. The election would give, or fail to give, a mandate for a particular national policy, and was welcomed or opposed as such. Public opinion was something to be mobilised behind a particular course of action. The conservative aspect to this view was that elections existed in order to return a government to power; as one pro-Treatyite put it: 'I believe in any country the one sure bulwark of stability – human nature is so imperfect – of peace and ordered government is that the will of the majority should prevail'.[74] The radical side emphasised the malleability of public opinion. Since 1916 republicans had believed that heroic leadership would galvanise a majority behind any particular course of action. Left to their own devices, however, the majority always choose the line of least resistance. Both radicals and conservatives tended to see elections as majoritarian levers for certain policy ends.

It seems natural then that the pro-Treatyites should interpret the election result as a decisive vote in favour of the Treaty. During the peace committee's sessions it was argued that an election was required to give the Dáil an opportunity to renew its representative character, and this was ultimately accepted by the anti-Treaty delegation. Pro-Treatyites maintained that the outlook of the second Dáil had been more radical than that of the population as a whole, and the election had just returned a more representative body. A breakdown of the vote for the coalition candidates confirms the accuracy of this judgement. Table 6.1 compares the anti-Treaty and the pro-Treaty vote in contested and uncontested constituencies. On the pro-Treaty side, 41 were elected in contested constituencies, and 17 in uncontested constituencies. Of the 58 anti-Treaty candidates, 36 were elected, 17 from uncontested constituencies. The most striking electoral statistic, however, is the large number of anti-Treatyites from the second Dáil who failed to get re-elected when faced with opposition. In all, 118 Sinn Féin candidates went forward for re-election from the second Dáil, 62 endorsing acceptance of the Treaty and 56 rejection. Of the 26 candidates that failed to get re-elected, 21 were opponents of the Treaty. Overall, of the 128 members of the second Dáil, only 18 members managed to reject the Treaty and subsequently keep their seats in a competitive election. It is not surprising that the result was interpreted by the pro-Treatyites as a mandate for the Treaty. Collins later remarked that 'the rejection of so many anti-Treaty candidates in spite of the protection offered them by the panel, and the system of proportional representation, and the smallness of their poll, are further, a protest against the "republican" tactics of the last six months'.[75]

Table 6.1 **Coalition candidates in the pact election**

	Contested constituencies		Uncontested constituencies	
	Pro-Treatyite	Anti-Treatyite	Pro-Treatyite	Anti-Treatyite
Number of candidates	48	41	17	17
Number elected	41	19	17	17
Number of these re-elected from Second Dáil[1]	39	18	17	16
Number of these defeated from Second Dáil	6	22[2]	0	0

1   Figures refer only to Sinn Féin candidates.
2   Excludes Dan Breen who was a joint candidate.

Source: B. Walker (ed.), *Parliamentary Election Results in Ireland, 1802–1902* (1978), pp. 101–8.

The idea that creating appropriate rules of the game requires the existence of an overarching consensus on fundamental matters of policy is rejected by di Palma:

> democracy's rules, being a means for coexistence, need not be more than a second best for the parties that negotiated their adoption. Rules can be a matter of instrumental agreement worked out among competing leaderships, even in the absence of a popular or elite consensus on fundamentals.[76]

The problem in Ireland stemmed from the fact that there was no consensus on fundamentals. The pro-Treatyites would renounce the pact rather than jeopardise the Treaty, and the anti-Treatyites would reject an election if it meant disestablishing the Republic. The legitimacy of the rules of the game was not extraneous to a consideration of policy ends. Although Collins was willing to make concessions on numbers, he was not willing to make them on principle. On the other side, a reduction in the numbers of republicans to be nominated to the coalition panel was resisted to avoid giving the impression that in the election 'the Treaty issue was being further determined'.[77] This was the 'fundamental position' of the anti-Treaty delegates.[78] The rules of the game were less important than the symbolic issues, such as the presence of the crown in the constitution and the oath to the crown. Neither side was willing to swap concern for substantive outcomes for short-term party advantages. This was also true of the army negotiations, the success of which was an essential precondition for the continuance of the pact. Early in June, Mulcahy had been warned that the anti-Treatyites would not accept unity 'unless an agreed election implied that the Dáil would continue as the Government of the Irish Republic and was solely responsible for the administration of the country – Ulster included'.[79] Even for Moylan and Lynch, who had been willing to accept the general scheme for army unification, the constitutional question and the question of army reunification could not be disentangled. The IRA Executive wanted to provide the Chief of Staff in order to guarantee that the army would not be used to subvert the Republic.[80]

The pact, underpinned by an agreement on army unity, might have delayed the outbreak of civil war. However, some conflict between the Provisional Government and the more extreme IRA men was inevitable. The issue of the Treaty had not been resolved by the pact. At the outset, the Dáil had been divided by a proposal that it accept the fact that the majority of the people accepted the Treaty. Likewise, after eleven sessions of the peace committee, a similar division arose over the pro-Treaty side's preamble which recommended acceptance of the fact that a majority of the Dáil and of the people accepted the Treaty. It was objected that the conference was not being used to secure peace and unity between the sides, but as an instrument for 'enforcing acceptance of the Treaty upon us'.[81] Indeed a member of the pro-Treaty delegation spoke of 'a very big difference' between the two sides' conceptions of coalition government. The pro-Treatyite conception was that the coalition would preserve all the advantages which the Treaty had brought. The republican conception was that the coalition government should evade the Treaty.[82] One member threw cold water on the viability of a coalition under such circumstances: 'If the anti-Treaty party go in to work the Treaty a coalition is possible, but if they go in to break down the Treaty government in opposition to it, a coalition is not'.[83]

In his negotiations with de Valera at UCD, Collins stressed that nothing could be done to endanger the Treaty position and insisted that the policy of the House would be the policy of the majority, in short the Treaty position. De Valera replied that the party spirit might disappear as the benefits of coalition were made clear. If not, Collins could rely on the support of the third parties.[84] De Valera's reassurances notwithstanding, there was no explicit agreement that the republicans on the coalition government commit themselves to protecting the Treaty. Likewise there was no agreement on the nature and name of the new assembly. Collins's own ambiguous attitude to the pact is revealed by his comment before the election that

> the people want to support the candidates who will do the best for the Treaty. At the back of all things I still have faith in the common people although at the moment when they are looking to me for guidance on this important point I have to be silent.[85]

Republican commentators have seen in the pact a genuine attempt at conflict-resolution which was undermined by British interference.[86] In this vein on 29 June, de Valera stated that, if adhered to, the pact would have given the Irish 'an opportunity for working for internal peace and of taking steps which would make this nation strong against the only enemy it has to fear – the enemy from outside'.[87] Another Fianna Fáiler, Gerry Boland, later argued that if Collins had resisted British pressure and waited for the third Dáil to meet before attacking the IRA in the Four Courts, there would have been no civil war and the anti-Treatyites would in due course have taken their seats in the third Dáil.[88] Even impartial accounts of the war accept that Britain was indirectly responsible for the breaking of the pact.[89] It does not follow, however, that the pact had long-term potential as a peace-saving device. Britain's position could only be tested by a united government, but there was little basis for such unity. Collins and de Valera did not have the full support of their own sides in making the pact. The constitutional status of the IRA remained to trouble the political elite and beyond that lay the question of Northern Ireland. If the pact had worked, unity might have been achieved, but if unity had been achieved, British military intervention might well have followed.[90]

Ultimately, the pact went against the grain of Irish political traditions. From the decision in the cabinet to allow the Dáil to decide by majority vote on the Treaty, a majoritarian solution to the crisis was the most likely outcome. If de Valera had been interested in a non-majoritarian solution, he should have accepted the offer on 4 January and avoided a Dáil vote on the Treaty. Both Collins and Griffith had agreed to the scheme whereby a Dáil vote would be avoided. Both became 'enthusiastic democrats' after the Dáil vote on the Treaty. Once the Dáil had decided in favour of the Treaty, a conflict between the views of the Dáil and the IRA was inevitable. A large section of pro-Treaty Sinn Féin, perhaps the majority, continued to regard the Dáil vote on the Treaty as 'the final consecration of the Treaty which nobody but traitors must ever call in question again'.[91] Throughout the peace committee's negotiations the pro-Treaty delegates never wavered from their insistence that their opponents recognise that there was a majority for the Treaty in the Dáil. The problem for constitutional engineers in Ireland derived from the fact that the Irish were majoritarian rather than pluralist democrats, and majority rule, as de Valera was soon to realise, provided the simplest base for political order.[92]

6.3   Voluntarist democratic theory and the failure of the pact

The analysis above requires us to ask how voluntarist theory can be usefully applied to situations where the transition to democracy and the transition to independence take place simultaneously. Between the signing of the Treaty and the ratification of the constitution of the Irish Free State by the British parliament the following December, an Irish state existed only in provisional and embryonic form. As such, the Irish case is altogether different from those inter-war polities discussed by Linz and Stepan, where the state had been consolidated well before the transition to democracy.[93] Inevitably the constraints within which political elites acted were different from those that existed within more established polities. Moreover, where the establishment of governmental authority over a territory is a primary focus of elite competition, the motivations of political actors may differ from those with established central institutions.

In the period between the signing of the Treaty and the civil war, effective diplomacy was conducted through informal and secretive channels but there was no routinised set of procedures for the regulation of conflict. As it turned out, *ad hoc* agreements did not prove binding on pivotal actors and they had a provisional and informal character about them. This was a reflection of the institutional incoherence of the Free State in the early months. Another aspect of that incoherence was that the Free State lacked the basic institution of parliamentary democracy, an executive collectively responsible to parliament. A number of proposals were made that would have created an executive responsible to the Dáil, but these were opposed by the Provisional Government itself. It had been suggested, for example, that the Dáil take responsibility for producing an agreed constitution. This might have bolstered the authority of a Dáil that had become merely 'a showpiece which preserved the trappings of republicanism'.[94] It might also have provided a more robust base for the defence of a republican constitution than the Provisional Government, but this idea was also opposed by members of the Provisional Government.

The autonomous status of the IRA was the most dramatic aspect of the institutional incoherence of the Free State, but one that was not surprising. Local brigades of the IRA had never been subject to effective central control. The closest the Provisional Government came to resolving the issue was to create an army council elected by an IRA convention. Even relative 'moderates' on the anti-Treaty side, like Liam Lynch, demanded that this convention be composed of the delegates entitled to attend the banned convention of 26 March.[95] Yet that proposal was unlikely to have satisfied the Provisional Government, never mind their British counterparts. An official Provisional Government memo later stated:

The Army Authorities went if anything further than they ought to have gone in their efforts to meet the idiosyncrasies of the Irregulars. In their anxiety for settlement without armed strife they made offers which would almost have menaced the principle stated above, namely, that the armed forces should be subject not to any clique but to the People. These offers were rejected by the Irregulars' leaders, who wanted to ensure that they would be able to control the Army and utilise it for purposes not sanctioned by the people. The people would never and could never sanction any lessening of their own full and absolute control over the armed forces.[96]

It follows that the consolidation of the system required a prior process of institutionalisation whereby certain institutional structures would become simplified, routinised, and authoritative. Between December 1921 and June 1922 the Provisional Government existed in a vacuum. Their ambition was 'to set up a new state based on law and freedom within the bounds of the Treaty'.[97] The Dáil vote on 7 January provided the starting point for that process. The election victory conferred a great deal of legitimacy on that ambition. By late spring, asserting the authority of the government was the chief concern for pro-Treatyites. As O'Higgins put it:

If things go on as they are going I do not know who is going to govern the country. I do not know who is going to collect the revenue of the country. I do not see who is going to keep any ordered fabric of Government or even of society existing in Ireland. That is the issue that you are faced with.[98]

The problem was that asserting the authority of the government cut across the logic of building bridges to the republicans. Asserting the authority of the state meant establishing an institutional monopoly over decision making and establishing a clear hierarchy within governmental institutions. Inevitably it also meant undermining those institutions that were associated with the Republic – the IRB, the IRA, the Republican Courts, and the Second Dáil.

At what point did the imperative of asserting the authority of the Provisional Government replace that of seeking compromise? From January onwards the Provisional Government was aware of its military vulnerability. Early in March de Valera told them that 'but for the majority of the Dáil you would not be talking as a member of the Provisional Government because you would be swept out of the country by the army'.[99] At this stage, to paraphrase Robert Dahl, the cost of suppressing the IRA far exceeded the cost of tolerating it. An attempt at repression would have jeopardised the very existence of the Provisional Government. On the other hand, by June, with a basic military organisation established, and a guarantee of a continued supply of British arms, the situation had changed. Britain had left little room for manoeuvre over the Treaty. The truce with the IRA, dating from 4 May, had failed to provide stability: 'robberies, assaults, shootings, attacks on national troops, commandeering of goods, raiding of houses and the taking out of prisoners, murders of British soldiers, bank robberies, etc', had all followed, apparently with the approval of the Four Courts Executive.[100] The IRA Executive's insistence on choosing the new Chief of Staff put paid to any possibility of army unity, and as the convention date approached, the possibility of British reoccupation was foremost in people's minds. At this stage the costs of toleration had become greater than the costs of suppression. O'Donnell and Schmitter argue that governments may choose to tolerate recalcitrant opponents up to a point, but if widespread violence occurs or if the existence of the opposition threatens 'the vertical command structure of the armed forces, the territorial integrity of the nation state, the country's position in international alliances, [or] . . . the property rights underlying the capitalist economy', repression soon follows tolerance.[101] All these factors influenced the Provisional Government's decision to attack the Four Courts.

Inevitably, the manner in which the Provisional Government asserted its authority in June led to accusations of bad faith by their opponents. Friendly contact had been maintained between Beggars Bush and the Four Courts right up to the outbreak of hostilities; the pact was never formally renounced by the Dáil, and the Provisional Government did not seek parliamentary approval for their initiation of the civil war until September, all of which enabled de Valera to claim later that they had carried out 'an executive coup d'état' in the summer of 1922.[102] There is clear evidence that as late as 26 June the Provisional Government were committed to convening the new Dáil at the RDS on 1 July, and the Ministry of Defence had already informed the IRA Executive that further negotiations on army unification were a matter for the new coalition government.[103] Hugh Kennedy, the chief law officer, had also advised the Provisional Government in April that the second Dáil should be dissolved by a vote unless it had in its constitution some other provision for its own dissolution.[104] The fact that it was never formally dissolved enabled republicans to claim that it remained the only legitimate legislative body in the country and this would remain a minority view until the late 1930s. The pact may have been the only way in which an election could take place, but its terms left the Provisional Government in a vulnerable position. On 20 July the republican newsletter argued:

> If the Griffith–Collins party be regarded as the war-party, that party would be in a minority of the Third Dáil, holding 58 seats out of 128. Of the remaining 70 the 36 Republicans voted for the Pact and peace, the pact deliberately violated by the Collins party – and the other 34, Treaty or no Treaty, certainly had a mandate for peace, not war.[105]

Republicans forgot that the reason the Provisional Government had no majority in the third Dáil was because of Collins's concession to them on 17 May, but as in other countries at this time the legality of the succession process in Ireland was 'sufficiently ambiguous' for them to then claim a position of moral superiority in the civil war.[106]

The Provisional Government had a dual transition to handle. On the one hand it was a transition to self-government. On the other it was a transition to electoral democracy. The first provoked the most dissension. Irish nationalists had a rather rudimentary conception of democratic politics and tended to view electoral politics through the prism of distinctly nationalist agendas. An election would either legitimise the Free State or disestablish the Republic. As such the June election became the crucial threshold for the establishment of a government under the terms of the Treaty. Irish recalcitrance was not the product of misgivings about the virtues of democracy, but more of a sense that the Free State represented for republicans a betrayal of national ideals. The problem for moderates on both sides was that the political game was not an attractive option if it failed to protect positions on the national question. Constitutional engineers were dealing with rather refractory material when it came to Ireland.

What di Palma has offered is a distinct set of tactical recommendations for political elites in transitional situations, but these tactics can only be applied successfully in certain situations. By and large Irish elites were sensitive to the need to find guarantees for rival political positions but were unable to guarantee substantial rewards for compliance. Finding the right rules of the game was not enough. The national aspirations of both sides had also to be protected and it was impossible for Collins to protect both the Treaty and anti-Treaty positions at the one time. Here British power was a crucial limiting factor and one that Collins tended to overlook. For his colleagues the need to establish an authoritative government was a more pressing concern than that of appeasing the republicans, and was probably held to be worth civil war. For the Provisional Government, majority rule, with its winner-take-all implications, was a far more attractive idea than the uncertainty promised by di Palma's *garantista* rules. Majority rule was also deeply rooted in Irish elite political culture, although it was immediately attractive because it served as a means through which a stable institutional order could be rapidly constructed. Its attractions were as much psychological as cultural.

6.4 Conclusion

For decades after the civil war, impartial analysis of its origins was hampered by a paucity of original documents and also by the atmosphere of recrimination and bitterness which surrounded discussion. In the light of the available evidence, is it now possible to attribute blame to individuals or to particular decisions that were taken? Voluntarist theory assumes that elites can always have a decisive effect on political outcomes, but the bulk of the theory built up to support this proposition has been taken from states which already possessed authoritative central institutions. In the Irish case the absence of such institutions was crucial. The fall-out from the Treaty revealed 'the lack of effective relations between the various nationalist institutions which prevented any controlled, disciplined response to the Treaty'.[107]

Williams holds both de Valera and Collins responsible for the outbreak of civil war, the former for doing too little, the latter for doing too much.[108] Certainly de Valera did not do too much to distance himself from the stance of the Four Courts men, while Collins concentrated too much power in himself. However, given the position of the third parties, Collins did not deprive the pro-Treatyite position of majority support in the Dáil, and appeared to gain de Valera's consent to an agreement protecting the Treaty. On the other hand, de Valera had no authority over the IRA who, in his own words, had 'taken up an independent position in this matter'.[109] Certainly, Collins erred in underestimating British determination to protect the Treaty. He had been informed quite early on that Britain would not be flexible on the Treaty. On 12 May 1922 Churchill told him that 'every one of us will swing round with every scrap of influence we can command against a Republic or any inroad upon the Treaty structure'.[110] Why Collins still believed that a republican constitution would be accepted by the British is something of a mystery. More specifically, why he thought the British would accept the Governor General being called the Irish President in his constitution is beyond comprehension.

Collins also erred in exchanging the freedom to draft a constitution as the price of securing British acquiescence in the pact. In the long run the loss of a 'republican' constitution may have been more damaging to the cause of peace. Harry Boland, Liam Lynch, Sean Moylan, and de Valera, a representative sample of moderate republican opinion in the spring, had all expressed approval of the constitutional idea as a valid test of Collins's 'stepping-stone' interpretation of the Treaty. Furthermore, once the decisive phase of the civil war was over, an acceptable document might have encouraged moderate republicans to attend the Dáil in September when it was being amended.[111] However, the claim that Collins's colleagues in the Provisional Government did not defend his draft in conference with the British has to be seen in the light of the agreement of 27 May, when they all, regardless of personal opinions, defended the pact. Rather it seems that the pact 'frightened the British into inserting every unpleasant form into the new constitution', as O'Higgins later claimed.[112]

Collins's failure, however, only seems to confirm the validity of the argument that elites can prove decisive only in certain situations. In the Irish case the crucial period was the period between the signing of the Treaty and the Dáil debate on 7 January. The initial meeting between four pro and five anti-Treaty delegates on 4 January had led to eight of the conference accepting terms. After consultation with de Valera the next day, however, the anti-Treaty delegates' position had changed. It was 'immediately found that the agreement reached on the previous night did not now meet with the approval of the other side'.[113] Instead it was proposed that the conference ask the Dáil to give majority support to an alternative document, probably based on de Valera's 'Document No. 2', which would be submitted to the British. This was rejected by the pro-Treaty side. De Valera's intervention had been decisive in preventing agreement. Moreover, once he had attempted to rally public opinion against the Treaty he was inviting the IRA to do the same. He was also undermining the pivotal position of the Dáil cabinet.

A united cabinet responsible to the Dáil was the only way in which the split could have been contained within democratic politics. There was little point in de Valera attempting to reconstruct a united cabinet with the pact when he had effectively destroyed it four months earlier. A comparison can be made with the impact of the Kilmainham Treaty of 1882 on the alliance between the radical Land Leaguers and the Parnellite party. The agreement seemed to close off for good the radical route to social change, and closely identified the Irish parliamentary party with the Liberal Party. The split which ensued ran deep and might have been 'extremely serious in its results'.[114] However, the leaders of the radicals, Michael Davitt and John Dillon, loyally accepted the Treaty and thus helped secure Parnell's position. Forty years later the radical wing of the national movement quickly deserted those who had compromised and left the moderates identified as the agents of British policy in Ireland.

Of course the earlier Dáil cabinet had been deeply divided on personal and ideological lines and had not really functioned as a government during the War of Independence. For this reason it is important that a transition should benefit from a period of prior institutionalisation whereby decision-making structures become routinised and hierarchical. After that the more onerous hurdles of consolidation and legitimacy have to be overcome. Any analysis of the difficulties faced by Collins in his attempts to prevent civil war must come to the conclusion that the Irish independence movement's adherence to conventional forms of government was far more apparent than real. Viewed in the light of the enormous difficulties faced by Irish elites in the spring of 1922, di Palma's optimism and his recommendations seem rather unrealistic and superficial. The basic question – Who was to be the sovereign authority in the country? – was only answered by civil war. Before that Collins and others had attempted to improvise solutions to the Treaty split that reflected di Palma's suggestions. Majority rule was, however, too engrained in Irish political culture and in the logic of the situation for these tactics to be effective. From one point of view, that of the Provisional Government, the transition, both to self-government and to democracy, had been successful. From another point of view the civil war raised as many questions as it resolved. The resolution of these issues forms the subject matter of Chapter Eight.

Chapter 7

The Durkheimian interpretation of the civil war

'Every man and every woman within the nation has normally equal rights, but a man or a woman may forfeit his or her rights by turning recreant to the nation.' **Pádraig Pearse, n.d.**

The civil war of 1922–23 was a crucial moment in Irish social and political development. Only seven months after the signing of the Anglo-Irish Treaty in December 1921, the new Irish state found itself embroiled in an intense conflict in which the Provisional Government struggled to gain control of the 26 counties of 'southern Ireland' in the face of a widespread insurgency campaign. In explaining why the new state found itself so quickly in the throes of civil war, two types of interpretation can be detected. The first emphasises the contingency of events. The civil war was the result of individual actions, ideological confusion and external pressure that followed from the decision to sign the Anglo-Irish Treaty on 6 December 1921.[1] A second interpretation, more recent in origin, offers a sociological explanation for the conflict. The civil war was an expression of an enduring and profound antimony in Irish political culture.[2] It reflected 'the long division of the Irish mind' between two subcultures, one communitarian and pre-modern, the other individualistic and modern, which represented two distinct reactions to the onset of modernity in post-Famine Ireland.[3]

It is with the second of these interpretations, the Durkheimian interpretation, that this chapter is concerned. Durkheim argued that in the course of modernisation social solidarity would gradually cease to be based on the existence of a pervasive moral consensus, and a new individualistic order would develop which allowed for the existence of a plural civil society. In that new social order the individual would replace the community as the source of authoritative social values. The Durkheimian interpretation of the Irish civil war sees the war as a conflict underpinned by the two types of social solidarity Durkheim outlined in his *Division of Labour*. The Treaty split revealed the existence of fundamentally different conceptions of social order among the Irish political elite, conceptions that are related to wider traditions of thinking about the state in Europe. In this sense the conflict was much more than an elite split over means rather than ends, but a conflict which expressed a deep-rooted schizophrenia in Irish political society.

From the Durkheimian perspective the Irish case represents something very unusual: a society where the cultural bases of a democratic order were defended by the state in a civil war. As a result of the victory of the Free State army in 1923, the Irish state acquired early on a degree of democratic legitimacy that the other successor states in Europe mostly lacked. The good order and stability of the Free State after 1922, then, owes much to this victory, an outcome that might be compared with that of the American civil war. In what follows I subject this interpretation of the civil war to an empirical and logical critique, and suggest that a central issue – not only in debates about the Irish civil war, but also in Durkheim's account of social development – that of the state is not adequately dealt with in this literature. Indeed my analysis of the Irish civil war suggests that the contrast in Durkheim's work between a society based on a strong *conscience collective* and a society where such a conscience is assumed to be lacking is, to some extent, a false one.

7.1   Durkheim and the two poles of Irish political culture

In his work on the division of labour Durkheim distinguished between societies in which social solidarity is based on the existence of strongly held moral beliefs, on a single *conscience collective*, and societies where such an all-embracing moral consensus is lacking. Such a *conscience collective* is found where strong collective beliefs are grounded in religious beliefs. To be sure, the new organic type of social order does not lack moral precepts entirely, but those precepts which exist express a different set of social relationships based upon relationships of exchange within a differentiated division of labour. Such a set of relationships 'creates among men an entire system of rights and duties which link them together in a durable way'.[4]

The difference between the two forms of social solidarity can be understood in terms of the importance of individualism in the latter type. In the mechanical division of labour the scope for individual freedom is limited. In these societies 'social conduct is controlled by shared values and beliefs: the collectivity dominates the individual, and there is only a rudimentary development of individual self-consciousness'.[5] In the organic division of labour, on the other hand, social conduct is guided by precepts derived from a system of moral individualism. Moral norms underpin a system which recognises the autonomy, dignity and freedom of the individual. The influence of collective beliefs is limited. The two forms of social solidarity also differ in the character of the sanctions imposed against deviant behaviour:

A society with mechanical solidarity is held together mainly through normative coercion; deviants are severely punished, and penal repressive law is important. With increasing division of labour, restitutive law, regulating relations of exchange, comes into the foreground. The necessity to punish deviants diminishes, and as a consequence, men are willing to grant each other more freedom and equality.[6]

'Repressive sanctions' are those associated with penal law and involve the infliction of punishment in the form of suffering on the transgressor, such as the loss of life or liberty. 'Restitutive sanctions', on the other hand, involve the restoration of the *status quo ante*. The object is not punishment but the restoration of a balance between individuals. The existence of repressive laws is an index of the presence of strongly held moral beliefs: 'the greater the preponderance of repressive over restitutive law, the more unified and inclusive is the *conscience collective*'.[7] The *conscience collective* is most all embracing in the simplest form of society where strongly held collective beliefs are grounded in religion. Violation of the moral code invokes a religious sanction and is severely punished.

Organic solidarity is defined as the interdependence of individuals or groups in systematic relations of exchange with one another. The replacement of a mechanical with an organic form of social solidarity comes with an increase in the complexity of the division of labour. Organic solidarity presupposes not the similarity but the growth of differences between individuals.[8] In primitive societies individuals are tied to one another through sameness: solidarity derives from a similarity of sentiment of belief. Society is merely an aggregate of individuals sharing the same outlooks and beliefs, rather than a system of mutually dependent elements. 'The parts of the whole are connected mechanically, rather than forming an organic unity as the parts of a biological (and social) system do'.[9] The disappearance of this type of social solidarity is predicated upon the disappearance of the 'segmentary' form of society in which the population of a territory is divided into a number of internally homogeneous segments with rigid boundaries separating them.[10] As more movement and interaction take place between these segments, and the partitions dividing them become more permeable owing to an increase in the 'moral density' of society, so the division of labour becomes more advanced. This follows a number of social changes: the most important of which are population increase, the spread of town life, and finally improvements in the means of communication.

The civil war split in Ireland has been explained in ways that reflect Durkheim's dichotomy. For Prager, the inability of the nationalist elite to maintain a common front in the first half of 1922 reflected a disagreement over much more than the terms of the Treaty. The split revealed 'the presence of sharply divergent conceptions of the meaning of the Irish nation and distinct understandings of who were the rightful members of that nation and of the social relations that ought to prevail among its members'.[11] The two cultural traditions – the Irish Enlightenment and the Gaelic Romantic tradition – both offered their own solutions to the crisis of Irish modernity. Each had its own understanding of 'the proper course of affairs for the nation', and 'the appropriate relations among its members':[12]

> There was the Irish-Enlightenment tradition, deriving its original insights from the Anglo-Irish Ascendancy and articulating modern secular aspirations for the Irish nation. Here the objective was to construct a social order characterised by autonomous individuals and independent spheres of social life in which the Irish citizen could rationally influence the course of Irish affairs. On the other side there was a competing Gaelic Romantic set of thoughts and beliefs. Its aim was to promote a solidary nation without conflict and disharmony, imbued with a vivid sense of the past in the functioning of the present. Neither secular nor individualistic, this orientation expressed a yearning for a social order protective of the values and patterns of interaction putatively characteristic of the ancient Gaelic Ireland.[13]

The basis of freedom according to the Irish Enlightenment tradition was the autonomous rational individual. The basis for freedom in the Gaelic Romantic tradition was a social community based on authentic traditional values. For those who subscribed to the Anglo-Irish tradition, the new Ireland would be led by 'an elite committed to non-sectarian and urbane values'.[14] In contrast Gaelic Romantics offered a picture of the future that was 'far more detailed than any commitment to the free rule of individuals in an independent Irish community'.[15] They would create a self-sufficient agricultural state in which Gaelic patterns of social life would re-emerge and create a community free from the evils of modern capitalist society:

> The Gaelic-Irish conception of Ireland was that the nation ought to strive to re-create its past and resist those changes that seemed to challenge the basic meaning of Ireland as embodied in its traditions. Modern Ireland was to be celebrated as a pre-industrial nation; its identity was to be found in its rural character. The sanctity of the family was to be preserved, the Church was to remain a central social institution second only to the family, and the farm was to serve as the backbone for a healthy thriving society.[16]

The Gaelic Romantic tradition, in short, sought to preserve what was left of traditional Ireland, or reconstruct a new Ireland in accordance with the mythic patterns of the past. The new Ireland was to be 'a harmonious nation, communal and free from "modern" urban, British, and Anglican influences, from which it was currently suffering'.[17] In 1922 republicans intended to maintain a type of primordial solidarity among the Irish nation that would be lost if the Treaty were accepted. For the pro-Treatyites, as inheritors of Irish Enlightenment thinking, acceptance of the Treaty was a means of achieving an independent state composed of equal and free individuals. It was a state that would discard the mechanical solidarity of an undifferentiated rural order.

In Garvin's *1922: The Birth of Irish Democracy*, the civil war split is also explained in ways that echo Durkheim's theory of the division of labour. The split 'tended to follow a divide that separated those who saw the Republic as a moral and transcendental entity analogous to the Church of Christ, an entity whose citizens were duty bound to defend it with their purses and their lives, from those who saw the Republic as a bargaining device in achieving rational-legal self-government for as much of Ireland as possible, regardless of formal political labels'.[18] Garvin suggests that the anti-Treatyites were aiming to establish a moral community rather than 'a nation state of citizens whose individual moral state, was subject to minimal legal restraints, a private rather than a public matter'.[19] Two identifiable political traditions within the nationalist community were expressed in the war:

> 1921–22 is the founding date of democratic Ireland's political life, not just because of the coming of the truce in July 1921 or the signing of the Treaty in December 1921, but because of the emergence, for the first time in Irish history, of popular expression of two poles of Irish Catholic political culture: the vision of the Republic as a moral community, as a community of equals submerging individual identity and self-interest for the common good on the one hand, and a non-magical, lawyer's pragmatic nationalism on the other, which saw Irish independence as a means to the construction of a commercialised, mechanically representative democracy on the other.[20]

For Garvin, then, the civil war division was between 'republican moralists' and 'nationalist pragmatists'. The former went hand in hand with an inability to handle differences of opinion and a tendency to view opposing political stances as motivated by unworthy considerations. Pragmatists saw politics in contrast as 'a process by which large numbers of people settled their differences non-violently, rather than a process by which human beings became better people'.[21] Garvin suggests that the 'pragmatist' and 'moralist' subcultures are ideal types but ones that reflect deep-rooted tendencies in Irish life. The republican moralist subculture derived from the type of puritanical Catholicism that was established in post-Famine Ireland, while the nationalist-pragmatist approach had its roots in the eighteenth-century Enlightenment. Garvin describes Irish society at the time as essentially a peasant society, although it was becoming 'a classic western free farmer society'.[22] A belief in communalism – in the family as the central unit of society, and in the preservation of rural life in the face of the forces of commercialisation – was typical of peasant societies everywhere.[23]

From the perspectives of both Prager and Garvin, then, the civil war was an expression of the value strains experienced by a society that was undergoing the throes of modernisation. More specifically, it was a conflict caused by the tension inherent in the transition from a society based on mechanical to one based on organic solidarity. Republicans had a 'mechanical' highly normative understanding of political order, while the pro-Treatyites defended an 'organic' or legalistic conception of political order. Democratic mechanisms for forging agreement were rejected by these republicans because they did not reflect traditional understandings of the public realm. As a result, democracy had to be imposed on the anti-Treatyites by the Provisional Government in 1922–23.

7.2   Uniformity and diversity within Irish nationalism

A tension between the two forms of social solidarity is common in developing societies. As Durkheim put it, advancement in the division of labour is due to the stronger pressures exerted by social units on one another, which leads them to develop in more or less divergent directions. However, 'at every moment this pressure is neutralised by a reverse pressure that the common consciousness exerts upon every individual consciousness'.[24] In societies where the nation-building process is in its active stage, the tension is increased. In order for different societies to be differentiated from one another 'they must be attracted or grouped together through the similarities that they display'.[25] In short, the need for each social segment to highlight its distinctiveness inhibits the development of organic solidarity:

> What draws men together are mechanical forces and instinctive forces such as the affinity of blood, attachment to the same soil, the cult of their ancestors, a communality of habits, etc. It is only when the group has been formed on these bases that co-operation becomes organised.[26]

The presence of mechanical solidarity is explained not just by the low division of labour, but also by this pressure towards uniformity. In a new nation it is to be expected that this pressure will be all the greater. Conversely, the greater the amount of exchange between individuals and the less the uniformity, the greater the degree of organic solidarity.

Allardt suggests that 'instead of saying, as Durkheim does, that mechanical solidarity is based on similarity and organic solidarity is based on the division of labour, we can assume that there are two separate variables that can be used together to explain both types of solidarity'.[27] Allardt derives four propositions from this choice of variables.[28] The first is *that the less developed the division of labour and the stronger the pressure towards uniformity, the less the likelihood of legitimacy conflicts.* In this situation a state of mechanical solidarity obtains, which can happen only in undeveloped societies. The second is *that the less developed the division of labour and the weaker the pressure towards uniformity, the greater the likelihood of legitimacy conflicts.* Such conflicts may exist in pre-industrial societies that are weakened by religious schism as in seventeenth-century Britain. The third is *that the more developed the division of labour and the stronger the pressure towards uniformity, the greater the likelihood of legitimacy conflicts.* This situation existed in independent Ireland in 1922. Lastly, *the more developed the division of labour and the weaker the pressure towards uniformity, the less the likelihood of legitimacy conflicts.* In such a state a situation of organic solidarity prevails.

Independent Ireland was in situation three in 1922, when a relatively high division of labour co-existed with strong pressures towards uniformity. A chief source of pressure towards uniformity was the historical religious cleavage, 'the cultural division of labour', between Protestants and Catholics, which left Catholics as a relatively homogeneous minority community within the UK. The existence of religious discrimination and shortage of higher educational opportunities had blocked social mobility for Catholics. As a result the Catholic community remained less socially differentiated than its Protestant counterpart. Moreover, since industrialisation took place mainly in the north-east, nationalist Ireland did not develop an urban industrial enclave separate from its rural surroundings. As Hechter suggests, 'the lack of enclave hinterland differences in southern Ireland permitted the development of a solidary and broad-based political party capable of effecting independence'.[29] Land reform was another factor. Garvin argues that 'republican moralism' in Ireland resembled the conformist and puritanical cultures that 'owner occupier free farmers seem to create whenever they form a dominant social group'.[30] By 1922 the vast majority of Irish farms were owner-operated.[31]

In addition to these structural factors there was a political one. While nationalists continually challenged the authority of the British state, the Irish nationalist community represented itself as a community of equals and not as an entity that contained different interests. In the British majoritarian political system it was always to the advantage of nationalists to emphasise the homogeneity of Irish public opinion and the existence of strong solidary bonds between its members. This was to counter the claim that Ireland was composed of two nations, one Catholic and one Protestant, and to argue that Ireland's right to self-rule was based on the majority rule principle. That there were strong political pressures towards uniformity can be seen from the electoral history of Irish constituencies in the decades before independence. In large areas of Ireland, reflecting the dominance of the Home Rule Party, parliamentary seats went uncontested in as many as half of the elections that took place. Adapting Garvin's regional classification of Ireland, table 7.1. shows the number of contested elections by region between 1885 and 1917.[32] It suggests, significantly, that the nationalist party's electoral dominance reflected a sociocultural divide separating the north-east from the more traditional rural constituencies of the south and west. In the future area of independent Ireland only in the centre was there a robust tradition of contested elections and this was still low, scoring just over fifty per cent. In the heartland, and in

Table 7.1 **Contested parliamentary elections by region, 1885–1917**

Region	Number of elections	Number of elections contested	Percentage of elections contested
Centre	75	41	54.6
North-East Ulster	239	147	61.5
Heartland	338	121	35.7
Border Periphery	154	60	38.96
Western Periphery	154	55	35.7

Centre:
College Green, Harbour, Stephens Green, St Patrick's, University, Dublin North, Dublin County South.

North East Ulster:
Antrim North, Mid-Antrim, Antrim East, Antrim South, Armagh North, Armagh Mid, Armagh South, Belfast East, Belfast South, Belfast West, Belfast North, Down North, Down East, Down West, Down South, Fermanagh North, Fermanagh South, Londonderry City, Londonderry North, Londonderry South, Tyrone North, Mid Tyrone, South Tyrone.

Heartland:
Carlow, Cork City, Cork North, Cork North-East, Mid-Cork, East Cork, West Cork, Cork South, Cork South-East, Kildare North, Kildare South, Kilkenny City, Kilkenny North, Kilkenny South, Kings County: Birr and Tullamore, Limerick City, Limerick West, Limerick East, Meath North, Meath South, Queens Co.: Leix and Ossory, Tipperary North, Tipperary Mid, Tipperary South, Tipperary East, Waterford, Waterford West, Waterford East, Westmeath North, Westmeath South, Wexford North, Wexford South, Wicklow North, Wicklow East.

Border Periphery:
Cavan West, Cavan East, Donegal North, Donegal West, Donegal East, Donegal South, Leitrim North, Leitrim South, Longford North, Longford South, Louth North, Louth South, Monaghan North, Monaghan South, Sligo North, Sligo South.

Western Periphery:
Clare East, Clare West, Galway, Connemara, Galway North, Galway East, Galway South, Kerry North, Kerry West, Kerry South, Kerry East, Mayo North, Mayo West, Mayo East, Mayo South, Roscommon North, Roscommon South, Sligo North, Sligo South.

Source: B. Walker (ed.), *Parliamentary Election Results in Ireland, 1801–1922* (1978), pp. 325–83.

the border and western peripheries, uncontested elections were the norm. It is important to realise that the nationalist Sinn Féin party inherited this position of electoral monopoly in the 1918 general election, when the party won over two thirds of the seats in nationalist Ireland. In addition, 25 out of the 72 seats in the area of the future Irish state were uncontested.[33] This situation was even more dramatic in 1920 when all seats were uncontested in the future area of the Free State.

The peculiar history of Irish representation can be understood only by appreciating that Ireland was what Therborn terms 'a national mobilisation democracy' where democratisation is seized upon as a means of nationalist mobilisation.[34] In such democracies, where political elites use electoral contests as means of demonstrating the national will, they have a vested interest in downplaying the significance of social divisions among their supporters and in stressing the homogeneity of outlook among them. The 1918 election, the first democratic election to take place in Ireland, was thus seen as a national plebiscite, not as an election giving different sectors of Irish society a chance to represent themselves.[35] The founding fathers of the Irish state mostly believed that politics were there to serve the interests of the nation, not of discrete social groups. As Pádraig Pearse put it, 'a government of capitalists or a government of clerics, or a government of lawyers, or a government of tinkers or a government of red-headed men, or a government of men born on a Tuesday, does not represent the people and cannot bind the people'.[36]

Allardt suggests that the existence of strong pressure towards uniformity in a society derives from two sources: (*a*) existing norms are specific and related to strong sanctions that are applied with great consistency; and (*b*) there are no or very few conflicts between norms.[37] Between 1918 and 1921 there was little overt disagreement among nationalists about the aims of the nationalist movement, and in 1919 all elected deputies were asked to swear an oath of allegiance to the Republic. Moreover, most of the major interest groups in Irish society supported the move to independence, particularly when British counter-insurgency measures had the effect of alienating public opinion in the later stages of the war. The Second Dáil, which was elected in an uncontested election in 1921, contained a large number of fundamentalist republicans as a consequence. Michael Hayes, a pro-Treaty TD, later reflected that:

> The Second Dáil which was called upon to decide the Treaty issue was of an unusual character. Its members were all activists in a minority group which had obtained a sweeping majority vote. Few of them had any experience of either central or local government, or of the making of international agreements.[38]

After the Treaty was signed, the military and civilian wings of the Sinn Féin movement were split, the Catholic Church and the press now backed the

Treaty, and the third parties that contested the 1922 election also recommended abandoning the goal of the Republic, at least as an immediate objective. In response some of the anti-Treatyites resorted to the kind of repressive sanctions that they felt had galvanised public opinion behind them between 1919 and 1921. The wilder element smashed newspaper offices, prevented public meetings taking place, and intimidated opponents in the run up to the 1922 election. They rejected majority rule, 'by appealing to a theory of the electorate's expressed will being irrelevant and intimidated by various tyrannies, in particular, the apparatuses of thought control represented by the journalists and the clergy'.[39] De Valera, for example, later believed that the unity of the nationalist movement collapsed because the press, encouraged by the church, urged the independents to contest the pact election. In his view 'it was the interference of the Bishops that broke the unity of the Dáil and left us at sixes and sevens'.[40]

In short the Treaty split brought into the open the conflict between the conditional acceptance of electoral democracy espoused by Pearse and the reality that the nation was composed of different elements, each with its own agendas and interests. As has been analysed in the previous chapter, in the spring of 1922, having delayed the election until June, the Sinn Féin organisation then decided that it would field a joint panel of pro and anti-Treaty candidates for the election. Contests between Sinn Féin candidates would be kept to a minimum and the Treaty issue would not be discussed. A joint government would be formed afterwards. The Labour Party refused to be part of this government on the grounds that it was an independent party. Clause four of this electoral pact had allowed 'that every and any interest is free to go up and contest the election equally with the National Sinn Féin panel'. However, advertisements shortly appeared in the press stating that the national interest would be best served by voting for the Joint Panel candidates.[41] Furthermore, it was later alleged in the Dáil by a Labour candidate that 'many of the members sitting in these benches had revolvers and guns used against them by people who were party to that pact'.[42]

On the one hand the pact had seemed the only way of preventing the division over the Treaty culminating in civil war and of enabling an election to take place at all. On the other, Labour later complained that it was an agreement designed to make sure that 'the people would be given no opportunity of expressing any view except to return to power the two wings of the old party'.[43] In retrospect one reason why the pact fell apart was because it brought into the open the conflict between the two conceptions of democracy which existed in Ireland, one seeing elections as a means of demonstrating the national will, the other seeing them as a means of registering the preferences of a pluralist society. Michael Collins later reflected that:

The election was declared to be one in which the Treaty issue was not being decided. The people have chosen to declare otherwise. The Government made the Pact with the anti-Treaty party, believing that only by doing so could an election be held at all. The Pact appeared to muzzle the electorate. The Electors have not allowed it to muzzle them'.[44]

Table 7.2 **Changes in Dáil representation in constituencies where third party or independent candidates won seats in the pact election**

Constituency	1920			1922			+ −		
	Treaty	*Rep*	*3rd*	*Treaty*	*Rep*	*3rd*	*Treaty*	*Rep*	*3rd*
Carlow–Kilkenny	2	2	0	2	0	2	—	−2	+2
Cork Borough	2	2	0	2	1	1	—	−1	+1
Cork East and North-East	0	3	0	0	1	2	—	−2	+2
Cork Mid, North, South, South-East and West	4	4	0	3	2	3	−1	−2	+3
Dublin Mid	1	3	0	1	1	2	–	−2	+2
Dublin South	2	2	0	2	0	2	_	−2	+2
Dublin Co.	4	1	1	2	0	3	−2	−1	+2
Galway	4	3	0	4	2	1	—	−1	+1
Kildare Wicklow	1	4	0	1	1	3	—	−3	+3
Leix–Offaly	4	0	0	3	0	1	−1	—	+1
Longford Westmeath	3	1	0	2	1	1	−1	—	+1
Louth–Meath	4	1	0	3	1	1	−1	—	+1
National University	2	2	0	2	1	1	—	−1	+1
Tipperary, Mid, North and South	1	3	0	1	2	1	—	−1	+1
Waterford– Tipperary East	1	3	1	1	1	3	—	−2	+2
Wexford	0	3	1	0	1	3	—	−2	+2

Source: B. Walker, *Parliamentary Election Results in Ireland, 1801–1922* (1978), pp. 101–8.

The conflict between the two conceptions of democracy was rendered all the more dramatic because the third parties that emerged to contest the election were clearly two self-consciously interest-orientated parties, the

Labour Party and the Farmers' Party. A multi-party system represented far more of a threat to the anti-Treatyites than it did to the pro-Treaty candidates. It has often been suggested that the pact collapsed because the anti-Treatyites reneged on the promises to respect freedom of speech they made when signing the pact. Clearly the anti-Treatyites stood to lose more from a fair election than the pro-Treatyites. During negotiations over the pact it was pro-Treatyite delegates that argued that the country needed an election to renew the representative character of the Irish parliament and not merely to ratify the Treaty. It was significant that this argument originated on the pro-Treaty side since they proved to have least to fear from a free election.

Table 7.2 shows the changes in Dáil representation between 1921 and 1922 in those constituencies where third parties or independents won seats. The losers were usually anti-Treaty candidates. All in all, in the 16 constituencies in which third parties won seats, the republican side lost seats in 13, while the pro-Treatyites lost seats only in five. In total the republicans lost twenty-two seats while the pro-Treatyites lost six. The majority of anti-Treaty seats were lost to the Labour Party. Indeed Labour topped the poll in first preference votes in three constituencies, independent candidates topped the poll in two constituencies, while Farmers' candidates topped the poll in Cork East and North-East. In none of the sixteen constituencies did a republican candidate top the poll. The results in these constituencies are very important because anti-Treatyites would later claim that support for pro-Treaty candidates should be interpreted as support for the joint panel. However, the analysis offered here suggests that when offered a choice, the voters systematically voted against anti-Treaty panel candidates and not against pro-Treaty panel candidates. The republican position was thus undermined by the forces of electoral competition.

There was also a clear geographical pattern to these results. Independent candidates won seats in the urban constituencies of Cork and Dublin, as well as in the National University constituency, but not in rural constituencies. Farmers' Party victories were recorded in Carlow–Kilkenny, Cork Mid, North, South, South-East and West, County Dublin, Kildare–Wicklow, Waterford–Tipperary East, and Wexford. Overall they did not contest seats in the west of Ireland or in the border counties. Labour won 16 seats overall, six in the urban constituencies of Cork, Dublin and Galway, a total of five in the south-eastern constituencies of Carlow–Kilkenny, Waterford–Tipperary East and Wexford, and a total of five in the midlands constituencies of Kildare–Wicklow, Leix–Offaly, Longford Westmeath, and Louth–Meath. Labour's support base was both heavily eastern and urbanised, largely confined to the centre and heartland regions of Ireland. On the basis of this analysis one can argue that the degree of electoral competitiveness in 1922 was positively related to the degree of urbanisation. The anti-Treatyites were strong mainly in backward western constituencies which were politically underdeveloped. This fact reinforces the hypothesis that the presence of a relatively high division of labour in Irish society, combined with very strong pressures towards uniformity, lay behind the civil war conflict in 1922.

Since the main losers of the pact election were the anti-Treaty candidates, it was only a matter of time before the pro-Treatyites began to see the republican tactics since the Dáil vote on the Treaty as an attack on 'the people's rights'.[45] Once the anti-Treaty IRA seceded from the Ministry of Defence in March they had become dependent on raids and mutineering in order to finance themselves. This had a knock-on effect:

> The Wild West atmosphere was spread about by the gunmen at the bidding of leaders more culpable and a lot more foolish then themselves, and as a result of this the bonds of restraint common to civilised communities were torn asunder. Widespread brigandage made its appearance. Banks were robbed. Post Offices were raided. It was open to everyman to take what he could. Some took houses and land. Others more modest, only took motor cars.[46]

After the anti-Treatyite forces were defeated in conventional hostilities in August, they switched to guerrilla tactics designed to make the country ungovernable. This strategy only served alienate the public further from the anti-Treaty cause. The former Home Rule MP from Mallow, William O'Brien, recalled a meeting he had had with de Valera on 5 August 1922. O'Brien told de Valera that few people in his area were against the anti-Treatyites until they blew up the railway viaduct. De Valera replied that if that kind of thing went on much longer the public would begin to regard the anti-Treatyites as 'bandits'.[47] The government's perception of events had always had a social dimension to it and the nature of the anti-Treaty campaign after August only confirmed the veracity of this interpretation for those on the government benches. Cosgrave, who became Chairman of the Provisional Government in that month, declared 'that there is a state of woeful moral degradation abroad'.[48] The issues at stake were no longer purely political:

> What has got to be asserted in this country is not the mere term, the supremacy of parliament. It is the supremacy of the people's right to live their lives in peace, to possess whatever little they may have, to own a security that is the security of a free people, without any interruption by any armed despot with a revolver in his pocket or a bomb in his hand.[49]

The actions that had been taken to restore order were not for 'the mere formula of the supremacy of parliament' but 'a formula for the security of the people, or the security of their lives, and the value of their money in the country'.[50] It was a formula in other words for the preservation of moral individualism, parliamentarism, and with it, of the capitalist system.

As Garvin remarks, the possibility that the Free State army actually 'liberated' southern Ireland from the despotism of the anti-Treatyite IRA has never been discussed in Irish schoolbooks, principally because the losers in the civil war eventually ended up as the dominant political party in the state.[51] The Free State army did see itself as a liberator. For example an army report from Cavan for February 1923 reported little of note, 'if exception be made of the sack of the little town of Ballyconnell, the facts of which are now known all over the world – the defenceless people of which were robbed and murdered by the liberty-loving Irregular forces'.[52] Where the army was unable to establish its authority over local areas, anarchic conditions soon set in. For example, the evacuation of the military barracks in Tullow, Borris, and Bagnalstown, in County Carlow in February 1923, was soon followed by 'the activities of armed robbers who looted on a large scale, destroyed bridges, and felled trees across the roads'.[53] The urgent task for the military and the civic guard was thus the establishment of posts throughout the country and the demonstration that crimes would be met with resolute action. The army were in no doubt that such policies would meet with public approval even in areas, such as Cork East, where republican sympathies were strong:

> The situation may be summed up by saying that where the military and civic guard are in active occupation, matters are well and improve day by day – there follows first the passive attitude of the people, to be succeeded by the interested and helpful attitude. This is noticeable in small things – their obedience to the law as regards the Licensing Acts etc, and further by the assistance given the guards in their enquiries and prosecution in other cases.[54]

It follows, then, that the Free State authorities believed public support for the anti-Treaty cause was, to a considerable degree, the product of coercion. In July 1922 an official statement remarked that Waterford, Cork, Kerry, and Mayo, were in 'subjection' to the 'Irregulars' since the electoral result had shown that these counties were overwhelmingly in favour of the Treaty.[55] The following month Collins argued that the military defeat of his opponents in the areas in which they were strong was less important than the 'establishing of our forces in certain principal parts of that area with a view to shaking the domination held over the ordinary people by the Irregulars'. The people would thus be freed from their present 'cowed' position.[56] This type of analysis was extended to the 'Irregular rank and file', whom the Free State authorities believed had been 'duped' by their leaders. Richard Mulcahy remarked on 12 September that the 'Irregulars' were composed of three elements: 'people who may be classed as politicians; people who may be classed as honest soldiers, and people who may be classed as criminals'. In Mulcahy's view, the 'honest soldiers' had been 'misled', and were 'waiting for a word from the politicians that they are travelling the wrong road'.[57]

Even in those areas where hostility to the Free State was strongest, such as in Kerry, the Free State authorities still believed that the rank and file had been 'duped' by their leaders. One officer who visited Tralee Jail in late March 1923 remarked that the prisoners were 'mostly men who had been led astray and who really did not know what they were doing'.[58] Out in the field, the rank and file were generally 'sick of the business' and were 'held together only either by the personality and or intimidatory methods of their leaders'.[59] If public opinion in Kerry was hostile to the army, this could again be explained by the fact that the Irregulars had been able to shape perceptions of what was taking place outside the county. One army report described the malleability of public opinion in this way:

> On coming into actual contact with them the impression of hostility immediately evaporates, in fact the first impression was one of general friendliness – people seemed glad to have troops in their locality and treated them in most cases without reserve or suspicion . . . The actual feeling everywhere seemed to be a sense of genuine relief. The people had been living in complete isolation for months – their connection with the outside world had been cut off and their feelings of isolation had accentuated their fear of the Irregulars, and when our troops began to appear they were genuinely relieved . . . Inside this area the people lived completely at the mercy of the Irregulars, unaware of outside happenings, and depended on the Irregulars for information of outside events.[60]

It is difficult to judge the validity of this interpretation. The best indicator of public backing for the anti-Treatyites would be the first preference vote for republican candidates in the 1922 election, but this suffers from two flaws. Firstly, many of the republican candidates were returned in uncontested constituencies. Secondly, some of the vote for the pro-Treaty candidates can actually be interpreted as support for the joint panel, and not as an endorsement of the Treaty position at all. However, when you compare the results of the 1922 and the 1923 elections the distribution of electoral support for republican candidates follows a clear pattern.

I have again adapted Garvin's regional divisions of Irish society in the presentation of the electoral statistics in table 7.3. The regional means for the anti-Treaty share of the vote show clearly that the republican support base was strongest furthest away from Dublin, in the peripheral areas of Ireland. In the *centre* of Ireland, anti-Treaty support in 1922 averaged at around 16 per cent. In the *heartland* areas it just exceeded a quarter of all first preferences. In the *border periphery* anti-Treaty support averaged just under a third of all first

Table 7.3 **Mean percentage first preference support for anti-Treaty candidates in contested constituencies by region, 1922–23**

Region[1]	1922[2]	1923[3]	+ –
Centre[4]	16.23	17.47	+1.24
Heartland	25.39	24.00	–1.39
Border Periphery	32.81	28.06	–4.75
Western Periphery	32.8	40.26	+7.46

1   Since some constituencies were changed in 1923 and since regional boundaries and constituency boundaries do not always overlap, I have adopted the following categorisation.

Centre:
All Dublin constituencies plus Dublin University for both elections.

Heartland:
Carlow–Kilkenny, all Cork constituencies, Kildare–Wicklow, Leix–Offaly, Limerick City–Limerick East, Louth-Meath, Tipperary Mid, North and South, Waterford–Tipperary East and Wexford for 1922; Carlow–Kilkenny, all Cork constituencies, Kildare, Leix–Offaly, Limerick, Meath, Tipperary, Waterford, Wexford and Wicklow for 1923.

Border Periphery:
Cavan, Donegal, Longford–Westmeath and Monaghan for both elections; Leitrim–Roscommon North, Mayo South–Roscommon South and Sligo–Mayo East for 1922; Roscommon, Leitrim–Sligo and Louth for 1923.

Western Periphery:
Clare and Galway for both elections; Kerry Limerick West and Mayo North and West for 1922: Kerry, Mayo South and Mayo North for 1923.

2   The following constituencies were uncontested in 1922: Dublin University, Limerick City Limerick East, Donegal, Leitrim Roscommon North, Clare, Kerry Limerick West, Mayo North and West, Mayo South and Roscommon South.

3   Only the seats for Dublin University were uncontested in 1923.

4   I have not included figures for the National University.

Source: M. Gallagher, *Irish Elections 1922–44: Results and Analysis* (1993), pp. 1–54.

preferences, while in the *western periphery's* one contested seat the anti-Treaty vote was also just under a third. In 1923 the regional picture is rather similar, with the difference that the anti-Treaty mean in the *western periphery* where all elections were contested rises to a remarkable 40.26 per cent of the vote.

What about the figures for individual constituencies? Firstly, in the centre (Dublin), support for anti-Treatyite candidates was relatively low in both elections, seldom exceeding twenty per cent of first preferences. Excluding the National University as a Dublin constituency, support for anti-Treaty candidates varied between 0 to 19.9 per cent in 1922, and between 13.6 to 21.2 per cent in 1923. In the heartland, support for anti-Treaty Republicans was

higher, amounting to a quarter of the first preference vote in many constituencies, and reaching over forty per cent in areas of Cork and Tipperary in
1922. On the whole, support was higher in the southern agricultural countries
than in the midlands, but no clear pattern predominates. Support for anti-
Treaty candidates varied from 0 to 49.5 per cent in 1922 and from 16.9 to 30.7
in 1923. In the border periphery, support for Republican candidates seems to
average at around the quarter mark. In 1922 it varied from 0 to 56.4 per cent
and from 18.3 to 36.5 per cent in 1923. Lastly, in the western periphery support
for anti-Treaty candidates was very high. Many of these constituencies were
uncontested in 1922 but in 1923 it ranged from 33.5 to 45 per cent. It was
uniformly higher than practically anywhere else in Ireland in 1923, and anti-
Treatyites gained at least a third of the total first preference vote in practically
all the westerly constituencies in 1923. Only in this region did support for
anti-Treaty candidates rival that for government candidates.

A number of conclusions can be derived from this analysis. Firstly, support
for anti-Treaty candidates was nowhere negligible. Its national average of
around 20 per cent was a respectable figure for an anti-system party, if not for
a party whose military wing later claimed to be the legitimate government of
the country. If an exclusionary threshold of 10 per cent had existed at the
constituency level, as it often does for small parties at the national level, then
republican candidates in both elections would have exceeded this threshold in
every single constituency that they contested. This suggests that their cause
had a residue of hardcore support throughout the country. There was very
little dramatic variation, at the constituency level, in the level of support for
the anti-Treatyites between the two elections, even if their national first
preference vote increased in 1923. Secondly, strong anti-Treaty support existed
in two areas: in the west of Ireland, and in the southern 'Golden Vale' areas of
North and East Cork, Tipperary and Waterford. This distribution correlates
very well with areas where military opposition to the Free State was strongest
during the civil war, suggesting that the IRA had popular support in these areas.
Lastly, the figures for 1923 do little to reinforce the Provisional Government's
claim that the public in the south and west was 'cowed' into an anti-Treaty
attitude by the authoritarian tactics of the IRA. Overall support for the anti-
Treatyites was stronger in the 1923 election, a time when the IRA was disbanded, than in 1922. Furthermore, the anti-Treaty vote had less of a regional
profile in 1923 and had to some degree become standardised throughout the
country. In all the regions outside Dublin it averaged more than 23 per cent,
a remarkable figure considering that a great number of anti-Treaty candidates
were in prison or on the run.

It is more likely that popular support for anti-Treaty candidates in 1922
can be explained by social variables rather than by the intimidatory presence
of the IRA. The agricultural gradient running from the north-west to the

Table 7.4 **Numbers per thousand employed in agricultural occupations in 1926 by county**

Centre		*Border Periphery*	
Dublin Co. Borough	533	Cavan	749
Dublin Co.	10	Donegal	709
		Monaghan	685
Heartland		Leitrim	812
Carlow	334	Longford	634
Kilkenny	448	Sligo	705
Cork Co. Borough	11		
Cork Co East.	433	*Western Periphery*	
Cork Co. West	672	Galway	747
Kildare	127	Kerry	656
Wicklow	557	Clare	683
Laois	578	Mayo	801
Offaly	599	Roscommon	796
Limerick Co. Borough	20		
Limerick Co.	623		
Louth	733		
Meath	361		
Tipperary Co. N.R	613		
Tipperary Co. S.R.	534		
Westmeath	613		
Waterford Co. Borough	25		
Waterford Co.	579		
Wexford	563		

Source: Irish Free State Census 1926, table 3 (a), p. 15.

south-east of the country is obviously the most relevant. It was to the left of this line that opposition to the Free State was strong, while to the right of the line opposition to the Free State was weak. Garvin suggests that anti-Treaty support was strong in 'poorer and more remote areas' in 1923.[61] Table 7.4 shows the number of people employed in agricultural occupations per thousand by county in 1926. An analysis of these figures suggests that republican support was strongest in the western periphery where the vast number of people were involved in agriculture. In contrast, their support was weak where the economic structure was more diversified, as in most of the heartland of Ireland. The border counties, where anti-Treaty support was modest, are the only exception to this trend. Pyne notes that in 1923, 41 per cent of the anti-Treaty Sinn Féin party's seats came from the western area of the country, compared with 30 per cent of the Government's seats. Sinn Féin succeeded in getting a third or more of the poll in the five Connacht constituencies and in

Kerry and Clare. In all these areas the percentage of people living in urban areas was well below the national average. The party's share of the vote in the four counties with cities of 20,000 or more was below its national average.[62] In contrast Cumann na nGaedheal did well in urban constituencies, especially in Dublin. There is some connection between the rurality of the constituency and anti-Treaty support.

The analysis just provided supports the hypothesis that in areas where the division of labour was highest support for the Free State was strongest, while in areas where the division of labour was lowest support for the anti-Treaty sides was strongest. In addition, we have seen that support for anti-Treaty candidates was stronger in areas where the level of political competitiveness was low, and weak where it was high. In short, the Treaty split reflects differences in the division of labour throughout Irish society. In the east, south-east, and midlands there was a high division of labour, combined with little pressure toward uniformity, whereas in the west and south-west a low division of labour was combined with still strong pressures towards uniformity. Both Treaty positions then can be related to the type of social solidarity prevailing in different regions.

7.3   Solidarity, democracy and the state

The political orientations described by Garvin and Prager clearly belong to wider traditions of thinking about the state in Europe. Berki outlines what he sees as the 'two opposed philosophies of man as a member of a human community'.[63] *Transcendentalism* rests on the belief that man belongs primarily to a moral community which is ontologically prior to its members. Individuals are united together in pursuit of common and moral goals. The association of individuals has a public character to it, which 'expresses more than the aggregate of the interests of its members'.[64] The public interest delimits and defines the proper pursuits of individuals who form part of the community. Law is seen as the expression of the collective reason and moral purpose of the community. *Instrumentalism*, in contrast, assumes that man belongs primarily to an interest community. Association with a collectivity is accepted as a means of furthering individual interests and not primarily as an expression of moral feelings and aims. Membership of the community is conditional and based on consent. The association which results from the free association of members has no moral as opposed to legal personality: the collectivity is simply the sum of individual interests. 'Consequently the "authority" of the association derives solely from the rights of its members'.[65] Law is not seen as an expression of collective will, but as a means of maintaining rational agreement among the membership of the community.

As an unheroic philosophy of political behaviour, instrumentalism tends to be limited in its aspirations about human beings. In Ireland, acceptance of the Treaty was endorsed precisely in instrumental terms, even when acceptance meant a modification of previously held ambitions. Such a turnabout was justified in the name of the people's rights 'to regulate its development in accordance with hard military, economic, and political facts'.[66] Taken to extremes, the transcendental approach to politics will involve attempts to alter society radically since it assumes individuals will be moulded by collective purposes. It assumes that societies can be transformed by collective endeavour. This was reflected in the classic republican belief that the deaths of republicans in the civil war would reverse majority opinion on the Treaty and 'inspire the vast majority of our countrymen to fight until independence is achieved'.[67] In contrast, the instrumental approach will tend to reflect established social patterns and seek to protect the existing social fabric from disruption.

As each principle accepts that authority comes from the people, both can be considered democratic principles of statehood. The former sees democracy as a means of demonstrating the people's collective sovereignty, while the latter sees popular sovereignty not as the expression of a unified will, but as the result of a process of mutual readjustment between a collection of morally self-sufficient individuals. 'Transcendentalism, in other words, places more emphasis on "sovereignty", whereas instrumentalism accentuates the "contractual" basis of government.'[68] Analogously in Ireland the pro-Treatyites defended the Treaty as the choice of the majority, whereas for republicans such acceptance meant denying the sovereignty of the people – the general will – which under less constrained conditions would have resulted in a vote for a republic. The civil war clash can be seen then as a conflict between two conceptions of democracy, rooted in differing conceptions of popular sovereignty.

Berki suggests that the development of modern Europe has 'assumed an enduring pattern where variation can be usefully explained by the relative strength of state and society as institutions and as expressed through the relative position of predominance afforded to either of the two basic principles'.[69] Independent Ireland could be a case in which the predominance of society over the state was not the product of social evolution *per se*, but of a civil war in 1922. On the other hand, the manner in which the civil war involved an assertion of central state power raises some questions about the validity of such a judgement. From the very beginning of the civil war, the assertion of centralised authority over society was seen as the chief priority of the Provisional Government. Warning his colleagues of the tough times ahead, Kevin O'Shiel, a Provisional Government legal adviser, pointed out the lesson of recent political history, which was that practically every challenge against central authority 'has been overcome by prompt, effective, vigorous, and utterly ruthless action'. Specifically comparing the Irish situation with that of

Russia in 1917 and Germany in 1918, O'Shiel concluded that revolution succeeded where 'the hand that ruled was either unwilling or unable to strike at the challenge hard enough and effectively enough'. In what seems a curious choice, he believed the Provisional Government should model itself on the Red Government in Russia whose 'worldly power' he admired, and on the German Social Democrats who, like the Provisional Government *vis à vis* the Dáil departments, had been forced to crack down on the Workers' Councils by an external power.[70]

Durkheim's conception of the role of the state in a democratic system was an ambiguous one. On the one hand he accepted that the power of the state tended to increase as it became 'a prime institution concerned with the implementation and furtherance of individual rights'.[71] However, he also thought that the power of the state could be curtailed by the existence of secondary groups in society which intervene between the individual and the state. 'Thus that which makes the central power more or less absolute is the more or less radical absence of any countervailing force that is systematically organised with the intention of moderating that power'.[72] On the other hand, when faced with serious challenge to the social order the state had to react in a vigorous way: 'it is impossible for offences against the most fundamental collective sentiments to be tolerated without the disintegration of society, and it is necessary to combat them with the aid of the particularly energetic reaction which attaches to moral rules'.[73] In less developed societies such crime is interpreted as a religious transgression. This enables the 'absolutist' state to appropriate the religious quality of the moral reaction to legitimate the use of coercive power: 'offences against the state are treated as sacrilegious and hence to be violently repressed'.[74]

Durkheim did not discuss the possibility that this moral reaction could also be true of states in advanced societies. Certainly the ability of intermediary groups to limit the power of the state in the Irish civil war was very restricted.[75] For the first months of the civil war the Irish parliament was suspended; rigorous censorship was in operation later, and mass internment was introduced. The abuses of state power were numerous: 'making hostages of condemned men, tolerating murder by state forces, shooting unconvicted republican leaders as a deterrent, using civil war legislation and the army to quell social and industrial unrest'.[76] On 11 September 1922 Thomas Johnson, the leader of the Labour Party, remarked:

> Too many stories are coming to us from too many places to discount utterly the truth about the brutal treatment of prisoners; about the methods of terrorism and intimidation that are being carried out by the Government on the authority of the Government in the pursuit of their intention to vindicate the authority of parliament.[77]

Government policy raised two issues. In the first place, it led to the suspicion that the government was far more concerned with the protection of property rights than of rights *per se*, and that a crucial aspect of any democracy, the rights of individuals to be protected from the state, did not in fact exist during the civil war.[78] Secondly, it suggests that the Free State position was a statist one. The actions of the state may have been taken to defend a system of moral individualism, but they involved an extension of state power. As Cosgrave later put it, the 'supreme duty' of the Government was to provide the conditions in which people could live in peace and in which social progress was possible: 'an ordered state existence, respect for the laws of God and all authority derived from Him, come first among these conditions'.[79] For Durkheim too, a strong state was not antithetical to individual freedom: 'our moral individuality far from being antagonistic to the state, has on the contrary been the product of it' .[80]

The reaction of the Free State government to the anti-Treatyite campaign was distinctly one of moral outrage. When asked to reconsider a modified version of the electoral pact in April 1923, Cosgrave retorted:

> That means that you are asking that the people who want to burst up the present social fabric – the Communists – are to be allowed to get a constitutional position in the State. That the people who roast children, burst watermains, murder our men, will have to get a constitutional position in the state.[81]

In the Dáil debate on the necessity of civil war in September 1922, O'Higgins quoted a letter from a republican prisoner in which the prisoner looked forward with relish to the abduction of bank officials and railway clerks. This drew the comment: 'in that single document you have embodied the disintegration that is at present proceeding apace in the country, the moral disintegration'.[82] Another deputy suggested that the anti-Treaty campaign had 'extinguished the very moral principles that should be the basis of civilised society'.[83] Cosgrave himself saw a country beset with

> a moral desolation not merely in the ordinary acceptance of the term in which people think of dishonesty and disregard of individual rights, of reckless murder and general insecurity; but also the moral desolation in a blindly dishonest outlook and attitude towards the national position and the effect of the nation's Treaty of Peace.[84]

The civil war was a moral crisis for the government, which was itself not above impugning the motives of their opponents. An army report commented that the anti-Treatyites were supported by people who had in certain areas materially gained from the reign of the 'irregulars', and from those who were enabled to 'evade' their 'civic responsibilities' by the 'irregular' campaign, such as railway employees, post-office officials, and teachers.[85] This reaction suggests that the distinction in Durkheim's work between a society based on mechanical solidarity where social conformity is the result of a pervasive *conscience collective*, and a society based on organic solidarity where such a *conscience* is assumed to be lacking, is a false one. The existence of organic solidarity and of restitutive law 'cannot become wholly detached from the influence of the *conscience collective*'.[86] When defending the government's decision to introduce repressive legislation in 1931, Cosgrave stated that 'the whole work of this state is held up by a crowd of people who posture as nationalists, who pose as patriots, and who act in contravention of the law of the state, the law of God, and every law which any democratic State would set up'.[87] The only bulwarks against chaos were the Church and the State, and republicanism in the late 1920s aimed at 'the destruction of both'. In order to defend a system of moral individualism, or what Cosgrave later termed 'freedom without licence', the government felt that (*a*) a realisation by individuals of their responsibility to the state, and (*b*) adherence to Christian teaching, were both necessary.[88]

Clearly, in Cosgrave's thinking, 'a residuum of repressive law must continue to exist, regulating the moral codes necessary for the fulfilment of contracts, which is centred upon respect for the autonomy, dignity and freedom of the individual, i.e., moral individualism'.[89] An alliance between Church and state was thus necessary to counteract the moral decay in society. That need prompted Kevin O'Shiel to suggest in February 1923, that the pro-Treaty party

> link up therefore with some of the great class interests such as the Church or agriculture, that it should become in fact a Christian people's party to defend religion against the Atheist and the Freemason and property against the Bolshevik.[90]

This outlook formed the basis of the Cumann na Gaedheal 'law and order' position throughout the 1920s, and was the official reflection of the austere version of Catholicism that developed after the Famine.

The manner in which restitutive law comes to replace repressive law is not a unilinear process. Durkheim recognised that there were certain administrative and governmental functions 'where certain relationships are regulated by repressive law because of the special character marking the organ of the common consciousness and everything appertaining to it'.[91] When the authority of the state itself comes under attack, punishment takes on a symbolic aspect and is intended to bolster the authority of the central institutions. Thompson suggests that the relationship between social development and the preponderance of restitutive law is a curvilinear one. He sees a move from restitutive law in the most simple societies to repressive law in the early stages of the establishment of the state as it attempts to get a monopoly of the legitimate use of coercion, followed by a return to restitutive law when the State has become established and secure. Civil and restitutive law can predominate when there is a high degree of social solidarity and value integration, and criminal law can predominate when the emerging State has still to establish ideological hegemony.[92]

The Irish case confirms the truth of this hypothesis. Indeed, after the civil war Irish society became even more reliant on strong central institutions – the state, the Catholic Church, and the Gaelic Athletic Association – for the supply of social and moral cohesion.[93] An individualist and pluralist social order would not emerge for a very long time.

In short, the extent to which a transition from a society based on mechanical solidarity to one based on organic solidarity involves a change in the character of the moral codes regulating individual behaviour should not be overstated. In Ireland the philosophical basis for moral individualism lay in ultramontane Catholicism. The civil war gave expression to the two poles of Catholic political culture but it appears that both Garvin and Prager have made the Cumann na nGaedheal–Fine Gael tradition appear more liberal and more secular than it was. Moreover, there was much more common ground among the Sinn Féin elite than they are willing to admit. It was, according to Cosgrave, the objective of his government after the civil war not just to reassert the authority of the courts and confirm the supremacy of parliament, but to 'resuscitate the Gaelic spirit and the Gaelic civilisation for which we have been fighting through the ages and all but lost'.[94] For good or for bad, holy Ireland – the view of Irish society as a moral community – survived the Treaty split.

7.4 Conclusion

There is considerable empirical evidence to support the proposition that the civil war conflict in Ireland 'expresses the incomplete realisation of organic solidarity in the newly developing industrial order'.[95] Differences in the division of labour and differences in the degree of uniformity in various constituencies not only seem to provide part of the explanation for the civil war split, but also seem to be interrelated variables. During the 1922 election campaign there was a clear tension between the traditionally monolithic tendencies of Irish nationalism and the realities of social pluralism in a relatively advanced society. As a result, the transition to democracy contained two potentialities: the survival of a unified Sinn Féin party which would dominate parliamentary politics in the manner that the PRI dominated Mexican politics after the revolution, or the emergence of a multi-party system along the Finnish pattern, where the civil war did not wreck the pluralistic system that emerged in 1906. The collapse of the pact meant that the PRI outcome would not materialise in Ireland, while the course of 'civil war politics' afterwards ensured that genuine pluralism would not emerge either.

One merit of the Durkheimian interpretation is to relate the civil war conflict to the existence of rival and deep-rooted conceptions of the state which had developed in the century or so before independence. There are problems with the account of these conceptions given by Garvin and Prager, but their analysis helps dispel the illusion that Irish nationalism was somehow predicated on a monolithic set of philosophical assumptions about political life. The evidence suggests that these conceptions of the state can be related to wider orientations in European political culture and in that sense general principles, not merely local passions, were at stake in the Irish civil war. Yet the opposition between pro-and anti-Treatyites was not simply a conflict between proponents of a nation state proper versus supporters of a civic order composed of free and autonomous individuals, but also a conflict between those that saw the state principally in terms of political legitimacy and those that saw it primarily as a basis for social order. The tension between these two tendencies would persist into the 1930s and, as I argue later, it was Fianna Fáil's blending of the two, rather than the civil war, that resolved the issue in that decade.

Arguably, the relationship between democracy, social solidarity and the state was not adequately dealt with by Durkheim and is not sufficiently addressed by either Garvin or Prager. In Ireland both 'Free Staters' and republicans came to preside over the most centralised democratic state in western Europe, but the phenomenon of the state has not been seriously addressed by Irish social science. As late as 1941, Cosgrave remarked that there was 'a different conception of civic duty and civic responsibility' on the two sides of the Irish political spectrum.[96] We have today no clear idea of what these differences were based upon and where they originated. Clearly, the manner in which the state established its authority over Irish society forms a basic part in our understanding of the development of the Irish political system, but so far there has been very little analysis of the Irish state as a unitary actor. Unless we have some answers to these questions it is not likely that we will come to any real understanding of the nature of Irish social and political development since 1922.

Chapter 8

Reshaping the Free State: de Valera and the rise of constitutional republicanism

'Fianna Fáil was perhaps slightly constitutional, but only in the way that a woman two or three months into a pregnancy is slightly pregnant'.

Declan Kiberd, 'Eamon de Valera: the image and the achievement' in P. Hannan and
J. Gallagher (eds), *Taking the Long View: 70 Years of Fianna Fáil* (Dublin, 1996).

It was once a standard observation of political science that democratic regimes required strong leaders for the solution of particularly intractable political problems. The Italian Marxist, Antonio Gramsci, analysed situations in which 'Caesarist' political strategies were employed by political leaders to transform conflict-ridden systems into situations where the basic authority of the central government was not contested. Caesarism 'always expresses the particular solution in which a great personality is entrusted with the task of "arbitration" over a historico-political situation characterised by an equilibrium of forces headed toward catastrophe'.[1] Such a personality bases his claim to absolute authority on successful appeals for national salvation or unity. 'Caesarist' political strategies, and the patterns of authority associated with them, may not be confined to liberal democratic states, but they are employed to transform situations that fundamentally threaten regime stability – where civil conflict between the rival parties cannot result in the victory of one or other of the antagonists – into systems where normal political competition within the rules of the game can take place.

The analysis put forward in this chapter is based on the premise that the consolidation of a democratic system in inter-war Ireland was a classic case of what Linz and Stepan call democratic 're-equilibration'. Re-equilibration is defined by Linz as 'a political process that, after a crisis that has seriously threatened the continuity and stability of the basic democratic political mechanisms, results in their continued existence at the same or higher levels of democratic legitimacy, efficacy or effectiveness'.[2] The Irish case may be the classic instance of democratic re-equilibration this century, since the protagonists had only recently been involved in a civil war. The argument here is that de Valera's transformation of the Free State regime of the 1920s into the essentially republican regime of the late 1930s resulted in a political system with a higher degree of legitimacy and effectiveness than that under Cosgrave, without ever departing from democratic rules and methods. Re-equilibration involves a profound transformation of the existing regime, but not of democratic institutions.[3]

Inevitably, since the transformation of the Free State between 1932 and 1937 was undertaken by a leader with very clear ideas on the nature of Anglo-Irish relations, much of this chapter focuses on the role de Valera played in reconciling republicans to the new state. Although Fianna Fáil's entry into the Dáil in 1927 has been seen as a recognition of the legitimacy of the Free State parliament, and therefore as the defining moment in the process of consolidation, the situation was far more complicated at the time. Between 1926 and 1937 Fianna Fáil pursued a legitimising strategy, a stance which not only implies that the Free State was lacking legitimacy in their eyes, but which was also based on the assumption that the majority of anti-Treaty republicans would not come to accept the Irish state until the Treaty settlement had been revised. Since there was no guarantee in 1927, or indeed in 1932, that the British government would accept such changes to the Treaty, the constitutional republican project remained essentially an open-ended and highly contingent one. Ultimately, it was a combination of circumstances – the challenge posed by the Blueshirts in 1933, a thaw in Anglo-Irish relations in 1935, and the electoral failure of the opposition – that enabled Fianna Fáil to finally complete the transition from the politics of protest to the politics of government. This remarkable conversion took about ten years.

8.1   The re-equilibration model

The factors allowing re-equilibration to take place depend, according to Linz, on a 'unique constellation of factors'.[4] Linz's model is based on his analysis of de Gaulle's role in the transition from the Fourth to the Fifth Republic in France, but the conditions he outlines are broadly comparable with those that existed in inter-war Ireland. Inevitably, since re-equilibration involves a dynamic re-arrangement of the patterns of elite competition, it is necessary to concentrate on elite political strategies as the main variable in the process. In Linz's view, re-equilibration originates in a leadership outside a regime but one that is acceptable to many within it. At the same time, this new leadership is capable of bringing back into the regime many of its erstwhile challengers and isolating its most extreme opponents. For re-equilibration to occur, the new leadership must be committed to legitimising the regime by democratic means and to preserving democratic institutions once in power. Finally, re-equilibration occurs in the presence of an electorate that is willing to approve of and trust in the new leadership's capacity to solve the initial insoluble problem of the regime. Democratic change is approved of by the electorate, passively or actively.[5]

These conditions apply to independent Ireland in the inter-war era. The re-equilibration process saw a new political leadership, Fianna Fáil, emerge from the embers of the civil war. The party proved instrumental in bringing back into the political system many of those who remained hostile to the existence of the Free State as a result of the provisions of the Anglo-Irish Treaty of 1921 and the resulting civil war. What was crucial in Ireland was that Fianna Fáil proved capable of securing the tolerance of their former civil war enemies in Cumann na nGaedheal after 1926, while at the same time isolating those who remained doggedly hostile to the existence of the Free State. After 1932, not only was the Fianna Fáil party able to engineer a solution to the Treaty divide that was broadly acceptable to Irish political opinion, but in the process they also managed to marginalise those who were most hostile, not only to the Treaty, but arguably to the system itself – the anti-Treaty IRA.

Re-equilibration can be conceived of as a game involving strategic inter-actions between three types of political actor: those loyal to the regime, those semi-loyal to it, and those disloyal to the regime. For re-equilibration to succeed, those loyal to the regime have to be satisfied that an attitude of semi-loyalty to the regime on the part of the civil war losers is sufficient reason to tolerate the semi-loyal opposition, while those who are semi-loyal to the regime have to become more powerful or more pivotal in the system than those that remain basically disloyal. In other words, 'the responsible opposition' has to reposition itself. Its task becomes not so different from that of democratic opposition parties in authoritarian regimes; it is 'to change the relations among all the component parts of the non-democratic regime in such a way as to weaken the regime while simultaneously improving the conditions not just for regime change but specifically for democratisation'.[6] The role of the semi-loyal opposition is thus the independent variable in the re-equilibration process. The manner in which it consciously alters perceptions of what is feasible in a political system creates the possibility for re-equilibration and thus for a consolidation based on changeover. For this reason the bulk of this chapter is concerned with the repositioning of the anti-Treaty opposition to the Free State between 1923 and 1932.

8.2   The emergence of Fianna Fáil

During the civil war, opposition to the Free State consisted of four over-lapping elements:

(1) The rank and file of the IRA who remained largely loyal both to the Second Dáil and to their own Executive.

(2) Anti-Treaty TDs who regarded the existence of the Free State parliament as a usurpation and supported the republican government established in October 1922. After the war, a republican Dáil, *Comháirle na dTeachtai*, was formed to assist this government in its work.

(3) Those elements of Irish civil society that were republican in sympathy but which refused to take sides in the civil war. The most important such group was the Neutral IRA Association, which claimed a membership of over 25,000. As the war continued, its leaders became alienated from the Cosgrave government and ultimately considered forming their own republican party in the spring of 1923.[7]

(4) The section of the electorate that supported the anti-Treaty side. While effective military opposition to the Free State was concentrated geo-graphically, the anti-Treatyites retained a hard core of electoral support throughout the country.

The fact that the republicans lacked the support of the majority of the people during the civil war was recognised by de Valera as their chief weakness:

> If the republicans stand aside and let the Treaty come into force, it means acquiescence in the abandonment of the national sovereignty and in the partition of the country – a surrender of the ideals for which the sacrifices of the past few years were deliberately made and the sufferings of these years consciously endured. If the republicans do not stand aside, and they must resist, and resistance means just this civil war and armed opposition to what is, as I have said, the desire of the majority of the people. For republicans the choice is therefore between a heartbreaking surrender of what they have repeatedly proved was dearer to them than life and the repudiation of what they recognise to be the basis of all order in government and the keystone of democracy – majority rule.[8]

The way out of this dilemma was to win majority electoral support for the anti-Treaty position. De Valera attributed the marginalisation of the republican position in 1922 to the fact that the republicans had lost control of their political party during the War of Independence:

> If members of the IRA, who were also members of Sinn Féin clubs had remained active members and kept the organisation imbued with the proper Republican spirit and outlook, the present struggle would probably never be taking place. It was because the rank and file of the organisation fell into weak hands, and so the way was prepared for the events which led to civil war.[9]

The reform of Sinn Féin into an effective electoral machine accordingly became de Valera's most pressing objective during the civil war. Although the anti-Treaty IRA would provide the basis on which he hoped to revive the party, it is also clear that de Valera intended to move them away from the militant republicanism that saw its heyday under the IRA Executive during the civil war. De Valera saw in the pro-Treatyite's decision in December 1922 to form their own party, Cumann na nGaedheal, an opportunity to relaunch Sinn Féin as a party which would fulfil the need for 'a broadly national organisation which will embrace all who put the cause of national independence and general national interests above all sectional or party interests'. In the spring of 1923, the concentration of anti-Treaty prisoners in jails and internment camps also provided 'a wonderful opportunity for political discussion and reorganisation'.[10] However, de Valera wanted to exclude those who were closely involved with the military campaign from the Sinn Féin reorganising committee. Their presence might serve as a pretext for harassment from the authorities, but it 'might also frighten off those we wish to attract into the organisation'.[11]

De Valera's own vision for the future of Sinn Féin was quite clear. The party was attractive because:

> it gave an opportunity for coming back to many who may now wish to do so. We must not close the door on these. Our aim is not to make a close preserve for ourselves, but to win the majority of the people again. I understand the difficulties but we must teach our people to be broad in this matter.[12]

What practical steps would achieve the twin objectives of harnessing militant opposition to the Free State behind a party that would be sufficiently broad to appeal to a wide strand of nationalist opinion? In the first place the name Sinn Féin was retained. Attempts to have the party rename itself the Irish Republican Political Organisation were resisted by de Valera, who insisted that 'we wish to organise not merely republican opinion strictly so-called, but what might be called "nationalist" or "independence" opinion in general'.[13] The Cumann na Poblachta party founded in January 1922 would remain in existence for those who would think that a revamped Sinn Féin party would be 'too broad' for them, and who would 'prefer accordingly to stick to the word Republic'.[14] Secondly, members of Sinn Féin would now have to declare their allegiance to the constitution adopted at the Sinn Féin Ard Fheis of 1917, so as to exclude those who stood for something less than the original demand for complete independence, as well as those who were willing to take the oath to the British crown.[15] Thirdly, IRA units were instructed to assist actively in the efforts at reorganising the party. IRA officers were to oversee the formation of Sinn Féin clubs in brigade areas and to encourage civilian supporters to join. It was stressed to them that the poor showing of the anti-Treaty side in the civil war was due to the fact 'that our civilian supporters were not organised to assist us'.[16] Lastly, a particular stress was put on electoral organisation. In this the demobilised IRA was again to play a central role. Company OCs were instructed to furnish reports on the state of local electoral registers as a means of estimating the likely first preference support for republican candidates in the coming election, and as a means of ensuring that the registers were sufficiently up to date.[17]

The 1923 election presented Cumann na nGaedheal with an opportunity to win public approval for its prosecution of the civil war, and every effort was made by anti-Treatyites to ensure that the election was contested. A highly militarised atmosphere continued to prevail and the authorities persisted in harassing republican candidates. As many Sinn Féin candidates were now imprisoned or on the run, 64 of the party's 85 candidates were unable to address their constituents during the campaign.[18] Sinn Féin's level of electoral organisation for this election was rudimentary and the party was derided as 'the women and childers party' by their opponents on account of the absence of males from the hustings. Nevertheless, the anti-Treatyites still received approximately a quarter of all first preference votes in the election, an indication that 'the sympathy of a strong minority of the population' remained with them.[19]

Publicly, de Valera continued to deny the legitimacy of the Free State, but did so on the basis of a political philosophy that was avowedly nationalist rather than republican. The problem was that the subtle distinctions apparent in his own political discourse were lost on many of his colleagues. The new Sinn Féin party proved to be very much a fundamentalist republican party resembling other contemporary political parties only in name. It saw itself as a national movement, not as a party committed to the representation of specific interests. Sticking to a strict abstentionist policy, the party also tried to keep its supporters as isolated as possible from the influence of the Free State. According to Pyne:

> With its own embryo executive, legislature, and judicial system, with the tacit support of the IRA and by the provision of economic, educational, and social

facilities for its members, the party was in fact attempting to duplicate, in so far as its resources permitted, many of the functions of the state.[20]

The party's elected TDs continued to attend their own Dáil and the republican government founded during the civil war still claimed *de jure* authority over the whole island. Should the party have gained a majority of support at the polls, these embryonic institutions would have become the official institutions of the Irish state.

Post-civil war anti-Treaty republicanism was articulated then, not in the context of a competitive party system, but rather in that of an underground movement aiming to replace the existing state apparatus with one of its own. Sinn Féin had been initially successful in attracting members, funds and votes, but if election results were to be believed, there was little prospect that the party would gain the majority that it needed to make its policy a success. The party's poor showing in a by-election in 1925 apparently convinced de Valera finally of the need to abandon the abstentionist policy.[21] Given that a decline in the party's fortunes was apparent from almost every indicator, it was not surprising that 'various elements within the republican movement began to question the party's performance and the efficacy of its policies'.[22] Mounting pressure for a reassessment of Sinn Féin's political strategy led to open signs of division within the republican movement. On the one hand, hardliners proposed that the role of the IRA within the movement be strengthened. The IRA feared that discussions over the abstentionist policy would split its ranks and, at its first post-civil war convention in 1925, it was decided that the IRA would withdraw its allegiance to the republican government and vest control of the organisation solely in its army council. The republican movement, which had been formally united since the establishment of a republican government in October 1922, was again divided into a political and a military wing.[23] At the first meeting of the new army council it was decided:

> That no members of the army council or GHQ Staff shall hold himself free to enter the parliament of 'Northern' or 'Southern' Ireland, or advocate the entrance of these bodies with or without the Oath of allegiance. Individual volunteers, as citizens, are free to express their views on political questions, provided that no such issues shall arise at Parades or staff or Council Meetings.[24]

On the other hand there was increased debate about the wisdom of the abstentionist policy among the politicians. An intelligence report on an 'irregular' convention held in June 1925 suggested that the majority of the republican TDs favoured entering the Dáil and would mount a publicity campaign against the oath to that end.[25] In December 1925, Frank Aiken, former Chief of Staff of the IRA, outlined the logic of their position to the new army council:

> It is, I maintain, an honourable policy to use the powers which the Free State or Six County governments possess, in order to achieve the independence of our country, provided we don't have to admit their legitimacy by any oath or declaration or by any other way whatsoever, and that we maintain openly that our object is to establish a lawful government for the Republic. I haven't the slightest sympathy in the world with people who would declare now that they will not agree to that policy and who would, when our present policy fails, either take oaths or declarations of allegiance themselves to these bodies or vote for others who would; neither have I much sympathy with people who would stake all the chances of national success in our generation on the extremely remote possibility of a coup d'état.[26]

In a series of newspaper articles between September 1925 and January 1926, Seán Lemass, the Minister of Defence in the republican government, argued the case for a fundamental reappraisal of Sinn Féin's policy. He stressed in particular the need to concentrate on a single achievable political objective, such as the abolition of the oath.[27] The articles caused considerable discussion within the movement, a debate which was intensified by the furore caused by the Free State's acceptance of the findings of the British government's Boundary Commission, signed on 3 December 1925. It had initially been hoped that the Commission would redraw the boundaries of the state to the advantage of Irish nationalists. Instead, the Commission's report actually recommended that the Free State cede some of its territory in Donegal to the northern parliament. The boundary crisis led to Clann Éireann, a splinter group, emerging from within the government's ranks. Labour tried to persuade Sinn Féin to take their seats in the Dáil for the vote on the Commission but was unsuccessful. A combined opposition, including Sinn Féin, would have been able to outvote the Cumann na nGaedheal government, but with Sinn Féin outside the Dáil, there was little hope of that happening. In the long run, however, the boundary crisis 'impressed upon de Valera and his associates the urgency of arriving at a decision, one way or the other, on the subject of a new policy'.[28]

On 6 January 1926 de Valera publicly announced his willingness to enter the Free State parliament if the oath to the British crown were removed. De Valera hoped to renew the fortunes of Sinn Féin by forcing a confrontation with the government on the question of the oath. The previous ambitions of the party had been 'too high and too sweeping'. The oath, on the other hand, was 'a definite objective within reasonable striking distance', and if he could move the people to smash it, 'I shall have them on the march again, and once moving, and having tasted victory, further advances will be possible'.[29] A resolution was circulated to all the branches of Sinn Féin proposing that if the admission oaths to the southern and northern parliaments were removed, 'it becomes a question not of principle but of policy whether or not republican representatives should attend these assemblies'.[30] The resolution was debated by an Ard-Fheis of Sinn Féin held in Dublin on 9 March 1926. A rival resolution, declaring that to attend any 'usurping legislature' would be inconsistent with 'the fundamental principles of Sinn Féin', was carried by a vote of 223 to 218. As a result, on 11 March de Valera resigned as President of Sinn Féin. His policy also divided Comhairle na dTeachtai which met on 28 March to discuss de Valera's resolution. The body split into two halves of equal sides. Defeated by a majority of one, de Valera then tendered his resignation as President of the Republic. After a joint committee failed to resolve the differences between the two sides over the abstentionist issue, the two wings of Sinn Féin agreed to split. Those delegates that supported de Valera's motion, a large minority, became part of 'Fianna Fáil: the Republican Party'.

8.3   Fianna Fáil in opposition

Fianna Fáil was founded on 16 May 1926 at La Scala Theatre, Dublin. Its programme was:

(1) Securing the political independence of a united Ireland as a republic.
(2) The restoration of the Irish language and the development of a native Irish culture.
(3) The development of a social system in which, as far as possible, equal opportunity will be afforded to every Irish citizen to live a noble and useful Christian life.
(4) The distribution of the land of Ireland so as to get the greatest number possible of Irish families rooted in the soil of Ireland.
(5) The making of Ireland an economic unit, as self-contained and self-sufficient as possible – with a proper balance between agriculture and the other essential industries.[31]

Long-term ambitions aside, the more immediate question facing de Valera was whether Fianna Fáil would take their seats in the Dáil. He hoped that by concentrating his attack on the oath he would expose 'England's ultimate control' of the situation and 'smash' the Treaty at the next election.[32] These words were picked upon by the press to suggest that de Valera wished 'to obtain power to smash the Treaty and plunge the country into war with England', but de Valera restated that Fianna Fáil were out to use 'none but constitutional means to reassert the sovereign independence of Ireland'. He substituted the word 'rescind' for 'smash', and argued that his policy of 'rescinding' the Treaty, 'complete or in its vital objectionable clauses', was in keeping with either a true republican or an 'honest' Free State outlook.[33]

In the run up to the June 1927 election, representations were made by the army council of the IRA proposing co-operation between 'all republican bodies' for the purpose of defeating the Cosgrave government.[34] Their strategy was based on the proposal that Sinn Féin would not 'insist on the immediate proclamation of the Republic should a majority be secured', and Fianna Fáil would agree 'not to enter the Free State legislature as a minority party'. The IRA leadership also proposed that a national board be established to approve anti-Treaty candidates and election addresses. In the event of a Fianna Fáil victory, the Free State army would be disbanded and disarmed while the army council of the IRA would become the army council of the Minister of Defence.[35] In the discussions which took place on 26 April 1927, Fianna Fáil were 'unwilling to agree that its candidates would guarantee not to enter if returned in a minority, even if the oath were removed'.[36] After the IRA's proposals were unanimously rejected by the national executive of Fianna Fáil, de Valera was approached personally by the IRA, but replied that he was in complete agreement with the views of his executive.[37] Fianna Fáil would fight the election alone and were committed to ending their abstentionist policy under the right circumstances.

In the election Fianna Fáil came close to equalling the government's share of seats, gaining 44 as opposed to Cumann na nGaedheal's 47 seats. On 23 June Fianna Fáil arrived at the Dáil to take their seats, but were prevented from doing so as long as they refused to take the oath. De Valera then turned to article 48 of the 1922 constitution, which allowed for referenda on constitutional questions if a petition signed by not fewer than 75,000 signatures were presented to the government. 'There was very little likelihood of the Irish public voting to retain a vote of allegiance to the British Crown'.[38] However, the assassination of Kevin O'Higgins on 10 July led to a dramatic change in government policy. The government introduced a bill requiring electoral candidates to promise in advance to comply with the oath. At a stroke, the whole basis of the abstentionist policy was destroyed. De Valera had already publicly rejected the idea that he would pledge himself 'in terms that appear to me to have no meaning'.[39] However, along with his party's TDs, de Valera decided to take the oath, albeit as an 'empty formula', and enter the Dáil, where Fianna Fáil became the largest opposition party.

The impact of Fianna Fáil's entry into the Dáil on Sinn Féin proved to be devastating. Sinn Féin had been able to put forward only 15 candidates for the June 1927 election as opposed to Fianna Fáil's 87.[40] Only five were elected. Sinn Féin were unable to put any candidates forward for the September 1927 election. Those who had left to form Fianna Fáil initially continued to attend the republican Dáil, although de Valera had resigned as President of the Republic. After entering the Free State parliament, their continued attendance became impossible. When the republican Dáil met on 11 December 1927, only half of those who had attended the previous year were invited to attend, as the other half had attended the Free State parliament. As a result the republican Dáil was reduced from its original strength of 128 in 1922 to a mere twenty. Moreover, the number of affiliated Sinn Féin Cumainn in 1927 was 87 compared to a figure of 232 for the year 1926.[41] There seemed little future for the party. The new President of the republican Dáil, Art O'Connor, remarked that:

> we are in a very difficult position since the Army decided to withdraw its allegiance in November 1925 – so that as a Government we were left without the physical force to carry out any orders or decrees we might be seeking to enforce with a strong hand, and with the departure of Fianna Fáil from the Dáil as a moral force we are greatly weakened, and the fact that a great many people who call themselves republicans do not give us any allegiance or support of any description is undoubtedly a great source of moral weakness to us.[42]

Not surprisingly, attitudes within Sinn Féin towards Fianna Fáil were often bitter: one speaker at their Ard Fheis in December 1927 demanded that Fianna Fáil candidates return the Sinn Féin election deposits that helped get them elected.[43] Yet between 1927 and 1932 it was difficult for Sinn Féin's leadership to stop its members participating in elections on behalf of Fianna Fáil. Some Sinn Féin politicians still invited Fianna Fáil politicians to speak on the same platforms and many members and supporters who initially remained loyal to Sinn Féin later joined Fianna Fáil, 'attracted by its dynamism and the political acumen of its leaders'.[44] Indeed it was later maintained that some IRA leaders who had opposed Fianna Fáil's policy before 1927 subsequently ordered their members to vote for Fianna Fáil even though the oath had not been removed.[45] So great was the tendency to drift, that it was proposed at Sinn Féin's Ard-Fheis in December 1930 that party members be forbidden to have contact 'for any purposes whatsoever' with those who had taken an oath of allegiance.[46]

Fianna Fáil was more than ever caught up in the logic of electoral politics. The results of the general election of June 1927 had left the balance of power in the hands of the smaller parties. Cosgrave formed a minority administration. A coalition of Labour and the National League, with Fianna Fáil backbench support, was proposed during the summer. De Valera indicated that if the recent Public Safety Bill were overturned and the oath removed by the would-be coalition, Fianna Fáil would not make an issue of constitutional questions during the life of the next Dáil.[47] With Labour and the National League now sharing a policy of appeasement towards the republican opposition, an alternative to the Cosgrave administration existed for the first time. However, on 10 August 1927 Cosgrave survived a no-confidence vote in the Dáil by one vote. Nevertheless, Fianna Fáil's performance at the resulting snap election of September 1927, when it lost not a single seat and increased its share from 44 to 57 seats, proved a vindication of 'the new departure'.[48]

Since 1922 the political life of the Free State had been polarised over the question of the Treaty. It was opposition to the Treaty, more specifically to the oath, that led Sinn Féin to abstain from the Dáil, and to deny the legitimacy of the Free State. The insufficiently nationalist policy of Cumann na nGaedheal also led to three splinter parties emerging from within its ranks between 1923 and 1927, and left the Fianna Fáil party in the position of being a semi-loyal party that shared more with the disloyal IRA than with those parties that supported the Free State. Cumann na nGaedheal's policy over the Treaty was to hope that improvements in Commonwealth relations would compensate for their lack of unilateral action over the Treaty: in 1927 Kevin O'Higgins told a meeting in Carlow that his government 'made no claim to be able to produce a republic from the hat of the Treaty'.[49] The Treaty was what Linz calls 'an insoluble problem', since the instability associated with it could not be alleviated by any coalition of forces for whom loyalty to the Free State took precedence over their preferred solutions to the problem. Moreover, the Treaty issue was a regime-threatening one: since the parties supporting the regime could not compromise on a solution, the possibility existed that one of them would attempt a solution with the support of the forces that were perceived as disloyal by the other parties, thus leading to a polarisation of the overall political situation. Again the essence of an insoluble political problem is that a solution acceptable to a majority of the regime-supporting parties cannot be found.[50]

A very different scenario unfolded once Fianna Fáil split from Sinn Féin and entered the Dáil. Instead of attempting to mobilise opposition to the Free State by relying on the promise of direct action by the IRA, Fianna Fáil almost managed to form a reformist alliance with the small parties that were hostile to the government's coercive policies. In the summer of 1927 a potential majority of the parties was committed to an alternative solution to the Treaty issue without relying on the support of the disloyal opposition. The insoluble problem had suddenly become soluble. This was an indication that the middle ground in the Irish political system was surprisingly malleable. As it was, the coalition government failed to materialise; if it had, it would surely have altered the subsequent pattern of Irish political development. A realigning coalition, where 'one or more segments on one side of the political divide become convinced that a different set of alliances, with groups on the other side, would be a more efficacious route to their distinctive objectives', is one of four ways identified by Lustick which allow insoluble issues to be over-come.[51] Pure chance determined that it would not be tried in the Irish case.

The failure of Fianna Fáil to replace the Cosgrave government did not force them back into the republican Dáil. On 22 August 1927 de Valera told an audience in Blackrock that:

> If we are to make any progress in the conditions in which we actually find ourselves, and not have one section of our people constantly hampering and fouling another section, there must be one unchallenged directing head to deter-mine national policy at every instant, and one unified machinery under that head for putting the policy into execution. That directing head can only be the body of the elected representatives of the people meeting together and arriving at a decision by majority rule.[52]

On the other hand, Fianna Fáil's attitude to the Free State was not free of ambiguity. From republicans they drew the criticism that their entry into the Free State parliament 'would stabilise British rule in Ireland'.[53] From their opponents they drew the criticism that they secretly wanted to destroy the Free State. De Valera told his opponents on the government benches:

> I still hold that your right to be regarded as the legitimate government of this country is faulty, that this House itself is faulty. You have secured a de facto position. Very well, there must be somebody in charge to keep order in the community and by virtue of your de facto position you are the only people who are in a position to do it. But as to whether you have come by that position legitimately or not, I say you have not come to that position legitimately. You brought off a *coup d'état* in the summer of 1922.[54]

However, de Valera also said he hoped to 'broaden and widen' the Free State parliament so that it would become 'the sovereign national assembly of the Irish nation'. In addition, a Fianna Fáil government would not stand for a policy of removing officials from positions of authority, but would assume that 'those who took service in the Free State did it believing they were right'.[55] Moreover, Fianna Fáil TDs were encouraged by the leadership to adopt a constructive attitude towards the Free State parliament and were told not to oppose the government merely for opposition's sake, but to do so only when the party had constructive criticism to make. De Valera told the delegates at the party's third Ard Fheis in 1928 to:

> Please remember that we are not in the same position as Parnell and his Party were. Over there in England, to disrupt the whole machinery was the obvious tactics; but in our case there would be reactions by the people which we could not face.[56]

Such steps as Fianna Fáil would take to undermine the Treaty settlement would only be taken in consultation with Irish public opinion. Pursuing that course de Valera again attempted to force the government to hold a referendum on the oath, but was prevented from doing so when the Cosgrave government removed the provision for referenda from the constitution. This reaction emphasised again to Fianna Fáil the necessity of undermining the Treaty settlement with the machinery of the state at its disposal rather than from the opposition benches. On the other hand, Fianna Fáil's years in opposition allowed the party to develop a detailed range of policies they could offer as an alternative to those of the Cosgrave government. Where the Cosgrave governments were sparing in their attitude to public expenditure, Fianna Fáil were almost Keynesian in their attitude to state intervention in the economy. Where Cumann na nGaedheal were in favour of free trade, Fianna Fáil believed in economic protectionism. Where Cumann na nGaedheal were exponents of tough law and order policies, Fianna Fáil were critical of attempts to force republicans into allegiance to the Free State. Indeed, Fianna Fáil saw themselves as spokesmen for the whole republican opposition, including the IRA. In power they would set aside forever the government's proposed Public Safety Bill, which, if passed, 'would one day deluge Ireland with the blood of some of its noblest men', according to one Fianna Fáil spokesman.[57] Fianna Fáil remained critical of attempts to force republicans into a position of allegiance to the Free State, which, it argued, only led to an increase in violent opposition. De Valera's view was that:

> If you deny people who are animated with honest motives, peaceful ways of doing it, you are throwing them back upon violent ways of doing it. Once they are denied the peaceful way they will get support for the violent way that they would never get otherwise. There is no use in my preaching that doctrine to the Executive Council. The Executive Council only know one way – the way of the big stick.[58]

What added to the normal process of political polarisation these divergences gave rise to was the government's perception that the Fianna Fáil programme was part of 'a widely organised conspiracy to overthrow by force the government of the state'.[59] Two politically motivated murders took place in 1929, three in 1931. A new left-wing organisation Saor Éire was established in 1931, which, government sources anticipated, would supersede Sinn Féin in winning the allegiance of the IRA.[60] This led the government to introduce amendment 17 to the constitution on 17 October 1931 allowing for the establishment of a five-man military tribunal with sweeping powers including the death penalty. The Executive Council was also empowered to declare organisations unlawful. On 20 October 1931 the IRA and ten other organisations were declared proscribed organisations. Of the radical organisations in the state, only Sinn Féin remained legal. Five seditious publications were also declared illegal by the Military Tribunal. [61]

As part of its electoral strategy for the 1932 election, the Cosgrave government chose to associate the Fianna Fáil party with this 'conspiracy' by suggesting that a Fianna Fáil government would not be able to control the gunmen. It emphasised the 'crypto-socialist' and 'slightly constitutional' character of Fianna Fáil.[62] During the election campaign one Cumann na nGaedheal candidate argued that if a Fianna Fáil government was elected, its leadership would not be able to control the 'bullies' and 'gunmen' who controlled the party, and the country would accordingly be driven back to the horrors of the civil war.[63] Eoin O'Duffy, head of the Gardai, believed that by acting as the spokesmen for radical movements Fianna Fáil were also undermining the loyalty of the average voter to the government:

> The plain man in the street is unable to see wherein those who have elected to continue the war are less justified than those who elected after a time to abandon it and are now not unlikely to secure no less unquestionable a tribute of public approval than that of being entrusted with the government of the country.[64]

While denying the allegations, Fianna Fáil opposed the government's introduction of the Public Safety Act in 1931 and demanded that republican prisoners be released from Irish jails. They also sought a majority mandate from the people to remove the oath. In both these policies Fianna Fáil undoubtedly received the support of local brigades of the IRA as well as the grudging approval of other republican associations. An IRA directive, taken just before the 1932 election, allowed IRA members to work and vote in elections and many did so in support of Fianna Fáil. The IRA army council denied that this was part of a deliberate change of policy, but it arose from the fact 'that hatred against the coercionist regime was so intense the Volunteers could not be restrained from working against their candidates'.[65]

Fianna Fáil approached the election cautiously, and were careful to make sure the party's public pronouncements left the opposition in no doubt that they were committed to a reformist path. In their 1932 election manifesto Fianna Fáil assured the electorate that under their government:

> All citizens shall be treated as equal before the law, and the individual will be protected in his person and his property with all the resources at the government's command. Ordinarily such promises would not be necessary. Apprehensions, however, have been aroused and it is necessary to allay them. We may add that we have no leanings towards Communism and no belief in Communist doctrines.[66]

The results of the 1932 election did little to vindicate the government's scare tactics. As Fanning remarks, the 'red scare' was far less effective in 1932, after

Fianna Fáil had spent five years in the Dáil as the main opposition party, than it would have been in 1927.[67] In the election Fianna Fáil emerged as the largest party, securing 44.5 per cent of the first preference support, higher than Cumann na nGaedheal ever achieved, even in 1923.[68] All the other parties lost support. The Labour Party enabled Fianna Fáil to form a minority government, once Fianna Fáil had promised that it would introduce some of Labour's policies.

8.4   Fianna Fáil in power

In power de Valera quickly precipitated an 'economic war' with the British government by his refusal to pay land annuities to the UK. Tenant farmers, who had borrowed money to purchase their farms under the land reform schemes of the late nineteenth and early twentieth centuries, paid land annuities. Under the Government of Ireland Act of 1920, these annuities were to form part of the income of the two governments, North and South. Nevertheless, since the Treaty, Irish governments had been handing over an annual sum of almost £3,000,000 to the British Exchequer. This arrangement was formalised by a meeting between Irish and British officials in March 1926. According to de Valera's official biographers, 'the total annual payment being made to Britain was over £5,000,000, or about one fifth of the total revenue of the Irish government'.[69] Now de Valera was refusing to pay the annuities to the British government, who in turn imposed tariff duties on Irish imports. A tariff war ensued which badly affected Irish exports.

The IRA were quick to see in the 'economic war' a chance to cement their alliance with Fianna Fáil. However, Fianna Fáil refused an offer of co-operation from the IRA immediately after the 1932 election. Instead it proposed that the IRA accept de Valera's 'Dump Arms' order of April 1923, when the IRA tried to sue for peace at the end of the civil war. Frank Aiken, now Minister of Defence, entered into discussions with the Chief of Staff of the IRA with a view to bringing the existence of the IRA as a distinct organisation to an end. Fianna Fáil now asked two questions of the IRA:

(1) Whether the Irish Republican Army of today will on its part accept these proposals (Cease Fire Proposals) if a Fianna Fáil government does so.
(2) May I take it that on a removal of the oath and the acceptance publicly of the 'Cease Fire' proposals by a Fianna Fáil government, the IRA will place their arms at the disposal of the elected representative of the people?[70]

The army council of the IRA offered each battalion these terms for discussion and all turned them down. The IRA committed itself to its continued existence as a distinct organisation with all its arms and equipment under its control.

The Fianna Fáil government in turn refused to go into conference with the army council to discuss their alternative interpretation of de Valera's 'Dump Arms order'. Frank Aiken later outlined the logic of Fianna Fáil's position:

> At the end of the Civil War I wanted to hold out until Mr. Cosgrave would agree to abolish the Oath. I stood out against surrendering arms to a Government bound by the Oath, and against the destruction of arms while the Oath remained. I have done my share to abolish the Oath, and now that an honourable constitutional way is open to secure a Republic without civil war, I intend continuing to oppose internecine strife, and to do my utmost to unite all wise, loyal and disciplined citizens to secure a Republic, governed on the National democratic principles of the cease-fire Proposals.[71]

On 18 July 1932, further attempts by the IRA to draw Fianna Fáil into an alliance came to nothing. Fianna Fáil rejected proposals for a joint policy on the grounds 'that the situation which had arisen had been created solely by Fianna Fáil, with no aid from us (i.e. the IRA), and that the direction and control must continue absolutely to be vested in the Fianna Fáil government'.[72] Moreover, Fianna Fáil was keen to avoid giving the impression of 'a government inside a government' and suggested instead that the IRA confine themselves to organising shows of public support for the policies of the government. Fianna Fáil again raised the possibility of bringing the existence of the IRA to an end. This did not unduly disturb the IRA but some of its more perceptive members realised that the writing was on the wall. One senior figure, George Gilmore, believed that 'practically all the republican and anti-Free State feeling is pro-Dev, and that Fianna Fáil are going to hold the fort for a long time to come'.[73]

The temporary alliance of the two organisations that were united in a desire to oust the Cosgrave government was coming to a close. One of the immediate acts of the new Fianna Fáil government in 1932 was to suspend the operations of the military tribunal and to free seventeen IRA prisoners from jail. However, the Fianna Fáil government did not suspend article 2A from the constitution, which allowed for military tribunals. The Free State's Criminal Intelligence Department, responsible for counter-insurgency, also remained in existence. Moreover, a former Cumann na nGaedheal politician, James Geoghegan, was chosen as Minister of Justice. Republicans observed him attending an inspection of the Gardai accompanied by the head of the Criminal Intelligence Department, David Neligan, who, in the opinion of republicans, was 'directly responsible for the murder of many republicans, while indirectly responsible for the murder of many others'.[74] Frank Aiken, former Chief of Staff of the IRA, also attended functions at the Curragh Army Barracks in his capacity of Minister of Defence, accompanied by none other than the Chief of Staff of the Irish Army. The Fianna Fáil government invited their former foes such as Ernest Blythe and Desmond FitzGerald to the annual commemoration of the 1916 Rising at Arbour Hill. A cynic remarked that it was difficult to tell which side would have been more uncomfortable. Other aspects of Fianna Fáil policy rankled with extreme republicans too. De Valera attended the Imperial Commonwealth Conference at Ottawa and declared that he was willing to see the annuities issue decided by arbitration, an indefensible position for republicans. On a more humorous note, 'the order issued by the Fianna Fáil party prohibiting its members from associating with Cosgrave's friends at the bar of Leinster House has been completely disregarded and the inevitable fraternal spirit has already been established'.[75]

In power, de Valera also came under pressure to use his position to oust former enemies from the Free State administration and replace them with republicans suffering from straitened economic circumstances. The continuance in public service of Eoin O'Duffy as Chief of Police, and David Neligan as head of CID, in particular, caused unease among both the IRA and Fianna Fáil. The Kerry contingent of the Fianna Fáil parliamentary party were reportedly 'up in arms' at the transfer of Neligan to the Land Commission since he had been allegedly involved in the 'murders at Kerry' in the later stages of the civil war.[76] In 1933 a confidante spelled out to de Valera the advantages of an alliance with the IRA. The IRA, 'paying no heed to public clamour', could do things the government could not accept responsibility for publicly, and an alliance would cement support for de Valera in the US.[77] De Valera rejected the alliance saying it would lead to 'disaster' and contradict the whole direction of his political strategy since 1923.[78] He was content merely to transfer Neligan and O'Duffy to uncontroversial posts and there is no recorded case of victimisation. De Valera's policy made perfect sense. In the troubled thirties Fianna Fáil could not rely fully on the Gardai to enforce order. A policy of retribution, even a small-scale one, would have seriously compromised the party's ability to maintain law and order in the years following its ascent to power, particularly since the Blueshirts were led by O'Duffy, a former head of the Gardai.

With the 'economic war' in full swing and strong domestic opposition to Fianna Fáil emerging, the IRA leadership were still reluctant to withdraw their support fully from the Fianna Fáil organisation. During the January 1933 election they again assured de Valera of their informal support on the grounds that a Fianna Fáil government 'would least jeopardise the national position and the economic development of the country'.[79] Afterwards, as revealed by a letter from Moss Twomey to an American supporter, the position of the IRA was one of critical, tactical, and temporary support for Fianna Fáil:

What everybody both in the US and here too is reluctant to admit is that the advent to power of the Fianna Fáil party has made a difference, not fundamentally, but in regard to the tactics which must be followed. While they stand in the same relation to the Republic so far, as the Cosgrave regime, they have not taken any positive action detrimental to the republican cause; theirs are sins of omission. We all realise that they are trying, through propagandist statements, to represent themselves as standing for far more than they are taking any active measures to accomplish, in time, if they will shirk action, they too will be exposed. But against the traitorous Imperialist parties, there should be little doubt as to where we should stand. A time may come when it may be immaterial to us which Treaty party is in office but that time is not yet. Our policy ought to be to take advantages of the very atmosphere they are keen on creating, namely that they are not antagonistic to republican ideals or republican organisations. If we avail of this opportunity we will be in a position later on to fight off any attack when directly made against us.[80]

On the other side of the political spectrum, the hardship caused by the economic war to powerful agricultural interests helps explain how a small 'Army Comrades Organisation', founded in 1931 to protect the interests of Irish ex-servicemen, became, under a variety of different names, the vehicle for a widespread protest movement against the policies of Fianna Fáil.[81] The movement became particularly strong after de Valera was returned with an absolute majority in the general election of 1933. The Blueshirts, as they were known, became a partner in the new Fine Gael organisation in 1933 and were accordingly impossible to suppress fully. Under the leadership of Eoin O'Duffy they committed themselves to the revitalisation of an opposition demoralised by successive defeats at the polls, to the protection of free speech for Fine Gael politicians, and ultimately to the prevention of annuity payments to the government. The government represented their actions as constituting collusion with an outside power against the national interest, but the Blueshirts were largely the product of domestic misgivings about the Fianna Fáil government.

Table 8.1 **Politically motivated outrages committed between 1 July 1934 and 31 May 1935 divided into two periods**

	1 July 1934– 31 May 1935	1 July 1934– 16 January 1935	16 January 1935– 31 May 1935
Number of outrages reported	718	604	114
Detection made	205	184	21
Persons arrested	570	536	34
Persons convicted	469	453	16

Source: 'Malicious damage to property; cutting of telegraph and telephone wires, blocking of roads, felling of trees – period from 1 August 1934 to 16 July 1935' (NA, D/J, D. 28/34).

The mid-thirties saw the re-emergence of seriously disordered conditions in the country, with a systematic attempt being made to prevent the collection of rates and land annuities. Paradoxically, for an organisation that was considered fascist by their opponents, the Blueshirts, in their opposition to Fianna Fáil policy, were resorting to tactics more reminiscent of the agrarian agitations of the nineteenth century. In this vein they were referred to as 'our left wingers' by James Dillon, a member of the Fine Gael party.[82] However, because their tactics ultimately placed them outside the law, the old Cumann na nGaedheal element within Fine Gael precipitated O'Duffy's resignation as President of Fine Gael in September 1934. From then on the radical element within Fine Gael was marginalised. As can be seen from table 8.1., which divides the politically motivated offences committed between 1 August 1934 and 16 August 1935 into two periods, the signing of an Anglo-Irish coal-cattle pact in December 1935 was a turning point in the decline of right-wing political violence. Certainly the high point of serious disorder had been reached by the end of 1935.

It may be, as Fanning speculates, that the long-term significance of the Blueshirts was merely to delay the confrontation between de Valera and the IRA.[83] In 1933 and 1934, confrontation with an IRA operating under the slogan 'no free speech for traitors' was the preserve of the Blueshirt organisation. Shortly before his resignation, O'Duffy told a group of his supporters in Tipperary that 'they must break the skull of anyone who said they were traitors'.[84] Yet after 1934, with the Blueshirts in rapid decline, confrontation with the IRA became the preserve of the official law enforcement agencies of the state. That there would be a confrontation was apparent from a radical change in IRA policy introduced by the general IRA convention held on 17 and 18 March 1933. Among the new charges brought against the Fianna Fáil government was that they represented 'the struggle of Irish capitalism for increased freedom from British Imperialism'.[85] The IRA was no longer behind Fianna Fáil's economic war and rescinded its resolution, carried at the army convention of 1932, to adopt a supportive attitude towards the government. It would now 'pursue its policy irrespective of its reactions on the policy of the Free State Government and other political parties'.[86] A new hard-line attitude reasserted itself. One speaker, Seán MacBride, soon to become Chief of Staff, declared that 'until the Republic for the 32 counties is established, my attitude remains unchanged'.[87]

In power, Fianna Fáil's strategy had shifted from the Fabian strategy pursued between 1926 and 1932, where issues were isolated from one another in order to minimise the opposition which the party confronted at any one time, to a blitzkrieg strategy, where any number of reforms are introduced before the opposition has time to mount sustained opposition.[88] Fianna Fáil's initial lumping together of the oath and the annuities issues, and then its conduct of 'the economic war', certainly had the effect of mobilising a combined opposition against them in 1933. Over the next two years a return to civil war conditions did not seem too far-fetched. As is shown in table 8.2, Fianna Fáil was cast in the role of governmental arbiter between left and right-wing paramilitary groups. In this period the two cleavages that divided the Irish parties, the constitutional and the economic ones, reinforced each other, and left a political system divided into two camps, with an extra-parliamentary organisation on each side. In such a context, asserting the authority of the centre and not seeming to be reliant on the disloyal opposition to the left became a priority for the government. Between 1933 and 1934 opposition spokesmen claimed that the government spent more time curtailing the activities of the Blueshirts, but after 1934 the Gardai turned their attentions more to the IRA.

Table 8.2 **Political spectrum 1933**

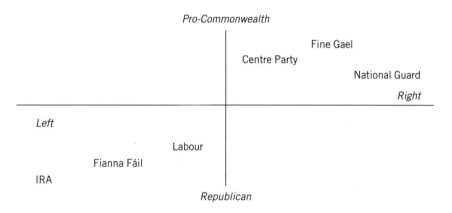

Various failed attempts by the government to suppress the Blueshirts had led to the reintroduction of trial by military tribunal in 1933. The official figures on convictions by military tribunal between 1933 and 1936, reproduced below in table 8.3, show that after 1934 trial by military tribunals led to more convictions of IRA men than Blueshirts. Whereas 347 Blueshirts were convicted as opposed to 102 IRA men in 1934, in 1935 the proportions had changed. In 1935, 116 IRA men were convicted by tribunal as opposed to only 76 Blueshirts. Arguably, these figures reflect two factors. Firstly, Blueshirt activity reached a peak in the second half of 1934, when O'Duffy was 'on the rampage', but died down dramatically in the first half of 1935.[89] Secondly, IRA offences actually increased in number in the first half of 1935 although they declined thereafter. In short, the demise of the Blueshirts allowed de Valera to identify the IRA as the main danger to the good order of the Irish state, and he showed himself no less ruthless in their suppression than his predecessors had been. This undoubtedly helped repair relations with his political opponents, who had hoped that the departure of O'Duffy would enable the 'saner elements within Fianna Fáil' to persuade de Valera to be more reasonable.[90] It also helped ensure a greater degree of middle-class support for the Fianna Fáil party who seemed the only ones capable of restoring order. By October 1935 senior Gardai believed that the IRA was declining.[91] It was declared a proscribed organisation in 1936.

Table 8.3 **Number of convictions by military tribunal, 1933–36**

Year	Blueshirts	IRA	Others
1933	11	34	
1934	347	102	4
1935	76	116	9
1936 (to 31 July 1936)		109	1
1936 31 July–3 November		14	3
Total	434	375	17

Source: 'Military tribunal statistics' (NA, D/J, D 29/36).

Political extremes aside, de Valera's main political opponent remained the British government. If he was to vindicate his strategy of achieving republican objectives by constitutional means, tangible gains in Anglo-Irish relations had to be made. The Removal of the Oath Bill, which became law on 3 May 1933, went some way towards fulfilling the government's ambition of establishing a government based on democratic principles 'and the complete absence of political barriers or tests of conscience of any kind'.[92] On the other hand, the reintroduction of military tribunals in 1933 represented a failure of de Valera's ambition to achieve 'internal peace without coercive legislation'.[93] Fianna Fáil were unhappy with their position as people 'who have given sufficient proof of their attachment to the republican ideal whom (*sic*) are now held up to obloquy as the "instruments of British oppression"'.[94] This quandary impressed upon de Valera the need to accelerate the more positive part of his campaign. Government pensions were introduced for members of the civil war IRA, IRA men were recruited into the new ancillary police force (the Broy Harriers), and the ranks of the new volunteer reserve in the Irish army were also filled with many former IRA men.[95]

Aside from the effects of coercive legislation, government measures were forcing the IRA into a constitutional position. To further this process a Garda memo suggested de Valera look to 'legislative acts directed towards the political and economic emancipation of our country'. In particular it argued that a new constitution 'will, I feel certain succeed in demilitarising the IRA, and remove the organisation as a serious menace to democratic government'.[96] In 1932 the IRA army council had stated that 'only a constitution in which are enshrined the rights and principles the (1916) Proclamation so fearlessly set forth can claim the allegiance of the Irish people'.[97] The creation of a new constitution, however, was only one of a broad range of changes in Anglo-Irish relations that were introduced by de Valera between 1933 and 1938. Taken together they undermined those aspects of Anglo-Irish relations that were considered incompatible with Irish sovereignty over the 26 counties. These changes are summarised in table 8.4.

Table 8.4 **Changes to the Anglo-Irish Treaty, 1933–38**

Date	Title	Content
3 May 1933	Constitutional Act	Removal of Oath to the British Crown from Constitution.
11 December 1936	Constitutional Act 57	All Mention of King and Crown's representative deleted from constitution.
12 December 1936	External Relations Bill	Provision made for the exercise by the King of certain functions in external matters as and when so advised by the Executive Council.
1 July 1937	Constitution Bill	Introduction of new constitution to replace that of 1922.
25 April 1938	Anglo-Irish Agreement	Control of Irish ports handed over to Irish authorities.

Amendment 27 of the constitution completed the emasculation of the office of Governor General, instigated in 1932 when de Valera had one of his own followers, a shopkeeper, Domhnall O'Buachalla, appointed to the office. The amendment also removed the King from the constitution, thus over-turning the chief republican criticism of the 1922 constitution. The passing of the External Relations Act in 1936 provided for the continuance of all existing relations, but the act was a simple statute repealable by ordinary legislation and not part of the constitution. Thus de Valera believed that 'we have in this state, internally a Republic, and so long as we have an act of parliament associating us in certain respects with the states of the British commonwealth we will have that association, and no longer'.[98] So de Valera's document no. 2, which formulated the idea of external association in 1922, bore final fruit after all. De Valera's constitution, unlike that of 1922, was passed by a referendum, with 685,105 voters approving, and 526,945 opposing. It was an unequivocal assertion of Irish sovereignty over the 26 counties, article 5 stating that 'Ireland' was 'a sovereign, independent, democratic state'. Finally, according to de Valera, the return of the ports to the Irish authorities in 1938 'recognises and establishes Irish sovereignty over the twenty-six counties and the territorial seas'.[99]

The crisis of the mid-1930s had given de Valera the opportunity to employ another mechanism which Lustick suggests allows regime-threatening issues to be handled within the rules of the game, 'regime-recomposition'. This occurs when the balance of power between forces in opposition to each other is 'intractable', and when trust must be placed in a particularly strong leader 'to achieve a crisis ending solution to the previously "unsolvable problem"'.[100] The crises raised by the economic war allowed de Valera to assert the authority of the centre between 1935 and 1937. His abolition of the senate in 1936, his introduction of the External Relations Bill which removed the crown from the constitution in December of the same year, and his introduction of a new constitution in 1937, signalled a recomposition of the Irish regime. By 1937 the popularity of the Fianna Fáil programme was forcing a rethink on the opposition benches. Fine Gael, who were initially a pro-Commonwealth party, were beginning to show signs of a change of attitude. In 1937 they actually abstained from the Dáil debate on retaining a link with the Commonwealth in the new constitution. The wheel had come full circle and the progress towards the Republic had become a normal issue of party political competition. This was a sign that the political system had become re-equilibrated.

8.3   Pre-conditions of the re-equilibration process

Linz identifies six basic conditions which enable re-equilibration to take place. First is the existence of a leadership uncompromised by the loss of legitimacy and efficacy of the existing regime in crisis, and committed to the creation of a new regime with new institutions to be legitimated by democratic means. The Fianna Fáil party provided such a leadership. While at times the party openly denied the legitimacy of the Free State, Fianna Fáil's actual intention was spelt out in June 1926 by Frank Aiken, former Chief of Staff of the IRA. Their policy was 'to use the powers possessed by the Free State so-called Parliament' to build up the Irish nation, 'without in any way recognising the British King's authority in Ireland or recognising the right of any county or counties to secede from the nation'. For Aiken this clearly meant experimenting with purely constitutional methods:

> For myself, I would much rather, if I had the choice, win our freedom in this way, peacefully and with the great majority of the people enthusiastically partaking in

the struggle, than to obtain a victory by a minority with arms, even though the latter were comparatively short and easy.[101]

Second, that leadership has to be able to gain the acceptance of those loyal to the existing regime as well as those who choose 'disloyalty in crisis' and were therefore potential supporters of a non-democratic regime. One way of achieving these objectives was to limit the demands the party made on behalf of its constituents. This is what Lustick calls 'decomposing' a political problem by breaking the regime-threatening issue down into its component parts and thus minimising the possibility of the full weight of the combined opposition being mobilised. Rather than declaring that once in power they would dissolve all existing relationships with the United Kingdom, Fianna Fáil limited their ambitions to the removal of the oath, and then to the oath issue, combined with the non-payment of annuities. As Huntington remarks, 'the problem of the reformer is not to overwhelm a single opponent with an exhaustive set of demands, but to minimise his opposition by an apparently limited set of demands'.[102] To do this Fianna Fáil focused on those aspects of the Cumann na nGaedheal regime that the other parties did not support, such as their reliance on coercive legislation.[103] This had the advantage of attracting the smaller parties to them in the summer of 1927 and breaking up any would-be coalition of interests against them. It also ensured the support of the Labour Party, which proved crucial in 1932 when Labour offered their support provided Fianna Fáil did not go beyond their manifesto commitments when in office. It also helped reassure their opponents that the changeover would not have drastic consequences.

The 'decomposition' of the Treaty issue was the perfect strategy to adopt between 1927 and 1932, when the new party was faced with a government that continually played on people's fears of what might happen if Fianna Fáil came to power. After 1933, however, this consideration no longer applied and the constitutional changes made could be presented as stabilising rather than revolutionary measures. The mix of strategies employed by de Valera between 1926 and 1937 is a perfect illustration of the argument that Huntington makes about reformist politicians:

> To achieve his goal the reformer should separate and isolate one issue from another, but, having done this, he should, when the time is right, dispose of each issue as rapidly as possible, removing it from the political agenda before his opponents are able to mobilize their forces. The ability to achieve this proper mix of Fabianism and blitzkrieg is a good test of the political skill of the reformer.[104]

A third precondition of the re-equilibration process is that the leadership of the regime that has lost its position must be able to accept that fact 'and

facilitate rather than oppose the transfer of power'.[105] Shortly after Fianna
Fáil's entry into the Dáil, the vote of no confidence in the government on
10 August 1927 had almost resulted in the termination of Cumann na
nGaedheal's period of political dominance. Only the decisive vote of the
Speaker of the House prevented the opposition forces from toppling the
government. Had two Labour deputies not been absent due to illness, or had
six Sinn Féin deputies not continued their abstentionist policy, then a change
of government would have been an inevitability. Even at that, had one
National League TD from Sligo, John Jinks, not been detained in the bar by
the editor of *The Irish Times* when he should have been voting in the Dáil,
then Cosgrave's period in office would have ended in 1927 and not five years
later. Recalling these events, Michael Hayes, speaker of the Dáil in 1927, wrote
that the Cumann na nGaedheal leadership saw in the entry of Fianna Fáil into
the Dáil the 'probability in such a situation of a change of government – after
a time'.[106]

Resuming power in September 1927 Cosgrave told the Dáil that he had
'no intention of accepting office in the mere capacity of a super-policeman to
maintain law and order while allowing the country to drift along, economically,
nationally and internationally'.[107] Before the 1932 election Cosgrave also
informed the Irish High Commissioner in London that it was his opinion
'that from all points of view it would be most unwise for the British government to adopt too aggressive an attitude or iron hand methods towards a
government made up of the Fianna Fáil party'.[108] There was no guarantee that
the changeover would not bring instability, but Cosgrave publicly declared
that his government 'were satisfied to leave judgement in the hands of the
people'.[109] As it was, the changeover still occurred in an atmosphere of considerable conflict and instability. The Irish experience between 1927 and 1933
does little to reinforce the argument that a successful transition can take place
only in the absence of popular mobilisation. Rather it supports the alternative
view that:

> pivotal elites opt for democratisation because they have been unable to control
> extremism themselves and are no longer willing to pay the high price of failing to
> provide political order. They forecast that democratic elections will be won by
> non-extremists and that ceding control to moderate actors in an electoral democracy
> is less risky than continuing with the status quo.[110]

A fourth and closely related precondition of the re-equilibration process,
is the willingness of the former leadership to subordinate the realisation of
its policy goals in order to save the substance of democracy. During the
September 1927 election campaign Cosgrave actually told voters in Kilkenny
that he was willing to forgive and forget the past provided that the people

decided the issue: 'I am standing for the peaceful alteration of the Treaty and we should do away with this political turmoil', he declared.[111] This willingness to contemplate a changeover on Cosgrave's part naturally presupposes some confidence in the democratic commitments of those to whom power is to be transferred. As early as March 1931 the republican newspaper, *An Phoblacht*, had warned that the Treaty could not be overthrown by 'mere votes' and that the leaders of Fianna Fáil must be prepared to shoot 'not the IRA but those who stand for English rule in Ireland'.[112] However, when in power, de Valera refused to allow the expulsion of public officials formally loyal to the Cosgrave regime. He was satisfied with the existing system of government and told the heads of the various departments he had no intention of replacing them.[113]

Fifth, Linz suggests that 'a certain level of indifference and passivity in the bulk of the population must exist in the final denouement of the crisis'.[114] To put it another way, large sectors of the population are unavailable for mobilisation by disloyal oppositions. The Irish case does vindicate the view that re-equilibration can only work when the electorate cannot easily be mobilised by extremist appeals, since Irish electorates did not reward anti-system parties. However, the conservative assumption that this requires the electorate to be passive or indifferent is disproved by the Irish experience. Part of Fianna Fáil's success in re-equilibrating Irish democracy lay in the fact that they were able to legitimate the changes they introduced by gaining a higher percentage of first preference votes virtually every time they contested an election. Indeed, from 1932 onwards the public seemed to be rewarding their strategy and the party was able to mobilise a much higher level of electoral support than their predecessors. This support was due primarily to the party's reassurances that any future change would not jeopardise the voters' sense of security. As de Valera recalled in 1936:

> The people supported Fianna Fáil because its policy was a practical one. It kept the ultimate objective of a free, united Irish nation clearly in view, but it concentrated successively on the nearer local objectives along the way, striving at each point to put upon the people only the strains which the people could bear.[115]

Sixth, Linz suggests that re-equilibration is only possible when the semi-loyal opposition is capable of controlling the disloyal opposition that is hostile not just to a particular regime, but to democracy itself. Re-equilibration is a game in which the semi-loyal actors in the regime consciously deceive the disloyal political forces whose challenge may have precipitated the fall of the previous regime and brought them to power.[116] Certainly, by a mixture of straightforward coercion and constitutional reformism the IRA was isolated within the political system to a greater degree than was the case in the 1920s, when what one republican called 'the police thuggery and ecclesiastical fire and brimstone of the Cosgrave regime', forced all republican organisations into a de facto alliance.[117] The changed attitude of Sean MacBride, a leading member of the IRA, is illustrative of the impact of Fianna Fáil on the organisation. In the early thirties he predicted that if Fianna Fáil succeeded in removing the oath and the office of Governor General the IRA would be in a difficult position.[118] By 1938 he had become convinced that the IRA had no real role to play in southern politics and ceased to be active in the organisation.

Whether de Valera and his colleagues had actually 'deceived' the IRA into thinking that the aims of the two organisations were identical is debatable. It seems more likely that at times circumstances determined a common outlook, but that once these temporary circumstances were removed, it became clear that the initial split had signalled a fundamental difference of outlook in the republican ranks. That this was the case was made clear in the run up to the 1932 election, when Fianna Fáil's Frank Fahy told voters in Tuam that for the past five years he had been advising young men in the country against the idea of resorting to force at this stage to achieve national freedom. In power he said Fianna Fáil 'will remove the oath, and say to those outside the Dáil to come in, and if that does not succeed they are going to govern'. More ominously, he added that 'anyone in the way of the Fianna Fáil government will be pushed out of it, because Fianna Fáil meant to govern nationally'.[119]

8.4   Conclusion

The model of the re-equilibration process put forward by Linz provides a useful model for analysing the manner in which Irish democracy became consolidated after the civil war. What is less clear is the causal weight that should be attributed to various factors in the re-equilibration process. At first glance, the emphasis put here on elite strategies and elite relationships suggests that a high politics approach is the most convenient one for the analysis of this case. On the other hand, de Valera's policies were ratified by popular assent, so the Irish case represents a – perhaps unusual – example of an elitist process being accompanied by waves of popular mobilisation. Another interesting question is raised by the role of the British government's appeasement policy in enabling de Valera to transform the constitutional basis of Free State politics. Since 1935 British policy towards 'the restless dominion' was strictly one of appeasement, as was revealed in a letter from Sir Haldane Porter, an Irish-born British civil servant, to Cosgrave in June 1937:

> As to what the attitude of the British Government is or will be towards the new Constitution, I cannot say; but they will probably take the line of least resistance, because I cannot suppose that in the present conditions of Europe they will not

do anything to precipitate a controversy with the Irish Free State: but one thing I do know and deplore is that, so far as my knowledge of the British public goes, they no longer take any interest in Irish affairs.[120]

As a result of British appeasement, the domestic consequences of Fianna Fáil radicalism were no longer as threatening as they had been, and opposition to the changes they introduced was largely conducted on parliamentary lines. De Valera's difficulties in the 1930s would surely have been compounded if the British government had been interventionist. As it was, the Blueshirt movement enjoyed few known links with the British government.[121]

A basic pre-condition for the re-equilibration process lies in the commitment of the new leadership to finding democratic methods for the resolution of particularly intractable political problems. This desire no doubt goes right back to the experience of civil war. As Fanning suggests, de Valera's commitment to the majority rule principle was more or less constant from this date onwards.[122] Indeed as early as June 1923 de Valera had signalled a clear preference for recognising the third Dáil:

> It may be advisable to regard the Second Dáil as still the legitimate Government of the country, though we have to face the fact that our opponents are now functioning as a de facto government. A definite decision on the question can not be taken until the Second Dáil has an opportunity of meeting . . . My own opinion is that more rapid progress will be made by constituting ourselves as free as possible from anything in the past that would entangle us and prevent us from facing the situation exactly as it is.[123]

The outlines of what was to become the Fianna Fáil party were already apparent from de Valera's attempted reorganisation of the Sinn Féin party at the end of the civil war. Ideological pragmatism combined with republican rhetoric, a concentration on socio-economic issues, and electoral efficiency (an internal memo stated that there should be no duds in this regard but appointment by ability) could all be said to date from this period.[124] They indicate that de Valera was intent on moving the military struggle onto the constitutional plane and that the fundamentalist republicanism of the IRA Executive was to be discarded for something more pragmatic.

Logically, defeat in the civil war was the wellspring for the democratic strategies employed by the anti-Treatyites afterwards. While a clear commitment to the constitutional path did not emerge until the split of 1926, there is no doubt that de Valera saw in the defeat of the anti-Treatyites in the civil war an opportunity to reassert his control over the republican movement. As early as 12 October 1922 he had signalled to the IRA Executive his willingness to work the Treaty 'without Ireland's *appearing* to agree to give away her sovereignty and to accept partition'.[125] The relationship between republicanism and democracy will long be a subject of controversy in Irish political science, but between 1932 and 1938 the Fianna Fáil party proved that many republican aspirations could be achieved by constitutional methods, which was a revelation at the time. Whether he could have done so had British policy been less conciliatory is more questionable. Had the Free State gone into the Second World War with the ports under British control, Irish democracy might have undergone another major crisis in the 1940s.

Chapter 9

'Majority rule' and the constitutional development of the Free State 1922–37

'The problem of democracy in Ireland was that most Irish people, whether Protestant or Catholic, were majoritarian rather than pluralist democrats.'

Tom Garvin, *1922: The Birth of Irish Democracy* (Dublin, 1996)

On 23 May 1954 Sean MacBride, leader of the small opposition party, Clann na Poblachta, wrote to the Taoiseach, Eamon de Valera, proposing the formation of 'a nationally representative government'. Such a government, composed of the main political parties, would help 'minimise the embittered play of party politics' and lead the political elite to co-operate in the serving of the common good. In MacBride's view, the Irish state had not known 'normal political development' since 1922 and Irish government had suffered from the want of 'constructive' and 'consecutive' policies as a consequence. The British 'party system of government' which had operated since 1922 was unsuited to Irish needs, because 'the factors which made the system a relative success in England had no application here'. The Free State would have been better advised 'to follow the political pattern of a smaller and more successful democracy such as Switzerland'.[1]

Although the Irish Free State had begun its life with elements of such a 'consensual' political system – a written constitution, a PR electoral system, a second house with some powers, and provisions for direct democracy on fundamental matters – by 1937 the situation had changed.[2] The 1922 constitution, amended by ordinary legislation over the previous 15 years, was now as flexible as the unwritten British constitution. The Senate had been abolished the previous year, and the new state had grown used to constant single-party government despite the use of STV for elections. MacBride's view contrasts with the orthodox interpretation of constitutional development in the period, which is that such changes were not only a 'relative success', but an absolute necessity. Indeed, it has been argued that the various crises which beset the state between 1922 and 1937 would not have arisen at all had Irish institutions been modelled more closely on the British model in the first place.[3]

In the wider debate on the relationship between political stability and institutional design in the inter-war era, the Irish case has been cited in support of the thesis that a combination of single-party government and a two-party system are conducive to democratic stability.[4] The constitutional history of the Free State vindicates the Westminster model in other words, and the Irish case is one of a number of states whose achievement of political stability can be explained by its British institutional legacy. This assumption, alongside the view that the 'westminsterisation' of the political system was a necessary part of the stabilisation process, has never been critically assessed. In what follows I suggest that stable coalition governments could have been formed in the Free State between the wars and that the conventional equation between the Westminster model and political stability was not as clear-cut as previously assumed. Indeed the constitutional life of the Free State was not placed on a stable footing until 1937, with the introduction of a new constitution which departed in significant ways from British precedents.[5]

9.1   The emergence of majority rule

Events themselves suggested that the relationship between majority rule and the consolidation of Irish democracy was a close one. The results of the 1922 general election had enabled the Provisional Government to claim that the majority of the people had supported the Treaty. The anti-Treatyites claimed in converse that the rights of the majority did not extend to the surrender of Irish national independence. From the outset the fundamental issue at stake in the Free State was the right of the elected majority to have its decisions taken as authoritative. When the anti-Treatyites offered to negotiate peace terms after ten months of civil war, the government replied that in future 'all political issues . . . shall be decided by the majority vote of the elected representatives of the people'.[6] At the Sinn Féin Ard Fheis in 1926, when a large minority of the delegates left to form Fianna Fáil, de Valera declared that 'the majority of the people were going to shape the future'.[7] In 1927, after the assassination of Kevin O' Higgins, the government passed legislation forcing electoral candidates to declare their willingness to take their seats if elected. As a result Fianna Fáil were forced to abandon their abstentionist policy, a move that had been on the cards for at least two years. Then, after gaining a majority of seats in 1933, de Valera gradually revised the Treaty on the basis of his parliamentary majority. His enactment of a republican constitution in 1937 'completed the reconciliation of majority rule with popular sovereignty'.[8]

Table 9.1 **Irish governments, 1922–38**

Date of Appointment	Government	'Prime Minister'	Single Party Majority	Single Party Minority
1922	Provisional Government	Michael Collins	9 Months	
1922	Provisional Government	William Cosgrave	11 months	
1923	Cumann na nGaedheal	William Cosgrave	3 years, 10 months	
1927	Cumann na nGaedheal	William Cosgrave		2 months
1927	Cumann na nGaedheal	William Cosgrave		4 years, 3 months
1932	Fianna Fáil	Eamon de Valera		10 months
1933	Fianna Fáil	Eamon de Valera	4 years, 4 months	
1937	Fianna Fáil	Eamon de Valera		10 months
1938	Fianna Fáil	Eamon de Valera	4 years	

Source: Chubb, *The Government and Politics of Ireland* (1970), table 6.5, p. 163.

Despite the close connection between these events and the majority rule principle, a majoritarian system was not a foregone conclusion. Under STV it had not been envisaged that single-party government would be possible, and for the most part Irish elections did not return clear parliamentary majorities. Between 1922 and 1938 there were nine Irish governments, which are shown in table 9.1. The first was a Provisional Government without full legislative powers. The second lasted for less than a year. The third (1923–27), like the second, would not have had a majority of its own supporters in the Dáil, if Sinn Féin, the largest opposition party, had taken their seats. The fourth, a minority government, lasted only a few months. The last Cumann na nGaedheal government (1927–32) was also a minority government. Between 1932 and 1933 the first Fianna Fáil government was dependent on Labour support. The only proper majority government before 1938 was that of Fianna Fáil between 1933 and 1937, and its share of the vote was still less than half, at 49.7 per cent. Again in 1937 it became a minority government, but this situation lasted only one year, until the 1938 general election returned a majority Fianna Fáil government to power.

If Irish elections did not return majority winners, how then did single-party government become the norm? One answer is that the continued dominance of the Treaty issue in political life reinforced the bipolar logic of political competition. The relationship between voting preference and party preference has been neatly captured by the 'directional model' of party choice.[9] This model suggests that once a basic line of division is established in a political system, voters tend to vote in terms of which side of the divide they are on, not in terms of how closely their opinions match those of the parties themselves. In this respect voting is not rational but directional, and the parties that situate themselves most clearly on either side of the middle ground tend to attract most votes. In the Irish case, despite strong support for 'neutral' candidates in 1922, once two parties emerged – Cumann na nGaedheal and Sinn Féin – which represented the two sides of the civil war split, the nature of voting was bound to be directional rather than rational. As a result the smaller parties' share of the vote dropped over time, falling from over 40 per cent in 1922 to under 15 per cent in 1938.

Table 9.2 **Results of each pair of general elections, 1922–38**

Year	Cumann na nGaedheal	Sinn Féin– Fianna Fáil	Total number of Dáil seats	Number required for majority	Civil War Parties % share of the vote	Others % share of the vote
1922	58	36	128	65	59.74	40.26
1923	63	44	153	77	66.37	33.63
1927	46	44	153	77	53.67	46.33
1927	61	57	153	77	73.86	26.14
1932	56	72	153	77	79.75	20.25
1933	48	76	153	77	80.17	19.83
1937	48	68	138	70	80.05	19.95
1938	45	76	138	70	85.25	14.75

Sources: C. O'Leary, *Irish Elections, 1918–77* (1979), Gallagher, *Irish Elections, 1922–44* (1993).

Even with 'directional voting' the two largest parties did not, however, achieve enough support to form single-party governments. To do this they would also have to take advantage of a basic flaw in the 1922 constitution, which did not outline the conditions under which a Dáil could be dissolved, except to say that 'Dáil Éireann may not at any time be dissolved except on the advise of the Executive Council'. The first extraordinary dissolution occurred in 1927 when the Attorney General, John A. Costello, advised

Cosgrave's minority government, which had done badly in the June election, that the constitution did not prevent the Executive Council from dissolving the Dáil without its consent.[10] This ruling was to prove of great benefit to the largest two parties. After each regular election held once a four-year period had elapsed, the Executive Council soon called another snap election in order to convert their initial plurality of seats in the Dáil into a majority. Table 9.2 shows the effects of these 'snap elections' on the smaller parties. Each time the governing party dissolved the Dáil, they gained an increase in seats which enabled them to form a single-party government. Except once, in 1933, each time they did this, the smaller parties' share of the seats declined. The civil war parties' share of the seats, which was less than 65 per cent in 1922, reached over 88 per cent by 1938.

Political practice would not have been reflected in constitutional law were it not for the ability of Irish governments to amend the constitution by ordinary legislation. This meant that the constitutional basis of the state also became strongly majoritarian. In new states the main problems with a written constitution as an instrument of restraint on government 'relate to its legitimacy and the source of its supremacy'.[11] In Ireland, article 2 of the 1922 constitution stated that 'if any provision of the said constitution or if any amendment thereof or if any law made thereunder is in any respect repugnant to any of the provisions of the Scheduled Treaty, it shall, to the extent only of such repugnancy, be absolutely void and inoperative'. This clause established the Treaty not the constitution as the fundamental law. On the other hand, the constitution also proclaimed that 'all powers of government and all authority, legislative, executive, and judicial in Ireland, are derived from the people of Ireland'.[12] This located sovereignty in the people of Ireland. As an instrument of restraint on elected majorities, the 1922 constitution was uniquely vulnerable. If it was subordinate to the Treaty, it could be amended to protect the Treaty. If it was derived from the people, it could be amended by the people. Thus in 1928 when de Valera tried to use the provision for referenda to remove the oath, and was prevented from doing so by Cosgrave, who simply removed the provision from the constitution, both could claim to be acting in the name of a higher constitutional principle.

In 1934 Mansergh wrote that 'it is becoming increasingly evident that in certain aspects the government of the Irish Free State stands in sharp distinction to its constitution'.[13] This disparity increased up to 1937. The relationship between this process and the bipolar thrust of party competition was systemic:

> with two large parties competing for majority support, that parliament moved even closer to its Westminster origins. Many of the experimental and continental features of the Irish Free State were abandoned virtually without trial. Few of the 'extern' Ministers were ever appointed; all were staunch party men. Neither the

referendum nor the initiative were ever used to ascertain the people's opinion; both were abolished when de Valera tried to invoke these constitutional provisions to jettison the Oath. The elaborate schemes to give the Senate some power and purpose were gradually modified. The constitution itself, although it was the fundamental law for fifteen years, remained throughout its life, like the British constitution, wholly flexible and subject to amendment simply by act of parliament.[14]

In total there were 27 constitutional amendments, roughly shared between the two parties. By 1936, 48 out of a total of 83 articles had been amended. All the amendments pointed in one direction: to the emergence of a political system based on the three key elements of British constitutional arrangements: 'parliamentary sovereignty untrammelled by reference to any higher law, a cabinet sustained by its parliamentary support, and a constitution as flexible as ordinary statute law'.[15] Between them, both Cosgrave and de Valera had whittled down the 1922 constitution to the essence of the British system: the 'fusion of the executive and the legislature in a single parliamentary chamber'.[16]

9.2   Majority rule and political stability

By 1937 the majoritarian stamp on Irish political life was clearly established. The question remains of how the evolution of this system affected the process of political stabilisation. It has been argued that the Irish experience supports the hypothesis that a non-proportional electoral system will lead to a two-party system which in turn will lead to cabinet stability.[17] Although STV was in theory a proportional system, in practice the relationship between votes and seats was not proportional. This has been attributed to the fact that Irish constituencies often had fewer than five seats, the minimum size at which proportionality is guaranteed.[18] Up to 1937 around forty per cent of Irish constituencies were smaller than this. Moreover, one might add that the effect of dissolutions was to penalise the smaller parties further, since they left choice of government the key issue in the second election. In this sense the Irish electoral system was rather like the French system for presidential elections, which forces the electorate to choose between the best two candidates the second time round.

From a comparative perspective the Irish system seems to conform fully to the model of political stability outlined by Hermens. Firstly, the electoral system was not proportional, but 'more in the nature of a compromise between the majority system and PR than of a clear PR system'.[19] Secondly, by 1939 the Irish state 'had one of the most concentrated party systems of all European democracies'.[20] Thirdly, Irish cabinet stability was unparalleled in the rest of inter-war Europe. According to Karvonen, 'there were only two different cabinets in the period until the second world war'.[21] Such a system hinged on the fact that STV did not produce proportional outcomes. If it had, Hermens suggests that there would probably have been no majority since 1927, and as a result 'no stable government leadership'.[22]

Table 9.3 **Party political spectrum in 1927**

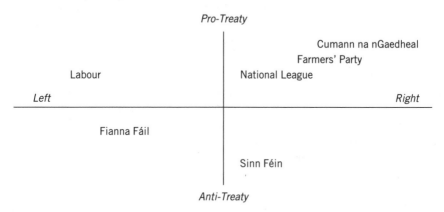

The assumption made by Hermens is that coalition government could not have provided a basis for political stability. Yet since the smaller parties were at times willing to support minority governments, durable coalition governments were also feasible. If the Farmers' Party had been willing to support Cumann na nGaedheal between 1927 and 1932, and, in the form of the Centre Party, amalgamate with them in 1933, a coalition of the two was possible. Likewise, Labour were willing to discuss entering into a coalition with Fianna Fáil in 1927, supported Fianna Fáil in office between 1932 and 1933, and Fianna Fáil reportedly remained dependent on Labour's support between 1933 and 1937.[23] Table 9.3 provides an ideological map of the political spectrum in 1927. Two lines of cleavage separated the parties, one over the Treaty, the other over economic policy. The fact that Fianna Fáil were the only party in the Dáil to oppose the Treaty initially ruled them out of any coalition. According to Thomas Johnson, Fianna Fáil's desire to remove the oath to the British Crown from the constitution was not 'to enable them to work the Treaty and Constitution with a clear conscience but to enable them to use their position as law-makers and makers of the Government to break the Treaty and make an entirely new constitution'.[24] As a result Labour were unwilling to join a Fianna Fáil coalition early in the summer of 1927,[25] although both parties stood to the left on the economic cleavage. Johnson declared that 'Fianna Fáil has published an economic programme the greater part of which is similar to the programme of the Labour Party. If the Fianna Fáil deputies enter the Dáil, Labour will join with them in getting their programme translated into actual force'. Johnson believed that Fianna Fáil's attitude to the oath had to change before a coalition was formed.[26]

Naturally, a coalition of the other parties on an economically conservative pro-Treaty position was possible, but because of Fianna Fáil's absence from the Dáil such a government was unnecessary before 1927. By then two of the smaller parties had begun to oppose what they considered the repressive politics of the Cosgrave government and favoured a policy of appeasement towards the anti-Treaty opposition. In 1927 de Valera believed that he could only achieve his objectives in combination with the other small parties. He told his party's third Ard Fheis:

> The Imperial forces are certain of every triumph. They defeat one section of nationalism within the Free State assembly. Then they combine with that section to defeat us – the other section outside. Victory for nationalism cannot come like that. Means must be found to bring the national forces together – together at least to this extent – that the two sections will in the main proceed along parallel lines and in a common direction so that the results of their combined effort may be the greatest possible.[27]

Between June and September 1927 discussions were based on the possibility of a minority coalition being formed between the Labour Party and the National League, with the support of Fianna Fáil backbenchers. However, Labour objected to the National League's desire for extra-representation in this coalition. Conversely, the National League defended its demands on the grounds that financial and business interests were apprehensive at the idea of a Labour-controlled government. Moreover, they required guarantees that the new government was not to be 'Labour in the saddle or Fianna Fáil in effective control or pulling the strings'.[28] Despite their differences, the party leaders agreed to support a motion of no-confidence in the Cosgrave government on 10 August 1927. De Valera had promised that if the recent Public Safety Bill were overturned and if the oath issue were overcome, Fianna Fáil 'would not force the issue on constitutional questions during the normal life of the present Dáil'.[29] Only the freak abstention from the vote of a National League deputy from Sligo prevented the government from being toppled.

So coalition government was a distinct possibility as early as 1927 and remained so until 1933. Would the rainbow coalition have been stable? If Labour had insisted on radical economic measures the National League would have been in an uncomfortable position. Johnson had committed himself to revising the oath but not to abolishing it, while Labour was split on the question of annuity payments.[30] Significant ideological differences still divided the would-be partners. But between 1927 and 1932 Labour moved towards the anti-Treaty camp on the constitutional question, while Fianna

Fáil continued to move leftwards on economic issues. Leadership changes (Johnson was replaced by T.J. O'Connell, and then O'Connell was replaced by William Norton), as well as the deepening economic recession, led the Labour Party to change its position on the Treaty. By 1932 the outlooks of Fianna Fáil and Labour were not so different. In 1932 all of Labour's TDs supported de Valera's 'Removal of the Oath Bill', which Norton called, like de Valera, 'a relic of feudalism'.[31]

The figures on voting transfers support the view that by 1933 two distinct 'blocs' had emerged within the system, one left-wing and republican in outlook, the other conservative and pro-commonwealth. Whereas in 1927 only 17.6 per cent of Labour transfers went to Fianna Fáil candidates in situations where there was no Labour candidate available to receive them, in 1933 this figure had risen to 72.7 per cent. Conversely, in 1927 only 14.9 per cent of Fianna Fáil transfers went to Labour candidates when there was no Fianna Fáil candidate available to receive them. In 1933 this figure had risen to 47.1 per cent. On the other side in 1927, in situations where there was no Cumann na nGaedheal candidate available to receive them, 25.1 per cent of the party's transfers went to Farmers' Party candidates and only 4.9 per cent to the National League. In 1933 the Centre Party received 37.3 per cent of the party's transfers in similar situations. In 1927 Cumann na nGaedheal received 29.3 per cent of the Farmers' Party transfers in situations where there was no Farmers' candidate to receive them. In the same election the party received 25.5 per cent of the National League's transfers where there was no National League candidate available to receive them. In 1933, in similar situations, Cumann na nGaedheal received 53.6 per cent of the Centre Party's transfers.[32] In other words, the pattern of transfers 'demonstrated emphatically that the party system consisted of two blocs, one composed of Fianna Fáil and Labour and the other of Cumann na nGaedheal and the National Centre Party'.[33]

That single-party governments in the Free State were durable does not prove that coalition governments would have been unstable. In the inter-war period, coalition governments were formed in Belgium, Czechoslovakia, France, the Netherlands, the five Nordic countries, and in the UK, without disastrous consequences. The number of parties and the number of issues dividing them were far greater in most of these states than in the Free State, but coalitions still proved compatible with political stability. Certainly, on the basis of policy issues and voting transfers, stable coalition governments could have been formed in Ireland between 1932 and 1937. Before that they were more feasible to the right of the political spectrum. The crucial question – whether a stable 'rainbow' coalition could have emerged from the vote of no confidence in Cosgrave on 10 August 1927 – can never be definitively answered. In the summer of 1927:

The alternatives then presented to the Parliament were a Government supported by a combination of Cumann na nGaedheal, the Unionists, and the Farmers' Party, and one supported by Fianna Fáil, Labour and the National League. Either coalition would have been obliged to pursue a policy of conciliation, avoiding, as far as possible, any action that would inspire a combined attack by the opposition parties. There would be no toleration of the dictatorial methods which have hitherto characterised Mr Cosgrave's Government.[34]

Nor does the fact that single-party cabinets proved to be durable prove that cabinet stability was the decisive factor in ensuring the stability of the Irish system. An alternative approach is to argue that cabinet stability was a source of stability, but that a bi-polar pattern of political competition was a source of instability. Majority rule, combined with the first past the post electoral system, could have enabled the anti-Treatyites to form a government on their own in 1927, only four years after the end of the civil war.[35] Thomas Johnson outlined one possible consequence of such a result:

> Suppose the impossible were to happen and the whole 101 candidates of Fianna Fáil and Sinn Féin were elected. The remaining 51 members of other parties, though lacking moral authority, would still have the legal right and power to elect a government and the Government so elected, and no other, would have the legal authority to govern the country. An attempt to set up a rival authority would probably cause division in the ranks of the Executive forces between those who would only obey the constitutional government and those who would follow the party elected as a majority by the votes of the people. Irrespective of the rights and wrongs of the question such a position must inevitably cause a constitutional crisis.[36]

Those who endorsed a majoritarian system when in office naturally became wary of it in opposition. When de Valera used military tribunals to deal with political subversives in 1935, Richard Mulcahy asked, 'Will the President say that there is any movement of violence in this country that can equal the Fianna Fáil party in practically wiping out the courts and wiping out the Seanad, and imposing against the widespread opinion of the country, burdens that they are not able to bear?'[37] In his comparative analysis of constitutional choices in the inter-war period Karvonen suggests that 'the strengthening of executive power in an ongoing process of polarisation is a risky manoeuvre in a parliamentary system'.[38] In 1929 an observer wrote that if de Valera assumed office, 'he could plunge the country into chaos without being unconstitutional or doing anything unprecedented'. This situation would never have arisen 'had the spirit and the letter of the constitution been adhered to rigidly'.[39] By 1937 the series of constitutional amendments had given de Valera the power to make whatever changes he wanted: 'it was a classic opportunity to establish a dictatorship'.[40]

It is often argued that in multi-party systems parties tend to stick to rigid principles and compete for an ideologically fixed section of the electorate, while in two-party systems pressures of political competition mean that parties' policy preferences tend to move towards the centre as they compete for the available middle ground of the electorate. This is known as the median voter theory of party competition. It contrasts with the 'radical elitist' model of party competition which argues that internal divisions within the larger parties in a bipolar political system will move these parties' policy positions closer to those of the party activists than to the centre ground.[41] Clearly in a situation where the two larger parties emerge out of a civil war, and where they are divided between hardline and conciliatory elements, two-party competition would not automatically lead to any convergence on the centre ground. In the Irish case, such convergence emerged only when the two opposing blocs split. Fianna Fáil split from fundamentalist Sinn Féin in 1926, and Fine Gael distanced themselves from the Blueshirt movement in late 1934. If there was basis for moderation it lay in the fact that the larger opposition parties needed some coalition potential under STV.[42] Notably in 1927, Fianna Fáil took its economic policies from Labour and agreed to limit its demands for constitutional change in return for concessions on the 1927 Public Safety Act by the would-be coalition. A similar agreement was made in 1932 in return for Labour support. On the other side, Cumann na nGaedheal had to amalgamate with the Centre Party, and after the demise of the Blueshirts Fine Gael was 'Cumann na nGaedheal all over again, without being very much inclined to extremism'.[43]

Garvin describes the consolidation of Irish democracy as a process of political 'deradicalisation'.[44] The crucial question is whether 'deradicalisation' was encouraged or hindered by the existence of multi-party competition. Linz argues that states which find themselves polarised into two camps can avoid further polarisation by adopting a multi-party system which might create sources of cross-cutting cleavages. In contrast, a two-party system would aggravate differences and maximise the ideological distance between the parties. Multi-party systems will only have a disintegrating effect where smaller parties act as disloyal oppositions and when the major parties follow them.[45] In Ireland the opposite process happened. While there was no pressure on Cumann na nGaedheal to take the views of the smaller parties into account before 1932, there is no doubt that Fianna Fáil had to moderate its stance between 1926 and 1933 if it wanted to have some coalition potential. In 1926 de Valera actually envisaged that, having got rid of the oath, Fianna Fáil would join with the other small parties in making a new constitution.[46] By 1932 Fianna Fáil's position was closer to that of the Labour Party than it was to Sinn Féin. This can only be considered a benign development.

9.3   Majority rule and the values of the Sinn Féin elite

Neither the development of a two-party system nor the existence of single-party government ought to be considered necessary preconditions of democratic consolidation in independent Ireland. Multi-party competition was conducive to democratic consolidation, while stable coalition governments could also have been formed given the requisite commitment on the part of political elites. If Irish democracy could have been stabilised under 'consensual' as well as 'majoritarian' institutions the state's institutional design cannot be the decisive factor in explaining the outcome. Much the same general conclusion has been reached by Karvonen in his analysis of the relationship between institutional design and democratic stability in inter-war Europe.[47] He found that both consensual and majoritarian systems proved compatible with democratic stability, but that attitudes to constitutions were decisive in explaining the fate of democracies in inter-war Europe.

In countries where the initial constitution-making was participated in by all sides, the political system enjoyed a sufficient amount of loyalty on the part of political elites to overcome later periods of instability. In states such as Austria, Germany, Estonia, and Latvia on the other hand, those that eventually came to office had been excluded from this process and subsequently rejected the constitution *in toto*. In the process of reshaping the constitutions, non-socialist parties invariably strengthened the degree of executive power, ultimately facilitating the emergence of authoritarian regimes. In states such as France, overall loyalty to the institutions of the Republic helped the state overcome its political crises. In this regard the long established democracies had a definite advantage over the newly established ones, as is evidenced from the fact that few new states retained parliamentary institutions in the period.

At first glance the relevance of the Irish case to Karvonen's theory seems clear. The anti-Treatyites did not participate in the process of constitution making and subsequently rejected the 1922 constitution. They thus contributed to the emergence of an executive-dominated system of government and to the political instability that came with those changes. However, the 1922 constitution was amended in equal proportion by both sides, which suggests that the Irish case was different. In 1930 Sean Lemass remarked that 'neither the Cumann na nGaedheal Party nor we are prepared to regard that Constitution apparently as anything but so much paper. It is only the Labour Party whose one desire is to be respectable in all things that attaches any importance to it.'[48] The nature of the constitutional changes made between 1923 and 1937 suggests that both the civil war parties had an alternative model in mind of how democracy worked.[49] Majority rule had formed a central plank in the propaganda campaign of Sinn Féin after 1918, which sought to convince international opinion of the overwhelming majority mandate for a 32 county

Republic. In the election of that year the party declared that once independence was achieved the public had a right to decide what form it should take. The pro-Treatyites then legitimised the disestablishment of the Republic declared in 1919, first by a parliamentary and then by an electoral majority. According to Collins, the Treaty would stand, 'unless in the whirl of politics' the anti-Treatyites 'became a majority in the country'.[50] This possibility formed the basis of the Fianna Fáil position from 1926 onwards.

As in the longer established cases, the Irish benefited from the fact that political practice could be based on a well-established constitutional tradition. Despite the innovations of the 1922 constitution, majority rule formed the basis of an unspoken constitutional consensus between the two sides. This is implied by Hogan, who argues that Cumann na nGaedheal's loss of a majority in 1927 threatened to overturn 'the entire constitutional edifice' on which the state was built. The crisis was then averted 'in a constitutional way' when the second election 'returned the Treaty party in sufficient strength to guarantee the continuance of stable constitutional government'.[51] In Hogan's analysis, majoritarian norms are equated with constitutional norms. Farrell also argues that respect for parliamentary majorities provided a secure base for democracy, because it was a reflection of the 'British style liberal-conservatism of the Irish rebel'. He explains the divergent fates of the Westminster system in Ireland in terms of two British traditions, one prevalent in the North, the other in the South. The conservative variant, or 'the Whitehall model', stems from experience of government, whereas the liberal model reflects 'the experience of men who have spent more time in opposition than in government'.[52]

Table 9.4 **Two variants of the Westminster model**

Core values of the Whitehall model	*Core values of the Liberal model*
Executive decision making	Control of government
the binding force of law	the need for consent
preservation of order	a stress on answerability
strong government	representative government

Source: B. Farrell (ed.), *The Irish Parliamentary Tradition* (Dublin, 1973), p. 213.

Table 9.4 contrasts the core values of these traditions. Farrell's contention is that 'the Unionist Party's bland assurance that its "natural" majority gave it a right to rule in perpetuity; its entrenched resistance to any attempt to attenuate the powers of its own executive . . . is intelligible within the conservative version of the British parliamentary model'.[53] This may be so, but between 1922 and 1937 the two wings of the Sinn Féin elite also progressively stripped their constitution of anything that limited executive power.

Civil liberties were encroached upon by Public Safety Acts which suspended habeas corpus, introduced internment without trial, trial by military tribunal, death sentences for the possession of firearms, and reprisal executions. Under the terms of the seventeenth amendment to the constitution in 1931, a military tribunal was empowered to give the death penalty for certain crimes, the only right of appeal being to the executive council. The need for governments to ratify constitutional amendments by referenda was circumvented by legislation extending the period in which it could amend the constitution by ordinary legislation. In 1928 the Governor General, having expressed doubts as to whether he could legally sign a bill deleting article 47, which gave both houses the right to refer bills to the people, was told he could act only on the advice of the Executive Council.

It would be more true to say that the Sinn Féin elite were 'Peelite' in their attitudes to the workings of the system. 'Peelites' traditionally saw parliamentary control as an unstable basis for government and believed that the executive, not the parliament, or through it the people, is responsible for public policy. A necessary condition for good government is that liberal or 'whig' mechanisms for enforcing governmental responsiveness are curtailed or simply ineffective.[54] The whole of Irish constitutional development up to 1937 can be summed up by saying that the mechanisms for ensuring responsible government on the liberal model were undermined in order that 'strong government' could exist. These 'Peelite' attitudes were well conveyed by Cosgrave's comment on Fianna Fáil's proposal to restore the referendum to the constitution in 1932:

> The majority of the people do not know what the initiative is, and they do not care about the referendum. Just imagine how you are going to have government in the State if you are going to have that sort of nonsense. As was said a short time ago, the initiative and the referendum have one thing in common – what the appendix is in the human body – they are there to be taken out.[55]

A purely majoritarian system also proved acceptable to the larger parties because both were also hostile to 'sectional' interests. The signatories to the pact in 1922 had stated that the national position necessitated the entrusting of government 'to those who had been the strength of the national situation during the last few years'.[56] Collins feared that 'the big businessmen and the politicians will come forward when peace was established and perhaps after some years gain control. Their interests will never demand a renewal of war'.[57] Cosgrave fought the June 1927 election on the issue of coalition government, a newspaper advertisement warning voters that by voting for Independents, Farmers, or Labour, they were voting for 'a weak government with no stated policy'.[58] Kevin O' Higgins was characteristically dismissive of smaller parties, remarking that 'all these wretched little parties vigorously sawing the bough they are sitting on is a sight to make angels weep and devils grin'.[59] On the other side, de Valera's reorganisation of Sinn Féin in 1923 was prompted by his fear that 'the national interest as a whole will be submerged in the clashing of rival economic groups'.[60] De Valera also had a shrewd appreciation of the strategic benefits of a single-party government, predicting in 1932 that the British Government would never negotiate with a government it expected to fall.[61]

Majority rule was also attractive to de Valera for a more mundane reason. According to Dahl, 'the stronger the expectation among the members of a political minority that they will be tomorrow's majority, the more acceptable majority rule will be to them, the less they will feel the need for such special guarantees as a minority veto and the more likely they are to see themselves as impediments to their own future prospects as participants in a majority government'.[62] Since 1923 de Valera had always anticipated that he would eventually mobilise an electoral majority against the Treaty much in the same way that Sinn Féin had mobilised a majority for the Republic in 1918. In 1923 many anti-Treaty candidates were on the run or in prison but Sinn Féin's vote was still impressive considering it had just lost a civil war. This may help explain why de Valera was happy to state in 1926 that in future all decisions would be made according to the wishes of the majority of the Irish people. De Valera may also have realised that the constitutional amendments being introduced by Cosgrave were laying the grounds for his assault on the Treaty. In 1928, for example, Cosgrave went against the spirit of the constitution by preventing the referendum on the oath. Several years later de Valera would do the same, when rejecting the Senate's proposal that he refer the Abolition of the Oath Bill to a referendum. Moreover, Cosgrave's extraordinary decision in 1929, to extend the period during which the constitution could be amended by ordinary legislation by another eight years, can only have encouraged de Valera to believe that majority rule would be his means of undoing the Treaty.

Another reason for the efficacy of majority rule lay in the number of political issues that were at stake. Table 9.5. adopts Lijphart's schema for classifying partisan issues and shows the issue-dimensions separating the parties in the Irish Free State. At first glance only two dimensions, those of regime support and foreign policy, can be considered as having been of high intensity. These dimensions can be considered as one, while the division over economic policy, though part of the overall division on Anglo-Irish relations, was also sufficiently great, particularly between 1933 and 1935, for it to be considered an issue of high intensity.[63] One contention of 'the competitive elitist model' of democracy is that a highly adversarial system can only be stable when elites compete over a narrow range of issues.[64] The Irish experience confirms the validity of this judgement. The efficacy of majority rule derived from the fact that it allowed one overarching issue, that of the Treaty, to be resolved in a democratic way. The main issues were put to the electorate who decided by plurality or majority vote who was to govern and what the direction of government policy would be. Arguably, majority rule encouraged the institutionalisation of the Treaty-split into party politics. Differences over the Treaty were recognised as legitimate, communities of interest emerged, and over time the protagonists became capable of compromise.

Table 9.5 **Issue dimensions of the Irish party system, 1922–37**

	Socio-economic	Religious	Cultural-ethnic	Urban-rural	Regime support	Foreign policy	Post-materialist	Number
Irish Free State	H				H	H		3

Note: H signifies a dimension of High salience.

Source: A. Lijphart, *Democracies: Patterns of Majoritarian and Consensus Government in Twenty-one Countries* (1984), table 8.1, p. 130.

An additional reason for the legitimacy and efficacy of majority rule lies in the ethnic make-up of the society. Asking why a government that defeated de Valera in the field allowed him to triumph through the ballot box in 1932, Munger points out that the two sides originated within the same party. He asks us to imagine an opposite possibility, where 'one of the parties had been a Sinn Féin party of the Republican tradition and the other a Unionist party with a past record of opposition to Irish nationalism. Northern Ireland comes inevitably to mind. It is difficult to believe that the transition should have been so smooth'.[65] Dahl also suggests that the more homogeneous a country 'the less likely it is that the majority will support policies that are harmful to a minority and the more likely it is that a broad consensus on the desirability of majority rule will exist'.[66] The Protestant minority amounted to around seven per cent of the population in 1926 and, separated from the large unionist population in the North, were not large enough to challenge the consensus on the desirability of majority rule by themselves. Majority rule could only have been challenged by an alliance between this privileged minority and Labour, but there was no obvious sympathy between the two.

Finally, Dahl argues that majority rule 'is more likely to be accepted by a minority if they are confident that collective decisions will never fundamentally endanger the basic elements of their way of life'.[67] In the Irish case there was a great deal of ideological common ground between the two Treaty sides. In terms of their view of society as 'a moral community', a wider consensus existed between the two sides. As John Whyte put it: 'Mr. Cosgrave refused to legalise divorce; Mr. de Valera made it unconstitutional. Mr Cosgrave's government forbade propaganda for the use of contraceptives; Mr de Valera's banned their sale or import'.[68] Both sides were committed to a degree of Gaelicisation, extending the process of land reform, and to improving upon the Treaty settlement. A winner-take-all system could be accepted by both because the basic values of the larger parties would not be threatened by a change of office. Experience of office narrowed the gap even further. In 1935 a Fianna Fáil cabinet document lamented 'the lack of a civic spirit' in Ireland in the same way that Cumann na nGaedheal had continually done throughout the 1920s. It also defined the Blueshirts' anarchical spirit, quite ironically, as the 'right of a minority to impose its will on the Irish people by force'.[69]

If an acceptance of majority rule was part of a broader consensus existing between the two Treaty sides, the fact that the evolution of the system still caused controversy suggests that the smaller parties did not share in the consensus on majority rule. For example, in 1926 a cabinet committee proposed wholesale changes to the constitution. The reforms, involving as they did the abolition of the referendum, did not just repair some fault in the existing constitution, as was claimed, but instead 'radically altered the constitution by abandoning one of the principles accepted in 1922 by the entire Constituent Assembly'.[70] It was objected by William Redmond, the leader of the National League, that the recent constitutional changes 'violated the spirit of the Constitution under which any eligible candidate could appeal to the electors on any programme whatsoever'.[71] Cosgrave could provide only an elitist justification for the suspension of the referendum, telling voters that the Amendment Bill had been 'introduced to ensure that that particular provisions enshrined in the Constitution would not be used by those who had not the interests of the public at heart'.[72] The exasperation of the smaller parties with Cosgrave's government was best expressed by Thomas Johnson:

> I have for five years consistently opposed the strong tendency of the Cumann na nGaedheal Ministry to arrogate to themselves excessive power by the automatic votes of the majority in the Dáil – so long as the Republicans refused to take their seats – to override the parties and groups forming the minority, treating opposition criticism as an impertinence .[73]

Fianna Fáil's use of parliamentary majorities was not free of controversy either. The 1922 constitution prescribed 'the principles of proportional representation' but did not define what those principles were. This proved significant when the government altered the electoral boundaries in 1935, resulting in changes to twenty of the thirty existing constituencies. The changes were devised by a cabinet committee composed of Eamon de Valera, Seán Lemass,

Seán T. O'Kelly and James Ryan. The guiding principle of the reform was supposedly demographic, to alter the boundaries in line with recent population changes. However, if one of the principles of proportional representation is to achieve proportionality between seats and votes, then the size of constituency becomes an important factor since the larger the constituency the more proportional the relationship between votes and seats. If a five-seater is the minimum size at which proportionality is guaranteed, as was believed at the time, then in 1933 18 out of 30, or 66 per cent of constituencies, did not disadvantage small parties, whereas in 1937 only a third, or ten constituencies, were large enough to ensure a proportional relationship between the number of votes gained and the number of seats won. It was objected in the Senate that these changes were inconsistent with earlier pledges guaranteeing minority representation that had been made to the southern unionists.[74] An alternative reform, which would have reduced the number of TDs to 138, but made the number elected from constituencies of less than five seats 36 rather than the planned 77, was proposed. The scheme was not debated in the Dáil.[75]

The tension between the Sinn Féin elite's majoritarian preferences and their attachment to general liberal principles was revealed by an exchange during the Dáil debate on the 1937 constitution between two members of the opposition and Fianna Fáil's Frank Donnelly, who was of the opinion that PR was 'a mathematical freak' introduced by the British to get the North to agree to partition:

MR DONNELLY: I do wish that the President would do what Lord Craigavon did and drop this proportional representation altogether . . . Any government that comes to pass Bills has to have a majority, and if the Government has the majority of the votes of the people they are entitled to put through what legislation they wish. No Government can act or get power without the votes of the people. If people are in a minority they are a minority by the votes of the people. It is the privileges of minorities to suffer. That is what they are for and it is for the majority to rule.

MR COSTELLO: Is that what the Deputy says about the North?

MR DONNELLY: We have to accept as a principle that the majority must rule.

MR COSTELLO: Does the Deputy accept it?

MR DONNELLY: I certainly do.

MR NORTON: That is certainly great consolation to the Northern Nationalists.[76]

In three ways the former Sinn Féin elite can be accused of majority tyranny.[77] Constitutionally, all three commitments made by Arthur Griffith to the southern unionists in 1921 were reneged upon by 1937: the use of PR for Dáil elections no longer ensured minority representation after the 1935 electoral reform; the second chamber was abolished; and finally university representation, which meant that Trinity College constituency returned three Dáil deputies, was also abolished. Electorally, majority rule was imposed against the majority principle, which dictates that if an election failed to produce a clear winner, then coalition government should be accepted rather than have recourse to a second election, which meant that all those who didn't vote for the eventual winner in the first election had wasted their vote. Socially, in terms of the relationship of the individual to society, it can be argued that a spiritual tyranny emerged, dominated by the norms of the Catholic Church and the Gaelgóir movement. Majoritarian rules were responsible for the ease with which legislation reflecting these values could be brought in and for the marginalisation of alternative ideological perspectives.[78]

Majority tyranny has been defined as 'the choice of a policy that imposes severe deprivation when an alternative policy could have been chosen that would have imposed no severe restrictions on anyone'.[79] Along these lines de Valera argued that there was no alternative to the abolition of the Senate which had blocked his bill abolishing the oath. De Valera claimed that the Senate 'stood in the way of national unity and willing obedience to the law, and that government by coercion had been the result of the preceding government in imposing the obligation'.[80] However, the full range of possibilities was not exhausted by de Valera before the decision to abolish the Senate. In particular he refused to submit the oath to the referendum, a stance which contrasts oddly with his declaration in 1926 that:

> For my part I am convinced that the oath will not be removed by any group or party acting within the Free State assembly. It will be removed only when the Irish people give an unequivocal mandate for its abolition, and when those who are elected will consequently refuse to take it. Then it will go and very soon afterwards in its train the other contrivances by which the English government make good their claim to interfere in our affairs.[81]

By 1933, however, in possession of a parliamentary majority, de Valera's attitude to plebiscites had changed. As with other aspects of Irish constitutional development in the inter-war era, majority rule served as an expedient decision-making rule for decisions that were in themselves highly controversial.

On the other hand, PR was retained in 1937 which meant that 'civil war politics' would only continue if the old guard remained electorally competitive. The adoption of PR across Europe has been explained as a rational bargain struck between smaller parties whose future existence seems threatened by universal suffrage and a potentially dominant party which is anxious to gain a foothold in the system.[82] This perspective is relevant to inter-war Ireland since, although single-party government led to a centralisation of power, the retention of STV meant that the basic existence of other parties was assured. A characteristic of STV is that while it limits tendencies towards fragmentation it also limits the potential for single-party dominance.[83] In terms of their freedom to introduce legislation and their length of time in office, both Cumann na nGaedheal and Fianna Fáil were dominant parties, but their electoral position was always vulnerable. The role of STV in countering the authoritarian tendencies of the period is an aspect of Irish political development curiously obscured by historical judgement.[84] In 1931 Ernest Blythe publicly recommended a reversion to the British system, arguing that first past the post would have settled the Treaty issue in 1923.[85] However, it was pointed out by a pro-Treatyite that the intervention of third party candidates in the pact election 'had indicated decisively the real opinion of the country and forced Collins and Griffith to decisive action'.[86] Moreover, after 1923 STV allowed voters who supported the Treaty but disagreed with Cosgrave to vote for candidates other than de Valera's. Indeed, the return of so many Labour and independent candidates to the Dáil after 1922 widened the arena of political discussion 'and prevented both Fianna Fáil and the government from turning the proceedings into a barren wrangle about what happened in 1921'.[87]

It was also important, if the Sinn Féin elite stand accused of majority tyranny, that the minority in question was a materially privileged one, and its views were increasingly identified with Fine Gael. The decline in minority representation which occurred between 1927 and 1933 was also due to the larger parties absorbing smaller organisations and their policies. Fianna Fáil absorbed existing Sinn Féin branches, IRA personnel, Labour Party policies, and from 1927 onwards, members of the Sinn Féin party came back with their tails between their legs. Fine Gael was an amalgamation of Cumann na nGaedheal, the Centre Party, and the Blueshirts. Its leaders were at pains to stress that it was much more than a revamped version of Cumann na nGaedheal and had absorbed a variety of distinct ideological influences.[88] Catch-all parties are not necessarily incompatible with minority representation. Arguably the political system became more democratic as the civil war parties ceased to be single-issue rump parties of Sinn Féin, absorbed other influences, and competed over more policy dimensions. Some have suggested that the system took on a left-right cleavage, others that the split reflected deep cultural divisions within society.[89] These divisions made the party system more responsive, even if they reinforced the Treaty divide.

Not only was the party system responsive to smaller parties, but the 1937 constitution also reversed the trend towards an 'elective dictatorship' that had begun under Cumann na nGaedheal. By 1937 Fianna Fáil had acquired an impressive array of repressive powers, and there were few effective restraints on the party in power.[90] The introduction of a constitution which would establish the office of President led to further fears that the constitution would herald the development of a personalised dictatorship under de Valera.[91] It was all the more important then that the new constitution would provide for the limitation of executive power and safeguard the rights of other parties. At first glance the constitution merely copper-fastened the majoritarian thrust of Irish constitutional development, but in other respects it was a reassertion of the constitutional liberalism of 1922, albeit with a greater cognisance of party interests. The decision to adopt the constitution by popular referendum rather than through the Dáil, where Fianna Fáil had an overall majority, signified a desire to establish a people's constitution, rather than a document tied to one political party.[92]

Indeed de Valera, 'the maker of the modern Irish polity in its mature form', left behind him a constitution that has proven remarkably adept at protecting the public from the despotism of elected majorities.[93] Firstly, de Valera argued that fundamental rights could not 'be changed by the Dáil except by a specified majority or an approval by the people by way of referendum' and ensured that the constitution could no longer be amended by ordinary statute law.[94] Secondly, the 1937 constitution prescribed not just the principles of PR but the STV system. When asked why the clause did not allow for a more flexible choice, de Valera replied that electoral arrangements were too fundamental to be left to the mercies of party politics.[95] Thirdly, the power to dissolve the Dáil no longer rested with the Cabinet but with the President, who was to take into account the wishes of Dáil Éireann. This was an important innovation, since, with a separately elected President, the decision could go against the governing party. Finally, the power to initiate referenda on controversial legislation, which had been removed from the constitution in 1928, was reintroduced in a new form.

The creation of such a constitution in 1937 indicated the extent to which de Valera was committed to the consolidation of a democratic system and not simply to the preservation of Fianna Fáil dominance. As Mair remarks, 'what remains striking in the 1937 constitution is the extent of its insistence that power be formally circumscribed'.[96] The role of the new President as head of state was to be largely symbolic and ceremonial and the President was to be elected by popular vote. This was surprising 'since the selection of a largely symbolic head of state in non-monarchical party democracies is often retained as the prerogative of members of parliament and party leaders'.[97] Moreover, key features of what we now regard as 'liberal' Irish democracy – an elected head of state, a powerful supreme court, and referenda on constitutional matters – are all a product of the constitution, although it is debatable whether anyone, including de Valera, could have foreseen how the system would develop. De Valera's constitution was all the more remarkable in that constitutional experimentation in most of the other successor states of inter-war Europe led to the emergence of authoritarian systems of government.[98] If it had continued the tendency, dating from 1922, to concentrate more and more power in the hands of the executive, then the possibility of a one-party state emerging would have been greatly increased. Such an outcome was hinted at by at least one outside observer in 1935.[99]

9.4   Conclusion

Garvin has described Irish political culture as a rather distinctive blend of liberal and authoritarian elements.[100] The institutional basis of that culture was distinctive too, combining a strong executive with a system of proportional representation. Paradoxically, the Sinn Féin elite were as committed to the cornerstone of the Westminster system – single-party government – as they were to its antithesis, proportional representation. The two co-existed very much against the odds between 1922 and 1937, and de Valera's threat to abolish PR during the 1938 election campaign suggests that the tension between them was not resolved by the new constitution. By and large the comparative literature on the relationship between institutional design and political stability stresses the merits of one model versus another, but the Irish case was really an intermediary case where a mixture of majority rule and STV provided an effective institutional arena in which democracy could be stabilised. Identifying the ingredients of that mixture has been the task of this chapter.

Ultimately any decision rule will be judged by the actions taken under it. In Lee's review of the performance of Irish governments since independence, he singles out the first Cosgrave and first de Valera governments for praise.[101] Between the wars the Sinn Féin elite succeeded in demilitarising politics, enhancing the legitimacy of the state, and creating new rules of the game in which political conflicts could be resolved. From this perspective majority rule certainly worked. However, even enthusiasts for majority rule, such as Locke or Rousseau, felt that though the decisions of the majority should be binding once a state was established, the original contract which established a state should require something closer to unanimity.[102] In Ireland the initiatives which attempted to preserve Sinn Féin's unity after the Treaty split failed to lead to a national cabinet commanding the allegiance of both sides. The initial decisions on the constitution were made without the participation of the anti-Treatyites and were then legitimised by majority rule. This introduced a source of weakness that was common to cases of democratic breakdown at the time. On the other hand, the Free State did not suffer from Karvonen's 'double discontinuity' in which 'the constitutions had next to no roots in earlier political structures and the governing coalitions were not those that had introduced the constitution'.[103] Majority rule, which was the unwritten constitution in the Irish case, harked back to the Dáil constitution of 1919 and beyond. In this sense the conventional emphasis on the advantage of constitutional continuity in Ireland is correct.

Whether majority rule, and with it single-party government, was a necessary condition for democratic consolidation is doubtful. My conclusion is that the Irish case confirms the standard hypothesis that majority rule may work in societies that are not deeply divided on ethnic lines. Needless to say the experience of Northern Ireland confirms the converse. What differentiates the southern from the northern experience between the wars was not different understandings of the Westminster model as such, but the fact that there was always a prospect of alternation of government in the Free State. Moreover, the threat posed by coalition government to political stability in the south lay more in the possibility that it could expose the latent conflict between nationalist conceptions of the state and the realities of pluralist politics, than in the possibility that small parties could be extremist. On the other hand, any stable socio-economic order must establish a balance between specific interests and wider collective solidarities.[104] Such conflicts affect states with a legacy of strong centralised authority, but the Irish case overcame them rather quickly, partly because it did not have to accommodate the preferences of a million unionists, partly because of the willingness of the smaller parties to allow the national question to take precedence, and partly because the 1937 constitution allowed a balance between the two impulses to be preserved.

Chapter 10

Conclusion

Independent Ireland has been a democracy for eighty years. While the early decades of independence proved a testing time for the new democracy, the degree of stability subsequently enjoyed by the Irish state has been exceptional. Not even the eruption of civil conflict in Northern Ireland over the past decades has fundamentally disturbed the highly stable state of affairs south of the border. Nor is there any evidence that this state of almost complete political stability is about to be overturned in the near future. Irish institutions are recognised as being legitimate by the vast majority of the population, and Irish political elites conduct their political lives within a set of rules that have changed little since 1937. De Valera's constitution, while it has proven to be controversial in many respects, has provided a remarkably stable framework for the conduct of peaceful political competition. It would have been difficult to believe that this was possible in 1937. Certainly those who saw in the constitution the possibility of a personalised dictatorship have proved very wide of the mark.

It may be, as Garret FitzGerald suggests, that the achievement of stable democracy is proof that the Irish 'have not been as unfortunate in the quality of the political leadership provided by all parties as these same citizens have been prone to assert'.[1] But to credit the political elite alone with the creation of a robust democratic system is to resort to the sort of theoretical simplification that social science is designed to avoid. If Irish elites acted to stabilise democracy between the wars, naturally elite variables must be relevant in some way. But this is circular reasoning. A systematic answer to the question of why democracy has fared well in independent Ireland involves much more than the automatic conclusion that democracy has thrived because Irish elites have enabled it to thrive. The level of economic development, agrarian class relations and the nature of civil society can also be important sources of democratic stability. While it would be too strong to suggest that any of these factors determined the political outcome after independence, it is impossible to locate the Irish case in the universal experience of democratisation without paying attention to them.

My basic assumption throughout this book has been that the options open to political elites, the problems they confront, and the alliances they can form with wider social groups, are still to a very considerable effect shaped by the kind of society they operate in. As one author put it:

> This is not to argue that individual choices made at particular points in time or all observable political outcomes can be specifically and neatly linked to pre-existing structures, but it is claimed that historically created structures, while not determining which one of a limited set of alternatives political actors may choose, are 'confining condition' that restrict or in some cases enhance the choices available to them.[2]

For that reason much of this book has been concerned with specifying the 'confining conditions' which enhanced or militated against the prospects for democracy in the new Irish state. My argument has been that these 'confining conditions' were undoubtedly favourable for democracy in 1921, a view which goes against the conclusion of a recent survey which suggests that Irish social conditions between the wars were no more favourable for democracy than those in Portugal and Poland.[3]

10.1   Favourable conditions

Naturally, if the political elite in 1921 were confronted with a 'still semi-feudal and pre-political populace', then the consolidation of a stable democratic system can be attributed to the skills and values of an exceptional political elite.[4] My analysis of Lipset's theory did not lead, however, to such a conclusion. Rather it suggested that Irish democracy emerged out of a society that was relatively educated and urbanised, and it was this which distinguished it from many of the states where democracy collapsed in the inter-war period. Certainly by 1921 Irish society had moved a long way from the situation it was in, when de Tocqueville observed in Ireland in 1835, a people 'poor, half savage, and overwhelmed by all the miseries by which God can strike man'.[5] The Irish case cannot be considered, like India, an exception to the rule that democracy emerges mainly in modern well-developed societies, but is a case where democratisation was underpinned by a relatively high level of economic development. What cannot be concluded from the analysis of Lipset's theory, however, is that Irish democracy was consolidated because of the state's economic performance after independence. The genesis of Irish democracy was no surprise: its survival cannot be explained by economic variables.

My analysis of Moore's theory in Chapter Four also led me to conclude that the class preconditions for the emergence of a democratic system were in place by 1921. Irish society had benefited from almost half a century of land reform, its agrarian class structure was relatively egalitarian, and it had much in common with other northern European cases where independent farmers remained a pivotal political actor into the twentieth century. Converting the rural poor into a stratum of independent property owners was precisely the solution to the Irish question the French scholar Gustave de Beaumont argued for in 1839, although it became a reality only well after his visit.[6] The fact that the Irish political 'revolution' between 1916 and 1921 was preceded by this social revolution explains, more than any other factor, why the polity and society that emerged from that revolution were essentially conservative. This was understood by the early leaders of the Free State, Michael Collins remarking in April 1922 that the stability of Irish society rested on 'the solid foundation of an industrious land-owning class'.[7] The experience of a civil war soon after, in which the element of social class conflict was relatively minor, again suggests that the class preconditions for the emergence of a democratic system were very much in place in 1921.

Much the same is true for the phenomenon of civil society, which I have treated in Chapter Five primarily as a sphere in which democratic practices could develop. From the early part of the nineteenth century, the habit of electing leaders, of holding them to account through special procedures, and of vesting decision-making power in annual meetings of members, were found in most Irish friendly societies, and they became the common currency of the various nationalist organisations that emerged in the final phase. Moreover, since the 1820s nationalist politicians had clearly understood that the main weapon they had against the British state was the mobilisation of public opinion, and by the 1880s the larger nationalist organisations were clearly trying to combine such central co-ordination with extensive practice in local democracy. As in Finland under Russian rule, civil society was the only sphere in which 'the will of the people' could be expressed and this momentum was increasingly tied to the general demand for democratisation.[8] The result was a democratic civil society that was national in scope, functionally specialised, and characterised by a high degree of reciprocity among its constituent parts. Although there is a tendency to regard these organisations simply as 'politics by other means', nearly all of these bodies survived the civil war to perform a non-political role in the 1920s and 1930s.

Even if we accept that the genesis and the consolidation of democracy are two distinct processes, we can still argue that the factors that further democratisation can also favour consolidation. Moore's work, for example, concerned itself with specifying the preconditions for the emergence of undemocratic systems of government. Since these conditions were noticeably absent in the Irish case, we have to ask what the likely alternatives to democracy were in inter-war Ireland. The rise of the Blueshirts in the 1930s does not mean that fascism was a clear alternative, since that movement was noticeably badly led and ideologically incoherent. Much the same could be said of the radical left, where the alliance between republicanism and socialism in the early 1930s resulted in pronounced internal divisions and ideological confusion.[9] The idea that there could have been some sort of 'Workers'

Republic' in inter-war Ireland is hopelessly naive. Indeed the most important political groupings that lost out after 1921 were not necessarily radical ones at all, but groups such as pro-Treaty republicans, Catholic Action groups, former Home Rulers, and the ex-Unionists who remained in the Free State.[10] All of these groups shared in a democratic culture that existed long before the establishment of the Free State.

On the other hand, the alternatives to democracy in inter-war Europe were not necessarily communism or fascism, but more often than not some form of traditional dictatorship in which bureaucratic, military, or landed elites were able to represent their interests as 'national' interests and thwart meaningful political competition.[11] In contrast to the fascist regimes, these authoritarian regimes, found throughout Eastern Europe, with the exception of Finland and Czechoslovakia, and perhaps Bulgaria, were not revolutionary regimes at all, but 'counter-revolutionary regimes that sought to preserve the interests of pre-war elites'.[12] In some ways the Irish state manifested similar features to these cases: a reliance on agriculture as the main source of employment, the dominance of nationalism as an ideology, and a low level of working-class organisation. However, in no sense was the Irish state dominated by pre-war social elites. These had largely been swept aside by land reform and the Sinn Féin electoral landslide in 1918. In the Irish case it was party elites and not bureaucratic or military elites that dominated political life. These elites were not 'instruments' of bureaucratic or military interests but were exceptionally autonomous.

In Eastern Europe, too, the main threat to the stability of the authoritarian regimes came from radicalised peasant movements, which were extremely important in Bulgaria, Romania, Lithuania, Latvia, Estonia, and, initially, in Hungary and Finland, but not in Ireland. Save for the harmless appearance of Clann na Talmhun in the late 1930s, there were no such movements in inter-war Ireland. The 'revolutionary potential' of the Irish countryside was limited, and no amount of wishful thinking on the part of socialist republicans could alter that fact. Also, the southern Irish state was ethnically homogeneous to a degree that was unusual in the successor states. The Anglo-Irish minority was less than seven per cent of the population in 1927. In such a context, nationalist ideology, which played on the existence of 'pariah' classes in Eastern Europe, was never as divisive as it was in a country like Poland, where almost thirty per cent of the population were not Polish. Even in contrast to a relatively homogeneous state like Finland, with a Swedish-speaking minority of around twelve per cent at independence, the Irish state seems to have been in an exceptionally advantageous position.

Does this imply then that the consolidation of Irish democracy was inevitable, and that there was no possibility of a reversal to authoritarian rule after 1921? I believe that environmental factors made the survival of democracy more likely than not, and that the process of land reform in particular differentiated the Irish case from most of its counterparts in Eastern Europe. It is significant that the one state 'geographically' in Eastern Europe that can claim to have retained a parliamentary form of government throughout the inter-war era – Finland – instituted a series of massive land reforms after independence. In Ireland the social order was accepted as a given by the main political actors and in this sense the Irish state was genuinely immune to the 'crisis of modernisation' experienced by European countries such as Italy, Spain and Germany between the wars. As James Hogan put it in 1938:

> If in Ireland we may look to the future with a greater degree of optimism than most of our fellow Europeans, it is precisely because we have not yet fully conformed to contemporary European standards, because the well nigh irresistible forces which are compelling western man towards some obscure destiny are as yet at some distance from us. There are still great reserves of religious faith and unspoiled imaginative energy on which we can draw. Problems, cultural and social, difficult, if not impossible, of solution elsewhere, do not exist for us or else exist in such a simple form as to be capable of swift and accurate solutions.[13]

Berg-Schlosser conceives of the inter-war crisis as a huge tidal wave that threatened to engulf all the European states at the same time. In societies that had undergone a thoroughgoing process of modernisation, however, historical and structural conditions meant that 'dikes' existed which softened the impact of these tidal waves.[14] This was certainly true of the Irish case, where the civil war, though polarising at the elite level, did not put into question the social and economic foundations of the state. It was also fortunate that the two periods of deepest crisis, that of the civil war in 1922–23 and that of the Blueshirt imbroglio between 1933 and 1935, were separated by a distance of some ten years, during which the two civil war sides spent over five years working in the same parliament. In the 1960s Michael Hayes commented that 'the ordinary work of a parliament smothered the fires of resentment and acted as a solvent for the emotional aftermath of the duel between brothers'.[15]

Berg-Schlosser's perspective has some bearing on our evaluation of the role of the civil war in Irish political development. In 1970 Fianna Fáil's Tom McEllistrim, who fought on the losing side in Kerry, reflected that the nationalist movement was 'chastened' by the experience of civil war, and he thought the civil war a 'godsend' to the country.[16] However, with the exception of Finland, which allowed some genuine pluralism after 1918, in every other European country which experienced a civil war in the twentieth century, what emerged was an authoritarian rather than a democratic system of government. In cases such as Austria, Greece, Hungary, and Spain, the post civil war polity remained fundamentally polarised between groups that were regarded as 'nationally minded' and groups tainted by their association with socialism or communism. The latter only found their way back into the system after a long authoritarian interlude, as in Spain, or after a long period of authoritarian and then conservative political dominance, as in Greece.

In the Irish case the losers came to power less than a decade after the civil war. In a European context this was unique, but was it unique because of the nature of Irish elite culture, or because of the structural characteristics of Irish society at that time?[17] The Irish civil war was not a deeply rooted class conflict, but a conflict fought among a nationalist elite which shared an overall consensus in many areas of public policy.[18] The prospect of the civil war losers regrouping and coming to power was never as threatening to the victors as it would have been in a more deeply polarised society. Indeed the aspirations of the losers had always had a great deal of legitimacy in Irish civil society, and the fact that the Catholic Church, the Gaelic Athletic Association and the Gaelic League survived the civil war intact arguably provided a basis on which they were reintegrated into society after 1923. What is remarkable about the Irish case is the ease with which both the Treaty sides were able to mobilise widespread electoral support behind their entirely different agendas within the space of ten years. This suggests that a certain volatility in the electorate and an absence of clear-cut social cleavages are favourable conditions for consolidation. It also indicates, as I have already suggested, that there was something superficial about the Treaty split, which in turn is attributable to the structural characteristics of the society. As suggested by Burton, Gunther and Higley, an electorate with a low level of ideological and class polarisation is more likely to exist in a relatively advanced society.[19]

The fact that Irish democracy rested on sound foundations between the wars was ultimately due to the historic interaction between the forces of Irish nationalism and the British state under the Union. The remarkable growth in primary education, the timing of land reform, and the emergence of a democratic civil society, were all consequences, in one way of another, of British policy, and were more tangible evidence of a positive imperial legacy than the inconstant parliamentary tradition highlighted by Farrell.[20] Indeed the whole problem with the tutelary perspective is that by allying itself with Ulster Unionists during the Home Rule crisis, the British state undermined a constitutionalist tradition that was then in a process of maturation. If a clear demonstration that extra-parliamentary methods were more effective than elected majorities in British politics were ever needed, then Ulster clearly provided it. As a result, after almost thirty years of waiting for Home Rule, and in a climate of growing disillusionment with political corruption, nationalist Ireland found itself suddenly radicalised and the events of the First World War ensured that this would have lasting effects. In the long run the constitutional tradition triumphed, but it took at least two decades of instability and violence before democracy was consolidated in the 26 counties.

10.2 Elites and democratic consolidation

In explaining why the process of consolidation was successful, structural factors can only provide necessary rather than sufficient conditions. A high level of socio-economic development, extensive land reform and a strong civil society may have made the consolidation of a democratic system more likely, but they certainly didn't guarantee it. According to Vanhanen, 'despite the limited scope of free choices in the process of democratisation, the strategies of political actors certainly matter, particularly so in transitional circumstances when social conditions do not clearly determine the nature of a country's political system'. The importance of these conscious strategies is greatest where 'social conditions are sufficiently favourable for democracy but do not yet guarantee democratisation'.[21] This is as succinct a summary of the Irish situation as I can find. Social conditions may have favoured one outcome more than another in 1921, but given the lack of authoritative institutions at the outset, the divisiveness of the Treaty issue, and the recriminations over the origins of the civil war, stable democracy could only come about as a result of a long-term process of consolidation in which political elites played a crucial role.[22]

Arguably the most important achievement of the pro-Treaty elite was that of subordinating the military to the civilian wing of the nationalist movement between 1922 and 1924. Despite the veneration of the republican tradition after the 1916 Rising, not only did the civil war see the defeat of the IRA for the first time, but also, once the civil war was over, the pro-Treaty elite systematically marginalised the republican elements within the Free State security forces, and reduced the National Army to a fraction of its civil war size. Together with the creation of an unarmed police force, and the establishment of an apolitical civil service, the insistence on professional standards in the army proved fundamental when Fianna Fáil assumed power in 1932. The pro-Treaty elite's strategy has parallels with India's treatment of the officers of the Indian National Army who had declared an Indian Republic during the Second World War. While imprisoned by the British, Nehru, who saw their revolt as motivated by the highest patriotic ideals, championed their cause. After independence, however, Nehru refused them positions in the Indian army on the grounds that they would politicise the force.[23]

On the other hand, Cosgrave remarked in 1931 that Irish people were only gradually 'realising that each individual citizen has definite obligations towards the state' and lamented 'the absence of a state sense among large sections of the people' which, he thought, explained why so many people were willing to support subversive groups and refused to serve on Irish juries.[24] Such remarks indicate the amount of work that still needed to be done if the state was to consolidate its authority in the 26 counties. In 1926, Frank Aiken claimed that Fianna Fáil's strategy of using the powers possessed by the Dáil to achieve their objectives did not involve a recognition of the legitimacy of that parliament, any more than Sinn Féin's possession of local government boards between 1918 and 1921 involved a recognition of the authority of the Local Government Board in Dublin or of the British King.[25] De Valera's key achievement after 1932 was to create a wider sense of ownership of Irish state institutions than the Cosgrave governments had been able to do, and in 1935 a Garda document advised that this was more important than relying on purely repressive means:

> The measures introduced by the Government such as the creation of the Volunteer Force; the granting of pensions to the old IRA; the legislative acts directed towards the political and economic emancipation of the country, have done more to force the IRA into constitutional alignment than coercive legislation could ever do.[26]

As Gramsci recognised, the issue in any 'Caesarist' transformation of a political system is whether revolution or restoration predominates, and the question is crucial to our evaluation of the role of Fianna Fáil after 1932.[27] Despite the expectations of republican hardliners there were certainly strong elements of restoration under de Valera. The explicitly majoritarian stance taken by Fianna Fáil after it came to power, the party's refusal to purge the public services of its former enemies, and the reintroduction of military tribunals to deal with subversives in 1934, are all signs that the element of restoration predominated in the Fianna Fáil regime. Arguably though, the real regime that de Valera sought to restore was not Cumann na nGaedheal's at all, but that of Sinn Fein between 1919 and 1921. A united nationalist movement with de Valera at its head, a set of institutions deriving their authority only from the Irish people, and a military wing clearly subordinated to the political leadership, were common aims of both Sinn Féin and Fianna Fáil, and between 1932 and 1938 de Valera went some way towards achieving them.

If Irish democracy had not been consolidated before the 1930s, can we say that there was one crucial turning point in the process? In Finland, Greece, and Spain, also countries with a civil war past, the experience of changeover was a fundamental event on their path towards stability. In Finland the moderate wing of the civil war losers, the Social Democrats, formed a short-lived administration in 1926, and, more dramatically, joined the Agrarian Union, who had been on the other side in 1918, in a 'red-earth' coalition in 1937. This coalition had a broader parliamentary base than any previous Finnish government and indicated that the political system in inter-war

Finland could only be consolidated by recognising the role and importance of the Social Democratic Party.[28] In Greece the socialist party PASOK came to power in 1981, an event that signalled the end of 'forty-five years of almost uninterrupted rule by the Greek right' and the inclusion of the hitherto excluded rural and working classes in the political system.[29] In Spain the landslide victory of the socialist PSOE party in the 1982 general election resulted in the formation of the first 'leftist' government in Spanish history since the 1930s. The smooth alternation 'underlined that the rules of the game were in force and indicated the system's ability to generate alternatives'.[30] In all three cases then, the civil war losers came to power after an initial period of dominance by conservative parties, and the experience of changeover broadened the representative base of the political system.

It is not uncommon for parties that pioneered the transition process to find themselves unable to maintain their dominant position within the system. In his analysis of the 'Third Wave' democratisers, Huntington suggests that 'the years after the first democratic government came to power were usually characterised by the fragmentation of the democratic coalition that had produced the transition, the decline in the effectiveness of the initial leaders of the democratic governments, and the growing realisation that the advent of democracy would not, in itself, produce solutions to the major economic and social problems confronting the country'.[31] In Ireland the coalition of interests that lay behind the establishment of the Free State had unravelled by 1927. Two splinter groups, the National League and Clann Éireann, had already broken away from the governing party by 1925, and the smaller parties seemed willing to enter into a coalition, with Fianna Fáil backbench support, in the summer of 1927. The deaths of Collins, Griffith and then of O'Higgins deprived the pro-Treatyites of their strongest leaders, and Cumann na nGaedheal were unable to come up with policies designed to counteract the depression. Between 1927 and 1932 the government had the reputation of being a 'lame duck' administration.[32]

Beetham has argued that a key aspect of democratic legitimacy is precisely the ability to vote in new governments at times when the poor performance of the government is creating widespread discontent with the system.[33] In the context of the depression, which hit Ireland as hard as any European country, it was clearly important that a party came to power that was willing to address the material hardships suffered by ordinary people. Changeover also implied that no 'reserved domains' of public policy existed, and that the pro-Treaty party would acquiesce in Fianna Fáil's revision of the Treaty. Such a situation could hardly have been foreseen in 1928 when Cosgrave prevented a referendum on the oath, an act which suggested that the Treaty was an unalterable part of Irish public policy. Ultimately, it is impossible to separate the consolidation process from that of democratisation, since the Fianna Fáil party also widened patterns of political participation, much in the same way that PASOK did in Greece in the 1980s. A successful changeover demonstrated that democratic rules would continue to apply, but also rewarded the party that was most interested in popular mobilisation with the spoils of office. This is not a unique occurrence but in the history of democratic transitions it is rare.

10.3   Comparative lessons

As an example of a successful democratic transition, the Irish case holds some perhaps unusual lessons for the comparative literature on democratic transitions. In the first place, it shows that a democracy can be consolidated without reaching explicit agreement on the rules of the game between the major political actors. An implicit consensus of sorts certainly existed between the civil war parties, but such a consensus was never made explicit. Neither the 1922 constitution nor the 1937 constitution, for all their merits, were supported by both sides of the civil war divide. Secondly, the Irish case proves that democracy can also survive intense adversarial party competition, a factor which undoubtedly led to the collapse of democracy in 1930s Spain. The current emphasis in democratic theory is on forming pro-democratic coalitions and elite pacts, but there are situations in which such tactics are impossible to employ. Rather, the Irish experience suggests that democracy can be consolidated by a successful changeover, if elites are willing to take the risks that such a process involves. Thirdly, the Irish case suggests that the employment of the correct democratic strategies is a necessary feature of the consolidation process. Although some of the strategies employed by de Valera after 1922 are contained in Lustick's work, on the whole de Valera's very deliberate reshaping of the Free State finds few parallels in comparative politics.[34] Finally, the Irish case suggests that exogenous factors can be just as relevant as endogenous variables in accounting for the success of the consolidation process. De Valera's ability to reform the Free State, and thus legitimise it in the eyes of most of its republican detractors, was dependent on Britain acquiescing in the revision of the Treaty. If Britain had opposed these moves, or tried to involve itself in the domestic conflicts of the early to mid-1930s, then the consolidation process would have been much more difficult.

Overall, the Irish experience supports the traditional contention that democratic consolidation is a dual process, involving both a process of institution building and the simultaneous growth of a favourable democratic culture. The state-building achievements of the Cosgrave governments in the 1920s have been widely praised by historians, but these institutions would not have led to stability had they not been accompanied by a corresponding growth in favourable attitudes towards them on behalf of their political opponents. The paradoxes of this process were revealed by a reflection of Fianna Fáil's Sean MacEntee in 1936:

> To my mind the political development which holds most prominence for the future well-being and progress of this country has been the acceptance by the vast majority of our people of the Oireachtas as the representative assembly of the State. Everything that Fianna Fáil has been able to do since 1927 has been consequent upon this. The abolition of the Oath, of the Appeal to the Privy Council, and of the Seanad as at present constituted, in my view would never have materialised but for the fact that the Oireachtas has been so accepted. And this occurred and indeed to an extent was compelled during Mr Cosgrave's regime.[35]

In 1936 MacEntee could not bring himself to accept that the anti-Treaty position in the spring of 1922 was an undemocratic one, but he was well aware that his opponents' elevation of majority rule to the status of a cardinal political principle in the civil war ultimately helped underwrite the position taken by Fianna Fáil against the IRA and the Blueshirts in the 1930s.

The Irish case, I suggest, represents a form of 'democratic elitism' whereby a dominant political elite proves able to absorb a variety of influences while at the same time maintaining their pivotal position within the system. For this reason future work on the Irish case might concentrate on the role of STV in shaping the political behaviour of the dominant political elite. Certainly from the 1922 election onwards STV has had a fundamental effect on political competition and it is as a combination of the Westminster system with STV that the Irish system is best understood in this period. Future work might also study the role of Irish sub-elites in the consolidation process. The role of the civil war political elite can be overestimated. There was a great deal of insecurity at the top, and democracy was consolidated in a society where the sub-elites – the media, the judiciary, and the army for example – were themselves supportive of democratic practices. More generally there has been little or no work on Irish civil society and its relationship to the democratic process. What role had organisations like the Gaelic Athletic Association in Irish political development, or did they survive the civil war only as de-politicised remnants of their former selves? Was Irish civil society funda-mentally retarded by the experience of civil war, or did it survive to shape the manner in which Irish politics subsequently developed? Finally, more work could be done on the nature of elite political culture in this period, since both the anti-Treatyites in 1922 and the Blueshirts in the 1930s had an ambiguous attitude to democratic principles. Indeed a key theme of this book is that both sides of the civil war divide were in some ways 'reluctant democrats', oscillating between democratic and authoritarian norms, and it was the resolution of this ambiguity, notably in the person of de Valera, that led to the consolidation of Irish democracy in the 1930s.

Whatever the answers to these questions the experience of Irish democracy after 1922 suggests that the model of democracy operating in the Irish Free State was what Held describes as 'the competitive elitist model' of democracy, a model that was capable of solving questions of political leadership and authority but not necessarily of social progress and individual freedom.[36] In this respect the Sinn Féin legacy was highly ambiguous. It provided leadership on issues of national freedom, but Sinn Féin had not developed a powerful critique of the state or of the market economy. This was due, I suggest, to the state's provenance as 'a national mobilisation democracy', whereby democracy was seized upon as a means of mobilising for national freedom, but not necessarily for individual or class freedom. The fact that the Treaty did not provide a permanent basis for Irish political development meant that 'the national issue' would remain dominant after 1921, and other issues were marginalised.

The experience of civil war in Ireland and the longevity of 'civil war politics' also suggest that the point of departure in each transition is crucial. The Irish case is unlike most of the cases that are analysed in recent comparative politics which have been peaceful transitions from authoritarian regimes. The Irish attempt to form a democratic system was accompanied by a violent revolt in a country which did not have developed indigenous political institutions. For that reason it was necessary to go through a period of institutionalisation first, in which central state institutions become effective and authoritative. After this process of institutionalisation, the hurdles of consolidation and legitimacy can be tackled. Particular problems are posed for democrats when the establishment of central state institutions and the establishment of democracy go hand in hand. There are few parallels in history for this and most of the post-colonial cases have ended in failure. The best comparable cases are probably Finland and Israel, but detailed comparisons have yet to be made.

To conclude, the fortunes of Irish democracy after 1921 were inseparable from the manner in which the civil war conflict worked itself out in peaceful party politics. The Cumann na nGaedheal elite managed to create a strong institutional base for the fledgling democracy, but between 1927 and 1932 the Irish state was still an unconsolidated system: consensus was low, attitudes were polarised, and the public was continually reminded of the chaos that might ensue if Fianna Fáil came to power. The fact that no such outcome materialised, and that de Valera finally succeeded in reconciling the two notions that seemed irreconcilable in 1922 – majority rule and popular sovereignty – meant that the progress of consolidation after 1932 was rapid. If the social preconditions for democracy were already in place in 1921, these should still be considered 'favourable conditions' for consolidation rather than determinants. There was nothing inevitable about the consolidation of

Irish democracy between the wars, and without a basic commitment to establishing a functioning democracy on the part of the political elites, there is no reason to believe that democracy would have been consolidated before 1939. Remarkably, much the same political elites who had failed to stop the slide towards civil war in 1922 were responsible for the consolidation of Irish democracy over the next two decades. Along the way they may have concluded that the task of creating a stable democracy in the 26 counties was the limit of one generation's capacity.

Notes

Abbreviations used in Notes and Bibliography

ASR	*American Sociological Review*
CP	*Comparative Politics*
D/T	*Department of An Taoiseach*
D/J	Department of Justice
D/E	Dáil Éireann files
ESR	*Economic and Social Review*
EJPS	*European Journal of Political Research*
FJ	*Freeman's Journal*
IHS	*Irish Historical Studies*
IPS	*Irish Political Studies*
JCH	*Journal of Contemporary History*
JIH	*Journal of Interdisciplinary History*
NA	National Archives
NL	National Library
PSQ	*Political Science Quarterly*
UCDA	University College Dublin Archive Department

Chapter One

1 T. Towey, 'The reaction of the British government to the Collins–de Valera Pact', *IHS* 22 (1980), p. 69.

2 Ibid., p. 66.

3 Lord Salisbury 15 May 1886, quoted in D. G. Boyce, *Englishmen and Irish Troubles: British Public Opinion and the Making of Irish Policy 1918–22* (London, 1972), p. 29.

4 Quoted in D. McCartney, *Irish Democracy and its Nineteenth Century Irish Critics* (Dublin, 1979), p. 16.

5 See R. B. McDowell, *Crisis and Decline: The Fate of the Southern Unionists* (Dublin, 1997), pp. 108–9.

6 K. O'Higgins, Memo, n. d. (NA, D/T, S 6695).

7 B. O'Leary and J. McGarry, *The Politics of Antagonism: Understanding Northern Ireland* (London, 1993), table 1. 1, p. 21.

8 'The north-eastern situation: chronological order of events since the signing of Collins–Craig Pact' (NA, Items Connected with Collins–Craig Pact of 21 Jan. 1922, D/T, S 1801).

9 Provisional Government Decision, 25 May 1922 (NA, D/T, S 2942).

10 O'Higgins, Memo.

11 N. d. (Fianna Fáil Archives, FF/22).

12 'General Aiken's opinion on republican policy', *Irish World*, 31 July 1926 (UCDA, Aiken Papers, P104/2574).

13 Republican attitudes to democracy are critically analysed in T. Garvin, *1922: The Birth of Irish Democracy* (Dublin, 1996), pp. 40–51.

14 See F. Munger, *The Legitimacy of Opposition: The Change of Government in Ireland in 1932* (Beverly Hills, 1975).

15 G. FitzGerald, 'Days of doubt long gone as State reaches 75th birthday', *The Irish Times*, 6 Dec. 1997.

16 F. Halliday, 'International society as homogeneity: Burke, Marx, Fukuyama', *Millennium* 21 (1992), p. 459.

17 Criteria are taken from M. Weiner, 'Empirical democratic theory' in M. Weiner and E. Ozbuddun (eds), *Competitive Elections in Developing Societies* (Durham NC, 1987), pp. 4–5.

18 *Irish Press*, 3 Feb. 1932.

19 C. Foley, *Legion of the Rearguard: The IRA and the Modern Irish State* (London, 1922), p. 104.

20 See M. Valiulis, 'The army mutiny of 1924 and the assertion of civilian authority in independent Ireland' *IHS* 13 (1983), pp. 354–67.

21 W.J. Stover, 'Military politics in Finland between the wars', *JCH* 12 (1977), p. 747.

22 R. Dahl, *Democracy and its Critics* (Yale, 1989), p. 232.

23 T. Vanhanen, *The Emergence of Democracy: A Comparative Study of 119 States, 1850–1979* (Helsinki, 1984), pp. 144–5.

24 Two works with the merit of treating a wide variety of European cases but which ignore the Irish case completely are D. Rueschmeyer, E. Stephens, and J. D. Stephens, *Capitalist Development and Democracy* (Cambridge 1992); G. Luebbert, *Liberalism, Fascism and Social Democracy: Social Classes and the Political Origins of Regimes in Interwar Europe* (Oxford, 1991). For an improvement see the essay by A. Zink in D. Berg-Schlosser and J. Mitchell (eds), *Conditions of Democracy in Europe 1919–1939* (Basingstoke, 2000), pp. 263–94.

25 For the former see J. Coakley, 'Political succession and regime change in new states in inter-war Europe: Ireland, Finland, Czechoslovakia, and the Baltic Republics', *EJPS* 14 (1987), pp. 187–207; and D. Kirby, 'Nationalism and national identity in the new states of Europe: the examples of Austria, Finland, and Ireland' in P. Stirk (ed.), *European Unity in Context: The Interwar Period* (London and New York, 1989), pp. 110–24. For the latter see B Kissane, 'The not so amazing case of Irish democracy', *IPS* 10 (1995), pp. 43–68; Garvin, *1922*, pp. 189–207.

26 See R. K. Carty, *Electoral Politics in Ireland: Party and Parish Pump* (Dingle, 1983); J. Prager, *Building Democracy in Ireland* (Cambridge, 1986); D. Schmitt, *The Irony of Irish Democracy: The Impact of Political Culture on Administration and Democratic Political Development in Ireland* (London and Toronto, 1973).

27 For a criticism see L. Kennedy, 'Modern Ireland: post-colonial society or post-colonial pretensions?' *Irish Review* 13 (1992), pp. 107–21.

28 See the argument advanced in Chapter Two.

29 See for example J. Lee, *Ireland, 1918–1985* (Cambridge, 1989); L. Mjoset, *The Irish Economy in a Comparative Institutional Perspective* (Dublin, 1992); J. H. Goldthorpe and C. T. Whelan, *The Development of Industrial Society in Ireland* (Oxford, 1992).

30 F. Hermens, *Democracy or Anarchy? A Study of Proportional Representation* (New York, London, 1972).

31 D. Berg-Schlosser, and G. de Meur, 'Conditions for democracy in inter-war Europe: a Boolean test of major hypotheses', *CP* 26 (1994), pp. 253–81.

32 See Garvin, *1922*.

33   For sophisticated integrated analyses see D. Berg-Schlosser, 'Conditions of authoritarianism, fascism and democracy in inter-war Europe', *International Journal of Comparative Sociology*, 39 (1998), pp. 335–77; V. Perez-Diaz, *The Return of Civil Society: The Emergence of Democratic Spain* (Cambridge, Mass., 1998); D. J. Yashar, *Demanding Democracy: Reform and Reaction in Costa Rica and Guatemala, 1870s–1950s* (Stanford, 1997).

34   B. Moore, *The Social Origins of Dictatorship and Democracy: Lord and Peasant in the making of the Modern World* (Harmondsworth, 1966).

35   Prager, *Building Democracy*, Garvin, *1922*.

36   Hermens, *Democracy or Anarchy*.

Chapter Two

1   See for example, J. A. Hobson, *Democracy and a Changing Civilisation* (London, 1934); W. Lappard, *The Crisis of Democracy: Lectures of the Harris Foundation* (Chicago, 1938); H. Laski, *Democracy in Crisis* (London, 1934).

2   A. Zink. 'Ireland: democratic stability without compromise', in D. Berg-Schlosser and J. Mitchell (eds), *Conditions of Democracy in Europe 1919–39* (Basingstoke, 2000), p. 293.

3   See Sinn Féin, *Ireland's Request to the Government of the United States of America for Recognition as a Sovereign Independent State* (Dublin, 1919).

4   See J. Coakley, 'The election that made the first Dáil' in B. Farrell (ed.), *The Creation of the Dáil* (Dublin, 1994), p. 36. See also the discussion in B. O'Leary and J. McGarry, *Explaining Northern Ireland: Broken Images* (Oxford, 1995), pp. 25–30.

5   R. Brubacher, *Nationalism Reframed: Nationhood and the National Question in the New Europe* (Cambridge, 1996), p. 79.

6   E. Hobsbawm, *Age of Extremes: A Short History of the Twentieth Century* (London, 1994), p. 125.

7   E. O'Malley, *The Singing Flame* (Dublin, 1978), p. 16.

8   *The Round Table* 23 (1923), pp. 261–2.

9   J. M. Regan, *The Irish Counter-Revolution 1921–36: Treatyite Politics and Settlement in Independent Ireland* (Dublin, 1999), p. 102.

10   See M. G. Valiulis, *Portrait of a Revolutionary: General Richard Mulcahy and the Founding of the Irish Free State* (Dublin, 1992); E. O'Halpin, 'The army and the Dáil – civil/military relations within the independence movement' in B. Farrell (ed.), *The Creation of the Dáil* (Dublin, 1994), pp. 107–23; T. Garvin, *1922, The Birth of Irish Democracy* (Dublin, 1996).

11   T. Garvin, 'Civil war took several billions out of economy', *The Irish Times*, 6 Dec. 1997.

12   *The Irish Times*, 4 Feb. 1932.

13   See M. Cronin, *The Blueshirts and Irish Politics* (Dublin, 1997), pp. 135–67.

14   *Dáil Debates*, col. 1860, 28 June 1928.

15   See L. Karvonen, *Fragmentation and Consensus: Political Organisation and the Inter-war Crisis in Europe* (Boulder, Colo., 1994).

16   Republican currents in Irish nationalist politics in the half-century before independence are analysed in T. Garvin, *Nationalist Revolutionaries in Ireland* (Oxford, 1987).

17   *IRA Daily Bulletin*, no. 27, 30 Dec. 1922.

18   R. A. Kann, 'The Case of Austria', *JCH* 15 (1980), pp. 37–53.

19   P. Preston, 'The origins of the socialist schism in Spain, 1917–31', *JCH* 12 (1977), pp. 101–33.

20   J. Coakley, 'Political succession during the transition to independence: evidence from Europe' in P. Calvert (ed.), *The Process of Political Succession* (Basingstoke, 1987), p. 27.

21   See R. Alapuro, *State and Revolution in Finland* (Berkeley, 1988), p. 187.

22   Coakley, 'Political succession during the transition to independence', p. 28.

23   'A Message from Eamon de Valera to the people of the United States', *Poblacht na hEireann,* War News no. 10, 4 July 1922.

24   B. Chubb, *The Government and Politics of Ireland* (London, 1970), pp. 44–5.

25   B. Farrell, 'The first Dáil and after', in B. Farrell (ed.), *The Irish Parliamentary Tradition* (Dublin, 1973), p. 24.

26   Ibid.

27   Quoted in D. Schmitt, *The Irony of Irish Democracy: The Impact of Political Culture on Administration and Democratic Political Development in Ireland* (London and Toronto, 1973), p. 40.

28   Farrell, 'The first Dáil and after', p. 212.

29   Ibid., p. 211.

30   Ibid., p. 218.

31   Quoted in R. Fanning, *Independent Ireland* (Dublin, 1983), p. 10.

32   Roy Foster reflects that 'Most historians who examine the record of the 1920s become "Free Staters"', R. Foster, 'More sinner than saint', *Independent on Sunday*, 17 Oct. 1994. See in particular, D. Keogh, 'Planting democracy in an island of hate', *The Irish Times*, 5 Oct. 1999; J. Lee, *Ireland 1912–1985* (Cambridge, 1989), pp. 171–4; F. S. L. Lyons, *Ireland Since the Famine* (Glasgow, 1983), pp. 484–504; O. MacDonagh, *Ireland: The Union and its Aftermath* (London, 1977), p. 107.

33   M. Weiner, 'Empirical democratic theory' in M. Weiner and E. Ozbudun (eds), *Competitive Elections in Developing Countries* (Durham, 1987), p. 19.

34   *The Round Table* 50 (1923), pp. 257–8.

35   Quoted in Lee, *Ireland 1912–1985*, p. 98.

36   *Irish Independent*, 16 Dec. 1922.

37   Quoted in Lee, *Ireland 1912–1985*, p. 98.

38   T. Garvin, 'Unenthusiastic democrats: the emergence of Irish democracy' in R. Hill and M. Marsh (eds), *Modern Irish Democracy* (Dublin, 1993), pp. 9–24.

39   C. C. O'Brien, 'The embers of Easter, 1916–1966', in O. Dudley Edwards and F. Pyle (eds), *The Easter Rising* (London, 1968), p. 229.

40   Cardinal Logue, cited in Foster 'More sinner than saint'.

41   E. O'Halpin, *Defending Ireland: The Irish State and its Enemies since 1922* (Oxford, 1999), p. 108.

42   J. A. Murphy, 'The achievement of Eamon de Valera' in J. P. O'Carroll and J. A. Murphy (eds), *The Life and Times of Eamon de Valera* (Cork, 1968), p. 2.

43   D. Thomson, *Europe Since Napoleon* (London, 1986), pp. 663–73.

44   C. S. Maier, *Recasting Bourgeois Europe: Stabilisation in France, Germany, and Italy in the Decade after World War One* (Princeton, 1988), p. 3.

45   Hobsbawm, *Age of Extremes*, p. 111.

46   On the Free State see Regan, *The Irish Counter-Revolution*, pp. 75–129.

47   Hobsbawm, *Age of Extremes*, p. 113.

48   *The Irish Times*, 5 Sept. 1927.

49   *Dáil Debates*, vol. 40 col. 49, 14 Oct. 1931.

50   Maier, *Recasting Bourgeois Europe*, p. 7.

51   G. Luebbert, 'Social foundations of political order in inter-war Europe', *World Politics* 34 (1987), pp. 449–78.

52   Maier, *Recasting Bourgeois Europe*, p. 4.

53   Ibid., p. 312.

54   Ibid., p. vii.

55 Ibid., p. 8.

56 Ibid., p. viii.

57 See P. Mair, *The Break-Up of the United Kingdom: The Irish Experience of Regime Change, 1918–49* (Glasgow, 1978), p. 18.

58 M. Hopkinson, *Green Against Green: The Irish Civil War* (Dublin, 1988), p. 4. See also O'Halpin, 'The army and the Dáil – civil/military relations', p. 113.

59 Garvin, *1922*, p. 194.

60 *Dáil Debates*, col. 175, 12 Sept. 1922.

61 O'Higgins to Cosgrave, n. d., 'Civil war: Mr. de Valera's ceasefire order' (NA, D/T, S 2210).

62 J. Linz and A. Stepan, 'Toward democratic consolidation' in L. Diamond, M. F. Plattner, Y Chu and H. Tien (eds), *Consolidating the Third Wave Democracies: Themes and Perspectives* (Baltimore and London, 1997), p. 14.

63 *The Irish Times*, 12 Sept. 1927.

64 With regard to the civil service this was less a case of administrative practice building on established British tradition than of Irish politicians and civil servants insisting on a meritocratic and apolitical Irish civil service for the first time. See E. O'Halpin, 'The civil service and the political system', *Administration* 38 (1991), pp. 283–303, and E. O'Halpin, 'The politics of governance in the four countries of the United Kingdom, 1912–1922' in S. Connolly (ed.), *Kingdoms United?* (Dublin, 1999), pp. 239–48.

65 Garvin, *1922*, p. 197.

66 'Voice recording made for the bureau by the Hon. George Gavan Duffy, President of the High Court', 20 Jan. 1951 (NA, Duffy Papers, 1125/15 no. 17).

67 See B. Kissane, 'Decommissioning as an issue in the Irish civil war', *Studies in Ethnicity and Nationalism* 1 (2001), pp. 8–16.

68 E. de Valera, 'Civil war 1922–24: historical summary by President de Valera' (NA, D/ T, S 9282).

69 *FJ*, 16 Aug. 1922.

70 Garvin, *1922*, p. 179.

71 Ibid., p. 32.

72 Ibid., p. 197.

73 Hopkinson, *Green Against Green*, p. 35.

74 O'Halpin, 'The army and the Dáil – civil/military relations', p. 114.

75 For a critique see B. Kissane, 'The not-so amazing case of Irish democracy', *IPS* 10 (1995), pp. 43–68.

76 R. K. Carty, *Electoral Politics in Ireland: Party and Parish Pump* (Dingle, 1983), p. 3.

77 D. Schmitt, *The Irony of Irish Democracy: The Impact of Political Culture on Administration and Democratic Political Development in Ireland* (London and Toronto, 1973), p. 88.

78 J. Prager, *Building Democracy in Ireland* (Cambridge, 1986), p. 29.

79 T. Garvin, 'Revolutionaries turned politicians: a painful, confusing metamorphosis', *The Irish Times*, 6 Dec. 1997.

80 Lee, *Ireland 1912–1985*, p. 69.

81 D. Rustow, 'Transitions to democracy: toward a dynamic model', *CP* 2 (1970), p. 362.

82 See B. Kissane, 'Explaining the intractability of the Irish civil war', *Civil Wars* 3 (2000), 71–4.

83 Rustow, 'Transitions to democracy', pp. 337–63.

84 Regan, *The Irish Counter-Revolution*, p. 31.

85 See J. Linz and A. Stepan (eds), *The Breakdown of Democratic Regimes* (Baltimore and London, 1978), p. 87.

86 See Farrell (ed.), *The Irish Parliamentary Tradition*, p. 211.

87 Lee, *Ireland 1912–1985*, p. 67

Chapter Three

1   R. Dahl, *Polyarchy: Participation and Opposition* (New Haven, 1971), p. 63.

2   R. Dahl, *Democracy and its Critics* (New Haven, 1989), p. 242.

3   J. Lee, *The Modernisation of Irish Society 1848–1918* (Dublin, 1989), p. 168.

4   See for example R. K. Carty, *Electoral Politics in Ireland: Party and Parish Pump* (Dingle, 1983);
J. Prager, *Building Democracy in Ireland* (Cambridge, 1986); and D. Schmitt, *The Irony of Irish
Democracy* (London and Toronto, 1973).

5   S. M. Lipset, 'Some social requisites of democracy: economic development and political
legitimacy', *APSR* 53 (1959), p. 72.

6   Ibid., p. 75.

7   Ibid., p. 80.

8   Ibid., p. 80.

9   Ibid., p. 75.

10   Ibid., p. 71.

11   J. Mokyr, 'Industrialisation and poverty in Ireland and the Netherlands', *JIH* 10 (1980), p. 451.

12   Cited in S. A. Royle, 'Industrialisation, urbanisation, and urban society in post-famine Ireland
1850–1921' in B. J. Graham and J. C. Proudfoot (eds), *An Historical Geography of Ireland* (London,
1993), p. 262.

13   Ibid., table 8.2, p. 263.

14   'Occupation of males in the present area of Saorstát Éireann in Each of the Years, 1881, 1891,
1901, and 1911', *Census of Population: vol. 10 General Report* (Dublin, 1926), Appendix A, pp. 153–63.

15   Lipset, 'Some social requisites', p. 96.

16   Lee, *Modernisation of Irish Society*, p. 14.

17   Royle, 'Industrialisation, urbanisation, and urban society, fig. 8.5, p. 288.

18   Lipset, 'Some social requisites', p. 83.

19   K. A. Kennedy, T. Giblin, and D. McHugh, *The Economic Development of Ireland in the Twentieth
Century* (London and New York, 1988), p. 198, table 1.1, p. 14.

20   Ibid., p. 15.

21   E. Gellner, *Nations and Nationalism* (Oxford, 1983).

22   See A. Banks, *Cross Polity Time-Series Data* (Cambridge Mass., 1971), segment 7, column A.

23   Lee, *The Modernisation of Irish Society*, p. 28.

24   Prager, *Building Democracy*, p. 29.

25   See the figures in T. Vanhanen, *The Emergence of Democracy: A Comparative Study of 119 states,
1850–1979* (Helsinki, 1984), appendix.

26   Lee, *The Modernisation of Irish Society*, p. 168.

27   Kennedy et al., *The Economic Development of Ireland*, p. 21.

28   Royle, 'Industrialisation, urbanisation, and urban society', fig. 8.5, p. 288.

29   Lipset, 'Some social requisites', p. 86.

30   Ibid.

31   Ibid., p. 90.

32   Ibid., p. 41.

33   Ibid., p. 91.

34   S. M. Lipset, 'Conditions of the democratic order and social change: a comparative discussion'
in S. Eisenstadt (ed.), *Democracy and Modernity* (Leiden and New York, 1992), p. 9.

35   J. Coakley, 'Political succession and regime change in new states in inter-war Europe: Ireland,
Finland, Czechoslovakia, and the Baltic Republics', *EJPS* 14 (1987), pp. 187–207.

36   Ibid.

37   M. Rintaala, *Three Generations* (Bloomington, 1962), p. 164.

38   D. Kirby, *Finland in the Twentieth Century*, (London, 1979), p. 98.

39   F. Singleton, *The Economy of Finland in the Twentieth Century* (Bradford, 1991), p. 34.

40   Ibid., p. 35.

41   A. Orridge, 'The Blueshirts and the "economic war": a study of Ireland in the context of dependency theory', *Political Studies* 31 (1983), p. 352.

42   B. R. Mitchell, *International Historical Statistics: Europe 1750–1933* (Basingstoke, 1991), Table A9, p. 130.

43   J. Linz, 'Transitions to democracy', *Washington Quarterly* 13 (1990), p. 160.

44   See B. Barry, *Sociologists, Economists and Democracy* (Chicago, 1978), p. 65.

45   Coakley, 'Political succession and regime change', abstract.

46   Barry, *Sociologists, Economists and Democracy*, p. 66.

47   O. MacDonagh, *Ireland: The Union and its Aftermath* (London, 1975), p. 127.

48   United Nations, *Economic Survey of Europe in 1959: with Study of Development Problems in Southern Europe and Ireland* (Geneva, 1961), ch. 7, p. 1.

49   M. Peillon, 'Placing Ireland in comparative perspective', *ESR* 25 (1994), p. 193.

50   F. Munger, *The Legitimacy of Opposition: The Change of Government in Ireland in 1932* (Beverly Hills, 1975), p. 34.

51   M. Dogan, 'Use and misuse of statistics in comparative research' in E. Dogan, and A. Kazancigil (eds), *Comparing Nations* (Oxford and Cambridge, Mass., 1994), p. 44.

52   P. Cutright, 'National political development', *ASR* 28 (1963), p. 5.

53   D. Berg-Schlosser and G. de Meur, 'Conditions of democracy in Inter-war Europe: A Boolean Test of major hypotheses', *CP* 26 (1994), pp. 253–79.

54   Ibid., p. 257.

55   Lipset, 'Some social requisites', p. 75.

56   See below table 3.10, p. 52.

57   H. Seton-Watson, *Eastern Europe between the Wars 1918–1941* (Cambridge, 1945), p. 306.

58   Lipset, 'Some social requisites', p. 4.

59   D. Neubauer, 'Some conditions of democracy', *APSR* 61 (1967), pp. 1002–9.

60   R. Jackman, 'Political democracy and social equality', *ASR* 39 (1974), p. 32.

61   See W. Goldfrank, 'Fascism and the great transformation' in K. Polanyi-Levitt (ed.), *The Life and Work of Karl Polanyi: A Celebration* (New York, 1990), pp. 87–93.

62   See A. Edwards, 'Democratization and qualified explanation' in G. Parry and M. Moran (eds), *Democracy and Democratisation* (London, 1994), pp. 89–106.

63   G. Schopflin, *Politics in Eastern Europe*, (Oxford and Cambridge, Mass., 1993), p. 16.

64   T. Garvin, *1922: the Birth of Irish Democracy* (Dublin, 1996), p. 196.

65   L. Mjoset, *The Irish Economy in a Comparative Institutional Perspective* (Dublin, 1992), p. 7.

Chapter Four

1   B. Moore, *The Social Origins of Dictatorship and Democracy: Lord and Peasant in the Making of the Modern World* (Harmondsworth, 1966).

2   For criticisms see J. Femia, 'Barrington Moore and the preconditions of democracy', *British Journal of Political Science*, 2 (1972), pp. 21–46; T Skocpol, 'A critical review of Barrington Moore's *Social Origins of Dictatorship and Democracy*', *Politics and Society* 4 (1973), pp. 1–34 ; J, Wiener,

'Review of reviews: the social origins of dictatorship and democracy', *History and Theory* 15 (1976), pp. 446–75.

3   See F. Castles, 'Barrington Moore's thesis and Swedish political development', *Government and Opposition* 18 (1973), p. 331

4   On small countries see S. Rokkan, 'Models and methods in the comparative study of nation-building' in T. Nossiter et al. (eds), *Imagination and Precision in the Social Sciences* (London, 1972), pp. 133–7.

5   On the small European cases see M. Alestalo, and S. Kuhnle, *The Scandinavian Route: Economic, Social, and Political Developments in Denmark, Finland, Norway, and Sweden* (Helsinki, 1984) p. 12. See also T. Tilton, 'The social origins of liberal democracy: the Swedish case', *APSR* 68 (1974), pp. 561–71.

6   Moore, *Social Origins of Dictatorship and Democracy*, viii.

7   A. Edwards, 'Democratization and qualified explanation' in G. Parry and M. Moran (eds), *Democracy and Democratisation* (London, 1994), p. 96.

8   P. Corish, 'The Cromwellian regime, 1650–60' in T. W. Moody, F. X. Martin, and F. J. Byrne (eds), *A New History of Ireland*, III, *Early Modern Ireland 1534–1691* (Oxford, 1991), p. 361.

9   I. Lustick, *Statebuilding Failure in British Ireland and French Algeria* (Berkeley, 1985), p. 29.

10   Ibid., p. 68.

11   J. Blum, *The End of the Old Order in Europe* (Princeton, 1978), p. 199.

12   J. G. Simms, 'Protestant ascendancy 1691–1714', in T. W. Moody, F. X. Martin and F. J. Byrne (eds), *A New History of Ireland* (Oxford, 1986), pp. 205–6.

13   P. Anderson, *Lineages of the Absolutist State* (London, 1979), p. 195.

14   Quoted in E. M. Johnston, *Ireland in the Eighteenth Century* (Dublin, 1974), p. 161.

15   P. Clayton, *Enemies and Passing Friends: Settler Ideologies in Twentieth Century Ulster* (London, 1996), pp. 2–3.

16   D. McCartney, *The Dawning of Democracy: Ireland 1800–1870* (Dublin, 1987), p. 118.

17   L. McBride, *The Greening of Dublin Castle: The Transformation of Bureaucratic and Judicial Personnel in Ireland 1892–1922* (Washington DC, 1992).

18   S. Clark, *Social Origins of the Irish Land War*, (Princeton, 1989), p. 186.

19   C. C. O'Brien, *Parnell and his Party 1890–90* (Oxford, 1957), p. 15.

20   Clark, *Social Origins of the Irish Land War*, p. 188.

21   B. O'Leary, and J. McGarry, *The Politics of Antagonism: Understanding Northern Ireland* (London, 1993), fig. 2.4, p. 82.

22   Rev. Monsignor Hallinan, *The Catholic Defence Society* (Dublin, 1907).

23   Moore, *Social Origins of Dictatorship and Democracy*, p. 429.

24   Ibid., pp. 422–32.

25   T. Hoppen, *Elections, Politics and Society in Ireland 1932–1885* (Oxford, 1984), p. 460.

26   D. Fitzpatrick, 'The disappearance of the Irish agricultural labourer', *Irish Economic and Social History* 7 (1980), p. 74.

27   *Irish Free State Official Handbook* (Dublin, 1932), p. 120.

28   D. Fitzpatrick, *Irish Emigration 1801–1921* (Dundalk, 1985), p. 1.

29   Ibid., p. 38.

30   On the broader effects of depopulation see ibid., pp. 38–9.

31   D. Fitzpatrick, 'Irish emigration in the later nineteenth century', *IHS* 26 (1980), p. 127.

32   T. Tilton, 'The social origins of liberal democracy: the Swedish case', *APSR* 68 (1974), p. 567.

33   F. Dovring, *Land and Labour in Europe in the Twentieth Century: A Comparative Survey of Recent Agrarian History*, 3rd ed. (The Hague, 1965), p. 241.

34 T. Mulhall, 'The state and agrarian reform: the case of Ireland 1800–1940' (PhD thesis, University of London, 1993), table 13, p. 250.

35 R. B. McDowell, *Crisis and Decline: The Fate of the Southern Unionists* (Dublin, 1999), p. 10.

36 Ibid., p. 15.

37 E. Strauss, *Irish Nationalism and British Democracy* (London, 1951), p. 275.

38 Ibid., pp. 275–6.

39 Tilton, 'The social origins of liberal democracy', p. 562.

40 E. M. Stephens, 'The constitution', *Irish Free State Official Handbook* (London, 1932), p. 72.

41 For a classic analysis see T. Garvin, *The Evolution of Irish Nationalist Politics* (Dublin, 1981).

42 Clark, *Social Origins of the Irish Land War*, p. 188.

43 T. Skocpol, *State and Social Revolution* (Cambridge and New York, 1973), pp. 439–41.

44 F. Wright, *Northern Ireland: A Comparative Analysis* (New Jersey, 1987), pp. 86–112.

45 On southern Irish Unionism see P. Buckland, *Irish Unionism 1885–1922* (London, 1973), p. 12.

46 Ibid., p. 5.

47 R. F. Foster, *Modern Ireland* (London 1989), p. 534.

48 See the essays in Boyce, D. G. (ed.), *The Revolution in Ireland 1879–1923* (London, 1988).

49 E. Rumpf and A. C. Hepburn, *Nationalism and Socialism in Twentieth Century Ireland* (Liverpool, 1977), p. 15.

50 For a critique see R. English, *Radicals and the Republic: Socialist Republicanism in the Irish Free State 1925–1937* (Oxford, 1994).

51 T. Garvin, *1922: The Birth of Irish Democracy* (Dublin, 1996), p. 155.

52 Speech to the Trinity College History Society, 21 Nov. 1967 (UCDA, Mulcahy Papers, P7/D/64).

53 'Civil war: army reports on general situation and organisation' (NA, D/T, S3361).

54 See *Agricultural Statistics*, Irish Free State, 1926. Maps 13 and 14.

55 Kevin O'Higgins, *Civil War and the Events Which Led To It* (Dublin, 1926), p. 34.

56 On peace proposals see B. Kissane, 'Explaining the intractability of the Irish civil war', *Civil Wars* 3 (2000), pp. 65–88.

57 P. Bew, E. Hazelkorn, and H. Patterson, *The Dynamics of Irish Politics* (London, 1989), p. 35.

58 Speech at Mansion House, 9 June 1922, 'Michael Collins: statements and speeches' (NA, D/T, S10961).

59 *Irish Independent*, 9 Apr. 1923.

60 L. Stone, 'News from everywhere', *New York Review of Books* 9 (1967).

61 'Number of persons in each occupational group', *Census of Population of Ireland 1946*: vol. II(Dublin, 1946), table I. A, p. 2.

62 E. Allardt, *Finnish Society: Relationship between Geopolitical Situation and the Development of Society* (Helsinki, 1985), p. 22.

63 Alestalo and Kuhnle, *The Scandinavian Route*, p. 26.

64 R. Alapuro, *State and Revolution in Finland* (Berkeley, 1988), p. 205.

65 Ibid.

66 'What the government of the Irish Free State has done', n. d. (UCDA, FitzGerald Papers, P35C/160).

67 J. Hogan, *Modern Democracy* (Cork, 1938), p. 84.

68 Allardt, *Finnish Society*, pp. 14–15.

69 Alapuro, *State and Revolution in Finland*, p. 47.

70 Fitzpatrick, 'The disappearance of the Irish agricultural labourer', p. 74.

71 See Lee's figures, table 4. 2 above.

72 M. Peltonen, 'From peasant holdings to family farms: impact of the agricultural depression of the 1880s–1910s on Finnish peasant farming' in L. Graberg and J. Nikula (eds), *The Peasant State: The State and Rural Questions in 20th Century Finland* (Rovaniemi, 1995), pp. 32–3.

73 Ibid., pp. 34–5.

74 O. Manninen, 'Red, white and blue in Finland, 1918: a survey of interpretations of the civil war', *Scandinavian Journal of History* 3 (1978), pp. 229–49.

75 Fitzpatrick, 'The disappearance of the Irish agricultural labourer', p. 84.

76 See G. Luebbert, *Liberalism, Fascism or Social Democracy: Social Classes and the Political Origins of Regimes in Interwar Europe* (Oxford, 1991), p. 11.

77 *Voice of Labour*, 6 May 1922.

78 *Voice of Labour*, 21 Jan. 1922.

79 *Voice of Labour*, 8 Sept. 1923,

80 Alapuro, *State and Revolution in Finland*, p. 206.

81 Ibid., pp. 204–5.

82 See T. Garvin, *Nationalist Revolutionaries in Ireland* (Oxford, 1987).

83 Ibid.

84 Dovring, *Land and Labour in Europe*, p. 345.

85 *The Irish Times*, 24 Jan. 1933.

86 J. Mylly, *Political Parties in Finland* (Turku, 1984), p. 107.

87 E. W. Polson Newman, 'The New Finland', *Contemporary Review* 137 (1930).

88 Ibid.

89 T. Vanhanen, *The Process of Democratisation: A Comparative Study of 147 States, 1980–1988* (New York, 1990), p. 37.

90 Ibid., p. 38.

91 Ibid.

92 R. Dahl, *Democracy and its Critics* (New Haven and London, 1989), p. 254. MDP refers to modern, dynamic and plural.

93 Luebbert, *Liberalism, Fascism or Social Democracy*, p. 47.

94 Alapuro, *State and Revolution in Finland*, p. 208.

95 T. Kettle, *The Philosophy of Politics* (Dublin, 1906), pp. 12–13.

96 See Alestalo and Kuhnle, *The Scandinavian Route*.

97 On this subject see Mulhall, 'The state and agrarian reform'.

98 D. Rueschmeyer, E. Stephens, and J. D. Stephens, *Capitalist Development and Democracy* (Cambridge, 1992), p. 280.

99 T. Garvin 'Political cleavages, party politics and urbanisation in Ireland – the case of the periphery-dominated centre', *EJPS* 11 (1974), pp. 307–27.

Chapter Five

1 T. de Vere White, *Kevin O'Higgins* (Dublin, 1948), p. 181.

2 Crucially, this chapter focuses mainly on the development of civil society in the future area of the Free State and the important linkage between popular Unionist politics and civil society is not explored.

3 J. Keane, *Civil Society: Old Images, New Visions* (Cambridge, 1998), pp. 36–7.

4 L. Diamond, 'Towards democratic consolidation' in L. Diamond and M. F. Plattner (eds), *The Global Resurgence of Democracy*, 2nd ed. (Baltimore and London, 1996), p. 229.

5   Paragraph based on *Thom's Irish Almanac and Official Directory* (Dublin, 1848).

6   F. Devine, 'The Irish Labour History Society Archive', *Saothar* 11 (1986), pp. 96–8.

7   *Thom's Irish Almanac*, pp. 285–6.

8   R. J. Morris, 'Civil society, subscriber democracies, and parliamentary government in Great Britain' in N. Bermeo and P. Nord (eds), *Civil Society before Democracy: Lessons from Nineteenth Century Europe* (Oxford, 2000), pp. 111–35.

9   P. Nord, 'Introduction' in N. Bermeo and P. Nord (eds), *Civil Society before Democracy: Lessons from Nineteenth Century Europe* (Oxford, 2000), p. xiv.

10   *Thom's Irish Almanac*, pp. 285–6.

11   *Rules and Regulations to be Observed by the Members of the Moira Society* (registered 1812) (NA, Registry of Friendly Societies, F260).

12   *Rules and Orders to be Observed by the Members of the Moira Society* (registered 1833) (NA, Registry of Friendly Societies, F260).

13   *Rules, Orders, and Regulations of the Ancient Moira Society* (1873) (NA, Registry of Friendly Societies, F260).

14   *Thom's Irish Almanac*, pp. 285–6.

15   T. Garvin, 'The politics of language and literature in pre-independence Ireland', *IPS* 2 (1987), p. 56.

16   'Constitution of the Gaelic League as revised by representative congress, 17 May 1900 (UCDA, MacNeill Papers, LA1E11).

17   'The Constitution of the Gaelic League as amended by the Ard Fheis, August 1921' (UCDA, O'Briain Papers, P83/307).

18   On Italy see R. D. Puttnam, *Making Democracy Work: Civic Traditions in Modern Italy* (Princeton, 1993); on Ireland see T. Garvin, 'O'Connell and the making of Irish political culture', in M. O'Connell (ed.), *Daniel O'Connell: Political Pioneer* (Dublin, 1991), p. 7

19   T. Skocpol, 'Unravelling from above', *The American Prospect* 25 (1996), pp. 4–5.

20   'List of Friendly Societies 1797–1844' (NA, Registry of Friendly Societies, Miscellaneous).

21   Morris, 'Civil society', p. 125.

22   *Rules and Regulations to be Observed by the Members of the Moira Society* (Dublin, 1812) (NA, Registry of Friendly Societies, F260).

23   *Rules and Regulations of the Emerald Society* (Dublin, 1844) (NA, Registry of Friendly Societies, F 480).

24   S. Keen, 'Associations in Australian history: their contribution to social capital', *JIH* 29 (1999), p. 647.

25   *Rules and Regulations to be Observed by the Members of the Protestant Pembroke Society of Tradesmen* (Dublin, 1848) (NA, Registry of Friendly Societies, F 470).

26   *Rules and Regulations to be Observed by the Friendly Brothers of Saint Jerome Society* (Dublin, 1850) (NA, Registry of Friendly Societies, F531).

27   *Rules of the Caledonian Benevolent Society* (Dublin, 1843) (NA, Registry of Friendly Societies, F59).

28   *Rules and Regulations to be observed by the Members of the Protestant Pembroke Society.*

29   *Rules and Regulations of the Deans Grange Christian Burial Society* (Dublin, 1861) (NA, Registry of Friendly Societies, F134).

30   *Rules and Regulations to be observed by the Members of the Protestant Pembroke Society.*

31   *Rules of the Caledonian Benevolent Society.*

32   *New Rules of the Caledonian Benevolent Society* (1860), (NA, Registry of Friendly Societies, F59).

33   *New Rules of the Caledonian Benevolent Society* (1888), ibid.

34   *Rules of the Caledonian Benevolent Society* (Dublin, 1906), ibid.

35   *Rules of the Irish National Foresters' Benefit Society 1878–1914* (Dublin, 1878) (NA, Registry of Friendly Societies).

36   *Irish National Foresters' Benefit Society: New General Rules* (Dublin, 1898), ibid.

37   *Draft Report of the Irish Agricultural Organisation Society, Ltd, for the year ending 31st March 1922* (NA, Registry of Friendly Societies, RF8 R88 A).

38   *Rules of the Irish Agricultural Organisation Society* (1912), ibid.

39   On the US see D. T. Beito, 'To advance the "practice of thrift and economy": fraternal societies and social capital, 1890–1920', *JIH* 29 (1999), pp. 585–612.

40   *Rules and Bye Laws of the Grocer's Assistants Friendly Association of Dublin* (Dublin, 1863) (NA, Registry of Friendly Societies, F174).

41   T. Garvin, *The Evolution of Irish Nationalist Politics* (Dublin, 1981), p. 50.

42   *Rules of the Metropolitan House Painters Trade Union* (Dublin, 1911) (NA, Registry of Friendly Societies, Misc.).

43   *Rules of the Irish Drapers' Assistants Benefit and Protective Association* (Dublin, 1905), ibid.

44   *Rules of the United Corporation Workmen of Dublin Trade Union* (Dublin, 1907) (NA, Irish Municipal Employees Trade Union, T260).

45   *Rules of the Dublin, Wicklow, and Wexford Railway Friendly Society* (1863) (NA Registry of Friendly Societies).

46   *Rules of the Ancient Guild of Incorporated Brick and Stonelayers* (Dublin, 1888) (NA, Ancient Guild of Incorporated Brick and Stonelayers, 1097/2).

47   *Rules of the Dublin Operative Poulterer's Trade Union* (Dublin, 1903) (NA, Registry of Friendly Societies, T224).

48   *Rules of the Operative Stonecutters of Ireland Trade Union* (Cork, 1902) (NA, M6801).

49   C. D. Greaves, *The Irish Transport and General Workers' Union: The Formative Years 1909–1923* (Dublin, 1982), p. 321.

50   Ibid., pp. 327–41.

51   'Dublin Trades Council' (NA, MS 12,779).

52   'Short history of the United Trades Council and Labour League of Dublin' (NL, Irish Trade Union Congress, 1894–1907).

53   Ibid., 27/28 Apr. 1894.

54   Report of the Fourth Irish Trades Congress, held in the City Hall, Waterford, 7, 8, 9 June 1897 (NL, Irish Trade Union Congress, 1894–1907).

55   Report of the Eighth Irish Trades Union Congress held in the Town Hall Sligo, 27, 28, 29 May 1901, ibid.

56   Morris, 'Civil society', p. 113.

57   See L. Diamond, 'Toward democratic consolidation', pp. 230–4.

58   F. O. Ashtown, *The Unknown Power Behind the Irish Nationalist Party: Its Present Work . . . and Criminal History* (London, 1907).

59   See J. Habermas, *The Structural Transformation of the Public Sphere: An Enquiry into the Category of Bourgeois Society* (Cambridge, 1992).

60   Morris, 'Civil society', p. 119

61   *Thom's Irish Almanac.*

62   Ibid., p. 284.

63   H. F. Berry, *History of the Royal Dublin Society* (London, 1915), pp. 14–18.

64   Morris, 'Civil society', p. 125.

65 *Thom's Irish Almanac.*

66 L. M. Cullen, *Princes and Pirates: The Dublin Chamber of Commerce 1783–1983* (Dublin, 1983), p. 56.

67 Ibid., p. 73.

68 Berry, *History of the Royal Dublin Society* (London, 1915), p. 31.

69 Ibid., pp. 265–627.

70 *The Royal Dublin Society and its Privileges versus Imperial Policy and Irish Public Right*: issued by a Committee for procuring signatures to a Petition for a Parliamentary Inquiry into the Royal Dublin Society, and the other subsidized Scientific Institutions of Dublin (Dublin, 1863), p. 5.

71 Ibid., p. 13.

72 Seanacus, 'The question of Catholic organisation', *Irish Rosary* 6 (1902), p. 726.

73 T. de Vere White, *The Story of the Royal Dublin Society* (Tralee, 1955), p. 179.

74 For a wide-ranging critique of Habermas's conception see G. Eley, 'Nations, publics, and political cultures: placing Habermas in the nineteenth century' in C. Calhoun (ed.), *Habermas and the Public Sphere* (Cambridge and London, 1994), pp. 289–339.

75 *The Royal Dublin Society and its Privileges*, p. 22.

76 De Vere White, *The Story of the Royal Dublin Society*, p. 119.

77 P. Beaslai, *The Story of the Catholic Commercial Club* (Dublin, 1958), p. 8.

78 S. Clark, *Social Origins of the Irish Land War* (Princeton, 1979), p. 67.

79 See J. Lee, *The Modernisation of Irish Society 1848–1918* (Dublin, 1989), p. 95.

80 Garvin, *Evolution of Irish Nationalist Politics*, p. 2.

81 F. O'Ferrall, *Daniel O'Connell* (Dublin, 1981), pp. 45–6.

82 E. Strauss, *Irish Nationalism and British Democracy* (London, 1951), p. 92.

83 Ibid.

84 Ibid.

83 Clark, *Social Origins of the Irish Land War*, pp. 88–9.

86 Ibid.

87 Garvin, *Evolution if Irish National Politics*, p. 46.

88 O. MacDonagh, 'Introduction: Ireland under the Union 1801–1870', in W. E. Vaughan (ed.), *A New History of Ireland*, v (Oxford, 1989), p. 1.

89 Clark, *Social Origins of the Irish Land War*, p. 102.

90 MacDonagh, 'Introduction: Ireland the Union 1801–1870', p. li.

91 O'Ferrall, *Daniel O'Connell*, p. 61.

92 Ibid.

93 See B. O'Duffy, 'Violent politics: a theoretical and empirical analysis of two centuries of political violence in Ireland' (PhD thesis, University of London, 1996).

94 N. Bermeo, 'Civil society after democracy: some conclusions' in N. Bermeo and P. Nord (eds), *Civil Society before Democracy: Lessons from Nineteenth Century Europe* (Oxford, 2000), p. 244.

95 T. Hoppen, *Elections, Politics, and Society in Ireland 1832–1885* (Oxford, 1984), p. 467.

96 S. Ó Riain, *Maurice Davin (1842–1927) First President of the GAA* (Dublin, 1994), p. 44.

97 Clark, *Social Origins of the Irish Land War*, p. 100.

98 Hoppen, *Elections, Politics, and Society*, p. 465.

99 *Ireland's Appeal for Amnesty: A letter to the Right Honourable W. E. Gladstone MP by Isaac Butt, President of the Irish Amnesty Association* (London, 1870).

100 Ibid., p. 99.

101 See Lee, *Modernisation of Irish Society*, pp. 89–99.

102 Clark, *Social Origins of the Irish Land War*, p. 247.

103 C. C. O'Brien, 'The machinery of the Irish parliamentary party, 1880–85', *IHS* 5 (1947), p. 51.

104 T. W. Moody, *Davitt and Irish Revolution 1846–82* (Oxford, 1981), p. 340.

105 Lee, *Modernisation of Irish Society*, p. 93.

106 M. Davitt, *The Fall of Feudalism in Ireland or the Story of the Land League Revolution* (London and New York, 1904), p. 116.

107 Ibid., p. 91.

108 Clark, *Social Origins of the Irish Land War*.

109 Ibid., p. 294.

110 Clark, *Social Origins of the Irish Land War*, p. 293.

111 Davitt, *The Fall of Feudalism in Ireland*, pp. 162–3.

112 *Proceedings of the Home Rule Conference held at the Rotunda Dublin* on 18, 19, 20 and 21 Nov. 1873, NL.

113 Garvin, *Evolution of Irish Nationalist Politics*, p. 81.

114 Ó Riain, *Maurice Davin*, p. 26.

115 O'Brien, 'The machinery of the Irish Parliamentary Party', p. 67.

116 *The Constitution of the Irish National League*, Form 1, 1882, NL.

117 P. Bull, 'The United Irish League and the reunion of the Irish Parliamentary party, 1898–1900', *IHS* 26 (1988), pp. 61–78.

118 *United Irish League: Constitution and Rules adopted by the Irish National Convention*, 19/20 June 1900, NL.

119 Ibid., p. 78.

120 *Gaelic Athletic Association: Constitution and Rules* (Dublin, 1885).

121 *United Irish League: Constitution and Rules*.

122 Ibid.

123 Eoin MacNeill, 'Gaelic League – future development – failure to publicize activities' (UCDA, MacNeill Papers, LA1/E/16, Eoin MacNeill Papers).

124 See Lee, *Modernisation of Irish Society*.

125 Garvin, *Evolution of Irish Nationalist Politics*, p. 91.

126 See A. S. Cohan, *The Irish Political Elite* (Dublin, 1972), p. 40.

127 *Report of the Registrar of Friendly Societies of Saorstát Éireann to the Minister for Finance for the Year Ending the 31 December 1923*, TCD.

128 *Ibid.*

129 S. Brooks, *The New Ireland* (Dublin and London, 1907), p. 15.

130 M. J. Waters, 'Peasants and emigrants: considerations of the Gaelic League as a social movement' in D. J. Carey and R. E. Rhodes (eds), *Views of the Irish Peasantry 1800–1910* (Hamden Conn., 1977), p. 161.

131 'Memorandum of Association of the Irish Industrial Development Association' (NA, Irish Industrial Development Association, 1091/3/1).

132 F. S. L. Lyons, The aftermath of Parnell, 1891–1903' in W. E. Vaughan (ed.), *Ireland Under the Union, A New History of Ireland*, VI (Oxford, 1996), p. 99.

133 P. O'Fearail, *The Story of Conradh na Gaeilge* (Dublin, 1975), p. 14.

134 Ibid., p. 30.

135 P. Murray, 'Irish cultural nationalism in the United Kingdom state: politics and the Gaelic League 1900–1918', *IPS* 8 (1993), p. 64.

136 Ibid., 59.

137 Ibid., 65.

138 O'Fearail, *The Story of Conradh na Gaeilge*, p. 39.

139 See T. Garvin, 'The politics of language and literature in pre-independence Ireland, *IPS* 2 (1987), pp. 49–63.

140 P. Murray, 'Irish cultural nationalism', pp. 55–73.

141 Douglas Hyde, *The Gaelic League and Politics: Pronouncement by Dr. Douglas Hyde – speaking at Cork on December 15 1914*, NL.

142 O'Fearail, *The Story of Conradh na Gaeilge*, p. 44.

143 P. Murray, 'Irish cultural nationalism', p. 69.

144 Ibid., p. 58.

145 R. C. Owens, *Votes for Women: Irish Women's Struggle for the Vote* (Dublin, 1975), p. 5.

146 Ibid.

147 R. C. Owens, *Smashing Times: A History of the Irish Women's Suffrage Movement 1889–1922*, (Dublin, 1984), p. 25.

148 Ibid., p. 53.

149 On Cumann na mBan see Sighle Humphrey, 'Diary', P106/909, Sighle Humphreys Papers, UCDA.

150 H. Sheehy-Skeffington, 'The women's movement, Ireland', *Irish Review* II (1912), pp. 225–7.

151 M. Jones, *These Obstreperous Lassies: A History of the Irish Women Workers Union* (Dublin, 1988), p. 42.

152 *Irish Women Workers' Union: Rules of Membership* (Dublin, 1921).

153 Catholic Defence Society, *The Catholic Defence Society* (Dublin, 1907).

154 See W. F. Mandle, 'The IRB and the beginnings of the Gaelic Athletic Association', *IHS* 20 (1977), pp. 418–38.

155 Garvin, *Evolution of Irish Nationalist Politics*, p. 99.

156 *Rules of the Irish Agricultural Wholesale Society Limited* (Dublin, 1913) (NA, Registry of Friendly Societies, R182).

157 *Rules of the National Land Bank Limited*, n. d. (NA, Registry of Friendly Societies, R1508).

158 *Rules of the Irish Farmer Limited* (1920) (NA, Registry of Friendly Societies, R 1530).

159 *The Constitution of the Gaelic League as amended by the Ard Fheis, August 1921* (UCDA, O'Briain Papers, P83/307).

160 'On the qualities needed in Gaelic League Workers and the importance given to social custom', n. d. (UCDA, MacNeill Papers, LA1/E/14).

161 Ó Riain, *Maurice Davin*, p. 149.

162 H. Plunkett, *Ireland in the New Century* (Dublin, 1982), p. 169.

163 O'Fearail, *The Story of Conradh na Gaeilge*, p. 6.

164 Ibid., p. 21.

165 O'Fearail, *The Story of Conradh na Gaeilge*, p. 17.

166 Jones, *These Obstreperous Lassies*, p. 3.

167 See L. Kennedy, 'The early response of the Irish Catholic clergy to the co-operative movement, *IHS* 21 (1978), p. 71.

168 *FJ*, 23 Feb. 1906.

169 S. Brooks, *The New Ireland* (Dublin and London, 1907), p. 15.

170 On the persistence of tradition theme see Garvin, *Evolution of Irish Nationalist Politics*, Hoppen, *Elections, Politics, and Society*, and R. K. Carty, 'From tradition to modernity and back again: party building in Ireland', in R. Hill and M. Marsh (eds), *Modern Irish Democracy* (Dublin, 1983), pp. 24–44.

171 Clark, *Social Origins of the Irish Land War*, pp. 351–71.

172 F. O'Ferrell, 'Liberty and Catholic politics 1780–1990', in M. O'Connell (ed.), *Daniel O'Connell: Political Pioneer* (Dublin, 1991), p. 42.

173 D. Lieven, *Empire: The Russian Empire and its Rivals* (London, 2000), p. 364.

174 *FJ*, 26 Sept. 1922.

175 V. Perez-Diaz, *The Return of Civil Society: The Emergence of Democratic Spain* (Cambridge, 1998), p. 28.

176 T. Kettle, *The Philosophy of Politics* (Dublin, 1906), p. 13.

177 These bodies were the Civic Survey, the Chamber of Commerce, the Institute of Architects, the Plot Holders Association, the Dublin County Committee of Agriculture, the County Dublin Farmers Association, the South Dublin Ratepayers and Development Association, the Dublin United Tramway Co, the County Dublin Joint Committee of Technical Instruction, and the Royal Society of Antiquaries, 'Greater Dublin Commission of Inquiry: Report' (NA, D/T, S 6532).

178 See B. Kissane, 'Civil society under strain: intermediary organisations and the Irish civil war', *IPS* 25 (2000), pp. 1–25.

179 J. J. Barrett, *In the Name of the Game* (Dublin, 1997).

Chapter Six

1   J. Linz, 'Crisis, breakdown and reequilibration' in J. Linz and A. Stepan (eds), *The Breakdown of Democratic Regimes* (Baltimore and London, 1978), p. 4.

2   G. di Palma, *To Craft Democracies: An Essay on Democratic Transitions* (Berkeley, Los Angeles, Oxford, 1990), p. 11.

3   The former view is contained in T. Garvin, *1922: The Birth of Irish Democracy* (Dublin, 1996), p. 129. For a different view see E. de Valera, 'Civil war 1922–24: Historical Summary by President de Valera' (NA, D/ T, S 9282).

4   See M. Hopkinson, *Green Against Green: The Irish Civil War* (Dublin, 1988), p. 272. For the latter interpretation see H. Lacey, 'There need never have been a civil war; what caused the tragedy?' *Irish Press*, 6 July 1958.

5   'Meeting between Pro-Treaty and Anti-Treaty Deputies in the House of Deputy S. T. O'Kelly, 2 Jan. 1922' (NA, 'Political disunity 1922: pre-election negotiations', D/T, S 2942).

6   De Valera, 'Civil war 1922–24'.

7   Cork Meeting, 19 Feb.1922 (NA, Eamon de Valera Speeches 1921–22, D/T, S2980).

8   *The Irish Times*, 19 Apr. 1922.

9   Hopkinson, *Green Against Green*, pp. 52–109.

10 Ibid. p. 66.

11 *FJ*, 1 May 1923.

12 Mulcahy to Collins, 25 Mar. 1922 (NA, Mulcahy Papers P7/B/192).

13 Suggestion by Fr. McCarthy, 12 Apr. 1922 (NA, 'Peace Proposal 1922: Suggestion by Fr. McCarthy & P. Daly, Cork', D/T, S 2978).

14 Appendix B 'Deputy Boland's draft', 10 May 1922 (UCDA, Blythe Papers, P24/45 (1)).

15 Ibid.

16 Aiken to O'Donoghue, 9 Mar. 1953 (UCDA, Aiken Papers, P104/1304 (2)).

17 H. Boland, *Dáil Debates*, col. 473, 19 May 1922.

18 D. McArdle, *The Irish Republic*, 2nd ed. (Dublin, 1951), p. 712.

19 M. Laffan, *The Resurrection of Ireland: The Sinn Féin Party 1916–1923* (Cambridge, 1999), p. 389.

20 C. D. Greaves, *Liam Mellowes and the Irish Revolution* (London, 1971), p. 329.

21 Provisional Government decision, 25 May 1922 (NA, D/T, S 2942).

22 Conference on Ireland, 10 Downing St. London, 27 May 1922 (NA, D/T, S 2942).

23 'Meeting at University College: report by Michael Collins', 18 May 1922 (NA, D/T, S 2967A).

24 Collins to Kevin O'Shiel, 29 May 1922 (NA, D/T, S 2967A).

25 'Leaders Appeal for Support of National Panel', A. Mitchell and P. O'Snodaigh (eds), *Irish Political Documents 1916–1949* (Dublin, 1985), p. 135.

26 Speech at Mansion House, 9 June 1922 (NA, Michael Collins: Statements and Speeches, D/T, S10961).

27 Ibid.

28 Press Statement, 13 June 1922.

29 *Cork Examiner*, 15 June 1922, Mitchell and O'Snodaigh, *Irish Political Documents*, p. 136.

30 Garvin, *1922*, p. 129.

31 *The Irish Times*, 17 June 1922.

32 Secretary Army Council to Secretary Dáil Éireann, 14 Apr. 1922 (NA, 'Liam Mellowes: Conditions of army unification', Dáil Éireann, 4/11/66).

33 'Proposals for army unity', 14 Apr. 1922 (UCDA, MacSwiney Papers, P48a/235).

34 Report of the republican delegation, 17 May 1922 (UCDA, Blythe Papers, P24/45 (4)).

35 Frank Aiken, 'Incidents in connection with IRA that had bearing on outbreak of civil war', n. d. (UCDA, Aiken Papers, P104/1253 (3)).

36 O'Malley to Mulcahy, 10 June 1922 (UCDA, Mulcahy Papers, P7/B/192).

37 Ibid.

38 O'Connor quote was from the *Cork Examiner*, 29 May 1922, 'Chronology of events leading to civil war' (UCDA, Mulcahy Papers, P7/B/192). On proposal of O'Duffy see Richard Mulcahy, 'Memorandum', 8 Sept. (1922) (Mulcahy Papers, P7/B/192).

39 P. G. Decision 5 June 1922 (PG 28) (NA, 'Army negotiations for unification 1922', D/T S 1233).

40 Mulcahy to O'Malley, 12 June 1922 (UCDA, Mulcahy Papers, P7/B/192).

41 'Resolutions passed at executive meeting held at 14/6/22' (NA, 'Army negotiations for unification 1922', D/T S 1233).

42 Mulcahy, 'Memorandum', 24 June 1922 (UCDA, Mulcahy Papers, P7/B/192).

43 M. Gallagher, 'The pact general election of 1922', *IHS* 21(1979), p. 419.

44 The military headquarters of the new national army was located at Beggars Bush.

45 'Extract from a notebook, the property of Sean MacBride, which was seized at Newbridge Barracks, July 1923' (NA, 'Army negotiations for unification 1922' (NA, D/T, S 1233).

46 E. Neeson, *The Irish Civil War 1922–1923* (Cork, 1995), p. 109.

47 MacBride, 'Extract from a notebook'.

48 Di Palma, *To Craft Democracies*, p. 27.

49 Ibid., p. 31.

50 Ibid.

51 Ibid., pp. 41–2.

52 Ibid., p. 46.

53 Ibid., p. 55.

54 Ibid., p. 87.

55 Ibid., p. 88.

56 *New York Herald*, 2 May 1922 (NA, 'Michael Collins: statement and speeches', D/T, S 10961).

57 'Meeting at University College: report by Michael Collins', 18 May 1922 (NA, D/T, S 2967A).

58 Report of the Republican delegation, 17 May 1922 (UCDA, Blythe Papers, P24/45 (4)).

59 *Dáil Debates*, col. 464, 19 May 1922.

60 *Dail Debates,* col. 429, 17 May 1922.

61 *Dáil Debates,* col. 361, 3 May 1922.

62 Seán O'Hegarty, *Dáil Debates,* col. 357, 3 May 1922.

63 T. P. Coogan, *Michael Collins* (London, 1990), p. 322.

64 Minute by Cosgrave, n. d., 'Peace proposal by F. Daly and Fr. McCarthy' (NA, 'Civil war 1922–24; Peace proposals', D/T, S 2978).

65 *Dáil Debates,* col. 464, 19 May 1922.

66 *Dáil Debates,* col. 464, 19 May 1922.

67 'Document No. 2', de Valera's alternative to the Treaty proposed a 26-county Republic, 'externally associated' with the British Crown as head of the Commonwealth.

68 Ernie O'Malley, *The Singing Flame* (Dublin, 1978), p. 246.

69 Di Palma, *To Craft Democracies,* p. 72.

70 Ibid., p. 73.

71 Churchill to Collins, 12 May 1922 'Civil War 1922 – Outbreak and immediately preceding events' (NA, D/T, S1322 B).

72 *Dáil Debates* , col. 437, 17 May 1922.

73 Eamon de Valera, *Dáil Debates* , col. 427, 17 May 1922.

74 Sean Milroy, *Dáil Debates,* col. 422, 17 May 1922.

75 Michael Collins, Memorandum, 26 July 1922 (UCDA, Mulcahy Papers, P/7 B/28).

76 Ibid., p. 30.

77 Dáil Peace Conference, 'Supplementary report by the Anti-Treaty members', 17 May 1922.

78 'Report of the Republican delegation', 17 May 1922 (UCDA, Blythe Papers, P24/45 (4)).

79 GHQ Staff Memo, n. d.. (UCDA, Mulcahy Papers, P7/B/100).

80 Frank Aiken, 'Incidents in connection with IRA that had bearing on outbreak of civil war', n. d. (UCDA, Aiken Papers, P104/1253 (3)).

81 Sean MacEntee, *Dáil Debates,* col. 434, 17 May 1922.

82 Seamus O'Dwyer, *Dáil Debates* , col. 417, 17 May 1922.

83 Dr MacCartan, *Dáil Debates,* col. 415, 17 May 1922.

84 'Report by Michael Collins, meeting at University College', 18 May 1922 (NA, D/T, S 2967 A).

85 Michael Collins, 'Difficulties of the constitution', n. d. (UCDA, Mulcahy Papers, P7 B/28).

86 See McArdle, *The Irish Republic,* pp. 720–7; Mary MacSwiney, *The Republic of Ireland* (Cork, n. d.), pp 2–25; H. Lacey, 'There need never have been a civil war; what caused the tragedy?' *Irish Press,* 6 July 1958.

87 Cited in A. Mitchell and P. O'Snodaigh, *Irish Political Documents 1916–1949* (Dublin, 1985), p. 140.

88 Boland to Hayes, 4 Apr. 1966 (UCDA, Hayes Papers, P53/279 (2)).

89 See J. Curran, *The Birth of the Irish Free State,* (Mobile AL, 1980), p. 220.

90 Ibid., p. 32.

91 William O'Brien, 'The Irish Free State: secret history of its foundation' (NL, O'Brien Papers, MS 4201).

92 Garvin, *1922,* p. 32.

93 J. Linz and A. Stepan (eds), *The Breakdown of Democratic Regimes* (Baltimore and London, 1978).

94 T. D. Williams, 'From the Treaty to the civil war' in T. D. Williams (ed.), *The Irish Struggle 1916–1926* (London, 1966), p. 125.

95 Lynch to O'Hegarty, 8 May 1922 (UCD, O'Hegarty Papers, P8/6).

96 'Typescript notes to be studied by each minister on the irregulars, armed forces, and the blowing up of the Four Courts', n. d. (UCDA, McGilligan Papers, P35c/159).

97 Ibid., p. 124.

98 Kevin O'Higgins, *Dáil Debates*, col. 417, 17 May 1922.

99 De Valera, *Dáil Debates*, col. 156, 1 Mar. 1922.

100 R. Mulcahy, 'Army truce May 4th' (UCDA, Mulcahy Papers, P7/B/192).

101 G. O'Donnell and P. Schmitter, 'Tenatative conclusions about uncertain democracies' in G. O'Donnell, P. Schmitter, and L. Whitehead (eds), *Transitions from Authoritarian Rule* (Baltimore, 1986), p. 15.

102 De Valera, 'Civil war 1922–24'.

103 On the RDS Provisional Government decision 36, 26 June 1922 (NA, D/T S 1332 B). On army negotiations see PG decision 12 June 1922 (PG 33), 'Army negotiations for unification 1922' (NA, D/T, S 1233).

104 Kennedy to Secretary Executive Council, 4 Apr. 1922, 'Third Dáil (Provisional Parliament), 1922: summoning and assembly' (NA, D/T, S 1332A).

105 *Poblachta na hÉireann*, 10 July 1922.

106 See J. Coakley, 'Political Succession and regime change in interwar Europe – Ireland, Finland, Czechoslovakia, and the Baltic Republics', *EJPS* 14 (1987), pp. 187–207.

107 Hopkinson, *Green Against Green*, p. 35.

108 T. D. Williams, 'From the Treaty to the civil war' in T. D. Williams (ed.), *The Irish Struggle 1911–1926* (London, 1966), p. 124.

109 De Valera, *Dáil Debates*, col. 368, 3 May 1922.

110 Churchill to Collins, 12 May 1922, 'Civil War 1922 – Outbreak and immediately preceding events' (NA, D/T, S1322 B).

111 At least this was the view of George Gavan Duffy, 'Voice recording made for the Bureau by the Hon. George Gavan Duffy, President of the High Court, 20 Jan. 1951', 1125/15 No 17, Gavan Duffy Papers, NA.

112 Kevin O'Higgins, Memorandum, n. d. (NA, D/T, S6695).

113 Michael Hayes (UCDA, Hayes Papers, P53, 27–30).

114 F. S. L. Lyons, *Parnell* (Dundalk, 1978), p. 13.

Chapter Seven

1 See T. D. Williams, 'From the Treaty to the civil war' in T. D. Williams (ed.), *The Irish Struggle 1911–1926* (London, 1966), pp. 117–29.

2 See T. Garvin, *1922: The Birth of Irish Democracy* (Dublin, 1996); J. Prager, *Building Democracy in Ireland* (Cambridge. 1986).

3 T. Garvin, 'The long division of the Irish mind', *The Irish Times*, 28 Dec. 1991.

4 E. Durkheim, *The Division of Labour in Society* (New York, 1933), p. 406.

5 A. Giddens, *Durkheim* (Glasgow, 1980), p. 25.

6 E. Allardt, 'Types of protest and alienation' in E. Allardt and S. Rokkan (eds), *Mass Politics: Studies in Political Sociology* (New York, 1970), p. 47.

7 Giddens, *Durkheim*, p. 25.

8 Ibid.

9 Ibid

10 Durkheim, *Division of Labour in Society*, p. 220.

11 Prager, *Building Democracy*, p. 30.

12 Ibid., p. 31.

13 Ibid., p. 16.

14 Ibid., p. 40.

15 Ibid., p. 44.

16 Ibid., p. 42.

17 Ibid., p. 43.

18 Garvin, *1922*, p. 143.

19 Ibid., p. 145.

20 Garvin, 'Long division of the Irish mind'.

21 Garvin, *1922*, p. 145.

22 Ibid., p. 145.

23 Ibid., p. 152.

24 Durkheim, *Division of Labour in Society*, p. 226.

25 Ibid., p. 219.

26 Ibid., p. 219.

27 E. Allardt ,'Types of protest and alienation' in E. Allardt and S. Rokkan (eds), *Mass Politics: Studies in Political Sociology* (New York, 1970), p. 47.

28 Ibid., p. 48.

29 M. Hechter, *Internal Colonialism: The Celtic Fringe in British National Development, 1536–1966* (Berkeley and Los Angeles, 1975), p. 293.

30 Garvin, *1922*, p. 147.

31 For comparative figures see F. Dovring, *Land and Labour in Europe in the Twentieth Century: A Comparative Study of Recent Agrarian History*, 3rd ed. (The Hague, 1965), p. 169.

32 T. Garvin *The Evolution of Irish Nationalist Politics*, (Dublin, 1981), p. 11.

33 J. Coakley, 'The election that made the first Dáil' in B. Farrell (ed.), *The Creation of the Dáil* (Dublin, 1994), pp. 31–47.

34 G. Therborn, 'The rule of capital and the rise of democracy', *New Left Review* 103 (1977), pp. 3–41.

35 See E. de Valera, *The Foundation of the Republic of Ireland in the Vote of the People* (Victoria, 1919).

36 P. Pearse, 'The sovereign people', *The Complete Works of P. H. Pearse: Political Writings and Speeches* (Dublin, n. d.), p. 341.

37 E. Allardt, 'Types of protest and alienation', p. 47.

38 Michael Hayes, 'Dáil Éireann and the Irish civil war', article in preparation for *Studies*, 1968–69 (UCDA, Hayes Papers).

39 Garvin, *1922*, p. 127.

40 Interview with William O'Brien, 5 Aug. 1922, William O'Brien, 'The Irish Free State: secret history of its foundation' (NL, O'Brien Papers, MS 4201).

41 A. Mitchell and P. O'Snodaigh, *Irish Political Documents 1916–1949* (Dublin, 1985), p. 135.

42 Deputy Davin, *Dáil Debates*, vol. 1 col. 101, 11 Sept. 1922.

43 Deputy O'Brien, *Dáil Debates*, vol. 1 col. 159, 12 Jan. 1922.

44 Michael Collins, Memorandum, 26 July 1922 (UCDA, Mulcahy Papers, P/7 B/28).

45 On the election results see, M. Laffan, *The Resurrection of Ireland: The Sinn Féin Party 1916–1923* (Cambridge, 1999), pp. 400–11.

46 Deputy Sears, *Dáil Debates*, col. 140, 11 Jan. 1922.

47 William O'Brien, 'The Irish Free State; secret history of its foundation' (NL, O'Brien Papers, MS 4201).

48 William Cosgrave, 'Oration at grave of President Arthur Griffith' (NA, D/T, S 5983/1).

49 William Cosgrave, *Dáil Debates*, vol. 1 col. 195, 12 Sept. 1922.

50 Ibid.

51 Garvin, *1922*, p. 127.

52 'Monthly report for February 1923', 20 Mar. 1923 (NA, Civil War 1922–23 army reports on situation and organisation, D/T, S 3361).

53 Ibid.

54 Report on Cork East, Monthly Report for February, 20 Mar. 1923, ibid.

55 *FJ*, 20 July 1922

56 Memo from Commander in Chief to Acting Chairman, GHQ, 5 Aug. 1922 (NA, Civil war army reports).

57 Richard Mulcahy, *Dáil Debates*, vol. 1 col. 174, 12 Sept. 1922.

58 'Report on Operations carried out in the West Cork and South Kerry Area', Apr. 1923 (NA, Civil war army reports).

59 'Report of the military situation, 31 Mar. 1923' (NA, Civil war army reports).

60 Ibid.

61 Garvin, *1922*, p. 135

62 P. Pyne, 'The third Sinn Féin party, 1923–1926', *ESR* 1 (1969–70), p. 236.

63 R. N. Berki, 'State and society; An antithesis of modern political thought' in J. Hayward and R. N. Berki (eds), *State and Society in Contemporary Europe* (Oxford, 1979), pp. 1–18.

64 Ibid., p. 3.

65 Ibid.

66 K. O'Higgins, *Civil War and the Events Which Led To It* (Dublin, 1926), p. 1.

67 Robert Barton, 1 July 1922, 'Memorandum of ambulance work & efforts for peace' (NA, Peace proposal J. F. Homan-Clontarf, D/T, S 8138).

68 Berki, 'State and society', p. 4.

69 Ibid., p. 5.

70 Memo, Jan. 1923 (UCDA, Mulcahy Papers, P/7B/107).

71 Giddens, *Durkheim*, p. 3.

72 Durkheim, *Division of Labour in Society*, p. 166.

73 Ibid. p. 397.

74 Giddens, *Durkheim*, p. 3.

75 See B. Kissane, 'Civil Society under strain: intermediary organisations and the Irish Civil War', *IPS* 15 (2000), pp. 1–25.

76 E. O'Halpin, *Defending Ireland: The Irish State and its Enemies since 1922* (Oxford, 1999), p. 38.

77 Thomas Johnson, *Dáil Debates*, vol. 1 col. 184, 11 Sept. 1922.

78 Cathal O'Shannon, *Dáil Debates*, vol. 1 col. 8, 11 Jan. 1922.

79 William Cosgrave, *Dáil Debates*, vol. 40 col. 48, 14 Oct. 1931.

80 Quoted in Giddens, *Durkheim*, p. 59.

81 William Cosgrave, 'Interview between the President and Donal Hannigan and M. J. Burke of Neutral IRA February 27 1923' (NA, 'Peace Proposals of Old IRA', D/T, S 8139).

82 Kevin O'Higgins, *Dáil Debates*, vol. 1 col. 98, 11 Sept., 1922.

83 Deputy Milroy, *Dáil Debates*, 11 Jan. 1922.

84 William Cosgrave, 'Oration at grave of President Arthur Griffith' (NA, D/T, S 5983/1).

85 Chief of Staff to Minister of Defence, 20 Sept. 1923 (NA, Civil war army reports).

86 Giddens, *Durkheim*, p. 29.

87 'Enforcement of Article 2A' (NA, D/J, D 29/36).

88 William Cosgrave, *Dáil Debates*, vol. 40 col. 49, 14 Oct. 1931.

89 Giddens, *Durkheim*, p. 29.

90 K. O'Shiel to Cosgrave, 2 Feb. 1923 (Mulcahy Papers, P7/8/100).

91   Durkheim, *Division of Labour in Society*, pp. 82–3.

92   K. Thompson, *Emile Durkheim* (London, 1982), p. 91.

93   T. Garvin, 'The aftermath', lecture given at seminar on Irish civil war 1922–23, Cathal Brugha Barracks, 13 Sept., 1997.

94   William Cosgrave, *Dáil Debates*, vol. 1 col. 77, 11 Sept. 1923.

95   Giddens, *Durkheim*, p. 31.

96   William Cosgrave, *Dáil Debates*, vol. 84 col. 1320, 9 July 1941.

Chapter Eight

1   A. Gramsci in Q. Hoare and G. N. Smith (eds), *Selections from Prison Notebooks of Antonio Gramsci* (New York, 1971), p. 219.

2   J. Linz and A. Stepan (eds), *The Breakdown of Democratic Regimes* (Baltimore and London, 1978), p. 87.

3   Ibid.

4   Ibid., p. 88.

5   Ibid.

6   A. Stepan, 'Democratic opposition and democratisation theory', *Government and Opposition* 32 (1997), p. 662.

7   B. Kissane, 'Civil society under strain: intermediary organisations and the Irish civil war', *IPS* 15 (2000), p. 19.

8   De Valera to McGarrity, 10 Sept. 1922 (NL, McGarrity Papers, MS 17,440).

9   'Reorganisation of Sinn Féin', Dept A/C to O/C All Divisions and Independent Bodies, 18 Jan. 1923 (NA, Sinn Féin: de Valera papers relating to the organisation of Sinn Féin 1922–23, D/T, S 1297).

10   De Valera to Donnelly, 22 May 1923 (NA, Sinn Féin, 1094/4/22).

11   Ibid.

12   De Valera to Minister for Home Affairs, 15 Jan. 1923 (NA, Sinn Féin, 1904/2).

13   De Valera to Organising Committee, 31 May 1923 (NA, Sinn Féin, 1094/1/11).

14   De Valera to A. L., 29 May 1923 (NA, Sinn Féin 1094/8/4).

15   Ibid.

16   Dept A/G to OCs of Divisions and Independent Brigades, 28 May 1923, (NA, Sinn Féin: de Valera papers relating to the organisation of Sinn Féin, 1922–23, D/T, S 1297).

17   To O/C Divisions and Independent Brigades, 27 July 1923 (UCDA, Twomey Papers, P 69, 74, 2).

18   M. Manning, *Irish Political Parties: An Introduction* (Dublin, 1972), p. 11.

19   E. Neeson, *The Civil War 1922–23* (Cork, 1995), p. 295.

20   P. Pyne, 'The third Sinn Féin Party: 1923–1926', *ESR* 1 (1969–70), p. 40.

21   Ibid., p. 42.

22   Ibid p. 42.

23   Ibid., p. 43.

24   'Evolution of Fianna Fáil and new Sinn Féin Party' (NA, D/T, S F 880).

25   'Civil war: army report 1925' (NA, D/T, S 4527).

26   Aiken to Chairman of Army Council, 11 Dec. 1925 (UCDA, Aiken Papers, P104 /1315 (1)).

27   Pyne, 'Third Sinn Féin party', p. 44.

28   Ibid., p. 45.

29   De Valera to McGarrity, 13 Mar. 1926 (NL, McGarrity Papers, MS 174 41).

30 Quoted in Pyne, 'Third Sinn Féin party', p. 45.

31 J. Lee and G. Ó Tuathaigh, *The Age of de Valera* (Dublin, 1982), pp. 62–3.

32 Ibid., p. 63.

33 Letter to press, 24 Feb. 1927 (UCDA, Twomey Papers, P69/48 (201)).

34 Secretary, Army Council to Eamon de Valera, 11 May 1927 (Twomey Papers, P69/48/30).

35 'Memorandum of suggested basis for co-operation between Republican bodies for General Election and after if a majority of Republicans are elected' (Twomey Papers, P69/48/35).

36 'Meeting of representative individuals of republican bodies to consider army council proposals for co-ordination for general election 26 Apr. 1927' (Twomey Papers, P69/48/35).

37 De Valera to Secretary, Army Council, 13 May 1927 (Twomey Papers, P69/48/29).

38 T. P. Coogan, *De Valera: Long Fellow, Long Shadow* (London, 1993), p. 400.

39 Interview with special correspondent of the *Irish World*, 21 Aug. 1926, ibid.

40 Coogan, *De Valera: Long Fellow, Long Shadow*, p. 398.

41 Cunnta an Runaidhe Onoraigh (NA, Department of Justice, 'Sinn Féin Ard Fheis' S 1/23).

42 'Report of Meeting of Dáil Éireann', 10 Dec. 1927 (NA, Department of Justice, 'Sinn Féin Ard Fheis' S 1/23).

43 Garda Report on Sinn Féin Ard Fheis held at the Rotunda House 11 Dec. 1927, 15 Dec. 1927 (NA, Department of Justice, 'Sinn Féin Ard Fheis' S 1/23).

44 Pyne, 'The third Sinn Féin party', p. 47.

45 'Comments on Mr MacBrides letter of the 16th instant and on Dr Cooney's letter of the 23rd', n.d. (UCDA, Aiken Papers, P104/1331 (3)).

46 *Irish Independent*, 1 Dec. 1930.

47 Speech by E. de Valera at Burgh Quay, 27 July 1927 (NL, Johnson Papers, MS 17169).

48 R. Fanning, *Independent Ireland* (Dublin, 1983), p. 99.

49 'Ireland: the political situation', *The Round Table* 59 (1925), pp. 552–62.

50 Linz and Stepan (eds), *The Breakdown of Democratic Regimes*, p. 50.

51 I. Lustick, *Unsettled States, Disputed Lands: Britain and Ireland, France and Algeria, Israel and the West Bank Gaza* (Ithaca, 1993), pp. 305–8.

52 Eamon de Valera, 'What Fianna Fáil stands for'– speech delivered at Blackrock Town Hall, 22 Aug. 1927 (UCDA, Aiken Papers, P104/1562).

53 M. MacSwiney to J. McGarrity, 12 April 1926 (NL, McGarrity Papers, MS 17441).

54 Quoted in The Earl of Longford and T. P. O'Neill, *Eamon de Valera* (Dublin, 1970), p. 263.

55 Ibid., pp. 260–1.

56 Fianna Fáil Archives, FF/22. On the party's concern with internal discipline see E. O'Halpin, 'Parliamentary party discipline and tactics: the Fianna Fáil archives, 1926–32', *IHS* 30 (1997), 581–91.

57 'Report of Meeting at Findlater Place' Fianna Fáil; Meetings, Speeches, 1929 (NA, D/T, S 5962).

58 Eamon de Valera, *Dáil Debates*, vol. 40 col. 56, 14 Oct. 1931.

59 William Cosgrave, *Dáil Debates*, vol. 40 col. 32, 14 Oct. 1931.

60 Garda Report on Sinn Féin Ard Fheis 1931, 10 Oct. 1931 (NA, Department of Justice, 'Sinn Féin Ard Fheis' D/J, S 1/23).

61 R. Fanning, *Independent Ireland*, 104. The proscribed organisations were Saor Éire, the Irish Republican Army, Fianna Éireann, Cumman na mBan, Friends of Soviet Russia, The Irish Labour Defence League, The Workers' Defence Corps, The Women's Prisoners Defence League, The Workers' Revolutionary Party, The Irish Tribute League, The Irish Working Farmers' Association, and the Workers' Research Bureau. The banned publications were *Irish World*, *An Phoblacht*, *Worker's Voice*, *Irish Worker*, and *Republican File*.

62 D. Keogh, 'De Valera, the Catholic Church, and the "Red Scare", 1931–1932' in J. P. O'Carroll and J. A. Murphy (eds), *De Valera and his Times* (Cork, 1983), p. 144.

63 *The Irish Times*, 5 Feb. 1932.

64 General Eoin O'Duffy, 'Memo-Implementing the proposed Treasonable Offences Act', 7 Oct. 1931 (NA, D/J, B. 22/35).

65 Army Council Dispatch no. 189, 7 May 1932 (UCDA, Twomey Papers, P 69/185/ 269).

66 C. Foley, *Legion of the Rearguard: The IRA and the Modern Irish State* (London, 1992), p. 101.

67 Fanning, *Independent Ireland*, p. 107.

68 Ibid.

69 Longford and O'Neill, *Eamon de Valera*, p. 262.

70 'Army council dispatch', no. 189, 7 May 1932 (Twomey Papers, P69/185/269).

71 *Irish Independent*, 8 June 1935.

72 UCDA, Twomey Papers, P 69/185/269.

73 Gilmore to Twomey, n. d. (Twomey Papers, P 69/53/368).

74 Clann na Gael Circular, 10 June 1932 (Twomey Papers, P69/185/288).

75 Ibid.

76 Twomey Papers, P 69/185 (21).

77 J. McGarrity to E. de Valera, 2 Oct. 1933 (NL, McGarrity Papers, MS 174 41).

78 De Valera to McGarrity, 31 Jan. 1934 (McGarrity Papers, MS 174 41).

79 Twomey, unpublished notes, n. d. (Twomey Papers, P69/186/1).

80 Twomey to Secretary Clan na Gael, 13 Feb. 1933 (Twomey Papers, P69/185/95).

81 See M. Cronin, *The Blueshirts and Irish Politics* (Dublin, 1997), pp. 135–67.

82 J. Dillon to F. MacDermott 15 Sept. 1934 (NA, MacDermott Papers, 1056/2/2).

83 R. Fanning, 'The rule of order': Eamon de Valera and the IRA, 1923–40', in J. P. O'Carroll and J. A. Murphy (eds), *De Valera and his Times* (Cork, 1983), p. 163.

84 J. Dillon to F. MacDermott, 25 Sept. 1934 (MacDermott Papers, 1065/2/4, p. 6).

85 Peadar O'Donnell, General Army Convention, 17 Mar. 1933 (Twomey Papers, P 69/186/1).

86 Resolution No. 25 carried at General Army Convention, 17 Mar. 1933 (Twomey Papers, P 69/186/1)).

87 Ibid.

88 S. Huntington, *Political Order in Changing Societies* (New Haven, Conn. and London, 1968), p. 346.

89 J. Dillon to F. MacDermott, 17 Oct. 1934 (MacDermott Papers).

90 J. Dillon to F. MacDermott, 25 Sept.1934 (MacDermott Papers, 1065/2/4, p. 7).

91 Garda Document marked 'Secret', Detective Branch HQ, 23 Oct. 1935 (NA, D/T, S 2454).

92 Ibid.

93 Fanning, 'The rule of order', p. 163.

94 'Notes on use of article 2A by present government' (NA, 'Constitution – Article 2A Operation 1933 + suspension', D/T, S 2454).

95 On the volunteer force see L. Joye, 'Aiken's slugs: the reserve of the Irish army under Fianna Fáil' in J. Augusteijn (ed.), *Ireland in the 1930s: New Perspectives* (Dublin, 1999), pp. 143–63.

96 Garda Document, Detective Branch H. Q., 23 Oct. 1935 (NA, D/T, S 2454).

97 Statement from the IRA Army Council, Easter Sunday 1932 (Twomey Papers, P 69/54/262).

98 Quoted in Fanning, *Independent Ireland*, p. 119.

99 Ibid., p. 120.

100 Lustick, *Unsettled States, Disputed Lands*, p. 306.

101 Frank Aiken, 'A call to unity', 19 June 1926 (Fianna Fáil Archives, FF/22).

102 Huntington, *Political Order in Changing Societies*, p. 347.

103 Lustick, *Unsettled States, Disputed Lands*, p. 305.

104 Huntington, *Political Order in Changing Societies*, p. 346.

105 Ibid.

106 Reflection by Michael Hayes on 10 Aug. vote (UCDA, Hayes Papers, P53/330 (7)).

107 Quoted in Fanning, *Independent Ireland*, p. 100.

108 Ibid., 109.

109 *Irish Press*, 2 Feb. 1932.

110 N. Bermeo, 'Myths of moderation: confrontation and conflict during democratic transitions', *CP* 29 (1997), 316.

111 *The Irish Times*, 9 Sept. 1927.

112 Cited in W. Cosgrave *Dáil Debates*, vol. 40 col. 35, 14 Oct. 1931.

113 Fanning, *Independent Ireland*, p. 109.

114 Ibid.

115 De Valera speech at Enniscorthy, 2 Aug. 1936 (UCDA, Aiken Papers, P104/1459).

116 Ibid.

117 George Gilmore, quoted in C. Foley, *Legion of the Rearguard: The IRA and the Modern Irish State* (London, 1992), p. 106.

118 General Army Convention, 17–18 Mar. 1933 (Twomey Papers, P 69/187 (92)).

119 *Irish Press*, 5 Feb. 1932.

120 *Irish Independent*, 28 June 1937.

121 See Cronin, *The Blueshirts and Irish Politics* (Dublin, 1997).

122 See Fanning, 'The rule of order', pp. 160–73.

123 Ibid.

124 'Organisation of election staff', 17 June 1923 (NA, Sinn Féin 1094/9/4).

125 De Valera to Chief of Staff and Members of Executive, 12 Oct. 1922 (NL, O'Donoughue Papers, MS 31,528). My emphasis.

Chapter Nine

1 Sean MacBride to Eamon de Valera, 23 May 1954 (NL, D/T, S 15655).

2 On consensus democracy see A Lijphart, *Patterns of Democracy: Government Forms and Performance in Thirty-Six Counties* (New Haven and London, 1996), pp. 31–47.

3 J. Hogan, *Election and Representation* (Cork, 1945), p. 47.

4 F. Hermens, *Democracy or Anarchy? A Study of Proportional Representation* (New York, London, 1972); L. Karvonen, *Fragmentation and Consensus: Political Organisation and the Interwar Crisis in Europe* (Boulder, Colo., 1993).

5 In this chapter I refer to 'majority rule' as a decision-making rule structuring executive-legislative relations, which requires that constitutional limitations on the power of elected majority or plurality governments be curtailed or simply do not exist.

6 M. Valiulis, *Portrait of a Revolutionary: General Richard Mulcahy and the Founding of the Irish Free State* (Dublin, 1992), p. 189.

7 R. Fanning, *Independent Ireland* (Dublin, 1983), p. 10.

8 B. Farrell, 'From first Dáil through Free State' in B. Farrell (ed.), *De Valera's Constitution and Ours* (Dublin, 1988), pp. 117–19.

9 P. Dunleavy, 'The political parties' in P. Dunleavy (ed.), *Developments in British Politics 4* (London, 1995), pp. 150–2.

10 C. O'Leary, *Irish Elections 1918–1977: Parties, Voters, and Proportional Representation* (Dublin, 1979), p. 24.

11 R. Nwabueze, *Constitutionalism in the Emergent States* (London, 1977), p. 23.

12 *Constitution of the Irish Free State* (Dublin, 1936).

13 N. Mansergh, *The Irish Free State: Its Government and Politics* (London, 1934), p. 331.

14 B. Farrell, 'From first Dáil through Free State', p. 219.

15 Ibid.

16 A. Ward, *The Irish Constitutional Tradition: Responsible Government and Modern Ireland* (Dublin, 1994), p. 238.

17 F. Hermens, *Democracy or Anarchy?: A Study in Proportional Representation* (New York, London, 1972).

18 J. Hogan, *Election and Representation* (Cork, 1945), p. 13.

19 Hermens, *Democracy or Anarchy?* p. 315.

20 Karvonen, *Fragmentation and Consensus*, p. 88.

21 Ibid.

22 Hermens, *Democracy or Anarchy?* p. 326.

23 Ibid., p. 315.

24 Thomas Johnson, 'Irish Labour Party's views on the oath of allegiance' (NL, Johnson Papers, MS 17 159).

25 'Statement by Thomas Johnson re coalition between Fianna Fáil and Labour Parties', 22 Aug. 1927 (Johnson Papers, MS 17 166).

26 'Two Speeches by Thomas Johnson 1926, 1927' (Johnson Papers, MS 17 164).

27 Fianna Fáil Archives, FF/22.

28 'Correspondence between T. Johnson and Wm. Redmond of National Party August 1927' (Johnson Papers, MS 17 165).

29 De Valera Speech at Burgh Quay, 27 July 1927 (Johnson Papers, MS 17 169).

30 E. McKay, 'Changing with the tide: the Irish Labour Party, 1927–1933', *Saothar*, 11, (1986), pp. 27–39.

31 Ibid., p. 28.

32 All figures from M. Gallagher, *Irish Elections 1922–1944: Results and Analysis* (Limerick, 1993).

33 Ibid., p. 157.

34 *The Irish Times*, 3 Sept. 1927.

35 D. Gwynn, *The Irish Free State 1922–1927* (London, 1928), p. 147.

36 Johnson, 'Two Speeches by Thomas Johnson 1926, 1927'.

37 Richard Mulcahy, *Dáil Debates*, vol. 59, no. 5, 1535, 27–29 Sept. 1935.

38 Karvonen, *Fragmentation and Consensus*, p. 164.

39 A. E. Malone, 'Party government in the Irish Free State', *PSQ* 44 (1929), p. 378.

40 Farrell, 'From first Dáil through Free State', p. 31.

41 P. Dunleavy, *Democracy, Bureaucracy and Public Choice: Economic Explanations in Political Science* (Hemel Hempstead, 1991), p. 117.

42 I am indebted to Professor Brendan O'Leary for this observation.

43 M. Tierney to F. MacDermott, 27 Sept. 1934 (NA, MacDermott Papers, 1065/4/4).

44 T. Garvin, 'Nationalist elites, Irish voters, and Irish political development: a comparative perspective', *ESR* 8 (1977), p. 165.

45 J. Linz, 'Crisis, breakdown and reequilibration' in J. Linz and A. Stepan (eds), *The Breakdown of Democratic Regimes* (Baltimore and London, 1978), pp. 24–27.

46 Speech at third Ard Fheis of Fianna Fáil (Fianna Fáil Archives, FF/22).

47 Karvonen, *Fragmentation and Consensus*.

48 *Dáil Debates*, vol. 34 col. 313–14, 2 Apr. 1930.

49 Ward, *The Irish Constitutional Tradition*, p. 238.

50 'Memorandum of ambulance work & efforts for peace' (NA, 'Civil war 1922–24: Peace proposal –
J. F. Homan/Clontarf', D/T S 8138).

51 Hogan, *Election and Representation*, pp. 23–5.

52 Farrell, 'From first Dáil through Free State', p. 213.

53 Ibid., p. 214.

54 A. Beattie, 'Ministerial responsibility and the theory of the British state' in R. A. W. Rhodes and
P. Dunleavy (eds), *Prime Minister, Cabinet and Core Executive* (London, 1995), p. 172.

55 *The Irish Times*, 12 Feb. 1932.

56 M. Gallagher, 'The pact general election of 1922' *IHS* 21 (1979), pp. 405–6.

57 Fanning, *Independent Ireland*, p. 13.

58 C. O'Leary, *Irish Elections 1918–1977: Parties, Voters and Proportional Representation* (Dublin,
1979), p. 24.

59 O' Higgins to MacDermott, 18 May 1927 (MacDermott Papers, 1065/1/1).

60 De Valera Memo, 16 May 1923 Sinn Féin 1094/8/1, NA.

61 Fanning, *Independent Ireland*, p. 114.

62 R. Dahl, *Democracy and its Critics* (New Haven, 1989), p. 161.

63 See M. Cronin, *The Blueshirts and Irish Politics* (Dublin, 1997), pp. 135–68.

64 D. Held, *Models of Democracy* (Cambridge, 1987), pp. 143–84.

65 F. Munger, *The Legitimacy of Opposition* (Beverly Hills, 1975), p. 25.

66 Dahl, *Democracy and its Critics*, p. 161.

67 Ibid.

68 Quoted in Fanning, *Independent Ireland*, p. 161.

69 'Notes on use of Article 2A by present government' (NA, Constitution 1922 – operation of
article 2A, 1933+ suspension, S 2454 D/T).

70 P. Fay, 'The Amendments to the Constitution Committee 1926', *Administration* 26 (1978),
p. 348.

71 Quoted in D. Gwynn, *The Irish Free State 1922–1927* (London, 1928), p. 142.

72 *The Irish Times*, 1 Sept. 1927.

73 Ibid.

74 D. O'Sullivan, *The Irish Free State and its Senate: A Study in Contemporary Politics* (London,
1940), p. 364.

75 Ibid., pp. 414–17.

76 *Dáil Debates*, vol. 68 col. 1351–1352, 11 June 1937.

77 See G. Sartori, *Democratic Theory* (London, 1958), pp. 98–9.

78 B. O'Leary and J. McGarry, *The Politics of Antagonism: Understanding Northern Ireland*
(London, 1993), p. 149.

79 J. Fishkin, *Democracy and Deliberation* (New Haven and London, 1991), p. 35.

80 Quoted in O'Sullivan, *Irish Free State*, p. 474.

81 Press Statement 18 Apr. 1926 (Fianna Fáil Archives, FF/22).

82 S. Rokkan, *Citizens, Elections, Parties: Approaches to the Comparative Study of the Processes of
Development* (Oslo, 1970), p. 157.

83 B. O'Duffy and B. O'Leary, 'Tales from elsewhere and a Hibernian sermon' in H. Margetts and
G. Smith (eds), *Turning Japanese: Britain with a Dominant Party of Government* (London, 1995),
pp. 193–210.

84 Although see Gwynn, *The Irish Free State 1922–1927*, pp. 143–9; Mansergh, *The Irish Free State*, pp 58–73; T. Garvin, 'Democratic politics in independent Ireland' in J. Coakley and M. Gallagher (eds), *Politics in the Republic of Ireland*, 2nd ed. (Limerick,1993), p. 254.

85 'Revision of Parliamentary constituencies' (NA, D/T, S 1817 A).

86 *Round Table*, no. 83, June 1931.

87 Ibid.

88 *Irish Independent*, 22 Mar. 1935.

89 On the economic divide see R. Dunphy, *The Making of Fianna Fáil Power in Ireland 1923–1948* (Oxford, 1995); P. Mair, *The Changing Irish Party System: Organisation, Ideology and Electoral Competition* (London, 1987); E. Rumpf and A. C. Hepburn, *Nationalism and Socialism in Twentieth Century Ireland* (Liverpool, 1977). On culture see T. Garvin, 'Political cleavages, party politics and urbanisation in Ireland – the case of the periphery-dominated centre', *EJPS* 11 (1974); J. Prager, *Building Democracy in Ireland: Political Order and Cultural Integration in a Newly Independent Nation* (Cambridge, 1986).

90 See Farrell, 'From first Dáil through Free State', pp. 18–32.

91 See M. Smith, 'The title *An Taoiseach* in the 1937 constitution', *IPS* 10 (1995), pp. 179–85.

92 See P. Mair, 'Consolidating Irish democracy: some reflections on Eamon de Valera and the transfer of power in Ireland in 1932', unpublished paper, 1999, p. 12.

93 T. Garvin, 'The enigma of Dev – the man from God knows where', *The Irish Times*, 10 Apr. 1998.

94 Quoted in D. O'Sullivan, *The Irish Free State*, p. 365.

95 See B. O'Duffy and B. O'Leary, 'Tales from elsewhere', pp. 193–210.

96 Mair, 'Consolidating Irish democracy', p. 12.

97 Ibid.

98 See Karvonen, *Fragmentation and Consensus*.

99 See K. Loewenstein, 'Autocracy versus democracy in contemporary Europe, II', *APSR* 29 (1935), p. 782.

100 T. Garvin, *1922: The Birth of Irish Democracy* (Dublin, 1922), pp. 123–56.

101 J. Lee, *Ireland: 1912–1985* (Cambridge, 1989), pp. 56–270.

102 Dahl, *Democracy and its Critics*, p. 135.

103 Karvonen, *Fragmentation and Consensus*, p. 173.

104 E. Allardt, 'Types of protest and alienation' in E. Allardt and S. Rokkan (eds) *Mass Politics: Studies in Political Sociology* (New York, 1970), pp. 45–64.

Chapter Ten

1 G. FitzGerald, 'Days of doubt long gone as State reaches 75th birthday', *The Irish Times*, 6 Dec. 1977.

2 T. Lynn Karl, 'Dilemmas of democratization in Latin America' *CP* 23 (1990), p. 7.

3 D. Berg-Schlosser and J. Mitchell (eds), *Conditions of Democracy in Europe 1919–1939* (Basingstoke, 2000), p. 464.

4 T. Garvin, 'The enigma of Dev – the man from God knows where', *The Irish Times*, 10 Apr. 1998.

5 Quoted in E. Larkin (ed.), *Alexis de Tocqueville's Journey in Ireland: July–August 1835* (Dublin, 1990), p. 9.

6 Ibid., p. 145.

7 *Irish Independent*, 27 Apr. 1922.

8 I. Liikanen, *Fennomania ja Kansa* (Helsinki, 1995), English summary, p. 349.

9   See R. English, *Radicals and the Republic: Socialist Republicanism in the Irish Free State 1925–37* (Oxford, 1994).

10   See the essays in M. Cronin and J. Regan (eds), *Ireland: The Politics of Irish Independence, 1922–49* (Basingstoke and New York, 1999).

11   See A. Janos, 'The one-party state and social mobilization; East Europe between the Wars', in S. Huntington and C. Moore (eds), *Authoritarian Politics in Modern Society: The Dynamics of Established One-Party Systems* (New York, and London), pp. 204–36.

12   G. Luebbert, *Liberalism, Fascism or Social Democracy: Social Classes and the Political Origins of Regimes in Interwar Europe* (Oxford, 1991), p. 259,

13   J. Hogan, *Modern Democracy* (Cork, 1938), p. 82.

14   D. Berg-Schlosser, 'Conditions of authoritarianism, fascism, and democracy in inter-war Europe: a cross-sectional and longitudinal analysis', *International Journal of Comparative Sociology* 39 (1998), p. 366.

15   M. Hayes, 'Dáil Eireann and the civil war', typescript in preparation for publication (UCDA, Hayes Papers, 1968/9, B85).

16   *The Irish Times*, 27 July 1998.

17   T. Garvin, *1922: The Birth of Irish Democracy* (Dublin, 1996), p. 45.

18   J. Regan, *The Irish Counter-Revolution: 1921–36: Treatyite Politics and Settlement in Independent Ireland* (Dublin, 1999), p. 69.

19   M. Burton, R. Gunther and J. Higley, 'Introduction', in J. Higley and R. Gunther (eds), *Elites and Democratic Consolidation in Latin America and Southern Europe* (Cambridge and New York, 1992), p. 29.

20   B. Farrell, *The Irish Parliamentary Tradition* (Dublin, 1973), p. 31.

21   T. Vanhanen, *Strategies of Democratisation* (Washington, 1992), p. 6.

22   On the contrasting conceptions of consolidation among the political elite see B. Kissane, 'Democratic consolidation and government changeover in the Irish Free State', *Journal of Commonwealth and Comparative Politics* 39 (2001), pp. 1–23.

23   S. Ganguly, 'Explaining India's transition to democracy' in L. Anderson (ed.), *Transitions to Democracy* (New York, 1999), p. 228.

24   *Dáil Debates*, vol. 40 col. 47–50, 4 Oct. 1931.

25   'A call to unity', 9 Mar.1926 (UCDA, Aiken Papers, P104/1499 (1)).

26   O'Coilte to Executive Council, 23 Oct. 1935, 'Constitution-Article 2A Operation 1933 and suspension' (NA, D/T S2454).

27   Hoare, Q. and Nowell Smith, G., *Selections from the Prison Notebooks of Antonio Gramsci* (New York, 1971), p. 219.

28   O. Jussila, S Hentila, and J. Nevakivi, *From Grand Duchy to Modern State: A Political History of Finland since 1809* (London, 1999), pp. 167–72.

29   P. Nikiforos Diamondorous, 'Prospects for democracy in Greece: 1974–1983' in G. O'Donnell, P. Schmitter and L. Whitehead (eds), *Transitions from Authoritarian Rule: Southern Europe* (Baltimore and London, 1986), p. 163.

30   J. M. Maravall and J. Santamaria, 'Political change in Spain' in G. O'Donnell, P. Schmitter, and L. Whitehead (eds), *Transitions from Authoritarian Rule: Southern Europe* (Baltimore and London, 1986), p. 102.

31   S. Huntington, *The Third Wave: Democratization in the Late Twentieth Century* (London, 1991), p. 256.

32   R. Fanning, *Independent Ireland* (Dublin, 1983), p. 100.

33   D. Beetham, *The Legitimation of Power* (London, 1991), pp. 140–60.

34   I. Lustick, *Unsettled States, Disputed Lands: Britain and Ireland, France and Algeria, Israel and the West Bank Gaza* (Ithaca, 1993), pp. 305–8.

35   MacEntee to Honorary Secretaries Fianna Fáil, 27 Jan. 1936 (UCDA, MacEntee Papers, P67/453).

36   D. Held, *Models of Democracy* (Cambridge, 1987), pp. 143–84.

Bibliography

Abbreviations

See p. 231.

Primary Sources

Dáil Debates

Government Papers
National Archives of Ireland
Dáil Éireann Files
Department of An Taoiseach Files
Department of Justice Files
Registry of Friendly Societies

Trinity College Dublin
Report of the Registrar of Friendly Societies of
Sáorstat Éireann to the Minister for Finance
for the Year Ending 31 Dec. 1923.

Report of the Registrar of Friendly Societies
for the Two Years ending 31 Dec., 1927.

Private Papers

National Library of Ireland
Dubin Trades Council
Irish Trade Union Congress
Thomas Johnson Papers
Joseph McGarrity Papers
William O'Brien Papers
Florence O'Donoghue Papers

National Archives of Ireland
Ancient Guild of Incorporated Brick and
Stonelayers Trade Union
Frank MacDermott Papers
Gavan Duffy Papers
Irish Industrial Development Association
Trade Union Records

UCD Archives
Frank Aiken Papers
Ernest Blythe Papers
Desmond FitzGerald Papers
Diarmuid Hegarty Papers
Sighle Humphreys Papers
Donnach O'Briain Papers
Ernie O'Malley Papers
Eoin MacNeill Papers
Sean MacEntee Papers
Mary MacSwiney Papers
Patrick McGilligan Papers
Richard Mulcahy Papers
Michael Hayes Papers
Moss Twomey Papers

Party Papers
Fianna Fáil Archives
Sinn Féin Papers (National Archives)

Periodicals
Catholic Bulletin
Éire/Ireland
Freeman's Journal
Irish Historical Studies
Irish Independent
The Nation
Irish Political Studies
Irish Press
Irish Rosary
The Irish Times
The Round Table
Saothar
The Separatist
Sinn Féin
Poblacht na hÉireann
Voice of Labour

Secondary Sources

Akenson, D. H., 'Was de Valera a Republican?' *Review of Politics* 33 (1971), pp. 233–54.
Akenson, D. H. and Fallon, J. F., 'The Irish civil war and the drafting of the Free State
        constitution', *Eire/Ireland* 5 (spring 1970), 10–26; (summer 1970), pp. 42–93; (winter 1970),
        pp. 28–70.
Alapuro, R., *State and Revolution in Finland* (Berkeley, 1988).
Alapuro, R. and Allardt, E., 'The Lapua Movement: the threat of a rightist takeover in Finland,
        1930–1932', in J. J. Linz and A. Stepan (eds), *The Breakdown of Democratic Regimes in
        Europe* (London, 1978), pp. 122–41.
Alestalo, M., *Structural Change, Classes and the State: Finland in an Historical and Comparative
        Perspective* (Helsinki, 1986).
Alestalo M., Andorka R. and Harcsa, I., *Agricultural Population and Structural Change:
        A Comparison of Finland and Hungary* (Helsinki, 1987).
Alestalo, M. and Kuhnle, S., *The Scandinavian Route: Economic, Social, and Political Developments
        in Denmark, Finland, Norway, and Sweden* (Helsinki, 1984).
Allardt, E., 'Types of protest and alienation' in E. Allardt and S. Rokkan (eds), *Mass Politics:
        Studies in Political Sociology* (New York, 1970), pp. 45–64.
Allardt, E., *Finnish Society: Relationship between Geopolitical Situation and the Development of
        Society* (Helsinki, 1985).
Anderson, P., *Lineages of the Absolutist State* (London, 1979).
Andrews, C. S., *Man of No Property* (Dublin and Cork, 1982).
Ashtown, F. O., *The Unknown Power Behind the Irish Nationalist Party: Its Present Work . . . and
        Criminal History* (London, 1907).
Banks, A., *Cross Polity Time-Series Data* (Cambridge, Mass., 1971).
Barrett, J. J., *In the Name of the Game* (Dublin, 1997)
Barry, B., *Sociologists, Economists, and Democracy* (Chicago, 1978).
Barry, F., 'Democracy from what point?' *Irish Review* 20 (1997), pp. 157–61.
Beaslai, P. *The Story of the Catholic Commercial Club Dublin 1881–1954* (Dublin, 1958).
Beattie, A., 'Ministerial responsibility and the theory of the British state' in R. A. W. Rhodes and
        P. Dunleavy (eds), *Prime Minister, Cabinet and Core Executive* (London, 1995), pp. 158–81.
Beetham, D., *The Legitimation of Power* (London, 1991)
Beito, D. T., 'To advance the "practice of thrift and economy": fraternal societies and social
        capital, 1890–1920', *JIH* 29 (1999), pp. 585–612.
Berg-Schlosser, D., 'Conditions of authoritarianism, fascism and democracy in inter-war Europe: a
        cross sectional and longitudinal analysis', *International Journal of Comparative Sociology* 39
        (1998), pp. 335–77.
Berg-Schlosser D. and de Meur G., 'Conditions of democracy in Interwar Europe: a Boolean test
        of major hypotheses', *CP* 26 (1994), pp. 253–81.
Berg-Schlosser, D. and Mitchell, J. (eds), *Conditions of Democracy in Europe, 1919–39* (Basingstoke,
        2000).
Berki, R. N., 'State and society; An antithesis of modern political thought' in J. Hayward and
        R. N. Berki (eds), *State and Society in Contemporary Europe* (Oxford, 1979), pp. 1–18.
Berman, S., 'Civil society and the collapse of the Weimar Republic', *World Politics* 49 (1997),
        pp. 401–29.
Bermeo, N., 'Myths of moderation: confrontation and conflict during democratic transitions',
        CP 29 (1997), pp. 305–23.

Bermeo, N., 'Civil society after democracy: some conclusions' in N. Bermeo and P. Nord (eds), *Civil Society Before Democracy: Lessons from Nineteenth Century Europe* (Oxford, 2000), pp. 237–61.

Bermeo, N. and P. Nord (eds), *Civil Society Before Democracy: Lessons from Nineteenth Century Europe* (Oxford, 2000).

Berry, H. F., *History of the Royal Dublin Society* (London, 1915).

Bew, P., *Land and the National Question in Ireland 1858–52* (Dublin, 1978).

Bew, P., Hazelkorn, E. and Patterson, H., *The Dynamics of Irish Politics* (London, 1989).

Blum, J., *The End of the Old Order in Europe* (Princeton, 1978).

Bowman, J., *De Valera and the Ulster Question 1917–1973* (Oxford, 1972).

Boyce, D. G., *Englishmen and Irish Troubles: British Public Opinion and the Making of Irish Policy 1918–22* (London, 1972).

Boyce, D. G. (ed.), *The Revolution in Ireland 1879–1923* (London, 1988).

Bromage, M., *De Valera : The March of a Nation* (London, 1956)

Brooks, S., *The New Ireland* (Dublin and London, 1907)

Brubacher, R., *Nationalism Reframed: Nationhood and the National Question in the New Europe* (Cambridge, 1996).

Buckland, P., *Irish Unionism, 1885–1922* (London, 1973), p. 12.

Bull, P., 'The United Irish League and the reunion of the Irish parliamentary party, 1898–1900', *IHS* 26 (1989), pp. 51–78.

Bunce, V., 'The historical origins of the east–west divide: civil society, political society, and democracy in Europe' in N. Bermeo and P. Nord (eds), *Civil Society Before Democracy: Lessons from Nineteenth Century Europe* (Oxford, 2000), pp. 181–209.

Carty, R. K., *Electoral Politics in Ireland: Party and Parish Pump* (Dingle, 1983).

Carty, R. K., 'From tradition to modernity and back again: party building in Ireland' in R. Hill and M. Marsh (eds), *Modern Irish Democracy* (Dublin, 1983), pp. 24–44.

Castles, F., 'Barrington Moore's thesis and Swedish political development', *Government and Opposition* 8 (1973), pp. 313–31.

Castles, F., *The Social Democratic Image of Society: A Study of the Achievements and Origins of Scandinavian Social Democracy in Comparative Perspective* (London, 1978).

Catholic Defence Society, *The Catholic Defence Society*, (Dublin, 1907).

Chubb, B., *The Government and Politics of Ireland* (Oxford, 1970).

Churchill, W. S., *The Second World War* (London, 1979).

Clark, S., *Social Origins of the Irish Land War* (Princeton, 1979).

Clayton, P., *Enemies and Passing Friends: Settler Ideologies in Twentieth Century Ulster* (London, 1996).

Coakley, J., 'Political succession and regime change in new states in interwar Europe: Ireland, Finland, Czechoslovakia and the Baltic Republics', *EJPS* 14 (1987), pp. 187–207.

Coakley, J., 'Political succession during the transition to independence: evidence from Europe', in P. Calvert (ed.), *The Process of Political Succession* (London, 1987), pp. 27–59.

Coakley, J., 'The election that made the first Dáil', in B. Farrell (ed.), *The Creation of the Dáil* (Dublin, 1994), pp. 31–46.

Coakley J. and Gallagher, M. (eds), *Politics in the Republic of Ireland*, 2nd. ed. (Limerick, 1993).

Coakley, J. and Gallagher, M. (eds), *Politics in the Republic of Ireland*, 3rd. ed. (London and New York, 1999).

Cohan, A. S., *The Irish Political Elite* (Dublin, 1972).

Collins, M., *The Path to Irish Freedom* (Dublin, 1996).

Coogan, T. P., *Michael Collins* (London, 1990).

Coogan, T. P., *De Valera: Long Fellow Long Shadow* (London, 1993).

Corish, P., 'The Cromwellian regime, 1650–60', in T. W. Moody, F. X. Martin, and F. J. Byrne (eds), *A New History of Ireland*, III, *Early Modern Ireland 1534–1691* (Oxford, 1991), pp. 353–85.

Cronin, M., *The Blueshirts and Irish Politics* (Dublin, 1997).

Cronin, M. and Regan, J. (eds), *Ireland: The Politics of Independence, 1922–49* (Basingstoke and New York, 1999).

Cullen, L. M., *Princes and Pirates: The Dublin Chamber of Commerce 1783–1983* (Dublin, 1983).

Cullen Owens, R., *Smashing Times: History of the Irish Women's Suffrage Movement 1889–1922* (Dublin, 1984).

Cumann Luthcleas Gael, *GAA: A Century of Service 1884–1984* (Dublin, 1984).

Curran, J. M., *The Birth of the Irish Free State, 1921–1923* (Mobile AL, 1980).

Cutright, P., 'National political development', *ASR* 28 (1963), pp. 253–64.

Dahl, R., *A Preface to Democratic Theory* (Chicago, 1956).

Dahl, R., *Polyarchy: Participation and Opposition* (New Haven, Conn., 1971).

Dahl, R., *Democracy and its Critics* (New Haven, Conn., 1989).

Davitt, M., *The Fall of Feudalism in Ireland or the Story of the Land League Revolution* (London and New York, 1904).

De Markievic, *Women, Ideals and the Nation* (Dublin, 1909).

De Valera, E., *The Foundation of the Republic of Ireland in the Vote of the People* (Victoria, 1919).

De Vere White, T., *The Story of the Royal Dublin Society* (Tralee, 1955).

De Vere White, T., *Kevin O'Higgins* (Tralee, 1965).

Devine, F., 'The Irish labour history society archive', *Saothar* 11 (1986), pp. 90–100.

Diamond, L. (1996), 'Toward democratic consolidation' in L. Diamond and M. F. Plattner (eds), *The Global Resurgence of Democracy*, 2nd. ed. (Baltimore and London, 1996), pp. 227–41.

Diamondorous, P. Nikiforos, 'Prospects for democracy in Greece: 1974–83' in G. O'Donnell, P. Schmitter and L. Whitehead (eds), *Transitions from Authoritarian Rule: Southern Europe* (Baltimore and London, 1986), pp. 138–65.

Di Palma, G., *To Craft Democracies: An Essay on Democratic Transitions* (Berkeley, Los Angeles, Oxford, 1990).

Dogan, M., 'Use and Misuse of Statistics in comparative research' in E. Dogan and A. Kazancigil (eds), *Comparing Nations* (Oxford, Cambridge Mass., 1994), pp. 35–72.

Dovring, F., *Land and Labour in Europe in the Twentieth Century: A Comparative Study of Recent Agrarian History*, 3rd ed. (The Hague, 1965).

Dunleavy, P., *Democracy, Bureaucracy and Public Choice: Economic Explanations in Political Science* (Hemel Hempstead, 1991).

Dunleavy, P., 'The political parties' in P. Dunleavy (ed.), *Developments in British Politics Four* (London, 1995), pp. 123–54.

Dunphy, R., *The Making of Fianna Fáil Power in Ireland 1923–1948* (Oxford, 1995).

Durkheim, E., *The Division of Labour in Society* (New York, 1933).

Durkheim, E., *The Division of Labour in Society* (London, 1981).

Dyson, K., *The State Tradition in Western Europe* (Oxford, 1985).

Edwards, A., 'Democratisation and qualified explanation' in G. Parry and M. Moran (eds), *Democracy and Democratisation* (London, 1994), pp. 88–106.

Eisenstadt, S. (ed.), *Democracy and Modernity* (Leiden and New York, 1992).

Eley, G., 'Nations, publics, and political cultures: placing Habermas in the nineteenth century' in C. Calhoun (ed.), *Habermas and the Public Sphere* (Cambridge, Mass., 1994), pp. 289–339.

English, R., *Radicals and the Republic: Socialist Republicanism in the Irish Free State 1925–1937* (Oxford, 1994).

Fanning, R., *Independent Ireland* (Dublin, 1983).

Fanning, R., 'The rule of order: de Valera and the IRA, 1923–40' in J. P. O'Carroll and J. A. Murphy (eds), *De Valera and his Times* (Cork, 1983), pp. 160–73.

Farrell, B., *The Founding of Dáil Éireann: Parliament and Nation-Building* (Dublin, 1971).

Farrell, B., 'The first Dáil and after' in B. Farrell (ed.), *The Irish Parliamentary Tradition* (Dublin, 1973), pp. 208–23.

Farrell, B.,'The paradox of Irish politics' in B. Farrell (ed.), *The Irish Parliamentary Tradition* (Dublin, 1973), pp. 13–26.

Farrell, B., 'From first Dáil through Irish Free State', in B. Farrell (ed.), *De Valera's Constitution and Ours* (Dublin, 1988), pp. 18–32.

Farrell, B. (ed.), *The Creation of the Dáil* (Dublin, 1994).

Fay, P., 'Amendments to the Constitution Committee 1926' *Administration* 26 (1978), pp. 331–52.

Femia, J., 'Barrington Moore and the preconditions of democracy' *British Journal of Political Science* 2 (1972), pp. 21–46.

Fenton, S., *Durkheim and Modern Sociology* (Cambridge, 1984).

Fishkin, J., *Democracy and Deliberation: New Directions in Democratic Reform*' (New Haven, Conn. and London, 1991).

FitzGerald, G., 'Days of doubt long gone as state reaches 75th birthday', *The Irish Times*, 6 Dec. 1977.

Fitzpatrick, D., 'The disappearance of the Irish agricultural labourer, 1841–1912', *Irish Economic and Social History* 7 (1980), pp. 66–92.

Fitzpatrick, D., 'Irish emigration in the later nineteenth century', *IHS* 22 (1980), pp. 126–44.

Fitzpatrick, D., *Irish Emigration 1801–1921* (Dundalk, 1985).

Fitzpatrick, D., *The Two Irelands 1912–1939* (Oxford, 1998).

Flora P. et al., *State, Economy, and Society in Western Europe 1815–1975: A Data Handbook*, 2 vols, II, *The Growth of Industrial Societies and Capitalist Economies* (London, 1987).

Foley, C., *Legion of the Rearguard: The IRA and the Modern Irish State* (London, 1992).

Foster, R. F., *Modern Ireland 1600–1972* (London, 1989).

Foster, R. F., 'More sinner than saint', *Independent on Sunday*, 17 Oct. 1994.

Gaelic Athletic Association, *Constitution and Rules*, (Dublin, 1885).

Gallagher, M., 'The pact general election of 1922', *IHS* 21 (1979), pp. 404–21.

Gallagher, M., *Irish Elections 1922–44; Results and Analysis* (Limerick, 1993).

Gamm, G. and Putnam, R., 'The growth of voluntary associations in America, 1840–1940', *JIH* 39 (1999), pp. 511–57.

Garvin, T., 'Political cleavages, party politics and urbanisation in Ireland – the case of the periphery-dominated centre, *EJPS* 11 (1974), pp. 307–27.

Garvin, T., 'Nationalist elites, Irish voters, and Irish political development: a comparative perspective', *ESR* 8 (1977), pp. 161–86.

Garvin, T., 'Revolutionaries turned politicians: a painful, confusing metamorphosis', *The Irish Times*, 6 Dec. 1977.

Garvin, T., *The Evolution of Irish Nationalist Politics* (Dublin, 1981).

Garvin, T., *Nationalist Revolutionaries in Ireland* (Oxford, 1987).

Garvin, T., 'The politics of language and literature in pre-independence Ireland', *IPS* (1987), pp. 49–63.

Garvin, T., 'O'Connell and the making of Irish political culture' in M. R. O'Connell (ed.), *Daniel O'Connell: Political Pioneer* (Dublin, 1991), pp. 7–13.

Garvin, T., 'Irish democracy and British rule' in M. Ní Dhonnchadha and T. Dorgan (eds), *Revising the Rising* (Dublin, 1991), pp. 21–9.

Garvin, T., 'The long division of the Irish mind', *The Irish Times*, 28 Dec. 1991.

Garvin, T., 'Unenthusiastic democrats: the emergence of Irish democracy' in R. Hill and M. Marsh (eds), *Modern Irish Democracy* (Dublin, 1993), pp. 9–24.

Garvin, T., 'Democratic politics in independent Ireland' in J. Coakley and M. Gallagher (eds), *Politics in the Republic of Ireland*, 2nd ed. (Limerick, 1993), pp. 250–62.

Garvin, T., *1922: The Birth of Irish Democracy* (Dublin, 1996).

Garvin, T., 'Civil war took several billions out of the economy', *The Irish Times*, 6 Dec. 1997.

Garvin, T., 'The enigma of Dev – the man from God knows where', *The Irish Times*, 10 Apr. 1998.

Garvin, T., 'Democratic politics in independent Ireland' in J. Coakley and M. Gallagher (eds), *Politics in the Republic of Ireland*, 3rd. ed. (London and New York, 1999), pp. 350–64.

Gaughan, J. A., *A Political Odyssey: Thomas O'Donnell MP for West Kerry 1900–1918* (Dublin, 1983).

Gellner, Ernest, *Nations and Nationalism* (Oxford, 1983).

Giddens, A., *Durkheim* (Glasgow, 1980).

Giddens, A. *Durkheim on Politics and the State* (Oxford, 1986).

Goldfrank, W., 'Fascism and the great transformation' in K. Polanyi-Levitt (ed.), *The Life and Work of Karl Polanyi: A Celebration* (New York, 1990), pp. 87–93.

Goldthorpe, J. H. and Whelan, C. T., *The Development of Industrial Society in Ireland* (Oxford, 1992).

Granberg, L. and Nikula, J., *The Peasant State: the State and Rural Questions in 20th century Finland* (Rovaniemi, 1995).

Greaves, C. D., *Liam Mellowes and the Irish Revolution* (London, 1971).

Greaves, C. D., *The Irish Transport and General Workers Union: The Formative Years, 1909–23* (Dublin, 1982).

Green, J. P., 'Social and cultural capital in colonial British America: a case Study', *JIH* 39 (1999), pp. 491–509.

Gwynn, D., *The Irish Free State 1922–1927* (London, 1928).

Habermas, J., *The Structural Transformation of the Public Sphere: An Enquiry into the Category of Bourgeois Society* (Cambridge, 1992).

Halliday, F., 'International society as homogeneity: Burke, Marx, Fukuyama', *Millennium* 21 (1992), pp. 435–61.

Hallinan, Rev. Monsignor, *The Catholic Defence Society* (Dublin, 1907).

Hancock, K., *Survey of Commonwealth Affairs*, vol. 1 (London, New York Toronto, 1937).

Hayward, J. and Berki, R. N. (eds), *State and Society in Contemporary Europe* (Oxford, 1979).

Hechter, M., *Internal Colonialism: The Celtic Fringe in British National Development, 1536–1966* (Berkeley and Los Angeles, 1975).

Held, D., *Models of Democracy* (Oxford, 1987).

Hermens, F., *Democracy or Anarchy? A Study of Proportional Representation* (New York, London, 1972).

Higley, J. and Gunther, R., *Elites and Democratic Consolidation in Latin America and Southern Europe* (Cambridge and New York, 1992).

Hoare, Q. and Nowell Smith, G., *Selections from the Prison Notebooks of Antonio Gramsci* (New York, 1971).

Hobsbawm, E., *Age of Extremes: A Short History of the Twentieth Century* (London, 1994).

Hobson, B., 'Introduction', in *Irish Free State Official Handbook* (London, 1932), pp. 15–17.

Hobson, J. A., *Democracy and a Changing Civilisation* (London, 1934).

Hogan, D., *The Legal Profession in Ireland 1789–1922* (Dublin, 1986).

Hogan, J., *Modern Democracy* (Cork, 1938), p. 84.

Hogan, J., *Election and Representation* (Oxford, 1945).

Hopkinson, M., *Green Against Green: The Irish Civil War* (Dublin, 1988).

Hopkinson, M., 'The Craig–Collins pacts of 1922: two attempted reforms of the Northern Ireland government', *IHS* 28 (1990), pp. 145–58.

Hoppen, T. K., *Elections, Politics, and Society in Ireland 1832–1885* (Oxford, 1984).

Horgan, J., 'Arms dumps and the IRA 1923–32', *History Today* 48 (1988), pp. 11–16.

Hugget, E., *The Land Question and European Society* (London, 1975).

Huntington, S., *Political Order in Changing Societies* (New Haven, Conn. and London, 1968).

Huntington, S., 'Will more countries become democratic?' *PSQ* 99 (1984), pp. 193–218.

Huntington, S., *The Third Wave: Democratization in the Late Twentieth Century* (London, 1991).

Inkwells, A., 'The effects of democracy on economic growth and inequality: a review' in A. Inkwells (ed.), *On Measuring Democracy: Its Consequences and Concomitants* (New Brunswick, 1991), pp. 125–57.

Jackman, R., 'Political democracy and social equality' *ASR* 39 (1974), pp. 29–45.

Janos, A., 'The one-party state and social mobilization; East Europe between the wars', in S. Huntington and C. Moore (eds), *Authoritarian Politics in Modern Society: The Dynamics of Established One-Party Systems* (New York and London, 1971), pp. 204–36.

Johnston, E. M., *Ireland in the Eighteenth Century* (Dublin, 1974).

Jussila, O., Hentila, S. and Nevakivi, J., *From Grand Duchy to Modern State: A Political History of Finland since 1809* (London, 1999).

Kann, R. A., 'The case of Austria', *JCH* 15 (1980), pp. 37–53.

Karvonen, L., *Fragmentation and Consensus: Political Organisation and the Interwar Crisis in Europe* (Boulder, Colo., 1993).

Keane, J., The politics of retreat', *Political Quarterly* 61 (1990), pp. 340–52.

Keane, J., *Civil Society: Old Images, New Visions* (Cambridge, 1998).

Keen, S., 'Associations in Australian history: their contribution to social capital', *JIH* 29 (1999), pp. 639–59.

Kennedy, K. A., Giblin, T. and McHugh, D., *The Economic Development of Ireland in the Twentieth Century* (London and New York, 1988).

Kennedy, L., 'The early response of the Irish Catholic clergy to the co-operative movement', *IHS* 21 (1978), pp. 55–74.

Kennedy, L., 'Modern Ireland: post colonial society or post-colonial pretensions', *Irish Review* 13 (1992–93), pp. 107–21.

Keogh, D., 'De Valera, the Catholic Church, and "the Red Scare", 1931–32' in J. P. O'Carroll and J. A. Murphy (eds), *De Valera and his Times* (Cork, 1983), pp. 134–159.

Keogh, D., *Twentieth Century Ireland: Nation and State* (Dublin, 1994).

Keogh, D., 'A broader picture of 1922', *The Irish Times*, 5 Oct. 1996.

Kettle, T., *The Philosophy of Politics* (Dublin, 1906).

Kiberd, D., 'Eamon de Valera: the image and the achievement' in P. Hannan and J. Gallagher (eds), *Taking the Long View: 70 Years of Fianna Fáil* (Dublin, 1996).

Kirby, D., *Finland in the Twentieth Century* (London, 1979).

Kirby, D., 'Nationalism and national identity in the new states of Europe: the examples of Austria, Finland, and Ireland' in P. Stirk (ed.), *European Unity in Context: The Interwar Period*, London and New York (1989), pp. 110–24.

Kissane, B., 'The not so amazing case of Irish democracy', *IPS* 10 (1995), pp. 43–68.

Kissane, B., 'Explaining the intractability of the Irish civil war', *Civil Wars* 3 (2000), pp. 67–90.

Kissane, B., 'Civil society under strain: intermediary organisations and the Irish Civil War', *IPS* 15 (2000), pp. 1–25.

Kissane, B., 'Democratic consolidation and government changeover in the Irish Free State', *Journal of Commonwealth and Comparative Politics* 39 (2001), pp. 1–23.

Kissane, B., 'Decommissioning as an issue in the Irish civil war', *Studies in Ethnicity and Nationalism* 1 (2001), pp. 8–17.

Kohn, L., *The Constitution of the Irish Free State* (London, 1932).

Lacey, H., 'There need never have been a civil war: what caused the tragedy?' *Irish Press*, 6 Aug. 1958.

Laffan, M., *The Resurrection of Ireland: The Sinn Féin Party 1916–23* (Cambridge, 1999).

Lappard, W., *The Crisis of Democracy: Lectures of the Harris Foundation* (Chicago, 1938).

Larkin, E. (ed.), *Alexis de Tocqueville's Journey in Ireland: July–August 1835* (Dublin, 1990).

Laski, H., *Democracy in Crisis* (London, 1934).

Lee, J., *The Modernisation of Irish Society 1848–1918* (Dublin, 1989).

Lee, J., *Ireland 1912–1985* (Cambridge, 1989).

Lee, J., 'On the birth of the modern Irish state: the Larkin thesis', in S. Brown and D. W. Miller (eds), *Piety and Power in Ireland 1760–1960: Essays in Honour of Emmet Larkin* (Belfast, Indiana, 2000), pp. 130–58.

Lee, J. and Ó Tuathaigh, G., *The Age of de Valera* (Dublin, 1982).

Lieven, D., *Empire: The Russian Empire and its Rivals* (London, 2000).

Liikanen, I., *Fennomania ja Kansa* (Helsinki, 1995).

Lijphart, A., *Democracy in Plural Societies: A Comparative Exploration* (New Haven, Conn. and London, 1977).

Lijphart, A., *Democracies: Patterns of Majoritarian and Consensus Government in Twenty-one Countries* (New Haven, Conn., 1984).

Lijphart, A., *Patterns of Democracy: Government Forms and Performance in Thirty-Six Countries* (New Haven, Conn. and London, 1996).

Linz, J., 'Crisis, breakdown and reequilibration' in J. Linz and A. Stepan (eds), *The Breakdown of Democratic Regimes* (Baltimore and London, 1979), pp. 3–124

Linz, J., 'Transitions to democracy', *Washington Quarterly* 13 (1990), pp. 143–65.

Linz, J. and Stepan, A. (eds), *The Breakdown of Democratic Regimes* (Baltimore and London, 1978).

Linz, J. and Stepan, A., 'Toward democratic consolidation' in L. Diamond, M. F. Plattner, Y. Chu and H. Tien (eds), *Consolidating the Third Wave Democracies: Themes and Perspectives* (Baltimore and London, 1997), pp. 14–34.

Lipset, S. M., 'Some social requisites of democracy: economic development and political legitimacy', *APSR* 53 (1959), pp. 69–103.

Lipset, S. M., 'Conditions of the democratic order and social change: a comparative discussion', in S. Eisenstadt (ed.), *Democracy and Modernity* (Leiden and New York, 1992), pp. 1–15.

Loewenstein, K., 'Autocracy versus democracy in contemporary Europe, II', *APSR*, 29 (1935), pp. 755–84.

Longford, The Earl of and O'Neill, T. P., *Eamon de Valera* (Dublin, 1970).

Luebbert, G., 'Social foundations of political order in Interwar Europe', *World Politics* 3 (1987), pp. 449–78.

Luebbert, G., *Liberalism, Fascism or Social Democracy: Social Classes and the Political Origins of Regimes in Interwar Europe* (Oxford, 1991).

Lustick, I., *Statebuilding Failure in British Ireland and French Algeria* (Berkeley, 1985).

Lustick, I., *Unsettled States, Disputed Lands: Britain and Ireland, France and Algeria, Israel and the West Bank Gaza* (Ithaca, 1993).

Lynn, Karl, T., 'Dilemmas of democratization in Latin America', *CP* 23 (1990), pp. 1–23.

Lyons, F. S. L., 'From war to civil war in Ireland: three essays on the Treaty debate' in B. Farrell, *The Irish Parliamentary Tradition* (Dublin, 1973), pp. 223–57.

Lyons, F. S. L., *Parnell* (Dundalk, 1978).

Lyons, F. S. L., *Ireland Since the Famine* (Glasgow, 1983).

Lyons, F. S. L., The aftermath of Parnell, 1891–1903' in W. E. Vaughan (ed.), *Ireland Under the Union, A New History of Ireland*, VI (Oxford, 1996), pp. 81–111.

Macardle, D., *The Irish Republic*, 3rd ed. (Dublin, 1951).

MacDonagh, O., *Ireland: The Union and its Aftermath* (London, 1975).

MacDonagh, O., 'Introduction: Ireland under the union 1801–70' in W. E. Vaughan (ed.), *A New History of Ireland*, V (Oxford, 1989), pp. lxv–lxvii.

MacPherson, C. B., *The Life and Times of Liberal Democracy* (Oxford, 1977).

MacSwiney, M., *The Republic of Ireland* (Cork, n. d.)

Maier, C. S., *Recasting Bourgeois Europe: Stabilisation in France, Germany and Italy in the Decade after World War One* (Princeton, NJ, 1988), p. 3.

Mair, P., *The Break up of the United Kingdom: Irish Experience of Regime-Change, 1918–49* (Glasgow, 1978).

Mair, P., *The Changing Irish Party System; Organisation, Ideology and Electoral Competition* (London, 1987).

Mair, P., 'Consolidating Irish democracy: some reflections on Eamon de Valera and the transfer of power in Ireland in 1932' (unpublished paper, 1999).

Malone, A. E., 'Party government in the Irish Free State', *PSQ* 44 (1929), pp. 363–78.

Mandle, W. F., 'The IRB and the beginnings of the Gaelic Athletic Association', *IHS* 20 (1977), pp. 418–38.

Manninen, O., 'Red, white, and blue in Finland, 1918: a survey of interpretations of the civil war', *Scandinavian Journal of History* 3 (1978), pp. 229–49.

Manning, M., *The Blueshirts* (Dublin, 1972).

Manning, M., *Irish Political Parties: An Introduction* (Dublin, 1972).

Mansergh, N., *The Irish Free State: Its Government and Politics* (London, 1934).

Maravall, J. M. and Santamaria, J., 'Political change in Spain' in G. O'Donnell, P. Schmitter and L. Whitehead (eds), *Transitions from Authoritarian Rule: Southern Europe* (Baltimore and London, 1986), pp. 71–109.

McBride, L., *The Greening of Dublin Castle: The Transformation of Bureaucratic and Judicial Personnel in Ireland 1892–1992* (Washington DC, 1992).

McCartney, D., *Democracy and its Nineteenth Century Irish Critics* (Dublin, 1979).

McCartney, D., *The Dawning of Democracy: Ireland 1800–1870* (Dublin, 1987).

McDowell, R. B., *Crisis and Debate: The Fate of the Southern Unionists* (Dublin, 1997).

McKay, E., 'Changing with the tide: the Irish Labour Party 1927–1933', *Saothar* 11 (1986), pp. 27–39.

McNamara, S., *Those Intrepid United Irishwomen: Pioneers of the Irish Countrywomen's Association* (Limerick, 1985).

Meenan, J., 'From free trade to sufficiency', in MacManus, F. (ed.) *The Years of the Great Test 1916–39* (Cork, 1967), pp. 69–80.

Merton, R., 'Division of labour in society' in Hamilton, P. (ed.), *Emile Durkheim: Critical Assessments*, I (London and New York, 1993), pp. 20–8.

Miller, K., *Emigrants and Exile: Ireland and The Irish Exodus to North America*, (Oxford, 1985).

Mitchell, A. and O'Snodaigh, P., *Irish Political Documents 1916–1949* (Dublin, 1985).

Mitchell, B. R., *International Historical Statistics: Europe 1750–1933* (Basingstoke, 1991).

Mjoset, L., *The Irish Economy in a Comparative Institutional Perspective* (Dublin, 1992).

Mokyr, J. 'Industrialization and poverty in Ireland and the Netherlands', *JIH* 10 (1980), pp. 429–58.

Moody, T. W., *Davitt and Irish Revolution 1846–82* (Oxford, 1981).

Moore, B., *The Social Origins of Dictatorship and Democracy: Lord and Peasant in the Making of the Modern World* (Harmondsworth, 1966).

Morlino, L., 'Democratic consolidation : definition and models' in G. Pridham (ed.), *Transition to Democracy: Comparative Perspectives from Southern Europe, Latin America and Eastern Europe* (Aldershot, 1991), pp. 571–90.

Morris, R., 'Civil society, subscriber democracies, and parliamentary government in Great Britain' in N. Bermeo and P. Nord (eds), *Civil Society before Democracy: Lessons from Nineteenth Century Europe* (Oxford, 2000), pp. 111–35.

Moynihan, M. (ed.), *Speeches and Statements by Eamon de Valera 1917–1973* (Dublin, 1980).

Mulhall, T., 'The state and agrarian reform: the case of Ireland 1800–1940' (PhD thesis, University of London, 1993).

Munger, F., *The Legitimacy of Opposition: The Change of Government in Ireland in 1932* (Beverly Hills, 1975).

Murphy, J. A., 'The achievement of Eamon de Valera' in J. P. O'Carroll and J. A. Murphy (eds), *The Life and Times of Eamon de Valera* (Cork, 1983), pp. 1–7.

Murray, P., 'Irish cultural nationalism in the United Kingdom state: politics and the Gaelic League 1900–18', *IPS* 8 (1993), pp. 55–73.

Mylly, J., *Political Parties in Finland* (Turku, 1984).

Neeson, E., *The Civil War 1922–1923* (Cork, 1995).

Nettl, P., 'The state as conceptual variable', *World Politics* 20 (1968), pp. 559–93.

Neubauer, D., 'Some conditions of democracy', *APSR* 61 (1967), pp. 1002–10.

Nugent, J. D., *The AOH and its Critics* (Dublin, 1911).

Nwabueze, R., *Constitutionalism in the Emergent States* (London, 1977).

O'Brien, C. C., 'The machinery of the Irish parliamentary party, 1880–85', *IHS* 5 (1947), pp. 55–85.

O'Brien, C. C., *Parnell and his Party 1880–90* (Oxford, 1957).

O'Brien, C. C., 'The embers of Easter 1916–66' in O. Dudley Edwards and F. Pyle (eds), *The Easter Rising* (London, 1968), pp. 223–41.

O'Brien, W., *The Irish Revolution and how it came about* (Dublin, 1923).

O'Connell, M. R. (ed.), *Daniel O'Connell: Political Pioneer* (Dublin, 1991).

O'Connell, T. J., *History of the Irish National Teachers Organisation 1868–1968* (Dublin, 1970).

O'Connor, F., *The Big Fellow* (Dublin, 1991).

O'Connor, U., 'Letter to the Editor: De Valera and the oath', *The Irish Times*, 11 Apr. 1994.

O'Crohan, T., *Island Cross-Talk: Pages from a Diary* (Oxford, 1986).

O'Donnell, G., Schmitter, P. and Whitehead, L. (eds), *Transitions from Authoritarian Rule* (Baltimore, 1986).

O'Donohue, F., *No Other Law* (Dublin, 1986).

O'Duffy, B., 'Violent politics: a theoretical and empirical analysis of two centuries of political violence in Ireland' (PhD thesis, University of London, 1996).

O'Duffy, B. and O'Leary, B., 'Tales from elsewhere and a Hibernian Sermon in H. Margetts and G. Smith (eds), *Turning Japanese: Britain with a Dominant Party of Government* (London, 1995).

O'Faolain, S., *King of the Beggars: A life of Daniel O'Connell* (Dublin, 1995).

O'Fearail, P., *The Story of Conradh na Gaeilge* (Dublin, 1975).

O'Ferrall, F., *Daniel O'Connell* (Dublin, 1981).

O'Halpin, E., 'The civil service and the political system', *Administration* 38 (1991), pp. 283–303.

O'Halpin, E., 'The Army and the Dáil– Civil–military relations within the independence movement' in B. Farrell (ed.), *The Creation of the Dáil* (Dublin, 1994), pp. 107–23.

O'Halpin, E., 'Parliamentary party discipline and tactics: the Fianna Fail archives 1926–32', *IHS* 30 (1997), pp. 581–91.

O'Halpin, E., 'The politics of governance in the four countries of the United Kingdom, 1912–1922' in S. Connolly (ed.), *Kingdoms United?* (Dublin, 1999), pp. 239–48.

O'Halpin, E., *Defending Ireland: The Irish State and its Enemies since 1922* (Oxford, 1999).

O'Higgins, K., *Civil War and the Events Which Led to It* (Dublin, 1926).

O'Leary, B. and McGarry, J., *The Politics of Antagonism: Understanding Northern Ireland* (London, 1993).

O'Leary, B. and McGarry, J., *Explaining Northern Ireland: Broken Images* (Oxford, 1995).

O'Leary, C., *Irish Elections 1918–1977: Parties, Voters and Proportional Representation* (Dublin, 1979).

O'Malley, E., *The Singing Flame* (Dublin, 1978).

Ó Riain, S., *Maurice Davin: First President of the GAA* (Dublin, 1994).

O'Sullivan, D., *The Irish Free State and its Senate: A Study in Contemporary Politics* (London, 1940).

Orridge, A., ' The Blueshirts and the 'economic war': a study of Ireland in the context of dependency theory', *Political Studies* 31 (1983), pp. 351–70.

Owens, R. C., *Votes for Women: Irish Women's Struggle for the Vote* (Dublin, 1975).

Owens, R. C., *Smashing Times: A History of the Irish Women's Suffrage Movement, 1889–1922* (Dublin, 1984).

Pakenham, F., *Peace By Ordeal: The Negotiation of the Anglo-Irish Treaty, 1921* (London, 1992).

Parekh, B., 'Ethnocentricity of the nationalist discourse', *Nations and Nationalism* 1 (1995), pp. 25–53.

Parmach, T., *Collapse of Liberal Democracy and the Rise of Authoritarianism in Estonia* (London, 1975).

Pearse, P. H., 'The sovereign people', *The Complete Works of P. H. Pearse: Political Writings and Speeches* (Dublin, n.d.)

Peillon, M., 'Placing Ireland in comparative perspective', *Economic and Social Review* 25 (1994), pp. 179–95.

Peltonen, M., 'From peasant holdings to family farms: impact of the agricultural depression of the 1880s–1910s on Finnish peasant farming' in L. Graberg and J. Jouko (eds), *The Peasant State: The State and Rural Questions in 20th Century Finland* (Rovaniemi, 1997), pp. 23–42.

Perez-Diaz, *The Return of Civil Society: The Emergence of Democratic Spain* (Cambridge, Mass, 1998).

Plunkett, H., *Ireland in the New Century* (Dublin, 1982).

Polonsky, A., *The Little Dictators: The History of Eastern Europe since 1918* (London, 1975).

Polson-Newman, E. W., 'The new Finland', *Contemporary Review* 137 (1930).

Prager, J. *Building Democracy in Ireland: Political Order and Cultural Integration in a Newly Independent Nation* (Cambridge, 1986).

Preston, P., 'The origins of the socialist schism in Spain, 1917–31', *JCH* 12 (1977), pp. 103–33.

Pridham, G., 'The international context of democratic consolidation' in R. Gunther, P. N. Diamandouros and H. Puhle (eds), *The Politics of Democratic Consolidation: Southern Europe in Comparative Perspective* (Baltimore, 1995), pp. 166–204.

Putnam, R. D., *Making Democracy Work: Civic Traditions in Modern Italy* (Princeton NJ, 1993).

Pyne, P., 'The third Sinn Féin party 1923–26', *ESR* 1 (1969–70), pp. 29–50, 229–57.

Pritchett, V. S., *Dublin* (London, 1991).

Redmond-Howard, L. G., *The New Birth of Ireland* (London and Glasgow, 1913).

Regan, J. M., 'The politics of reaction: the dynamics of treatyite government and policy, 1922–33', *IHS* 30 (1997), 542–64.

Regan, J. M., *The Irish Counter-Revolution 1921–36: Treatyite Politics and Settlement in Independent Ireland* (Dublin, 1999).

Rintaala, M., *Three Generations* (Bloomington, 1962).

Rokkan, S., *Citizens, Elections, Parties: Approaches to the Comparative Study of the Process of Political Development* (Oslo, 1970).

Rokkan, S., 'Models and methods in the comparative study of nation-building' in T. Nossiter et al. (eds), *Imagination and Precision in the Social Sciences* (London, 1972), pp. 121–57.

Royle, S. A., 'Industrialisation, urbanisation, and urban society in post-famine Ireland 1850–1921', in B.J. Graham and J. C. Proudfoot (eds), *An Historical Geography of Ireland* (London, 1993), pp. 258–88.

Rueschmeyer, D., Stephens, E. and Stephens, J. D., *Capitalist Development and Democracy* (Cambridge, 1992).

Rumpf, E. and Hepburn A. C., *Nationalism and Socialism in Twentieth Century Ireland* (Liverpool, 1977).

Russett, B. et al, *World Handbook of Political and Social Indicators* (New Haven, Conn. and London, 1964).

Rustow, D., 'Transitions to democracy: toward a dynamic model', *CP* 2 (1970), pp. 337–63.

Ryan, M. P., 'Civil society as democratic practice: north American cities during the nineteenth century', *JIH* 39 (1999), pp. 559–84.

Ryle Dwyer, T., *Michael Collins and the Treaty: His Differences with de Valera* (Cork and Dublin, 1981).

Sartori, G., *Democratic Theory* (London, 1958).

Schedler, A., 'What is democratic consolidation? *Journal of Democracy* 9 (1998), pp. 91–108.

Schmitt, D., *The Irony of Irish Democracy: The Impact of Political Culture on Administration and Democratic Political Development in Ireland* (London and Toronto, 1973).

Schopflin, G., *Politics in Eastern Europe* (Oxford and Cambridge, Mass., 1993).

Schoup, P., *The East European and Soviet Data Handbook: Political, Social, and Developmental Indicators, 1945–1978* (New York, 1981)

Seanacus, 'The question of Catholic organisation', *Irish Rosary* 6 (1902), pp. 726–9.

Seton-Watson, H., *East Central Europe between the two World Wars: 1918–1941* (Boulder, Colo., 1982).

Sheehy-Skeffington, H., 'The women's movement – Ireland', *The Irish Review* 11 (1912), pp. 225–7.

Simms, J. G., 'Protestant Ascendancy 1691–1714' in T. W. Moody, F. X. Martin and F. J. Byrne (eds), *A New History of Ireland* (Oxford, 1986), pp. 1–30.

Singleton, F., *The Economy of Finland in the Twentieth Century* (Bradford 1991).

Sinnott, R., *Irish Voters Decide: Voting Behaviour in Elections and Referendums since 1918* (Manchester, 1995).

Skinner, L., *Politicians by Accident* (Dublin, 1946).

Skocpol, T., 'A critical review of Barrington Moore's *Social Origins of Dictatorship and Democracy*', *Politics and Society* 4 (1973), pp. 1–34.

Skocpol, T., *State and Social Revolution* (Cambridge and New York, 1973).

Skocpol, T., 'Unravelling from above', *The American Prospect* 25 (1996), pp. 20–5.

Smith, M., 'The title An Taoiseach in the 1937 constitution', *IPS* 10 (1995), pp. 179–85.

Stepan, A., 'Democratic opposition and democratization theory', *Government and Opposition* 32 (1997), pp. 657–75.

Stephens, E. M., 'The Constitution', in *Irish Free State Official Handbook* (London, 1932), pp. 72–80.

Stone, L., 'News from everywhere', *New York Review of Books* 9 (1967).

Stover, W. J., 'Finnish military politics between the two world wars', *JCH* 12 (1977), pp. 741–59.

Strauss, E., *Irish Nationalism and British Democracy* (London, 1951).

Taagepera, R. and Shugart, M., *Seats and Votes: The Effects and Determinants of Electoral Systems* (New Haven, Conn. and London, 1989).

Tarrow, S., 'Making social science work across space and time: a critical reflection on Robert Putnam's making democracy work', *APSR* 90 (1966), pp. 389–97.

Taylor, C. L. and Hudson, M. C., *World Handbook of Political and Social Indicators* (New Haven and London, 1972).

Therborn, G., 'The rule of capital and the rise of democracy', *New Left Review* 103 (1997), pp. 3–41.

Thomson, D., *Europe Since Napoleon* (Harmondsworth, 1966).

Thompson, K., *Emile Durkheim* (London, 1982).

Tilton, T. 'The social origins of liberal democracy: the Swedish case', *APSR* 68 (1974), pp. 561–71.

Towey, T., 'The reaction of the British Government to the 1922 Collins–de Valera pact' *IHS* 22 (1980), pp. 65–77.

Townshend, C., 'The meaning of Irish freedom: constitutionalism in the Free State', *Transactions of the Royal Historical Society*, 6th series, 8 (1998), pp. 45–70.

United Nations, *Demographic Yearbook* (Geneva, 1956)

United Nations, *Statistical Yearbook* (Geneva, 1956)

United Nations, *Economic Survey of Europe in 1959: With Study of Development Problems in Southern Europe and Ireland* (Geneva, 1961).

Valiulis, M., 'The army mutiny of 1924 and the assertion of civilian authority in independent Ireland', *IHS* 13 (1983), pp. 542–64.

Valiulis, M., *Portrait of a Revolutionary: General Richard Mulcahy and the Founding of the Free State* (Dublin, 1992).

Vanhanen, T., *The Emergence of Democracy: A Comparative Study of 119 States, 1850–1979* (Helsinki, 1984).

Vanhanen, T., *The Process of Democratisation: A Comparative Study of 147 States, 1980–88* (New York, 1990).

Vanhanen, T. (ed.), *Strategies of Democratisation* (Washington, 1992).

Walker, B. (ed.), *Parliamentary Election Results in Ireland, 1801–1922* (Dublin, 1978).

Ward, A., *The Irish Constitutional Tradition: Responsible Government and Modern Ireland* (Dublin, 1994).

Waters, M. J., 'Peasants and emigrants: considerations of the Gaelic League as a social movement' in D. J. Casey and R. E. Rhodes (eds), *Views of the Irish Peasantry, 1800–1910* (Hamden, Conn., 1977), pp. 160–77.

Weiner, M., 'Empirical democratic theory' in M. Weiner and E. Ozbudun (eds), *Competitive Elections in Developing Countries* (Durham, 1987), pp. 3–34.

Wiener, J., 'Review of reviews: the social origins of dictatorship and democracy', *History and Theory* 15 (1976), pp. 446–75.

Williams, T. D., 'From the Treaty to the civil war' in T. D. Williams (ed.), *The Irish Struggle 1911–1926* (London, 1966), pp. 117–29.

Wilson, G., 'The Westminster model in comparative perspective', in I. Budge and D. McKay (eds), *Developing Democracy* (London, 1994), pp. 189–202.

Wright, F., *Northern Ireland: A Comparative Analysis* (Dublin, 1987).

Yashar, D. J., *Demanding Democracy: Reform and Reaction in Costa Rica and Guatemala, 1870s–1950s* (Stanford, 1997).

Index